HOLDING THE WORLD TOGETHER

Women in Africa and the Diaspora

Stanlie James and Aili Mari Tripp

Series Editors

HOLDING THE WORLD TOGETHER

African Women in Changing Perspective

Edited by
Nwando Achebe and Claire Robertson

THE UNIVERSITY OF WISCONSIN PRESS

The University of Wisconsin Press
1930 Monroe Street, 3rd Floor
Madison, Wisconsin 53711-2059
uwpress.wisc.edu

Gray's Inn House, 127 Clerkenwell Road
London EC1R 5DB, United Kingdom
eurospanbookstore.com

Printed in the United States of America

This book may be available in a digital edition.

Library of Congress Cataloging-in-Publication Data

Names: Achebe, Nwando, 1970- editor. | Robertson, Claire C., 1944- editor.
Title: Holding the world together : African women in changing perspective /
    edited by Nwando Achebe and Claire Robertson.
Other titles: Women in Africa and the diaspora.
Description: Madison, Wisconsin : The University of Wisconsin Press, [2019] |
    Series: Women in Africa and the diaspora | Includes bibliographical references
    and index.
Identifiers: LCCN 2018045763 | ISBN 9780299321109 (cloth : alk. paper)
Subjects: LCSH: Women—Africa—Social conditions. | Women—Africa—Economic
    conditions. | Women—Political activity—Africa.
Classification: LCC HQ1787 .H645 2019 | DDC 305.4096—dc23
LC record available at https://lccn.loc.gov/2018045763

CONTENTS

HOLDING THE WORLD TOGETHER

PROLOGUE

Holding the World Together

∽ Abena P. A. Busia

"What do we know and how do we know it?"

I

How do they speak of us, and what do we say?
How do we work to shape our own self display
While holding the world together?

II

Holding the world together, asking,
What sacred systems do we share, when and how divined?
When do we shield our arms and when do we field them?
What fears or faiths do we hold, and when do we yield them?
How do we mobilize, around what do we rally?
Then when we stand or run, what is our tally?

III

When we've been bought and sold, who is valued, who's martyred?
And when we buy and sell, who sorts out what's bartered?
Who tells us what to learn, and who stops to listen?
Who shows us where to go and what stops the flow?
What burdens do we share to bear all lives that matter,
While holding the world together?

IV

Holding the world together, asking,
Who loves or loves me not, and who calls me home?
Who names or names me not, and who calls me out?
Who cheats and beats and shouts, who harms my soul?
Who shares in the care to transform and make me whole?
These are our stories:

INTRODUCTION

~ Claire Robertson and Nwando Achebe

What do we know and how do we know it? African women's and gender studies has contributed much to rethinking categories often taken for granted. This project is dedicated to those engaged in this enterprise. We have recruited scholars across generations, nationalities, disciplines, race, gender, ethnicity, continents, and religions to bring enhanced interdisciplinary perspectives to an ever-changing field. In the last twenty years or so the field has matured and featured more scholarship by African women, fully represented here. Their increased input has provided heightened sensitivity to the production and Africanizing of knowledge, as well as the power of naming and speaking for others.

Here we both challenge the category "African women" and use it as an organizing mechanism. Because of the enormous cultural, historical, geographical, economic, and social variations among African populations, it is difficult to place all African women in a single analytic framework. An intersectional approach has dominated much recent feminist theory, in which experiences of multiple oppressions by race, gender, sex, education, nationality, ethnicity, age, class, and sexual preference create identifiable categories, such as working-class Ghanaian black lesbians or middle-class heterosexual white college-educated South African women. Such theory works well particularly in societies characterized by high inequalities and divided by discrimination, a reality in some African societies before European colonialism but furthered everywhere by it. Global white supremacy imposed racially defined Euro-American colonial rule on all but four countries worldwide, redrew African boundaries without regard to previous history or nations, and distorted local economies to deport profits to metropolitan countries. It was most firmly ensconced from the mid-nineteenth century to about the 1970s, at which point multinational corporate dominance superseded national interests, with prominent players including the Japanese, Arabs of various nationalities, and especially the Chinese, who have sought and achieved much influence by supplying or building needed infrastructure such as roads, railroads, and hospitals in developing nations. Thus, intersectional theory has become relevant for contemporary African nations, especially with regard to oppression by class, sex and gender, sexual preference, and ethnicity. Racism is more salient where European-origin whites are present in large numbers, as in South Africa or in diasporic locations, and sexism was not always a factor in Africa. Nowadays racism can be located in daily life in contemporary Africa often through mass media advertising, encouraging skin whitening, for instance, as an opportunistic expression of multinational dominance of the world capitalist economy, which impoverishes many Africans, including millions of women and children.

We cannot assume that all women are or were oppressed; here various authors have identified, for example, African women who are or were rulers, wealthy slave owners, successful warriors or politicians, or prosperous business-women. Those roles performed in the past indicate a different historical trajectory for African women than for Euro-American women. When working- and middle-class seventeenth- and eighteenth-century European women were being labeled housewives, their work devalued and delimited in scope, codified in discriminatory laws, women in Africa more often had power and authority and full rights to own property, operate a business, and so on, regardless of religious differences, especially in West Africa. The imposition of effective colonial rule in the twentieth century took away such women's legal rights and forced socioeconomic changes harmful to women. In this sense, European colonial rule imposed on women whose precolonial roles were highly varied the imagined subordinated monolithic category "African women," which attempted to confine them in body, dress, sexuality, work, property rights, and religious and political authority.

By choosing "African women" as a construct explored in this text, we neither privilege biological determinism nor impose an artificial, historically created category. Like societies worldwide, precolonial Africans had categories established by perceived biological sex differences, although these were sometimes not binary. Such categories were recognized in various ways from food restrictions to medically prescribed cures. They could vary widely from society to society and change over time. Equally malleable were prescribed gender roles, in some places at certain times highly segregated and at others only slightly differentiated. Notions of sexual difference and gender roles were strongly impacted by European colonial rule, which began early in southern

Africa but in most countries in the late nineteenth century (Ethiopia was an exception, with brief Italian colonial rule from 1936 to 1941), most stringently between World Wars I and II.

Modern (as opposed to Greek and Roman) historical European colonialism, which resulted in world domination by the British, French, Dutch, Portuguese, Spanish, Russians (across Asia), Americans, and Germans, had a heavy impact on the African continent, especially from the late nineteenth century to the 1950s through 1970s, depending on location. In southern African white settler colonies a pattern familiar to most in the Americas prevailed, with early settlement by Europeans in the sixteenth or seventeenth century and movements by white settlers along frontiers that closed in the nineteenth century. However, unlike in North America, indigenous peoples always outnumbered white settlers in Africa, and the establishing of strong controls over a majority of the population preoccupied Dutch, British, French, Spanish, and Portuguese invaders all over Africa.

Effective colonial rule in white settler colonies was usually implemented in the nineteenth century with the imposition of European laws that were Victorian in their ideology with respect to proper gender roles and responsibilities. Less formally, Christian missionaries of various sects tried both to convert Africans from indigenous religions and change their ways of living, including dress and deportment, especially for women. Stereotypical racialized notions of oversexualized Africans bred fear of a "black peril"—black males raping white women—and invasive efforts were instituted to control African women's sexuality, childbirth practices, and hygiene customs. Even sympathetic Europeans, observing the strenuous physical labor of African women farmers, often depicted them as powerless, overworked victims, given that such labor in Europe was coded male by prevailing gender norms, even though performed by many women.

The British, French, Portuguese, and Dutch were foremost in constructing, as many scholars have pointed out, not only the category "African women" but also the continent of Africa, its fifty-five countries combined into one place (most Americans refer to events in "Africa" but not, say, in "Europe"; rather, in France or Poland). The new category of African women included for colonialists—victims, powerless objects oppressed by their cultures and men, the legal property of men, as in Europe, subjected to medically justified bodily inquisitions (which they resisted) and urban arrests in colonial-established towns—were taught to be proper European-style housewives (actually domestic servants for European women), undereducated as in Europe, and modified in sexuality and dress by missionaries to suit European notions. They were taught that masculinity rather than seniority was a valid basis for claiming authority. After colonial political rule ended, neocolonialism continued Africa's economic subordination to the capitalist world economy, while women continued their vital economic roles, often with diminished returns accompanied by discrimination, increased responsibilities, and worsening diets. Mass media saturated by sexualized images of women and girls and consumer goods fads, along with ageism, sexism, racism, and ethnocentrism, devalued African women's status and abilities. Our contributors document the construction of African women into one category, but they also show how real African women contest that category, in film and literature, politics and economy, and society and sexuality, across the African continent.

The field of African women's and gender studies is more than abstractly engaged in the daily lives of those it studies, delineating contemporary political, economic, and social implications of African realities. Thus, our *changing perspectives* are driven not just by, for instance, the desire to contest ongoing negative stereotypes, but also by contemporary history. Recent African women's and gender scholarship has emphasized political activism and women's empowerment, in line with rising political power by women in some countries. Researchers join the subjects of their studies in seeking improvements in the situations of ordinary African women in a variety of contexts. Driving this activist impulse is the perception (and reality) that many African women face increasing threats to their well-being with respect to legal, political, economic, and social factors. Decisions made elsewhere in the world capitalist economy often distort African local economies, and political agency and choices are curtailed by outside pressures, corruption, and an electorate often with little formal education. Economies falter in the face of man-made and natural disasters and political corruption, while a rapid pace of social change involving urbanization, social and geographical dislocations, and religious movements fosters innovations in forms of organization. Contributors engage these issues as they relate to women and gender in Africa, paying particular attention to changing notions of gender identity and African women's perceptions.

We adopt a continent-wide perspective on Africa, including North, West, South, Central, and East African material, a nonstandard approach, given that most texts synthesizing African materials use a division that originated in nineteenth-century scholarship inflected by racial and ethnic categories that considered Arabs and Egyptians to be separate from, and often superior to, sub-Saharan Africans. Among many subjects not conforming to this division are the matrilineal Berbers, one of the largest ethnic groups in North Africa and the majority population of Morocco, whose skin color varies from light to dark, and whose armies controlled much of Spain in medieval times, as well as West African territory to the south, thus confounding many Euro-American stereotypes.

Eschewing geographical and chronological segregation, we divided the book into topical sections, with each contributor employing historical and/or cross-cultural examples, the focus on women and gender providing a unifying principle. Since the 1980s there has been scholarly consensus that European colonial rule imposed relatively uniform Victorian ideas about women and gender onto tremendous African diversity in terms of gender role expectations, changes, ideas about women, and so forth; therefore, the socioeconomic status and physical well-being, power, and authority of most African women were lowered, while their workloads and responsibilities increased. Our contributors elaborate on this history, adding contemporary data, while focusing further on areas that have received more scholarly attention in recent years: representations of women and gender in literature and film; precolonial, colonial, and contemporary political and religious organizing; the roles of women in, and impact on women of, religious fundamentalisms and globalization; and women's health and sexuality, including alternative sexualities. Most chapters provide historical material essential to understanding contemporary developments and are multidisciplinary, a characteristic of African women's and gender studies. Here history is as likely to have been written by anthropologists and social structural analysis by historians, for instance, while contributors from different disciplines use novels to illustrate their points.

Rather than seeking a universal theory to explain African women's gendered experiences, this volume derives organically from its authors' contributions, which include variously postmodern, intersectional, structural-functional, materialist, and women and gender development theoretical approaches. Three themes emerge in most of the chapters: the first concerns African women's agency, which is evident religiously, politically, culturally, socially, and economically; second, African women's history is explored over the ages, particularly to illuminate the foundations of contemporary situations; third, it is clear that African women and girls face rising challenges in many areas, often due to colonial-introduced economic distortions and neocolonial exploitation, but also that women have and will organize to meet those challenges, in African and diasporic locations.

The volume is divided into four parts dealing with representations of and by African women; religion and politics; economy and society; and love, marriage, and women's bodies. The first part includes analyses of representations and misrepresentations of African women, historically and in the present.

New scholarship has demonstrated that Euro-Americans' racist or simply inaccurate misrepresentations of Africans have seriously distorted most ordinary folks' perceptions. Europeans' misunderstandings affected colonial rule and laws. Accordingly, chapters 1 and 2 begin the volume by debunking colonial notions about African women through analyzing images of, and by, them in literature in chapter 1 and film in chapter 2. Elizabeth M. Perego in chapter 1 selected four novels by talented contemporary novelists Nadifa Mohamed, Leila Slimani, Chimamanda Ngozi Adichie, and NoViolet Bulawayo, who build on the stereotype-breaking tradition established by older African authors. Interestingly, several authors analyzed by Perego include specifically diasporic perspectives, illuminated further on in the volume by Cassandra Veney in chapter 12, where more analysis of the racialized experiences of new African immigrants in the United States is provided. Mohamed, Slimani, Adichie, and Bulawayo foreground such contemporary themes as identity, trauma, globalization's effects on women, and community fracturing and displacement.

In chapter 2 Cajetan Iheka gives readers an ambitious analysis of cinematic images of, and by, African women, produced by francophone, lusophone, and anglophone directors, with attention to Nollywood productions. By including Ousmane Sembene's *Xala*, Iheka explores feminist themes from the point of view of a prominent male director. The heart of the chapter concerns filmmakers Safi Faye, Assia Djebar, and Nollywood directors Chineze Anyaene and Wanuri Kahiu. These filmmakers have overcome the general lack of financial resources that has encouraged moving into the production of videos rather than films. Collectively, filmmakers and videographers have used the camera lens to express uniquely gendered experiences, becoming cultural readers of female realities in the process, while embodying female agency. These two chapters begin with a critique of negative stereotypes and then progress to emphasize the artistic success, creativity, and relevance of literature and film to contemporary social issues so cogently provided by the examples selected for our delectation.

Part II begins with Nwando Achebe's analysis in chapter 3 of the unique contributions by African women rulers to precolonial polities, which were characterized by a unity of political and religious or spiritual authority. She contends that spiritual authority and political power were indivisible and as a result were particularly vested in women in many African nations. African forms of rule viewed from this perspective were unique in featuring women. Elsewhere in the world until the late eighteenth century, when the American and French Revolutions produced republics in which religious authority and political power were specifically separated, most polities did not make that separation but nonetheless vested most authority in men. Achebe gives us instead many examples from the religio-political sphere of African women having authority that was both spiritual, with an emphasis on religious symbolism and practices, and powerful politically. Her description of women rulers as successful military leaders is striking—no wonder then that on the other side of the Atlantic, Harriet Tubman in the United States and Flore Bois Gaillard in St. Lucia, for instance, not only led people out of slavery but also were military leaders. This understanding then illuminates colonial-era African rebellions, several of which were organized by women, who were seen by the colonialists as solely religious leaders but who formed independent Christian churches and carried out Islamic jihads that threatened the power of colonial regimes.

In chapter 4 some of these movements are analyzed by Kathleen Sheldon, demonstrating the many shifting forms of African women's organization and resistance to colonial rule. Colonial authorities regularly underestimated women's organizing and thus were surprised when some of the most successful resistance movements to colonial rule had women leaders, such as the Yaa Asantewaa War in Gold Coast (Ghana), Ogu Umunwanyi (the Igbo Women's War) in Nigeria, the Harry Thuku demonstration in Nairobi led by Mary Nyanjiru, Anlu in Cameroon, and the anti-pass movement in South Africa. When independence movements became wars of liberation, women often played important roles, modifying usual gender roles to suit the situation, as in Algeria, Angola, Mozambique, Zimbabwe, and Kenya. Sheldon ably critiques the trope of the African woman as universal victim.

In chapter 5 Ousseina Alidou considers the impact on women and gender roles of various contemporary forms of African religious fundamentalisms, deriving from Christian, Islamic, and indigenous traditions. Religious fundamentalism can be defined as believing truth to be fixed and absolute, not contingent, and insisting on strict conformity to rules, more often than not established by a charismatic leader. Alidou uses a definition that also includes male dominance as a key characteristic of religious fundamentalism. Historically Africa experienced waves of Islamic incursions with the Ottoman Turks and the Arabs across North Africa, Omani Arabs along the East African coast, and many Sahelian jihads from medieval times onward with Moroccan and other invasions, as well as the rise of indigenous reformers such as Usman 'dan Fodio. European colonial expansion entered the Sahel in the wake of nineteenth-century militant Islamic reformist movements, meaning that colonialists had to accommodate the wishes of strong local rulers, who were more likely to cooperate if religious and other "domestic" arrangements, such as having slaves as servants, were not challenged. While Christian missionaries flooded into other areas, they were often discouraged or forbidden by colonial authorities to proselytize in Islamic areas, where literacy in European languages was rarely acquired by locals.

Alidou documents many similarities among fundamentalist sects across religions in their imposition of new restrictions on the lives of women and girls, situating these within historical interactions between religions and local indigenous religious traditions, but moving away from women's prophetic authority documented by Achebe. Through the foundation of independent schools, influencing public schools including universities, witch hunts, and introducing or stoking homophobia incorporated into laws, fundamentalisms have exercised growing influence. Nonetheless, contrary to the stereotype of the oppressed Muslim or Christian woman, some women have found new ways of living and organizing that are satisfying and sometimes offer authority. If, for instance, on the one hand, some new forms of Christianity have introduced new restrictions in areas where women historically had more authority, on the other, some syncretic sects have extended old prophetic traditions for women in new ways, while competitive Christian piety has offered some women methods for controlling errant husbands and extending authority.

In chapter 6 Alicia Decker and Andrea L. Arrington-Sirois offer an overview of myriad forms of women's organizing in contemporary Africa. Any analysis of contemporary African politics must take into account the huge diversity and burgeoning of women's groups across the continent. In some nations women are playing vital political roles and have provided essential support in electing a president; in many nations grassroots development groups address the plethora of problems connected to neocolonial economies. Decker and Arrington-Sirois focus on the impressive alphabetical proliferation of women's organizations from the 1980s on, from AAWORD to WRDF, and on university women's initiatives in establishing women's and gender studies programs and departments. They document contemporary African women's activism surrounding HIV/AIDS, female genital cutting, and women's grassroots issues in relation to women and economic development, also touching on women's empowerment through fundamentalist venues. African women's talent for effective organization, so manifest historically, continues to the present, with ever-widening continental initiatives. From micro-lending to other ingenious ways of providing mutual help, in whatever realm women occupy, they often conceptualize and implement new ways of handling intractable problems, which the world would do well to appreciate and emulate.

Aili Mari Tripp in chapter 7 focuses more specifically on African women's political organizing in making a persuasive argument that contemporary Africa leads the world in sheer numbers of women who hold elective office. She documents political implications for women of the transitions in many African countries from authoritarian to mixed "hybrid" regimes including democratic rule. The emergence of women's political organizations that are independent of state-ordained political parties, pressures from international actors such as the UN and regional groups, donor aid, and the decline of conflict are all relevant to increasing women's political power and rewriting constitutions to incorporate women's rights. Obstacles to women's holding office are also highlighted, however. In Liberia the first female president seemingly did not advance an agenda specifically aimed at, and for, women and thereby incurred criticism. It seems that on paper many countries are more progressive than in practice.

Part III captures African women's crucial and changing key economic and social roles, beginning with Gracia Clark's delineation of the essential precolonial, colonial, and contemporary economic roles of African women in chapter 8. She provides a historical description of women's farming and foraging activities followed by an analysis of the impact of economic distortions imposed by colonial, independent, and multinational corporate (MNC) rule. Women's agricultural roles have become more difficult, while women's small business opportunities are often limited by unevenly shared family obligations and an imbalanced division of labor assigning more labor-intensive tasks to women. More inequality is fostered by MNCs. Meanwhile, economists have great difficulty assessing the performance of African economies because most Africans are self-employed in the informal sector, and national official statistics are often grossly incomplete. But economists rarely do grassroots surveys and therefore ignore most women's economic activities. Such problems have necessarily entailed negative impacts of most "development" projects on women, whose lives, labor, and economic well-being have been damaged by them. Since African women, 61.9 percent of whom are economically active (the highest rate in the world), provide nearly 70 percent of agricultural labor and produce almost 90 percent of all food supplies, the undermining of their work has had negative effects. Lack of access to education and capital explains the dearth of women in the formal waged economy. Although in postcolonial Africa large-scale entrepreneurship has been very difficult to access for women, a limited number of women now run private companies with millions of dollars in profits, from Togo to Senegal, Cameroon to Uganda, as well as in Tanzania.

Chapter 9 focuses on women's importance in the history and continuing phenomenon of slavery in Africa. Claire Robertson links women's key economic roles to the high valuation of women slaves for their labor and their capacity to increase lineages through childbearing. Since most agricultural work was done by women, free women were the most frequent users of slave labor—to alleviate their burdens. Forms of slavery practiced in Africa rarely included Euro-American style chattel slavery. Frequently African slaves could marry, own property (even slaves), and transgenerational slavery was rare— the goal of much African slavery was to increase the free population, not permanently enslave an underclass. Nonetheless, the impact of the transatlantic slave trade shifted some forms of African slavery toward chattel slavery. Although many think of slavery as a past phenomenon, under colonial and independent governments the world capitalist economy has generated a sex trade in women and children, and an export and domestic market for servants, often kept in slave-like conditions. Contemporary socioeconomic conditions have produced new forms of slavery in Africa, linked to the past and challenged in the present.

In chapter 10 Josephine Beoku-Betts assesses the status of African girls and women in primary, middle, and secondary education. Her statistics demonstrate that although substantial progress has been made at the elementary and middle school level regarding access by girls to Western-type formal education, the impact of poverty and male-dominant norms has diminished further access, limiting secondary school attendance. She analyzes causes of lack of progress, while evaluating the effectiveness of different approaches to formulating policies. Looking at such factors as male privilege, sexual harassment, unequal labor demands (girls are expected to do more household chores and agricultural work than boys), early marriage, few rural schools and wage jobs, and the impact of religious fundamentalisms, she emphasizes the necessity for scholars to center the voices of girls and women in order to improve educational deficits.

Teresa Barnes in chapter 11 explores the historical roots of Africa's strongest contemporary socioeconomic trend, urbanization, arguing that African urban spaces are structured by gender. Africa was mainly rural before colonial rule until the late twentieth century with notable exceptions (coastal areas, old cities in the Sahel, Egypt, Great Zimbabwe, and Nigeria). With colonialism came foundation of new towns in many areas in the African interior; this development ushered in heightened class formation and inequalities in wealth and access to key resources. In white settler-founded new colonial cities such as Nairobi and Johannesburg, African women were forbidden to enter unless employed by whites but routinely contravened such regulations, while all Africans faced new legal disabilities imposed by European rule. Contemporary Africa has the highest urbanization rate of any continent, partly because of the collapse of many rural economies, which have suffered as a result of uneven distribution of development resources and the failure to reward women, the chief rural workers, with the profits of their labor. Women urban migrants often use urban profits to support rural households. Barnes considers continuities and discontinuities in the impact of urbanization on experiences of ordinary Africans during and after colonial rule. Urbanization has impacted economic and physical mobility, marriage, and divorce. Barnes notes many paradoxes of urbanization for women—from more autonomy (men complain about women being out of control) to more risk of poverty and violence, from anti-mini-skirt campaigns to fashion mavens, from powerlessness to organizing around relevant issues, and from overwhelming work burdens to new urban recreational opportunities, ending with a look at the implications for women of contemporary urban city planning efforts.

In chapter 12 Cassandra Veney looks at African women in the new diaspora in the United States. Whereas the old diaspora involved for most Africans impressment into slavery in the period from the seventeenth century to 1865, African women in the new diaspora often migrate voluntarily but then face all the obstacles imposed by historically rooted racism, sexism, classism, and ethnocentrism. The new diaspora gathered force from the 1990s on with reforms of U.S. immigration laws that got rid of discriminatory quotas and accepted more Africans as immigrants and refugees. Veney provides important information about changes in immigration laws including distinctions in the ways immigrants and refugees are treated but points out that legal citizenship is difficult to obtain, even more so with Trump administration "reforms." She considers the geographic distribution of new African diasporan women, their work, their contributions to churches, mosques, and school reforms, and their remittances to African relatives. They draw on African linguistic skills, professional training, organizational skills, and traditions of activism on behalf of families and communities. In the linkages between old and new diaspora women, we can see the emergence of a new form of Pan-Africanism, solidified partly by the widespread persistence of racism and discrimination that has led to many incidents of police brutality, including murders of new diaspora African men and women. Organizing against such violence has promoted necessary alliances among descendants of old diaspora immigrants and new diasporans, who have become active in many community struggles for dignity and equitable access to resources.

Part IV explores African experiences with courtship, love, loving, family, and marriage, segues into African sexuality and gender in its multitudinous forms, delves into the pressing subject of violence against women, and ends by showing that African women's health matters. In chapter 13 Rachel Jean-Baptiste and Emily Burrill focus on the evolution of marital and consensual unions historically to the present. African creativity and innovation have always been evident in highly varied kinship forms within and across societies and ethnicities. Historically lineage families dominated most of Africa, with marriage valued often mainly for producing new lineage members and political alliances for the elite. Women generally had customary rights that protected them from abuse and guaranteed land access, but colonial rule took away those rights, often forcing male urban migration to earn cash to pay taxes. Complementary or segregated gender roles disappeared when men left rural labor, leaving most roles to women. Over time marriage has been elevated in ceremonial and legal importance through European influence, having had different valance historically, but divorce has continued to be a viable option for many women. Jean-Baptiste and Burrill explore changes in different forms of love, loving, and marriage in Africa, including monogamous, polygynous, and woman-to-woman marriages, Christian and Islamic marriages, child marriage, and "new" gay marriages in parts of southern Africa. Their contemporary sources include lively debates in newspapers and online regarding topics affecting Africans such as love and loving, bridewealth and bride service, infidelity and polygyny. Their discussion of gay marriage in South Africa is a fitting segue to chapter 14.

In chapter 14 Signe Arnfred mines recent scholarship to bring attention to varied notions of gender and sexuality in Africa that contradict Western binary categories assumed by early to mid-twentieth-century British anthropologists. She explores the flexible and fluid nature of socially derived gender categories in Africa, which contrast sharply with the biologically determined nature of sex and dual categories of male and female assumed by colonialists. "Married" or "unmarried" was another dual category imposed by Europeans baffled by the processual nature of African marriage customs. Homoeroticism is also analyzed with a different slant than usually prevails in the United States. She looks at cross- and transgendered practices and masculinities, as well as femininities and sexuality. Sexual diversity characterized many African societies and is expressed in contemporary forms. Arnfred pays close attention to the new "language of love" expressed in African mass media, "companionate" marriage, and love letters, all seen as desirable by young urban professionals. She ends with a discussion of same-sex relationships and their criminalization in some parts of Africa under the influence of American fundamentalist missionaries. In many cases African practices demonstrating sexual ambiguity survive under the radar of intolerant overlays.

Henryatta Ballah and December Green in chapter 15 focus on domestic and state-sanctioned violence against African women. They point out that Africa has the highest average rates of domestic violence against women (VAW) in the world. VAW across Africa varies in incidence, as do laws against it and their enforcement. While VAW is against the law in twenty-one countries, there are big difficulties with enforcement. The chapter explores precipitating situations such as wars, refugee camps, and poverty, as well as those that discourage VAW. In the past, women's organizations resisted it and elders defused it, but male dominance was usually not challenged. Whether or not women are considered to be men's property is a key factor determining levels of violence, as well as women's economic autonomy or power. Colonial-imposed laws that deprived women of full citizenship sometimes have been perpetuated. Also relevant are women's strategies to combat violence, mechanisms such as those promoted by the solidarity of women's groups.

Ballah and Green look keenly at violence against women sponsored and implemented by the state or the military, with particular attention to Liberia, Mozambique, Rwanda, Guinea, and Sierra Leone, bringing women's experience in warfare into focus, including VAW perpetrated by UN "peacekeepers." Women's peacekeeping efforts and experiences as survivors of violence are discussed as well as women as perpetrators of violence. Nonetheless, the huge majority of contemporary combatants are male; a big problem for women is the impunity achieved by men for war crimes, when rape is not defined as a war crime. To succeed, efforts to end violence against women must include men at every level.

In chapter 16 Karen Flint analyzes pressing issues regarding women's health and well-being in Africa, situating them carefully within historical, environmental, and political circumstances. She considers the impact on women of major diseases, old and new, especially AIDS; female genital cutting; and other practices. She focuses on structural causes and constraints of health issues, especially emphasizing poverty (Africa now has a third of the world's poor), with women bearing the brunt of Africans' health challenges. Some successes have occurred as a result of the developing and merging of creative relationships between Western-influenced and indigenous medical practices, or folk medicine, but colonialism disturbed ecology, economy, nutrition, and disease environments without providing adequate biomedical services to remedy damages. Flint focuses particularly on changing sexual and birth practices with their health implications, female genital cutting, HIV/AIDS, and child-birth, emphasizing that positive changes must arise from a wide array of basic measures such as better infrastructure, reliable land access for women, and income generation. As with other authors, she prioritizes research that is locally based, and she listens to the voices of women.

This volume highlights both the diversity and the unity of African women's experiences in various contexts, beginning with an emphasis on the need for balanced and accurate representations of African women and girls in the media. Clearly, old and new stereotypes are inaccurate and do not serve well either the women they misrepresent or the world community. If some of the most optimistic and creative strategies have emerged from African women's experiences—in political and economic organizing, creative and social agency—some of the direst human tribulations are also evident. By concentrating on the historical circumstances underpinning contemporary conditions for women and on increasing challenges faced by African women and their agency in overcoming them, our contributors have laid out a broad spectrum of changing perspectives on African women involving increasingly notable cultural contributions by women to rethinking women and gender relations; increasing political participation and leadership by African women and grassroots organizing that particularly address increasing inequalities; heightened international awareness of inequalities; substantive challenges to African women's health and well-being posed by diseases, warfare, and violence against women; lack of access to key resources and resultant food insecurity; the rise of Islamic, Christian, and indigenous religion fundamentalist sects, and the persistence or development of flexible sexual and gender norms in the face of intolerance. Given that humanity as a whole shares a prime project of survival with dignity, the experiences, strategies, achievements, and abilities of African women relevant to achieving this goal are too valuable to be ignored within the human lexicon of possibilities.

PART 1

REPRESENTATIONS OF AND BY
AFRICAN WOMEN

Figure 1.1. Nigerian author Chimamanda Ngozi Adichie graces the summer 2014 cover of *Ms.* magazine, a leading American feminist publication. The editorial board's choice to feature Adichie in a cover story signals how well her novels and other works of fiction have resonated with international readers.

1

FRONT AND CENTER ON THE GLOBAL STAGE

African Women in Contemporary Novels

Elizabeth M. Perego

This chapter considers how contemporary African women authors portray women and gender and places this aspect of their works in historical perspective. I analyze representations of women, gender, and sexuality in four novels by contemporary women writers from a variety of backgrounds and locations.[1] The chapter begins with a brief history of representations of African women in colonial-era novels with particular attention to Karen Blixen/Isak Dinesen's *Out of Africa*, which exemplifies distortions imposed by the European colonial gaze. Overthrowing such simplified negative stereotypical images, African women authors do justice to the complexities of the characters and experiences of past and contemporary women in the works analyzed here: Nadifa Mohamed's *Orchard of Lost Souls*, Leila Slimani's *Chanson Douce*, Chimamanda Ngozi Adichie's *Americanah*, and NoViolet Bulawayo's *We Need New Names*. These works, published between 2013 and 2016, have garnered widespread attention and have been included on a number of lists of the best fiction written by African authors or African women authors, and so provide outstanding influential examples for my purpose.[2] In doing so they join the ranks of notable African women novelists such as Mariama Ba, Fatima Mernissi, Grace Ogot, Bessie Head, Ama Ata Aidoo, Buchi Emecheta, and others. Like Tsitsi Dangarembga, another prominent contemporary author, these authors provide women's perspectives on such contemporary themes as intersectional identities, vulnerabilities to violence against women and discrimination, and displacement of communities and individuals by migration, globalization, love, and trauma.

Here I include North and sub-Saharan literature in the same analytical framework, attempted only occasionally due to artificial colonial and contemporary geographical divisions, but their commonalities and differences do not correspond to such geographical or cultural divides. This chapter also provides literary dimensions that elaborate on Cassandra Veney's socioeconomic analysis of the experiences of new diasporic U.S. African women (chapter 12) by looking at France as depicted in Leila Slimani's work and U.S. diasporic women in the works of Chimamanda Adichie and NoViolet Bulawayo.

As Touria Khannous aptly noted, the designation of all women with ties to the African continent who compose fiction as "African women writers" risks obscuring the variety of experiences of women from Africa's vastly heterogeneous societies and communities. This categorization may insinuate as well that the "African" facet of these authors' identities takes precedence over other aspects such as class.[3] My analysis of African women novelists' depiction of women's experiences and how they engage with sexuality and gender demonstrates precisely how women writers are breaking with previous depictions of African women in literature. Thus, the value of placing works by female authors linked to Africa under the umbrella of "African women's writings" lies in how such an exercise permits us to identify these authors' response to earlier colonial-era representations of African women and how they illustrate African women grappling with key issues today.

Precolonial and Colonial Representations of African Women

The earliest representations of African women in the modern novel depicted them as homogeneous, unreflective, superficial objects of contemplation and wonder for European readers. European writers did not shape these negative depictions haphazardly or without purpose; from the nineteenth century on these works generally served to sexualize and exoticize Africans as a way of drawing support among populations in Europe for slavery and colonial rule. Through postcards, traveling exhibits, paintings, and other types of media, Europeans propagated images of the African continent as a place of intrigue and mystery but also an environment inhabited by a supposedly ignorant, inferior "race." Many interpretations of "Africa" and African peoples by artists and writers working for states or private interests relied upon fallacious and imagined accounts of sex, sexuality, gender, and women to render Africa an "Other," that is, an entity essentially different from and inferior to Europe. Pursuing this theme in their representations of African women, European writers, including state-commissioned depictions, showed African men as dominating and oppressing African women as a way of highlighting the supposed "backwardness" of African peoples. Precolonial and colonial authorities and entrepreneurs placed African women's bodies on display as objects of curiosity in a process that robbed them of their personhood. In the earliest representations of African women in European novels, female Africans are usually silenced, with writers fixating instead on their bodies presented as objects defined by European observation.[4]

Isak Dinesen's famous *Out of Africa* exemplifies how colonial-era literature about "Africa" presented African women as nameless, sexualized beings, lacking voices and subjectivities. Dinesen was a Danish aristocrat, the Baroness von Blixen, a planter, who lived near Nairobi in Kenya from 1913 to 1931. She intended *Out of Africa* to serve as a memoir about her experience on her "African farm." By constantly referring to her experience in "Africa" rather than specifying where she lived exactly, Dinesen obscures the diversity of the continent. She presents herself as a purveyor of knowledge about Africa and its peoples. She never admits the possibility that, as an outsider, she might not have access to certain forms of knowledge or her conclusions might be false. Furthermore, although she describes Maasai, Somali, and Kikuyu, any ethnic differences remain superficial, and the reader gains no insight into the perspectives of mostly unnamed non-European characters, even though her tone is often ethnographic.

When it comes to the various African/Kenyan women whom she describes in the work, like other European artists and writers of her day with female African objects, Dinesen sexualized and exoticized them. In her chapter "The Somali Women," she writes about her servant Farah's sisters-in-law. The women, who remain unnamed, wear ample skirts as a sign, in Dinesen's view, of their modesty and their "demureness." She writes, "Inside these masses of stuff [the skirt material] their slim knees moved in an insinuating and mysterious rhythm." She then goes on to cite a French poem, ostensibly describing what is going on under the women's skirts:

Your noble legs, under the ruffles that they hunt
Torment obscure desires and irritate them
Like two witches who
rotate a black philter in a deep vase.[5]

Her poem entices European readers to imagine the space under the women's skirts. She writes about the women's legs as sensually desirable and the women themselves as practitioners of black magic, surely a way to mark the women as sinister "Others."[6] Dinesen additionally describes the relationship of women and men as unequal, with men possessing and fiercely guarding the virginity of young women. The "Somali women" are referred to as "Farah's women" as she expounds upon the importance of their maidenhood at length.[7] Dinesen depicts Somali women collectively as alike while sexualizing them, a practice replicated throughout the novel.

Contemporary African Women Authors' Novels

Such sexualizing and superficial depictions are absent from the contemporary works analyzed here. There are three notable patterns in the ways that Mohamed, Adichie, Bulawayo, and Slimani portray African women. To begin with, the authors all stress the plurality of women's experiences as well as their agency in responding to circumstances imposed on them by their communities. Mohamed, Slimani, Adichie, and Bulawayo likewise depict women as diverse and fully fledged human beings who act as independent agents. Finally, the contemporary female novelists whose works are examined here represent women as having mature intellects, capable of analyzing their situations in world terms. Mohamed, Adichie, Bulawayo, and Slimani all portray female African characters who engage critically with broader issues of globalization, postcoloniality, migration, and gendered, racialized, and ethnicized political economy, using new forms of technology. In doing so, they continue earlier trends in African women's literature.[8] These threads illustrate a common, gendered humanity in representations of African women by such prominent female African writers.

Nadifa Mohamed, *The Orchard of Lost Souls*

Unlike the portrayal of "the Somali women" in *Out of Africa*, Nadifa Mohamed's *Orchard of Lost Souls* illustrates Somali women as diverse, strong, and expressive individuals who are capable of commenting critically on the state of their country and communities. The novel focuses almost exclusively on the experiences of women and girls and highlights problems facing Somali women in the city of Hargeisa amid mounting tensions between President Siad Barre and armed opponents in the late 1980s. Mohamed's narrative centers on the stories of three women—Kawsar, Deqo, and Filsan—of different backgrounds, who encounter varying travails due to their gender over the course of the narrative. Mohamed shows the intersectional relationship of oppression by gender and class, while emphasizing the difficulties of survival by women regardless of status under an oppressive postcolonial regime.

Kawsar is an elderly widow of a former police officer who lives comfortably in a villa. Despite her secure economic situation, Kawsar is haunted by the loss of her daughter some years before and upset about the political state of the country. Filsan is a young ambitious female soldier from a wealthy and well-connected family in Mogadishu. She strongly upholds the views of the state and seeks to support them. Deqo, finally, is a homeless orphan girl from a refugee camp who has to fight on a daily basis for her survival. Such diverse characters bring to life women's highly varied experiences in Somalia in the late 1980s, while emphasizing the complex nature of their personalities and multiple identities.

Several instances of gender-based violence occur throughout the novel; these dangerous encounters between the female protagonists and a male-dominant system further allow readers to perceive the women's fortitude. Men's power over women pervades the narrative. At several turns in the plot, Mohamed shows that men are, and women can be, subjected to violence at any point in time. Deqo, owing to her status as a homeless girl without family, is most vulnerable to patriarchal threats throughout the novel. During one particularly harrowing scene, she is almost raped in the house of a woman involved in sex work, who kindly takes her in.[9]

Filsan similarly experiences gender discrimination and violence at several points in the novel. General Haaruun, who in one scene sings the praises of Somali women to an American diplomat, is shown in the next scene attempting to use his influence to coerce Filsan into sleeping with him. This scene subverts any claim on the part of the postcolonial Somali state to have liberated women through independence or by having women involved in state institutions such as the military—a direct challenge to the state feminism that Mohamed portrays Haaruun as lauding. Later in the novel Filsan recalls an instance when her father beat her brutally for bringing home a boy late at night, which also prompts Filsan's father to demand that his housemaid check Filsan's underwear to ensure that she is still a virgin. In sum, the male-dominant values and practices of the state, the military, and her father inflict stark violence on her for refusing to sleep with a man when she does not want to and for jeopardizing her reputation as a virgin. Yet Mohamed further fleshes out the personalities of her female characters by having Filsan beat Kawsar when the older woman is arrested for defying the authorities at the October 21 commemoration.[10] Here, Mohamed shows women as capable of being both victims and perpetrators of violence (see chapter 15), a further sign of the complexities of their identities and personalities.

As with Filsan and Deqo, gender discrimination and the difficulty of being a woman in her society impacts Kawsar. Her daughter Hodan committed suicide after being arrested for attending a protest as a student and, Mohamed hints, raped in prison, causing her depression and eventual suicide. The loss of her daughter through gender-based violence causes immense suffering for Kawsar shown throughout the work, despite its having happened years before the events depicted in the novel.[11]

The three women—through their shared hardships, the twists of fate that bring them together, their will to survive, and their willingness to assist one another—transform their connections by the end of the novel into a pseudo-relationship of mothers and daughters. When the women reach Ethiopia after escaping Hargeisa in flames from the conflict, a refugee camp worker asks Deqo who is with her, and she responds, "My mother and grandmother." This impromptu construction of an intergenerational fictive female kinship network represents a refusal on the part of these women to be bowed by the harsh realities of the conflict unfolding around them as well as the oppression their society inflicts upon them as women. Moreover, Filsan's decision to abandon the army marks a break in her reliance on men and her desire to please or outdo them, which she previously sought through army enlistment. She was never able to achieve recognition due to the patriarchal underbelly of that institution. As she abandons her post, Filsan ponders that her father would not approve of her decision.[12]

As is typical of other authors discussed here, Mohamed portrays her main female protagonists as thinking critically about postcoloniality, globalization, and similar issues. At the beginning of *Orchard*, Kawsar runs into trouble during a celebration of the regime's anniversary that she is forced to attend. Mohamed depicts the older woman feeling disgusted with the postcolonial government during the events of the day, even spitting when she catches a glimpse of General Haaruun. Mohamed also mentions, as though Kawsar thought this herself, that the regime has brought women to the state's display of its glory because "it needs women to make it seem human," an accusation that the regime has not treated Somali people well.[13] *The Orchard of Lost Souls* tells the story of women who struggle to survive in an environment hostile to their well-being, and who question and challenge the obstacles that they encounter, including the harsh realities of the postcolonial state.

Leila Slimani, *Chanson Douce*

Leila Slimani's *Chanson Douce* (Lullaby) recounts the brutal murder in France of two small children at the hands of their white nanny. Of all of the novels examined here, Slimani's includes the fewest female characters with ties to the African continent. Unlike Adichie's *Americanah*, which puts the Nigerian, female, black, immigrant, and then repatriated status of Ifemelu front and center in the story (see below), Slimani eschews having her main character, a woman of Moroccan origin, emphasize her identity as a woman with ties to the African continent. Still, this novel, like others examined here, depicts the heterogeneous and global nature of African women's experiences, challenging gender restraints placed upon them by different societies.

While describing Myriam's need for a nanny and search for a caretaker, Slimani provides subtle clues to Myriam's ethnic, national, and religious background as well as to her views of her position as a woman of Maghribi descent married to a white Frenchman. When Myriam and her husband Paul determine the types of women they would like to hire as a nanny for their children, Paul states that, among other things, he would like to avoid hiring women who smoke or wear a veil (most likely the Islamic hijab); Myriam appears to agree with these criteria. Slimani exposes Myriam's unwillingness to hire an old or veiled woman or illegal immigrant immediately before she discusses the character's outrage when her similarly affluent friend Emma suggests that Myriam search for an immigrant woman without children. Emma states that women with children may be less likely to be available to watch the children in the evenings. In her dismissal of this subgroup of potential nannies, Myriam's white bourgeois friend states that it would be better for such women and their children to "be in their countries."[14] Myriam views Emma's words disdainfully, ostensibly because they indicate her willingness to discriminate against immigrant women with children, a category including Myriam. This statement indicates that the women assume that many of the nannies will naturally be from "Third World" developing nations.

In another scene Myriam's subject position as a woman from North Africa or of North African descent becomes clear when she adamantly refuses to hire "a Maghribi woman" as their nanny. Slimani states Myriam's reasoning as follows: "She fears that an unspoken complicity, a familiarity would be established between them. That the other would start making remarks to her in Arabic. Start talking about her life, and, soon, start asking a thousand things out of their common language and religion. She always was suspicious of what she called the solidarity of immigrants."[15] Presumably, by "Maghribi woman" the character means women with connections to France's former colonies of Morocco, Algeria, and Tunisia. With this passage, Slimani indirectly reveals Myriam's status as a North African woman, most likely Muslim (the majority of Maghribi adhere to the Islamic faith), with ties to at least one Maghribi country.

Finally, the only other point in the novel that addresses Myriam's status as a woman of North African origin occurs when Myriam, the burned-out mother, goes to an employment agency to seek help with hiring a nanny. The manager, seeing Myriam, assumes that as a Maghribi or Franco-Maghribi woman, she is seeking employment, and brusquely lists all the paperwork required for her to be a candidate for employment as a nanny, as if to deter her from applying. When Myriam explains that she is a potential client, not a would-be nanny, the manager's demeanor changes, and she speaks politely to her. Reflecting on the incident afterward, Myriam notes that the woman's ethnocentrism bothered her.[16] We can infer that Slimani intended for this passage to highlight Myriam's awareness of ethnocentrism and that she occasionally suffers from discrimination as a woman with family roots in North Africa, while profiting from a relatively privileged class position.

Given the back-to-back placement of scenes presenting Myriam's refusal to hire a woman who wears a veil and her anger at Emma's comment about not hiring a woman with children, Slimani perhaps sought to underscore Myriam's hypocrisy. She places Myriam within upper-middle-class French society and emphasizes that class dynamics rather than her Maghribi background influence her actions in the novel. In interviews with the press, Slimani stated her intention to have Maghribi characters but write as a universal author rather than an ethnically Maghribi one.[17] Her purposeful skimping on material that fleshes out their Maghribi origins suggests that Maghribi women would not see their connections to North Africa as a prominent feature of their identities or a driving factor behind their actions. Here, Slimani may be attempting to undercut certain stereotypes regarding immigrant Maghribi women, namely that the very nature of their belonging to marginalized groups precludes the possibility of their discriminating against these same groups or others like them. Slimani portrays a woman of Maghribi descent engaging in blatant discrimination against women of a background similar to her own.

Slimani also recognizes the reality that some individuals connected to France's former colonial territories can achieve higher socioeconomic status than some French citizens of uniquely European origins. Myriam and Paul eventually hire Louise, a white French woman who at first seems to be a dream come true for the couple. At one moment Paul even jokingly refers to her as "Mary Poppins," a testament to how pleased the couple is with their new nanny. As the reader learns later on in the novel, Louise is a struggling widow whose husband left her heavily burdened with debt upon his death. By the novel's end, she is facing eviction and has started meddling in the marriage of her employers. Her sanity slowly unravels as she contemplates her poverty. Most of the other nannies that Louise meets in the park are women immigrants of color, who find the "white nanny" a curiosity.[18] Louise is an anomaly among her peers, a white woman employed by a woman of color, who is ultimately incompetent as a nanny and dangerous due to her fragile identity and negative experiences.

As with the other novels analyzed here, *Chanson Douce* addresses various types of sexism and violence that male dominance inflicts on women. To begin with, Myriam's discrimination against elderly, veiled, and Maghribi women constitutes a form of violence. Thus, as with *The Orchard of Lost Souls*, we see here that women can perform the dual roles of victim and perpetrator of violence. The greatest gender-based violence or conflict in the novel arises from the unequal expectations of broader French society as well as family toward Myriam regarding her roles as household manager and as mother in the family. The narrative describes societal roles including Myriam performing duties that her husband Paul is absolved from, gender-segregated expectations. The beginning of *Chanson Douce* details Myriam's travails as a new mother who wants to spend time with her children but also finds herself exhausted and nostalgic for her career when staying home. Paul, in contrast, keeps working to support his family and advance his career. Slimani portrays Myriam as conflicted over whether or not to work; she initially refuses to let anyone else care for her children and then struggles to reconcile her desire for a career and time away from her children with her desire to protect them. When she begins working for a law firm run by her law school friend, Myriam adopts an all-or-nothing approach to the question of whether to work or stay home with her children. To prove herself, Myriam works longer hours than any of her colleagues in the firm, going above and beyond what she technically has to do to keep her job.[19]

Another instance where Myriam finds herself constrained by her gender emerges after the brutal death of her two children. The defense lawyer in Louise's murder trial describes Myriam in court as an "absent mother" while there is no indication that Paul faced a similar indictment. Instead, Louise's lawyer tries to paint Myriam as "having pushed" Louise to the edge of reason, as though Myriam's position as mother in the family makes her more responsible for taking care of her children and the person in the couple more likely to have been in contact with Louise. The attorney's take on events leading up to the murder of Myriam's children serves as a sign that women are often still expected to be sole caretakers in the home. This observation coheres with other sections of the book where the question of whether Paul would perform childcare duties instead of Myriam or a nanny never arises.[20]

Chanson Douce acknowledges the gendered struggles and violence that women immigrants from Africa sometimes endure. The only other woman with ties to the African continent that Slimani portrays extensively is Wafa, a garrulous friend of Louise who works as a nanny in the same neighborhood. Wafa receives her visa to France through a sexual relationship in Morocco with an elderly Parisian. This man brings her to France, but their relationship crumbles when his children, fearful that she is only looking for money, insist that she leave his home. Once Wafa is kicked out of the old man's house, she seeks to enter a marriage of convenience to obtain legal immigrant status in France, just as Obinze does in the UK in *Americanah*.[21] Slimani recounts how Wafa is nearly raped by the man whom she wants to wed to obtain her papers.[22]

These glimpses into Wafa's background underscore her vulnerability as both woman and immigrant. To get to France, Wafa relied on the support of a man to whom she sold sexual favors (we are not told if Wafa had previously tried other ways to go to France or whether she chose sex work out of necessity or personal choice). Then, she is almost raped while trying to negotiate an illicit deal to achieve legal status in France. As an immigrant with limited resources, she takes a position that forces her to be at the perpetual disposal of a wealthier couple. All these instances of violence and transgression stem at least in part from Wafa's multiple identities, with her gender foremost among these.

Chanson Douce also highlights tensions arising from contemporary lifestyles and differences between classes, national origins, races, and genders. At its core, the novel tells the story of a bourgeois millennial couple hiring a woman who has worked longer than they have and still has less, and the struggle of balancing work with personal life. With the characters of Myriam and Wafa, Slimani paints a complex picture of Maghribi women while emphasizing the double standards that women still face when it comes to parenting and trying to make a way for themselves in the world. Wafa represents a counterexample to Myriam, a woman with ties to the Maghrib lacking resources to live the kind of lifestyle that Myriam enjoys. Whereas the latter belongs to the upper-middle-class echelon of French society, Wafa is solidly working class and vulnerable to exploitation by her employers; Wafa remarks that her employers pay her rent in return for her making herself available at all times to take care of their children, a situation that hints at exploitation.[23] In sum, Slimani's portrayals of African women in *Chanson Douce* provide a broad view of the complexities of the lives of Maghribi immigrant women in France today (see also chapter 12), while also foregrounding the tragedy associated with Louise's nonstereotypical ethnicized role.

Chimamanda Ngozi Adichie, *Americanah*

In her third, much acclaimed, novel, *Americanah*, Chimamanda Ngozi Adichie paints a veritable tapestry of different characters and personalities across three continents. African women, however, arguably take up the most space of any subset of people throughout the eight-hundred-page work. The women portrayed by Adichie in *Americanah* are highly diverse, with some women advancing what could be defined as feminism and others upholding male dominance. Adichie draws strong contrasts between Ifemelu's mother and her Aunty Uju as well as Obinze's wife Kosi and Ifemelu, the novel's main character. Ifemelu's mother proves straitlaced while her aunt is open about sexuality with Ifemelu and revels in her position as the mistress of a powerful general. Regarding Ifemelu and the wife of her ex-boyfriend Obinze, Kosi, the latter is pleased when others mention the light tone of her skin while Ifemelu composes a blog post characterizing African American and African men's preference for lighter-skinned women as "bullshit." Adichie also confronts and criticizes the "white savior complex" head-on and calls attention to misconceptions about "Africa" that white Americans hold. For instance, a white woman who knows little about Ifemelu expresses pity toward her and, by extension, for the entirety of the African continent, a situation that makes Ifemelu highly uncomfortable.[24]

Americanah generally portrays African women as fully capable of voicing their opinions and occupying positions of power and privilege. First and foremost, in Adichie's novel the power to travel, observe, critique, or admire lies with a Nigerian woman like Ifemelu, who observes and comments on the world around her as a blogger, liberally and publicly. Using this medium, she pushes back against portrayals of "Africa" as a place of suffering by highlighting the problems that exist in the United States, while undercutting representations of Africa as poor. For instance, in addition to the example above about the "white savior complex," Adichie notes that a good proportion of the Nigerians who emigrate are not doing so out of stark economic necessity or due to violence, but because they could not live the lives they wanted at home.

Ifemelu critiques lives led in Nigeria as an "oppressive lethargy of choicelessness."[25] At several points in *Americanah* women linked to the African continent suffer gender-based discrimination and violence. The beginning of the novel illustrates how Ifemelu experiences this kind of discrimination during her childhood. At one point she speaks back to a female leader in her church, prompting her mother to exclaim, "It would be better if she was a boy, behaving like this." Ifemelu grew up with gender norms that proscribed certain behavior for young girls that society permitted for boys.[26]

A telling scene early in the novel shows Obinze's wife, Kosi, unwilling to hire a young woman as a housekeeper because she discovers condoms while rifling through the woman's bag. The girl tells Kosi that she brought the condoms because her previous employer's husband "was always forcing" her to have sex with him. The inclusion of this detail about Kosi in the novel acknowledges that a housemaid could be raped by her employer and that employers could turn a potential female worker away for attempting to prevent pregnancy if the situation repeated itself in a new household, a terrible reality that underscores the precarious position of and potential violence inflicted on economically disadvantaged young women in Lagos.[27]

Americanah's Ifemelu is eventually forced to admit that her success in America hinged at a key moment on her connection to a man. Upon her return to Nigeria after thirteen years in the United States, she publishes a blog post criticizing Lagosian women who chase after wealthy men to ensure their economic stability. Her friend Ranyinudo, the woman whose story Ifemelu admits she used as the foundation for the think piece, turns on the blogger, pointing out that she too benefited greatly from the assistance of a man; her white American ex-boyfriend, Curt, had arranged for her to have an interview with a company that eventually sponsored her green-card application, a difficult obstacle that many international students in the United States face upon finishing their studies if they wish to remain legally in the country (see chapter 12). Here, Ranyinudo reminds Ifemelu of her initial insecurity in the United States and that the power to render that position more secure lay with a wealthy white man. Similarly, in the first few months of her studies in Philadelphia, Ifemelu struggles to find a job to cover her expenses so she performs a sexual service for a man in exchange for cash. Thus, even a woman as intelligent and insightful as Ifemelu finds herself in a position where, against her wishes, the only way for her to procure money, as an international student with a scholarship that fails to cover the cost of her studies but without the legal right to work, is to sell sex.[28]

Whereas Slimani renders Myriam's background as mostly irrelevant to the story of the murder of her two children, Ifemelu as a blogger and activist immigrant to the United States from Nigeria spends most of the novel exploring her place in the world while commenting critically on her experiences in her childhood in Nigeria, her thirteen-year period living in the United States, and finally her return to Lagos. The book's title comes from the name that Nigerians call women who have spent time abroad. By selecting this term to represent the novel as a whole, Adichie draws attention to the immigrant Nigerian, female-gendered character of the protagonist. The novel shows Ifemelu engaging with a number of key issues concerning globalization, the postcolonial and neocolonial world order, and migration. For example, throughout the novel the protagonist analyzes, questions, and teases out issues of intersectionality and various types of privileges and perspectives. In a blog post, Ifemelu draws attention to how women of color experience race differently in the United States according to their ethnicity and the color of their skin. Adichie also deals critically with class issues in a major portion of the novel that describes Ifemelu's visit to a hair salon. In it Ifemelu situates her own status as an educated female African immigrant compared to that of other African women immigrants. Unlike Ifemelu, the women salon employees struggle with English and do not possess green cards or citizenship.[29] They also do not have the kind of wealth or education that Ifemelu enjoys, even though, as mentioned above, she too has suffered from want in America and was forced to do things against her will. Thus, Adichie gives us a strong character fully enmeshed in contemporary issues and fully capable of analyzing problems arising from intersectional identities.

NoViolet Bulawayo, We Need New Names

In her debut novel, We Need New Names, NoViolet Bulawayo depicts African women as complex, fully fledged characters going through a variety of experiences in contemporary Harare, Zimbabwe, and then in the United States. Her main character is Darling, who at the beginning of the novel lives in Paradise, a shantytown. Also portrayed are her friends, young girls, each with distinctive personalities. Darling's primary caretaker, Mother of Bones, joins her church congregation in shaming and assaulting a "loose woman" while Darling's mother and aunt have lovers. This distinction shows a variety ways in which women relate to sexuality. Darling herself, it should be noted, experiments with her sexuality and deplores her evangelist minister raping a woman in church to punish her for supposed immorality.[30]

As with Americanah, parts of We Need New Names are a critique of certain aspects of American society. For example, Darling converses with her friend Kristal about her use of Ebonics and how it is not, in Darling's opinion, "proper English." Darling likewise comments on the outrageous cost of jewelry in a Michigan mall and how much people are willing to pay for simple things like watches.[31] Thus, in this case a Zimbabwean adolescent girl is highly critical of her circumstances and fully capable of analyzing different environments, including "Western" ones.

We Need New Names addresses violence that girls and women can experience due to their gender. At the beginning of the novel, one of Darling's friends, Chipo, reveals in childlike terms that her grandfather raped her one day while her grandmother was away from home. Prior to this, upon being asked who "put it [the baby] in there [her stomach]," Chipo has only remained mute and cried quietly. In fact, Chipo generally refused to talk at the time that the novel is set, a condition that Darling links to her pregnancy and by extension to the aggression by her grandfather.[32]

One of the major female figures in the book, MotherLove, a woman who lives in the same community as Darling, suffers from a near breakdown as a consequence of the gender-based violence and dangers that girls and women in her community face. She discovers Darling and the female members of her gang of friends as they are "playing doctor" and trying to remove Chipo's unborn fetus with a hanger. The idea for this action comes from their friend Forgiveness, another ironically allegorical name, after she overhears her sister talking about how to terminate a pregnancy and the children learn of another woman in the village dying in childbirth. Darling's group of friends feels compelled to perform the procedure to save Chipo's life. When they explain this to the startled MotherLove, she responds by looking stunned, and "her body heaves downwards, like a sack falling."[33] Her rocklike nature (see below) cannot stand up to the stark reality of children trying to perform an abortion because of the dangers of childbirth present in their community. The scene additionally emphasizes the precariousness of being female in an environment where a girl as young as eleven could be the victim of rape and incest and then possibly die when she gives birth.

At other points in the novel, women are portrayed as more powerful and accustomed to difficulties of life in ways that men are not. One chapter describes people returning from voting after their loss in the elections and having to go to Paradise (an ironic name for a makeshift camp) when the government demolishes their homes in retaliation for their political opposition to the regime. Bulawayo describes the dispossessed group after their electoral loss: "And when they returned . . . they stuck hands deep inside torn pockets until they felt their dry thighs, kicked little stones out of the way, and erected themselves like walls again, but then the women, who knew all the ways of weeping and all there was to know about falling apart, would not be deceived; they gently rose from the hearths, beat dust off their skirts, and planted themselves like rocks in front of their men and children and shacks, and only then did all appear almost tolerable."[34] In this passage, women appear strong despite the hardships that they face. At the same time, though, it seems that there is an expectation for women to be strong and for them alone to carry the weight of the country's history and instruct their children in it. This trope of strength of African women is common, and critiqued here, since reality may place a burden upon the women to remain steadfast despite the horrors unfolding around them, yet another form of violence that they endure. Furthermore, the women are portrayed here as overcoming adversity precisely because they are accustomed to facing difficult circumstances as a result of their gender.

The critiques of the postcolonial state that the displaced individuals voice in this part of the novel, reciting their migration to Paradise, segues into another major aspect of representation of women in *We Need New Names*. In addition to describing different forms of violence and restrictions that women confront, the novel comments critically on issues of postcoloniality, globalization, immigration, and how these influence the lives of women born on the African continent. As in the passage just cited, at many points in the novel Bulawayo highlights the failures of the postcolonial state. The phrase "things fall apart" rings as a chorus throughout the novel when its characters, especially Darling, contemplate the lamentable state of Zimbabwe. The repeated statement constitutes a reference to Chinua Achebe's 1958 *Things Fall Apart*, a seminal work in African literature. Achebe's novel details the challenges and suffering of its main protagonist, Okonkwo, that result from the imposition of British colonial rule on Igboland. The title of the novel evokes the unraveling of his life and his eventual suicide as a direct consequence of the pressures stemming from European colonial encroachment.[35] Therefore, Bulawayo's frequent allusion to Achebe's work, set at the beginning of the colonial period in Nigeria, in discussing postindependence Zimbabwe draws parallels between colonial rule and the postindependent state. *We Need New Names* portrays Darling as fully conscious of the failures of the postindependent state and highly critical of the political situation in her country.

Beyond the struggles of postcoloniality, the novel wrestles with globalization and how it impacts women. In her experiences in Paradise and in a wealthy Zimbabwean community termed Budapest by her and her friends, Darling encounters pro-Rhodesia white residents, a woman of Zimbabwean origin from London visiting the country of her father, Chinese construction laborers, and NGO (nongovernmental organization) workers who exploit their images but give them things in return, primarily much-needed food. Moreover, many of the men in her community, including her own father, cross the border into South Africa to work. The children are also highly aware of Zimbabwe's place as well as their own in the world. They play "country-game," in which they list the pecking order of countries according to their level of wealth and power. Furthering her ironic images, Bulawayo also has the children singing "Lady Gaga" and participating in a game called "Kill Bin Laden," further proof that, regardless of their poverty, the children of Paradise are highly cognizant of world affairs and exposed to global cultural trends.[36]

Importantly, the children in Paradise, as well as Darling once she gets to the United States, challenge and question inequalities that arise from globalization. When an NGO comes to their town, the photographer who accompanies the group starts taking photos of the children without their permission. Darling wonders whether the NGO workers are viewing Chipo as a sort of Paris Hilton and that is why they want her photo. Clearly, Chipo's state as a displaced pregnant child does not evoke the images of wealth and luxury that Paris Hilton generally symbolizes. One can assume that Bulawayo includes this detail to insinuate that the NGO photographer wants to use the image of a pregnant, young Chipo as a purported sign of the level of poverty or problems in the country.[37]

In addition to postcoloniality and globalization, the novel addresses the struggles of African women upon immigrating to the United States. Like many other new immigrants to America, Darling struggles to adopt new cultural norms. For example, she causes a stir at a wedding when she hits a child for misbehaving because corporal punishment is not acceptable in the United States. There is also a discussion of the difficulties of mastering English in an anecdote about Aunt Fostelina's attempt to purchase a Victoria's Secret bra when she has problems pronouncing the word "angel."[38]

Conclusion

Taken in the aggregate, *The Orchard of Lost Souls*, *Chanson Douce*, *Americanah*, and *We Need New Names* represent women with connections to the African continent as heterogeneous individuals who approach and respond to problems in different ways. Female African writers today are continuing earlier trends of tackling questions of postcoloniality and pushing back against representations of African women as a voiceless, monolithic group. Several characters depicted in the novels evaluated here face gender discrimination and gender-based violence. How they respond to these situations varies according to character. In general, the women presented in these novels are acutely aware of gender and sexuality and how their intersectional status as women and members of other marginalized groups has held them back, sometimes to the point of actively speaking out against stereotypes of "Africa" or "African women." Finally, African female writers today are depicting women and girls in Africa and of recent African origin as immigrants to Western nations as confronting issues of globalization, postcoloniality, and migration in innovative ways and with new forms of technology. Although the origins of the authors NoViolet Bulawayo, Chimamenda Adichie, Nadia Mohamed, and Leila Slimani vary, their themes cohere and proclaim them as distinctive voices of African contemporary women, whose contributions to world literature not only overthrow colonial limitations but also provide new definitions, and describe new aspects, of human experiences.

Notes

1. I am focusing on novels here rather than other forms of literary expression in order to allow for a comparison of longer volumes that permit extended character development. Despite the rich tradition of oral narration that exists in many communities around Africa, this chapter exclusively addresses modern novels published by women about the African continent, predominantly recent works that have achieved acclaim.

2. For instance, NoViolet Bulawayo's *We Need New Names* was nominated for the *Guardian's* First Book Award and Booker Prize. Part of the novel also received the Cain Prize for African Writing in 2011. Concerning the authors' inclusion on lists of best African writers and novels, see, for example, Minna Salami, "7 Great Novels by African Women Writers," *MsAfropolitan* (blog), March 20, 2014, http://www.msafropolitan.com/2014/03/review-books-african-women-writers.html. One of the anonymous reviewers for this manuscript correctly pointed out that many of the works analyzed here were composed by women from the African continent living abroad about their experiences beyond "African" spaces. It is not my intention through the inclusion of these works to place diasporic literature on a higher echelon of worth than work produced in and focusing on local African contexts. Instead, it appears that international attention has narrowed in on diasporic literature by African women.

3. Touria Khannous, *African Pasts, Presents, and Futures: Generational Shifts in African Women's Literature, Film, and Internet Discourse* (Lanham, MD: Lexington Books, 2013), xi–xii.

4. Several academic works have addressed colonial-era depictions of African women and gender. See, for example, Malek Alloula, *The Colonial Harem* (Minneapolis: University of Minnesota Press, 1986); Anne McClintock, *Imperial Leather: Race, Gender, and Sexuality in the Colonial Contest* (New York: Routledge, 1995); and Natasha Gordon-Chipembere, ed., *Representation and Black Womanhood: The Legacy of Sarah Baartman* (New York: Palgrave Macmillan, 2011). The term and concept of "Othering" here comes from Edward W. Said, *Orientalism* (New York: Pantheon Books, 1978).

5. Isak Dinesen, *Out of Africa; and, Shadows on the Grass* (New York: Vintage International, 1989), 296, translated from French by the author. All translations in this chapter are mine unless otherwise indicated.

6. Said, *Orientalism*.

7. Dinesen, *Out of Africa*, 293, 296–99.

8. These authors' chief female protagonists here (with the exception of Mohamed's characters in *The Orchard of Lost Souls*, which is set in the late 1980s) all deal with present-day issues and problems.

9. Nadifa Mohamed, *The Orchard of Lost Souls* (New York: Farrar, Straus and Giroux, 2014), 114–16.

10. Mohamed, *The Orchard of Lost Souls*, 239, 19–45.

11. Mohamed, *The Orchard of Lost Souls*, 4, 14, 174.

12. Mohamed, *The Orchard of Lost Souls*, 334, 330. Mohamed shows Filsan recognizing that over the course of her life at critical points she depended on men's decisions and actions and so was complicit in upholding the patriarchal state order. See also p. 8.

13. Mohamed, *The Orchard of Lost Souls*, 5.

14. Leïla Slimani, *Chanson Douce* (Paris: Gallimard, 2016), 16.

15. Slimani, *Chanson Douce*, 28.

16. Slimani, *Chanson Douce*, 25.

17. In an interview with *France24*, Slimani stated after publishing her first book, "When a young North African publishes a first novel, it needs to be about Islam, identity, Maghreb, immigration, etc. I also wanted to say that a North African in France has access to universal experiences and is not obliged to mention dunes, camels and mosques." See Sarah Leduc, "Dark Novel on Female Sex Addiction Wins Prize in Morocco," *France24*, September 29, 2015, http://www.france24.com/en/20150929-novel-leila-slimani-book-sex-addiction-prize-morocco.

18. Slimani, *Chanson Douce*, 35, 190–96, 203–9.

19. Slimani, *Chanson Douce*, 18–24, 40–42.

20. Slimani, *Chanson Douce*, 84, 131–32.

21. Chimamanda Ngozi Adichie, *Americanah*, ebook (New York: Alfred A. Knopf, 2013), 648–55.

22. Slimani, *Chanson Douce*, 115–17.

23. Slimani, *Chanson Douce*, 115–17.

24. Adichie, *Americanah*, 58, 505, 353.

25. Adichie, *Americanah*, 647.

26. Adichie, *Americanah*, 127.

27. Adichie, *Americanah*, 87–88.

28. Adichie, *Americanah*, 962–63, 361–69.

29. Adichie, *Americanah*, 155–56, 290, 843–44.

30. NoViolet Bulawayo, *We Need New Names: A Novel* (New York: Back Bay Books, 2014), 32–41, 65–66, 201–16, 283.

31. Bulawayo, *We Need New Names*, 222–24, 231.

32. Bulawayo, *We Need New Names*, 6, 28.

33. Bulawayo, *We Need New Names*, 80–90.

34. Bulawayo, *We Need New Names*, 78–79.

35. Chinua Achebe, *Things Fall Apart* (London: Heinemann, 1958).

36. Bulawayo, *We Need New Names*, 93, 51, 64.

37. Bulawayo, *We Need New Names*, 54–55.

38. Bulawayo, *We Need New Names*, 184–85, 196–98.

Suggested Readings

Assiba d'Almeida, Irène. *Francophone African Women Writers: Destroying the Emptiness of Silence*. Gainesville: University Press of Florida, 1994.

Boyce Davies, Carole, and Anne Adams Graves, eds. *Ngambika: Studies of Women in African Literature*. Trenton, NJ: Africa World Press, 1986.

Browdy de Hernandez, Jennifer, ed. *African Women Writing Resistance: An Anthology of Contemporary Voices*. Madison: University of Wisconsin Press, 2010.

James, Adeola, ed. *In Their Own Voices: African Women Writers Talk*. London: J. Currey, 1990.

Makuchi Nfah-Abbenyi, Juliana. *Gender in African Women's Writing: Identity, Sexuality, and Difference*. Bloomington: Indiana University Press, 1997.

FIGURE 2.1 Scene from *Ije*, 2010 film directed by Chineze Anyaene. Film still used by permission of Chineze Anyaene.

2

CONTRASTING VISIONS

Filmic Representations of African Women

Cajetan Iheka

In 1810, Sara Baartman, a Khoikhoi woman from the Eastern Cape of South Africa, was exhibited in London as an ethnographic spectacle due to her "large" buttocks. The racist and sexist connotations of the use of Sara Baartman as an exhibit in nineteenth-century Europe have been widely analyzed in scholarly literature.[1] They represent the dominant image of African women in the Western colonial imaginary. Her handlers constructed Sara as the embodiment of the hypersexualized African. In this schema, her "abnormal" body composition was evidence of her freakish nature, but more importantly of her difference from the normal, rational Westerner. As an African, Sara was at best an inferior woman, or an animalistic creature in their eyes, one who lacked the accoutrements of the Enlightenment subject.

Depictions of Africans in colonial cinema retained the trope of the abnormal or savage African undergirding Baartman's exhibition. African women in particular bore the brunt of this misrepresentation due to their portrayal as sexualized objects. Olivier Barlet captures the essence of these films when he writes, "Colonial cinema fed the European audience's appetite for fantasy, escape, and exoticism with picturesque, sensational material."[2] Melissa Thackway notes that black women were "portrayed as sexually rampant creatures who ensnare unwitting white men, accelerating their downfall."[3] This stereotyping was not restricted to films made for a colonialist audience; the ones made for those colonized equally included many negative traits. Manthia Diawara opines that European filmmakers "considered the African mind too primitive to follow the sophisticated narrative techniques of mainstream cinema. Thus, they thought it necessary to return to the beginning of film history—to use uncut scenes, slow down the story's pace, and make the narrative simpler by using fewer actors and adhering to just one dominant theme."[4] Whether in

Tarzan films or *King Solomon's Mines*, there was an effort to negate a shared humanity in colonialist films by "othering" Africans. When they were not entirely elided or silenced, as in *Out of Africa* or *Heart of Darkness*, African women were subject to hypersexualized representations.

African filmmakers stepped into the picture in the 1950s to correct misconceptions of the Western gaze. Preoccupied with showing images of Africa and Africans that upheld their dignity and humanity, filmmakers such as Ousmane Sembène enlisted the camera in the project of decolonization. Adopting the creed of Third Cinema, stipulating that Third World *cinéastes* eschew the principles of Hollywood and European cinema and produce "imperfect" cinema geared toward raising social consciousness and inspiring anticolonial revolutions, early African filmmakers used the medium of film to critique colonial policies and highlight postcolonial disillusionment with the incompetence of the national elites.[5] Many such filmmakers—men and women—depicted layers of exploitation women faced in Africa because of colonialism but also because of the repressive bent of indigenous, or newly formulated under colonial impact, male-dominant structures.

Although African filmmakers loosened their ideological commitment to nationalist politics starting in the 1970s, many continued to highlight the plight of women and to portray them in a more positive light than the reductive representations in colonial films. The 1970s also marked the appearance of films directed by African women. This does not mean that women did not produce films before then. Efua Sutherland of Ghana, for instance, made films for television in the 1960s. Rather, the 1970s marked the appearance of Safi Faye's *Kaddu Beykat* (1975), the first film by an African woman to gain commercial and critical acclaim, as well as an unprecedented number of other well-received films by women.[6] Since then, women have occupied central roles not only as subjects of African films but also as producers and directors.

In this chapter I consider the multiple roles of women in African films by male and female *cinéastes*. While African male filmmakers have successfully illuminated the challenges of women and portrayed female agency, they sometimes share with colonial films the elision of women's subjectivities as well their objectification. Overall, African women film directors have disputed both colonial and postcolonial male representations by emphasizing women's agency as subjects of films, violence against women, the importance of their labor, and their environmental activism. First I analyze *Xala* (1974) by the "father" of African cinema, Ousmane Sembène.[7] Next, I examine the works of early women filmmakers, including Safi Faye's *Kaddu Beykat*, Sarah Maldoror's *Sambizanga* (1972), and Assia Djebar's *La Nouba des Femmes du Mont Chenoua*

(1977).[8] Following these sections, I take up the productions of contemporary filmmakers whose experimental styles transcend the nationalist paradigm of their predecessors. Chineze Anyaene's New Nollywood film *Ije* (2010) and Wanuri Kahiu's science fiction film *Pumzi* (2009) are scrutinized as examples of the latest cinematic trends in Africa.[9]

Women in African Films by Men: Ousmane Sembène's *Xala*

I begin with eminent filmmaker and feminist Ousmane Sembène, who was perhaps the most progressive among the earliest African filmmakers regarding representation of women. Successive filmmakers have built on *Xala*'s success in highlighting the challenges of women in patriarchal societies and positing a strong female personality in Rama. The opening scene of Sembène's *Xala* depicts a change of leadership in the Senegalese Chamber of Commerce when the male indigenous elite interrupt a meeting of the Chamber and dismiss the French incumbents. The empowered local elite, in a move reminiscent of Frantz Fanon's national bourgeoisie, replaces their customary garb with suits, making them like Europeans except for skin color. Like their European pre- decessors, the new members are men, suggesting that the change is merely cosmetic. The opening shots raise the question of the status of women in the film and in the postindependence dispensation, a question for which we find answers soon after.

The first meeting of the nationalized Chamber of Commerce ends with the announcement of El Hadji's marriage to his third wife later that day. At the lavish wedding where El Hadji's profligacy is displayed, there is substantial food and drink, and a live band entertains the audience. Later that night, however, El Hadji is impotent due to a curse placed on him. Disgraced, he explores several costly cures, which deplete his finances. Consequently, his business crumbles, and he cannot meet his financial obligations to the Grain Board and the bank. A healer removes the curse but then reimposes it when El Hadji's check bounces. A beggar then promises to cure him and invites fellow mendicants to the businessman's house. In the film's final sequence, we see "the wretched of the earth" gathered in El Hadji's house. They ask El Hadji to undress and let them spit on him to neutralize the spell. A reluctant El Hadji obeys the beggars, who accuse him and his class of dispossessing them. The failed businessman, whose other houses and cars have been seized by the bank and whose membership in the Chamber is already terminated, suffers his humiliation in silence.

Ultimately, El Hadji's financial woes are traceable to his lavish lifestyle shared with other nationalists who replaced the colonizers only to maintain the status quo regarding corruption and impoverishment of the masses. El Hadji demonstrated his ostentatious lifestyle in his decision to marry a third wife. In critiquing the corruption of the bourgeois class, the film problematizes the practice of polygyny and highlights its deleterious impacts on women. As the wives of El Hadji show, jealousy is a human emotion that does not go away simply because marrying more than one wife is permissible within a culture. So, after leaving the Chamber meeting, El Hadji goes home to his first wife, Adja, to prepare for his marriage. The camera then cuts to Adja and her daughter, Rama, who asks her mother not to validate the marriage by attending. While Adja chooses to suffer silently as her husband takes another wife, Oumi, the second wife, openly expresses her misgivings about her husband's decision to marry again. She scolds him, pushes him around, and requests money from him. Sembene stages the emotional impact of polygyny by highlighting the suffering of women like Adja and even of Ngone, the youngest wife, who marries El Hadji because his wealth is critical for her family's social recognition and upward mobility. Before the wedding reception commences, her relative displays some of the bridewealth, the gifts from El Hadji, showing that these material items played no small role in facilitating the marriage.

When El Hadji is unable to maintain an erection on the wedding night, the entire focus of the film shifts to his travails. Left out of this frame is the young bride whose desire (or lack thereof) is not articulated. As Kenneth Harrow describes it, she "functions as the excluded term on which the male center depends."[10] The only time she speaks is to inform her mother that the relationship is not consummated the first night. When El Hadji's other wives are shown in the film, it is to highlight the negative impact of polygyny on them. The new wife is only brought into the film when displayed on the wedding day by El Hadji, as he would any property and later that night when his manhood fails.

So far, I have positioned El Hadji's wives as victims of polygynous arrangements in *Xala*, but that should not be interpreted as the definitive representation of women in the film. In fact, Rama, Adja and El Hadji's daughter, occupies one end of a spectrum, with the other end holding her mother and stepmothers. She frowns on polygyny and discourages her mother from attending the wedding. In a remarkable scene before the nuptials, she rises to confront her father after declaring that "men are dirty dogs." Although El Hadji slaps her for her effrontery, she continues to be a strong voice for her mother and for nationalist values. When she visits her father's office later in the film, she rejects his offer of money, which is all the more significant because El Hadji rests the success of his relationship with his wives and children on his ability to meet their material needs. In rejecting his money, Rama remarks that her mother's happiness is her only demand of El Hadji, thereby rearranging marital and familial priorities to put emotional satisfaction at the apex (see also chapters 13 and 14).

Rama is not only remapping the cartography of the domestic sphere; the film equally portrays her as a nationalist. In differentiating the young woman from her submissive mother, Josef Gugler argues that "Rama, their daughter, embodies the future, reborn Africa, a society that will draw on its own language and culture while emancipating women from patriarchal traditions."[11] In an era where El Hadji and members of his class have traded their traditional garb for suits and briefcases filled with cash and appear dependent on foreign goods—cars, air conditioners, and even bottled water—Rama rejects her father's offer of bottled water, reminding the patriarch that she detests imported water. Earlier on, we learn that she promotes Wolof as the national language and supports academic work in this regard. The film ends with the humiliated El Hadji wearing the spittle of beggars he once ordered removed from the streets, with his former colleagues entrenched in their corrupt ways, so the viewer's attention shifts to Rama, who exerted agency in seeking positive change in the domestic and public spheres.

Sembène's feminist inclinations extend beyond Rama's role in *Xala*. His skillful combination of nationalist issues with feminist concerns is a hallmark of his works, whether literary or filmic. Other male filmmakers such as Med Hondo in *Sarraounia* (1986) and Idrissa Ouédraogo in *Yaaba* (1989) give empathetic views of women.[12] Lindiwe Dovey argues that the remarkable effort of these male filmmakers "to celebrate women and to critique men—can be considered part of a broader, progressive postcolonial trend of self-critique by African artists."[13] In their sensitivity to issues affecting women, these male filmmakers anticipate the productions of their female counterparts.

The Matriarchs of African Filmmaking: Safi Faye, Sarah Maldoror, and Assia Djebar

Diana Maury Robin and Ira Jaffe accurately describe the films analyzed in this section in their proposal that Third World women's films are concerned with the "repositioning and reempowering of women both in front of the camera and behind it; the rediscovery and retrieval of women's histories and subjectivities; the role of women in promoting the ideals of community; and, last but not least, the assumption by women of a more oppositional stance toward colonial and patriarchal forces."[14] In this category is Faye's *Kaddu Beykat*, which articulates a critique of colonial policies in Africa, although it was funded by the French government. The film is symptomatic of the Janus-faced character of early African filmmaking in francophone Africa. While these filmmakers endorsed the tenets of Third Cinema, centered on the notion of decolonization and liberation from the colonialist impulses of Hollywood and European cinema, they nevertheless relied on the generosity of France to produce their films.

Kaddu Beykat is primarily set in a Senegalese village where agriculture is the mainstay of the economy. As a result of French colonial policies that discouraged diversification in the agricultural sector while encouraging specialization in cash crops, this community depends on groundnut (peanut) production. Kaddu Beykat opens with shots of the environment, the land, and the trees, successively. From there the film cuts to three successive shots of women in domestic spaces. Two of them show women emerging from their houses with babies on their backs, while in the third, another woman is returning with firewood. The first shots of people in the film show women doing domestic labor. Women then appear going for water from the stream and repeatedly working in the fields, by themselves and with men. At intervals, the voice-over pauses to let the viewer focus on the task or the voice of a character such as a woman singing as she works in the field. Using close-ups among other techniques, Faye allows the viewer to dwell on women in a way not permitted by Sembène's focus on El Hadji in Xala.

The film's conflict arises when the crop fails because of drought, a situation that further impoverishes the community. In this environment, Ngor, betrothed to Coumba, cannot afford to pay the bridewealth. Kaddu Beykat is a documentary, but as is characteristic of Faye's work, she stretches the limits of the genre by also incorporating fictional elements to enrich the film. Ngor's move to the city and his disillusionment there disclose the disruption of rural life by colonial modernity and the fact that the city fails to live up to its promise for those who seek fortune there. On his return to the village, the couple perform the customary marriage rites. Whereas earlier in the film the couple spend time together in public, later in the film the focus moves from the celebration of the marriage to a scene where they are portrayed sharing an intimate space. Faye's film is slow paced, mirroring the slowness of life in the rural setting, just as the black-and-white images foreground the realities as they are, without the embellishments of color. Life in the village is portrayed as drudgery, embodied in manual labor, especially for women. Some scenes with only slight variations are repeated to delineate monotonous country life.

Although rural women are depicted primarily in relation to their domestic labor (see chapter 8), the city provides a space for subverting gender roles.

Ngor's boss in the city is a good example; her mobility is not restricted by domestic labor. Rather than working in fields and in the domestic sphere like rural women, she drives a car to work away from her home, leaving the male protagonist to shut the gate and undertake domestic chores, including doing laundry. Compared to rural spaces, urban spaces seem to provide wider latitude for women, even though the film suggests that wealthy city dwellers, like Ngor's employer, use their power to swindle the poor out of their earnings.

Rural women in the film are mainly absent from the public sphere. Besides holding sway in their homes, the women appear in the fields and on their way to other errands. Their social life is wholly connected to their work. In contrast, men (young and old) are shown spending leisure time in public spaces. In the final scene, for instance, a public gathering of men uses the opportunity of listening to Ngor's story of the city to discuss the importance of planting trees and diversifying agricultural produce. Given the important roles that women play in various ramifications of social life in this community—domestic, agricultural, and so on—their absence from this meeting, which rails against the exploitative practices of colonial rule and proposes future paths to economic and environmental sustainability, is telling. Yet one can argue that portraying rural women in relation to their labor enables Faye to emphasize their contributions to this local community alongside the gendered impacts of drought and colonial agricultural policies. Read this way, Faye's approach illustrates that women cannot afford the leisure activities indulged in by men.

In documenting the lives of members of the community, Faye also illumi-nates her role as a filmmaker whose voice-over throughout the film orients the viewers to the people and mise-en-scène. Her attentiveness to various facets of this African community contradicts simplistic depictions of Africans in the colonial filmic imaginary. Also, unlike colonial filmmakers and even many male African ones, Faye promotes a participatory style of filmmaking where members of the community influence content during production.[15] *Kaddu Beykat* captures voices of peasants, whose views are integral to the making and composition of the film.

Two years after Faye's film appeared, in 1977 Assia Djebar performed a similar feat when she underscored the experiences of ordinary women in *La Nouba*, the first Algerian film directed by a woman. Writing in "La nouba des femmes du Mont Chenoua," Réda Bensmaïa reads Djebar's film as a "cin-ematic fragment," arguing that the film's disjointed, fragmented style is consis-tent with the feminist vision of a filmmaker determined to decenter the male gaze and subvert the androcentricity characterizing Algerian freedom films.[16]

For Bensmaïa, a male story or film revolves around a central plot, usually that of masculine strength and valor, while a female-centered film like La Nouba departs from this convention. His astute comment is useful for situating La Nouba's unique style and indicative of the fact that the film continues the project of foregrounding marginal voices that Djebar started in her literary works. Like Sembène, Djebar turned to film to expand beyond a literary audience. The film is composed of five different fragments, like a musical suite. The first suite presents the story of Lila, her husband, Ali, and their child. In the second and third suites, we hear the stories of the women of Mont Chenoua. In the fourth suite, the viewer is drawn to the larger ecosystem, as encapsulated in the land and the sea, while the final one draws on archival records of the war of national liberation to illuminate the violent repression of that conflict.

Djebar's film, by highlighting female perspectives on the Algerian war, perhaps was inspired by Sarah Maldoror's Sambizanga (1972). Maldoror's film is set at the beginning of the Angolan war of independence, which pitted Portuguese Armed Forces against nationalist movements, including the People's Movement for the Liberation of Angola (MPLA), between 1961 and 1974. Maldoror, a Guadeloupan married to Mário de Andrade, a leader of the MPLA, utilizes film as a medium for articulating physical and psychological distress imposed by the war on women and their families. The film's opening scene introduces viewers to a family composed of a nationalist, Domingos Xavier, his wife, Maria, and their little child. In one scene, Domingos has just returned from his work as a tractor driver on a construction site and joins his wife for dinner. Maldoror's film paints the image of a close-knit family with the couple sharing smiles and laughter even when Maria objects to her husband's tardiness. The significance of this early scene becomes clearer after Domingos is arrested by agents of the colonial administration and taken to Luanda, separating him from his distraught wife and helpless child.

The film is then concerned with the clandestine activities of the nationalist movement, the torture endured by Domingos because he will not incriminate the other nationalists and their white sympathizers, and his death among fellow prisoners after a torture scene. Yet Maldoror's approach makes it impossible to forget the impact of the repression on women such as Maria. As Sheila Petty observed, Maldoror stresses gender interconnection by "panning from Domingos to Maria and back again," cutting back and forth between the struggle to tie Domingos in the vehicle after his arrest and the scene where women are comforting his wife, allowing viewers to perceive the feelings of men and women alike.[17]

Maldoror's film aligns with the ideological project of *La Nouba*, which also focuses on the war-time experiences of women. Although Maldoror's film enables the viewer to see the brutalization of the male body in ways that *La Nouba* does not, it is still particularly attentive to the plight of women in war. We follow Maria's long trail and trial, for instance, as she searches for her husband from one jail to the other, only to be turned back or physically assaulted. In one such scene, her face appears distressed while the somber background song heightens the emotional toll of her husband's arrest. When she finally learns of her husband's death and comes out of an imposing colonial building weeping, many women appear to console her, their immediate action suggesting they are relatives of other men imprisoned alongside Domingos. When they console Maria, the viewer can appreciate the collective implications of colonial repression, not just for individuals or families but also for the larger social fabric of communities.

Djebar's *La Nouba* shares with *Sambizanga* an attentiveness to the condition of women and their perspectives on the war for independence. The camera often tracks women from a distance and then close up, focusing viewers on their actions, including their work. It is possible to read Djebar's film in relation to Faye's *Kaddu Beykat*, which also positions women in terms of their labor. Besides this shared thematic thread, it is striking that Faye and Djebar deploy a mixture of documentary and fiction in their films. As for the popularity of the documentary form for female filmmakers, Beti Ellerson opines that it is "perhaps out of a genuine interest in addressing the pressing issues in their societies and relating stories that would otherwise not be told."[18]

Two women in the opening shot of *La Nouba* appear to be carrying exacting loads. A third woman shows up, reminiscent of the woman in Faye's film carrying what looks like firewood. Most women shown are physically encumbered by some form of burden. Lila's husband, in the first fragment, is confined to a wheelchair due to an accident. In his interpretation of Lila's role, Bensmaïa muses positively when he writes that after the accident, "Lila is able to detach herself, affording herself the means to meditate, to dream, to wander. She is able to re-forge not only the bonds that link her to other women, but also those that reconnect her to herself."[19] One can take this reading seriously and acknowledge the burden that the accident imposes upon her. Having lost unrestricted mobility, Ali needs Lila to wait on him. In one remarkable scene, she angrily drops his crutches when he gestures for her to keep quiet. Lila's attitude here is symptomatic of her frustration at being circumscribed by her husband. The women in other fragments without disabled husbands must tend to their children. Even when not shown tending children directly, the presence of many young ones milling around draws attention to the labor involved in raising them. We also see women outside the home as they work in fields, their backs bent wielding short-handled hoes as they till the soil. Together, the women in the film's fragments are circumscribed by their labor, evident in the load they carry on their backs and hands.

Furthermore, layered into the film is a psychological burden that is a consequence of the Algerian war of independence. The testimonies illuminate the heroic role of women in the war, the fact that they were major participants even if "his/story" often relegates their perspectives to the background. Besides actively participating in the war, the women equally bear the psychological burden of losing loved ones in battle.

I have shown the ways that *La Nouba*, *Sambizanga*, and *Kaddu Beykat* illuminate the burdens, physical and psychological, of women in their respective societies, thereby emphasizing the significant contributions and sacrifices they make for nation building. Yet there is a signal difference between Faye's and Djebar's film worth mentioning. Whereas Faye's film reveals the limited space for female socializing outside their work sites and the absence of women in the final scene of male camaraderie, in contrast, a group of women sing and dance as Djebar's film ends. The camera zooms in on one dancer at a time and pans across the larger group, showing women carefully in their individuality and as a collective. In this moment, they seem free of the burdens affixed to them throughout the film when they lose themselves in dance.

Viewers of *La Nouba* cannot miss shots that pan the landscape and the sea, or the way that female bodies are situated within expansive space. Unsurprisingly, then, critics have offered interpretations of the film's spatial logic. Bensmaïa, for instance, argues that "what emerges now is a turning outward, an infinite unfolding toward the external world and toward others."[20] The freedom that this critic associates with external space is echoed in Mani Sharpe's position on representation of space in Djebar's film. In outlining the significance of Mont Chenoua for Djebar's filmic text, Sharpe contends that it be "considered as a wider site of resistance against a history of patriarchal, sociospatial domination."[21] Bensmaïa and Sharpe agree that exterior spaces provide a counterpoint to constrictions of domestic space in the film. But it is also in these external spaces that the women grapple with the weight of burdens carried on their backs and hands. The landscape may be liberating, but its space also allows Djebar to expatiate on women's burdens. In some landscape shots of found archival documents, the destruction wrought by wartime explosions is obvious, showing much environmental damage. It is possible to argue that the film intertwines the fate of women with that of nature.

Both conceptual categories are constructed as heavily impacted by war. Yet the resilience of the women, who have the courage to tell their stories and occupy space in a graceful manner, suggests that we should not consider them as mere victims. The weight they continue to bear is testament to their strength just as the beauty of the Algerian landscape in *La Nouba* shows its resilience despite the ravages of war.

Commercial Filmmaking: Examples from Nollywood

When women filmmakers such as Faye, Maldoror, and Djebar were making waves in African cinema in the 1970s, alternatives to their social realist ideological films were also emerging, the kind that Roy Armes calls "alternative or experimental films."[22] As Frank Ukadike puts it, the "'new breed' African filmmaker seeks to advance cinematic strategy beyond the ideologies that have defined the contours of didactic sociopolitical films."[23] Without strong technical and financial support that France continued to provide for filmmakers in its former colonies, celluloid film production failed in many parts of the continent, including Nigeria. Afolabi Adesanya, a Nigerian filmmaker, has noted that the "economics of celluloid film production and marketing have been the bane of Nigerian filmmakers."[24] In its place, Nigerian filmmakers have embraced shooting the cheaper video while favoring "commercial popular cultural forms."[25] The commercial appeal of Nigerian films is most apparent in the successful Nollywood industry that expanded tremendously since the 1990s to become one of the largest film industries in terms of output. Differentiating videos from the lengthier francophone African films, Manouchka Kelly Labouba has noted that celluloid "films rarely break even commercially, and are also more easily available outside the continent, in film libraries or academic institutions in North America and Europe." In contrast, Labouba says, video filmmakers are "mostly interested in making their money back, because their films are financed locally by the directors themselves, or by patrons or by businessmen."[26] Nollywood films are aimed at popular audiences, inviting viewers to identify with consumerism and overconsumption, even while they live well below the lifestyle portrayed.

One consequence of the consumerist drive in these films has been the objectification of women. In Chris Obi Rapu's *Living in Bondage* (1992), regarded as the first Nollywood film, Andy (Kenneth Okonkwo) remains poor despite strong efforts to achieve economic success, until he meets a friend, Paulo.[27] Paulo has made it and belongs to an exclusive club that he invites Andy to join. Andy later learns that this club is a secret cult requiring the sacrifice of his dearest family member, his wife in this case, to obtain wealth.

Andy deceives his dutiful wife, Merit (Nnenna Nwabueze), into attending the meeting. Merit is killed after Andy's initial attempt to sacrifice a prostitute fails. As Andy is being scolded for his deceptive behavior, other members proudly announce their sacrificial victims, many of them women. Chief Omego (Kanayo O. Kanayo), for example, gave his mother in exchange for his wealth. Whether it is Omego's mother, Merit, or the prostitute that Andy tries to substitute for his wife, what is clear is the substitution of women for money. Other women in the film are portrayed as objects to be flaunted by men, with no emotional connection since relationships are pursued for the material benefits accruing from them. It is symbolic that the woman who becomes Andy's wife after Merit's death is named *Ego*, the Igbo word for money. It appears that money and women are interchangeable in *Living in Bondage*. The film's women are portrayed as "metaphors for pure consumption," to use language from Carmela Garritano's analysis of a similar phenomenon in Ghanaian videos.[28]

In a more recent Nollywood film, *Formidable Force* (2002), women are not subjected to the kind of objectification in Rapu's film but still play a secondary role to men.[29] This political action thriller shows Bill (Hanks Anuku) as a videographer who happens upon a sensitive conversation between a politician and police commissioner and films it. Nike (Genevieve Nnaji) appears in the film to support the male protagonist. The film's real agency is located in Bill, whose heroic endeavors are crucial for uncovering political corruption. His masculine body is foregrounded via close-ups, which emphasize his heroism in the face of torture. As I argue elsewhere, although "Nike is definitely not sexualized or eroticized" like the women of *Living in Bondage*, "her role is still dependent on Bill 'making things happen.' In other words, it is Bill whom we recognize as the primary hero of the film, the driver of its narrative."[30]

A corrective to Nollywood movies that position women as objects of the male gaze can be seen in the work of female filmmakers who have transformed the role of women from objects to subjects while proposing "new models of social and economic achievement for Nigerian women."[31] One example is Chineze Anyaene, whose *Ije* (2010) is a remarkable success in terms of both quality and box office earnings. *Ije* is a prime example of New Nollywood films differentiated by the adoption of more sophisticated cinematic techniques. Nollywood critics have lamented the abysmal quality of the films that are quickly put together, the bad acting, and the almost predictable storylines. New Nollywood's concern with quality is therefore attributable to the need to transcend what Jonathan Haynes calls "a gross disjunction between the poor quality of the images and the shiny products they represent."[32] As articulated by scholars familiar with the industry, other characteristics of New Nollywood include an abiding interest in transnationalism, in terms of thematic preoccupation and/or global circulation, as well as initial release in theaters before DVD rollout.[33]

Considering its premium quality, its transnational dimensions, and its initial screening at cinema houses before appearing on disk, *Ije*, which explores the lives of two sisters, Anya and Chioma, fits the lineaments of New Nollywood. The film opens with a crime scene set in the United States, which involves Michael Michino, Anya's husband, and his two friends who have been shot. As the camera moves away from Michael, Anya appears holding a gun. She is soon arrested and charged for the murder of her husband and the other men. The prosecution's argument rests on portraying Anya as an opportunist who kills her successful music producer husband to inherit his wealth. As Anya awaits trial in jail, she writes to her sister, Chioma, who arrives in the United States to pursue justice. Anyaene's film can be understood as an indictment of the justice system especially for immigrants and people of color (see chapter 12) but also of the practice of objectifying women that spans the Atlantic. The bias against foreigners, especially Nigerians and other Africans, is noticeable even during Chioma's flight, where she undergoes additional surveillance due to her nationality or skin color. Chioma learns on arrival that Anya's lawyer, Mrs. Barron, wants her to plead guilty to manslaughter charges to avoid the harsher penalty of a guilty verdict. In Chioma's conversations with the lawyer, it becomes evident that Anya's race and national affiliation are fundamental to the reasoning of Mrs. Barron, who is aware of the pitfalls of a system that disadvantages people of color.

Whereas Nike appears as a secondary character, an appendage to Bill's muscular body in *Formidable Force*, Anyaene locates agency in Chioma, played by the same actor, Genevieve Nnaji. Ultimately, Chioma convinces an African American lawyer, Mr. Turner, to take up Anya's case and argue for her innocence. Through Anyaene's skillful use of flashback, the viewer learns of Anya's abuse at the hands of Michael, including that she was raped on the night of the murder, and that in self-defense she shot the men who killed her husband. Anyaene wants to problematize the silence surrounding rape by making Anya hide that vital information from her testimony even if it is pivotal to her exoneration. Other flashbacks in the story trace the shame to her childhood experience of an abusive father, who "returns" his wife, Anya's mother, to her family after she is raped during a crisis. As Chioma explains to Mr. Turner, the fact of rape turned her mother into "damaged goods." Cognizant of the stigma of rape in her culture, doubly victimized Anya chooses to hide the truth in order not to offend the sensibilities of her father. Anyaene's flashbacks are skillfully and purposefully manipulated to demonstrate the lasting effects of childhood abuse but also the fact that rape is a form of violence against women everywhere (see chapter 15).

Women are critical to the resolution of the conflict in *Ije*. It is easy to claim that Mr. Turner's defense strategy helped win the case, but to extend such credit to him is to diminish the role of Chioma, who braves the odds of the unfamiliar American justice system to fight for her sister's cause. Besides firing Mrs. Barron and convincing Mr. Turner to take the case, she finds an object belonging to Carolina Vasquez that proves there was a witness to the crime in that house. Vasquez's testimony is then pertinent to the resolution of the case. Chioma and Carolina, both women of color and foreigners in the United States, work together to make possible Anya's release, to the consternation of the prosecutor.

Conclusion: *Pumzi*, Environment, and Female Agency

The experimental style of contemporary African cinema is arguably most evident in the increasing number of science fiction films set in Africa. Women have played a big role as both filmmakers and characters in this film genre. One sci-fi film that readily comes to mind is the celebrated *Pumzi* (2009) by Wanuri Kahiu. *Pumzi* is set in the future, thirty-five years after World War III, in a community sealed off from a contaminated earth. In this fabricated ecosystem, there is a water scarcity such that urine and body sweat are recycled to meet water needs. This manufactured ecology is the grounds of the Natural History Museum, powered with self-generated electricity, a world of science and technology, with Asha, the film's protagonist, working as curator in this high-tech museum. Kahiu's film warns of the consequences of rapacious destruction of the earth. Considering its planetary focus, Kahiu's film transcends the "nationalist frameworks" that Alexie Tcheuyap argues "historically overdetermined the incipient phase of African cinema."[34]

Ending this chapter with a discussion of *Pumzi* is appropriate not just because the film represents a recent trend in African filmmaking but also because it brings together many of the issues discussed here. The film's ecological theme, for instance, builds on an issue that earlier films addressed. Faye's *Kaddu Beykat* is set during a drought that impoverished the Senegalese village, while in Djebar's *La Nouba* the environmental impact of war in Algeria is emphasized. Furthermore, both films devote considerable attention to the land and sea, as if to underscore the entanglement of nonhuman members of the biosphere with human characters, which Françoise Pfaff has described as the "lyrical intimacy of man and nature" in a reading of Faye's *Kaddu Beykat*.[35] At the very least, *Pumzi* fleshes out the proto-environmental inclination of those earlier films. The drought of Faye's film and the impact of war on the environment in *La Nouba* are replicated in *Pumzi* but at an extreme level, making it possible to read the latter project as the culmination of the earlier works. While there is still water and the land retains a degree of fertility in the earlier films, the wastelands of *Pumzi* alongside the absence of water suggest that environmental disaster has struck. Considering the films together, one recognizes an abiding environmental interest in the works of female African filmmakers in the early period, when the issue was yet to become an attractive topic, and further development of the subject in films produced at the turn of the century.

The portrayal of Asha as a transformative character in *Pumzi* also aligns it with films such as *Ije*, where women assume primary roles and have agency, often related to physical mobility. In Maldoror's *Sambizanga*, Maria goes in search of her husband and uncovers the brutalities of the colonial administration. Maria journeys from the country to the city, while Chioma's transatlantic journey takes her from Nigeria to the United States to facilitate the acquittal of her sister. In the process, Chioma also makes visible the illusions of the American dream for immigrants (see chapter 12). *Pumzi* replicates a similar pattern with Asha breaking out of the enclosed community to locate the origin of the fertile soil sample she received from an unknown source, a breakout occurring after her request to leave is denied by her handlers. Asha's walk takes her through the contaminated land and desert until she sees a tree. The film ends when Asha fades away as a tree blossoms on the exact spot where she lies after putting the plant in the ground. The blossoming tree represents the possibility of ecological rejuvenation, a feat made possible by Asha's determination to brave the perils of the contaminated earth.

To understand fully the rearticulation of older themes and styles in more recent productions such as *Pumzi*, we can turn to MaryEllen Higgins's work on what she calls "the winds of African cinema." Differentiating winds from the notion of waves of African cinema, which she argues always involve a European base or root, Higgins contends that "African cinema winds shift directions, deterritorialize, remember ancestral breaths, transport them, gather new breaths, take new and unexpected aesthetic turns."[36] Following Higgins, we can locate in *Pumzi* the "ancestral breaths" of the earlier filmmakers who have addressed environmental themes and portrayed heroic women, even as the work extends to accommodate stylistic innovations. Kahiu may be as concerned with ecological devastation triggered by human factors as earlier filmmakers were, but she utilizes a distinctive film language particularly relevant for the contemporary era.

As we traverse the first decades of the twenty-first century, the increasing number of women filmmakers and female actors with significant positive roles is heartening. The works of Wanuri Kahiu (Kenya), Ariane Astrid Atodji (Cameroun), and Nicole Amarteifio, the creator of *An African City*, the popular web series on the lives of five women in Accra, Ghana, are a testament that women are flourishing in the industry. Outside cinema, African women are also doing well in other aspects of visual culture. Njideka Akunyi Crosby, for instance, made headlines in 2016 when her painting sold for a record $1.1 million at Sotheby's, while Zina Saro-Wiwa is becoming renowned as a video artist. In photography, Zanele Muholi has devoted her career to making visible black lesbian women in South Africa. The list is inexhaustible of female visual artists articulating the voices and images of Africa, including those of women in their beauty, intelligence, strength, and challenges. The works of these women are significant for inscribing their agency but also for excavating often marginalized voices, as well as for the corrections they provide to colonial Western scripts and male-dominant archives.

Notes

1. See Janell Hobson, *Venus in the Dark: Blackness and Beauty in Popular Culture* (New York: Routledge, 2005).

2. Olivier Barlet, *Decolonizing the Gaze* (London: Zed Books, 2000), 5.

3. Melissa Thackway, *Africa Shoots Back: Alternative Perspectives in Sub-Saharan Francophone African Film* (Oxford: James Currey, 2003), 34.

4. Manthia Diawara, *African Cinema: Politics and Culture* (Bloomington: Indiana University Press, 1992), 4.

5. Teshome H. Gabriel, *Third Cinema in the Third World: The Aesthetics of Liberation* (Ann Arbor, MI: UMI Research Press, 1982).

6. *Kaddu Beykat*, directed by Safi Faye (Senegal: Safi, 1975).

7. *Xala*, directed by Ousmane Sembène (Senegal: Filmi Doomireew, 1974).

8. *La Nouba des Femmes du Mont Chenoua*, directed by Assia Djebar (Algeria: Algerian Television, 1977); *Sambizanga*, directed by Sarah Maldoror (Angola: Isabelle Films, 1972).

9. *Ije*, directed by Chineze Anyaene (Nigeria: Xandria Productions, 2010); *Pumzi*, directed by Wanuri Kahiu (South Africa and Kenya: Inspired Minority Pictures, 2009).

10. Kenneth W. Harrow, *Postcolonial African Cinema: From Political Engagement to Postmodernism* (Bloomington: Indiana University Press, 2007), 4.

11. Josef Gugler, "African Writing Projected onto the Screen: Sambizanga, Xala, and Kongi's Harvest," *African Studies Review* 42, no. 1 (1999): 86.

12. *Sarraounia*, directed by Med Hondo (Burkina Faso and Mauritania: Les Films Soleil, 1986); *Yaaba*, directed by Idrissa Ouédraogo (Burkina Faso: Arcadia Films,

1989). For a discussion of the representation of older women in African film, see Suzanne MacRae, "The Mature and Older Women of African Film," in *African Cinema: Post-Colonial and Feminist Readings*, ed. K. Harrow (Trenton: Africa World Press, 1999), 241–54.

13. Lindiwe Dovey, "New Looks: The Rise of African Women Filmmakers," *Feminist Africa* 16 (2012): 21, African Film Festival (AFF), http://www.africanfilmny.org/2014/new-looks-the-rise-of-african-women-filmmakers/.

14. Diana Maury Robin and Ira Jaffe, eds., *Redirecting the Gaze: Gender, Theory, and Cinema in the Third World* (Albany: State University of New York Press, 1999), 13.

15. Nancy J. Schmidt, "Sub-Saharan African Women Filmmakers: Agendas for Research," in Harrow, *African Cinema*, 287.

16. Réda Bensmaïa, "La nouba des femmes du Mont Chenoua: Introduction to the Cinematic Fragment," *World Literature Today* 70, no. 4 (1996): 877–79.

17. Sheila J. Petty, "How an African Woman Can Be": African Women Filmmakers Construct Women," *Discourse* 18, no. 3 (1996): 78.

18. Beti Ellerson, "African Women in Cinema Dossier African Women and the Documentary: Storytelling, Visualizing History, from the Personal to the Political," *Black Camera: An International Film Journal* 8, no. 1 (2016): 223.

19. Bensmaïa, "La nouba," 878.

20. Bensmaïa, "La nouba," 878.

21. Mani Sharpe, "Representations of Space in Assia Djebar's *La nouba des femmes du Mont Chenoua*," *Studies in French Cinema* 13, no. 3 (2013): 222.

22. Roy Armes, *African Filmmaking: North and South of the Sahara* (Bloomington: Indiana University Press, 2006), 111.

23. Frank Ukadike, *Black African Cinema* (Berkeley: University of California Press, 1994), 252.

24. Afolabi Adesanya, "From Film to Video," in *Nigerian Video Films*, ed. J. Haynes (Athens: Ohio University Press, 2000), 39.

25. Jonathan Haynes, ed., *Nigerian Video Films* (Athens: Ohio University Press, 2000), 5.

26. Manouchka Kelly Labouba, "The Essence of African Cinema: Diverging Media Ideologies in Sub-Saharan African Cinema," *Film International* 13, no. 2 (2015): 80.

27. *Living in Bondage*, directed by Chris Obi Rapu and Kenneth Nnebue (Nigeria, 1992).

28. Carmela Garritano, *African Video Movies and Global Desires* (Athens: Ohio University Press, 2013), 63. For further discussion of the nexus between women and consumerism in Nollywood films, see Kenneth Harrow, "Women in 'African Cinema' and 'Nollywood Films': A Shift in Cinematic Regimes," *Journal of African Cinemas* 8, no. 3 (2016): 238–39.

29. *Formidable Force*, directed by Teco Benson (Nigeria: Reemy Jes, 2002).

30. Cajetan Iheka, "Nollywood and the Nigerian Dream: The Example of Teco Benson's Formidable Force," *Global South* 7, no. 1 (2013): 128.

31. Alessandro Jedlowski, "The Women behind the Camera: Female Entrepreneurship in the Southern Nigerian Film Industry," in *Cultural Entrepreneurship in Africa*, ed. U. Röschenthaler and D. Schulz (New York: Routledge, 2016), 258.

32. Jonathan Haynes, *Nollywood: The Creation of Nigerian Film Genres* (Chicago: University of Chicago Press, 2016), 45.

33. Moradewun Adejunmobi, "Neoliberal Rationalities in Old and New Nollywood," *African Studies Review* 58, no. 3 (2015): 34; Connor Ryan, "New Nollywood: A Sketch of Nollywood's Metropolitan New Style," *African Studies Review* 58, no. 3 (2015): 59; Jonathan Haynes, *Nollywood*, 285.

34. Alexie Tcheuyap, *Postnationalist African Cinemas* (Manchester: Manchester University Press, 2011), 1.

35. Françoise Pfaff, "Five West African Filmmakers on Their Films," *Journal of Opinion* 20, no. 2 (1992): 33.

36. MaryEllen Higgins, "The Winds of African Cinema," *African Studies Review* 58, no. 3 (2015): 77–92.

Suggested Readings

Diawara, Manthia. *African Cinema: Politics and Culture*. Bloomington: Indiana University Press, 1992.

Dovey, Lindiwe. "New Looks: The Rise of African Women Filmmakers." *Feminist Africa* 16 (2012): 18–36.

Garritano, Carmela. *African Video Movies and Global Desires*. Athens: Ohio University Press, 2013.

Harrow, Kenneth. "Women in 'African Cinema' and 'Nollywood Films': A Shift in Cinematic Regimes." *Journal of African Cinemas* 8, no. 3 (2016): 233–48.

Thackway, Melissa. *Africa Shoots Back: Alternative Perspectives in Sub-Saharan Francophone African Film*. Oxford: James Currey, 2003.

PART 11

RELIGION AND POLITICS

Figure 3.1. Statue of Princess Oma Idoko, Idah, Kogi State. Photo by Nwando Achebe, July 2007.

3

POLITICO-RELIGIOUS SYSTEMS AND AFRICAN WOMEN'S POWER

Nwando Achebe

This chapter offers a searching overview of the gendered systems of symbolic politico-religious power and authority created by African women and the female principle during precolonial and colonial times. It begins with the premise that one only captures a portion of African women's and gender history by focusing exclusively on the human visible realm. Therefore, using case studies drawn from across Africa, I explore the workings of these spiritual- and human-centered female-managed and controlled politico-religious systems that resulted in effective power based on gender or individual characteristics, paying particular attention to women's power ordained by the female spiritual principle (goddesses, prophetesses, spirit mediums, etc.) exercising power in different African contexts.

Many African politico-religious systems operated within a dual-sex or complementary system of organization, meaning that men and women, as well as male and female spiritual forces, shared leadership responsibilities in their societies in a complementary manner. I argue elsewhere that during the precolonial era, the real rulers of African towns and communities were the spirits; human beings were merely there to interpret the will of the gods.[1] In precolonial Africa, politics, religion, and economics were intrinsically connected. This interconnectedness between the spiritual and human realms is the focus of this chapter. I explore the roles of women and the female spiritual principle in African human and spiritual politico-religious systems, termed here the human and spiritual political constituencies, and highlight that interconnectedness.

Regarding the female spiritual principle's place within African worldviews and indigenous beliefs, African peoples identify two worlds—the human or physical/visible world of human beings, natural forces, and phenomena; and the nonhuman or spiritual/invisible world of divine beings, good and bad spirits, and departed ancestors. Among the Igbo of Nigeria, these worlds are called *uwa* and *ani mmo*, respectively. They are not separate but, like two half circles or halves of a kola nut, connect to make one fluid, continuous, complete, and whole African world. Furthermore, African cosmological structure operates within a cyclical movement of time, which explains the belief of most African peoples in the never-ending cycle of life—birth, death, and rebirth.

The visible and invisible worlds commune with each other. These interactions and interconnectedness can be witnessed in the act of pouring libation and presenting offerings to the spirits and ancestors. It also reveals itself in beckoning of the ancestors, the dead who have come back to life for the good of the community. Among the Zulu, for instance, the *ukubuyisa idlozi* rite brings home an ancestor after a period of mourning. West, west central, and southern African peoples, including the Dogon, Igbo, Ekperi, Tiv, Bamileke, Okpella, Mande, Chokwe, and Lunda, invite the dead back to life as masked spirits, who protect and police their communities and serve as courts of justice and arbitration. The African spiritual world is inhabited by so many spirits; there are too many for one person to know, thus, mediums—diviners, priests, priestesses, prophetesses, and spirit mediums—are necessary. They are persons endowed with spiritual skills to help explain the universe. This chapter highlights the role, power, and authority of two mediums in the politico-religious systems of their societies.

The complementarity of realms translates into politics, giving rise to two distinct constituencies—the human and spiritual political constituencies. The spiritual political constituency is made up of divinities, male and female functionaries, who derive their political power and clout from association with the spiritual world. The human political constituency is peopled by human beings, who achieve their political potential as human actors in the physical realm.

Female Politico-Religious Power in the Human Political Constituency

In the human political constituency, African women played a variety of leadership roles as queens, market queens, queen mothers, princesses, and even kings. In ancient Egypt, for instance, Hatshepsut came to the throne around 1473 BCE as the fifth pharaoh of the eighteenth dynasty. The earliest famous woman known to history, she was one of Egypt's most successful pharaohs.[2] Hatshepsut, the only child of King Thutmose I and his wife, Queen Ahmose, was twelve when her father died in 1495 BCE. Shortly thereafter, she married her half brother Thutmose II and became queen. The union was blessed with a daughter, Neferure. Fifteen years later, King Thutmose II died; and his infant son, born of a concubine, Isis, became heir apparent. Since Thutmose III was too young to assume the throne; Hatshepsut stepped in as regent, a role she performed during the first years of their rule. However, by the end of the seventh year, she was crowned pharaoh herself, bearing that position's full titles. She adopted characteristic regalia familiar to us from ancient Egyptian statues—a *shendyt* kilt, *nemes* headdress with its *uraeus* and *khat* head cloth, and a false beard. Being a female pharaoh was unprecedented, thus Hatshepsut had herself depicted as male, a directive that affirmed her place as king. The coding of politico-religious authority as male appears frequently in the examples cited below.

Hatshepsut was a consummate politician and stateswoman, as well as charismatic ruler. She handpicked a group of loyal officials, including Senenmut, who saw to the successful running of the state under Hatshepsut. Senenmut oversaw all royal works and served as a tutor to Neferure. Hatshepsut ruled peacefully so Egypt prospered. She sent a trade expedition to Punt in present-day Somalia, which returned with gold, ebony, ivory, spices, animal skins, baboons, and myrrh trees. She launched an extensive building and restoration program in Egypt, which saw the construction of a series of temples to honor the national god Amon-Re in Thebes and a rock temple in Middle Egypt, known to the Greeks as Speos Artemidos. She had the Al-Karnak temple remodeled, adding pillars and the Red Chapel. Her greatest accomplishment, however, was the construction of the Dayr al-Baḥrî temple, named also for Amon-Re, which included chapels dedicated to the royal ancestors and a number of significant Egyptian deities. When Hatshepsut died in 1458 BCE, she was interred in the Valley of the Kings next to her father.[3]

Meroë, considered Africa's second-greatest ancient civilization, had so many female rulers that the outside world believed it had never had a king. The first "Queen Candace" ruled the Kushites of Meroë as early as 23 BCE. She appears in Acts of the Apostles, 8:27, which tells of a Kushite man who visited Jerusalem. He was said to be the queen's treasurer and was described as "a man of great authority under Candace." In 61 CE, a writer sent to Kush by the Roman Emperor, Nero, noted that the kingdom was ruled by Queen Candace. Although little historical evidence about these leaders has survived, we do know that Meroë had at least seven queens, usually called by the title of Candace. The word "Candace" was actually a corruption of the Meroitic title *kdke*, given to kings' wives, queen mothers, and reigning queens, so all Meroitic queens probably had this title. These included Bartare (284 BCE–275 BCE), who was buried in one of the three pyramids in Meroë's south cemetery, and Shanakdakhete, who reigned from 177 BCE to 155 BCE, and whose tomb was inscribed with the first known Meroitic hieroglyphs. Queen Amanerinas might have ruled jointly with her husband, Prince Akinidad, while Queens Amanishakete and Amanikhatashan are also known to history.[4]

In Igalaland (in present-day southeastern Nigeria), one of the earliest Attah-Igalas (rulers) in living memory was Ebulejonu, a name meaning "woman that became chief or king." Known as Ebule, for short, she was the first and last *female* king, who was said to have reigned in the sixteenth century. The Igala monarchy was one of the oldest and most formidable kingdoms in central Nigeria, centered around the office of the Attah-Igala, who was regarded as the "father" of all Igala people.

Attah-Ebulejonu was the daughter of Attah-Abutu Eje, who, according to tradition, was half human and half leopard. Attah-Abutu Eje was born to a love-struck princess of the Jukun Kwararafa kingdom and her handsome young man/leopard husband suitor. Abutu Eje was said to have grown up in Wukari to become a man of great courage and charm. His insecure father-in-law king eventually drove him away for fear that the younger man might usurp his throne. One legend relates that Abutu Eje then went to Idah, where he established a royal throne. Because he was so powerful, he impressed the Igala people around him, who addressed him as Attah (father). Another version of this oral tradition states that Abutu Eje did not make it to Igalaland but died en route, thus paving the way for his only child and daughter, Ebule, to rule as *female* king. Attah-Ebulejonu, like Hatshepsut of Egypt before her, ruled as— and was remembered as—a king, not a queen, perhaps setting the precedent for the coronation of another Nigerian *female* king, Ahebi Ugbabe, some four centuries later.[5]

Princess Inikpi of the Igala kingdom was born to Attah-Ayegba during the last quarter of the seventeenth century. Attah-Ayegba is credited with defining the external and internal boundaries of the Igala kingdom and the creation of the title system around which the kingdom evolved. During Ayegba's reign, the Igala moved to free themselves from the yoke of the Jukun kingdom. In the last decade of the seventeenth century, when the Jukun king sent his emissaries with containers to collect annual tribute from the Igala, the latter filled the containers with stones and dung and sent his messengers back with a warning that the Igala people would no longer pay tribute. On receiving this insult, the Aku was enraged and decided to teach Ayegba and his Igala kingdom a lesson by declaring war.

Because the Jukun kingdom was the stronger of the two, Igala defeat seemed like a foregone conclusion. To prevent this, Attah-Ayegba consulted a diviner who revealed that if the Igala kingdom wished to win the war, then Attah-Ayegba would have to sacrifice to the gods the child he loved the most, his beloved daughter, Inikpi. A shaken Ayegba kept this chilling prophecy to himself and did nothing, but Inikpi heard rumors that her father had visited a diviner and wanted to know what the diviner had revealed. A stoic Ayegba refused to communicate the prophecy to her. However, the Attah under-estimated Princess Inikpi's persistence. Refusing to be deterred by her father's silence, she questioned intensively any confidantes who might know the diviner's revelation, found out the message, and took action as brave as it was swift. Having ordered a large hole be dug near the banks of the Niger and Benue Rivers, to the horror of her subjects, Princess Inikpi descended into it, accompanied by nine slaves, and then ordered the workers to tamp down the earth tightly, covering the hole. Thus, at her own order, Princess Inikpi was buried alive, along with her slaves.

Her courage and selflessness caused young Inikpi to be elevated by her people to the rank of a goddess. She presently straddles human and spiritual political constituencies as chief intermediary between the Igala and their Great God, Ojo. Inikpi has become the spiritual protector of all Igalas, a merciful mother who safeguards and intercedes on behalf of her children in time of trouble. She is also venerated as a goddess of fertility, who is believed to grant children to barren Igala women. Each year during the Igala Kingdom's most important festival, Ocho, the Attah and his senior chiefs offer sacrifices at Princess Inikpi's shrine. Today her statue stands at the Idah marketplace, near the confluence of the Niger and Benue Rivers, marking the spot where she gave her life to ensure the well-being of her people.[6] Leaders, both male and female, sacrificing themselves or being sacrificed for the communal good is a common theme of legends in many African and non-African societies; it is done to protect the sanctity of the nation.

In Abomey, capital of the eighteenth- and nineteenth-century West African kingdom of Dahomey, a group of uniformed women, armed with muskets, swords, and clubs, guarded the kings. Some were more than six feet tall, and all were of superior strength. The Europeans called them Amazons after the women warriors (probably Scythians) so feared by the Greeks. They were not only an elite corps of palace guards but by the nineteenth century had become professional soldiers, more disciplined, fearless, and daring than Dahomey's finest male soldiers. They became all-female military regiments, fighting for the kingdom as early as 1708 and leading Dahomey to many victories. In 1724 one European visitor saw as many as two thousand Amazons on parade in

Abomey. Three years later, they defeated the aggressive slaving kingdom of Whydah. These female soldiers, up to six thousand strong, were largely successful in battles.[7]

Most Amazons were foreign-born slaves taken from neighboring Yoruba kingdoms. After an 1818 coup in Dahomey brought King Gezo to the throne, he increased the recruitment of Yoruba slaves to serve as royal guards in his palace as well as populate his female battalions because they would have no ties to his enemies within Dahomey and therefore would not support attempted usurpations. They also could help the casualty-depleted male army defend his kingdom (which, unusually for Africa, was heavily involved in supplying slaves to the Atlantic trade). Initially, the Amazons were used to enhance the number of Dahomean soldiers. By dressing as men and standing behind the male soldiers, they formed a huge army, which intimidated the enemy, as did their use of large, extremely sharp razors as prime weapons. King Gezo then used them as soldiers and gave them more elaborate and standardized uniforms, as well as honors and rights that set them above male soldiers. By 1889 Amazons were serving as official state executioners.[8]

Amazon women lived in barracks protected by the high walls of the king's palace and were guarded by eunuchs sworn to protect their chastity. Training began between the ages of thirteen and fourteen, when the girls swore an oath of chastity and celibacy to prevent pregnancy and emotional ties to children and lovers. If an Amazon inductee happened to become pregnant, she was tortured until she revealed the name of her lover or was relegated into the "gate opening force" to lead an attack, so she was usually among the first casualties. New conscripts for the army were subjected to indoctrination designed to ensure loyalty to the king. As apprentices to older women soldiers, they were subjected to harsh discipline. To underscore their devotion, Amazon recruits sang martial songs such as "May thunder and lightning kill us if we break our oaths" and "Let us march in a virile manner, let us march boldly like men." In fact, Amazon women were believed to have become men: "As a blacksmith takes an iron bar and by fire changes its fashion, so have we changed our nature. We are no longer women."[9]

Much strenuous Amazon physical training took place in the forest, where they were taught strategic and tactical methods, along with moral and religious instruction. They were taught to imitate birdcalls, cope with hunger, thirst, and dangerous animals, treat wounds, and leap over enemy thorn bush fences. They learned to harden their nails in brine and then make them into weapons with sharp points. In addition to their nails and razors, they used muskets and short swords. They greased their bodies with palm oil to make them slippery. Understandably, they were much feared as ferocious enemies by neighboring peoples, who were constantly raided and whole villages enslaved.[10] They were, however, finally defeated by the French during the period of colonial conquest in 1892, probably because machine guns were not available to Dahomeans (the Berlin Treaty of 1885 set up the parameters for the eventual partition of Africa arbitrarily among Europeans and forbade sale of firearms to Africans).

In promoting the institution of a women's army, Dahomean rulers followed their well-established dual-sex system practice of shadowing in which every male government official had a female counterpart. Uniquely, Dahomey also had compulsory military service for both women and men, with local chiefs compelled to keep a record (in stones dropped into pottery vessels) of youth of suitable age available for the draft. The single exception to the shadowing principle, of course, was with the king himself, who had absolute power and countenanced no opposition, a characteristic enabled by the custom of taking slave wives, who had no local families to organize rebellions.[11]

In some societies, a system of joint sovereignty existed whereby leadership responsibilities were shared between a king and a female counterpart in a complementary fashion, as in the Asante empire. Queen mothers co-ruled with male kings, deriving their power from a matrilineal principle expressed in their social organization. They were not necessarily mothers of rulers but rather selected based on ability from among members of royal lineages. At the very top of the empire was the female *asantehema* and the male *asantehene*. Under them were paramount chiefs governed by paramount queen mothers, called *ohemaa*, and paramount chiefs, *omanhene*. The *ohemaa* had joint responsibility with the male paramount in all affairs of state. Under the paramounts were the towns, each governed by its own queen mother, called the *oba panin* and king, *odikro*. The *oba panin* were female rulers of lesser status, who occupied one of the two stools of state, the visible symbols of political authority. Under the towns were eight clans governed by subchiefs, *abusuapanyin*.

The queen mother exercised authority in many domains, but her most important duty was her responsibility with regard to her male counterpart, the king. As royal genealogist, she determined the legitimacy of all claimants to the vacant stool. When a king died, the *asantehema* nominated a candidate for the golden stool. She had three chances to nominate a candidate, who then had to be approved by a council of state. The queen mother also guided and advised the king on all matters of state, custom, and religion. She determined when community taboos had been breached and had the unfettered right to rebuke the king in public. The queen mother was a member of the governing council or assembly of state; her presence was required whenever any important matter of state was considered. Each queen mother had her own court in which she was assisted by female counselors and functionaries. She heard all judicial cases involving sacred oaths of the state and had independent jurisdiction over all domestic matters affecting women and members of the royal family. Male litigants could apply to have their civil cases transferred from the king's court to the queen mother's court. If they did, judgments meted out by the queen mother and her council were final. The queen mother oversaw female governance in the empire and performed important rituals for the community. She was present during important ceremonies such as funerals and performed initiation rites for young women, who had to be brought to the queen mother at the beginning of their menses.[12]

The British found few nations as difficult to conquer as they did the Asante. They launched a series of wars against them, remembered as the Anglo-Asante Wars or the "Hundred Years' War," which began in 1805. For almost a century the Asante defeated the British army, and they were only finally defeated in 1896 by a combination of treachery and superior weaponry. One cause that propelled their final war of resistance was the British treatment of Asantehene Prempeh I, who rejected British protectorate status in 1891, which would have guaranteed British control over Asante. The war dragged on, and in 1897 Prempeh was exiled, but not before the British declared that he could never return. In 1899, in a further attempt to humiliate Asante people, the British sent Governor Sir Frederick Hodgson to Kumasi to demand the golden stool, *sika dwa*, the primary symbol of Asante unity. That evening the chiefs held a secret meeting in their capital, Kumasi, their aim being to demand the return of their *asantehene*. Yaa Asantewaa, Queen Mother of Ejisu, was present. Observing that the chiefs were cowed, Yaa Asantewaa issued her now famous challenge:

> How can a proud and brave people like the Asante sit back and look while white men took away their king and chiefs and humiliate them with a demand for the Golden Stool? The Golden Stool only means money to the white man; they searched and dug everywhere for it. . . . Is it true that the bravery of the Asante is no more? I cannot believe it. . . . If you, the chiefs of Asante, are going to behave like cowards and not fight, you should exchange your loincloths for my undergarments. . . . If you the men of Asante will not go forward, then we will. We the women will. I shall call upon my fellow women. We will fight the white men. We will fight till the last of us falls in the battlefields.[13]

That was the beginning of the Yaa Asantewaa War. The final battle began on September 30, 1900. It ended in the bloody defeat of the Asante and the British gaining control of the Asante hinterland. A key element in this and other defeats was the confrontation between machine guns and muzzleloaders. Yaa Asantewaa was captured and deported to the Seychelles Islands, where she died around 1921. Her leadership and determined resistance revived the spirit of pride among the Asante and caused her to be revered now as a hero.[14] It is notable that female leadership in Asante was not cloaked in masculine symbols as shown elsewhere, even in Dahomey, where male/female dual authority ruled at all levels.

In 1918, in British Nigeria, a woman named Ahebi Ugbabe was appointed warrant chief, a departure from British colonial practice, which had never before offered a warrant chief position to a Nigerian woman. Her position was earned in recognition for past services, including her services as headman. Ahebi Ugbabe would be the first and last woman to hold this office in Nigeria. Chief Ahebi was eventually crowned king by an Igala monarch—her third in a series of gendered transformations. This, however, would not be enough for the ambitious and talented Ahebi. In her attempt to achieve "full manhood," she invaded and violated the ultimate sanctuary of Igbo men—the masquerade society. Masquerade societies in many West African societies symbolized that which separated men from women, and men from "full" men. Male members of this Igbo gerontocratic society did not believe in individual or autocratic leadership, a feeling expressed in the adage *Igbo enwe eze* (the Igbo have no kings). They reined her in, proving that there were indeed limits to how far women rulers could achieve gendered transformations and demonstrating the foundational masculinizing of power in Igbo society. In 1948 Ahebi Ugbabe died; she was the first and last king, male or female, to rule in Enugu-Ezike, northern Igboland, Nigeria (see chapter 13).[15]

After documenting the actions of many African female kings, queens, queen mothers, princesses, and warrior women, it is important to look at other expressions of female power and authority in African societies. In some systems in the human political constituency, women held power because of their relationship to the ruler in question, especially as mother, daughter, or sister. The mother of the *fon* (male ruler) of the Kingdom of Kom, West Cameroon, advised him and watched over the children of the palace. In the Mossi Kingdom, the eldest daughter of the king dressed in king's attire and had royal power until the next ruler was installed. Among the Yoruba of southwestern Nigeria, the *iyaoba* (queen mother), the *olori* (head wife of the *oba* or king), and the *iyalode* (ceremonial minister of social affairs) all held significant political power, exerting considerable influence over men's offices while participating actively in policymaking and government (see chapter 13).

Like others documented here, the small-scale Igbo peoples had a dual-sex political system, in which each sex managed its own affairs. In this joint system of male and female government, on the female side, organizations called the *otu umuada* (daughters of the lineage) and the *otu inyomdi* (wives of the lineage) emerged as supreme political bodies. The *otu umuada* featured as the community supreme court of arbitration; the Igbo had no male equivalent.[16]

West African open-air markets typify the interconnectedness between economics, religion, and politics in African systems (see also chapter 8). Most old marketplaces were considered to be in the charge of market deities.[17] Igbo town markets were owned by women and held every four days. Each had its government, made up of the *omu* or market mother, her council of women officials called the *ilogu*, and its policewoman, *awo*, who enforced market rules and regulations, arrested all wrongdoers, and brought them to the market court. West African markets were thus not only places of buying and selling but also politico-religious environments that upheld community values and norms. Indeed, West Africa had a number of notable market or merchant queens. Madam Efunroye Tinubu (ca. 1805–87) of Nigeria, who translated her enormous economic power into political influence, was one such woman; so were the Asante market queens of Ghana and Omu Okwei of Osomari (1872–1943), who became one of the wealthiest and most prominent women traders south of the River Niger.[18]

Female Politico-Religious Power in the Spiritual Political Constituency

In considering many precolonial, and a few colonial, examples of female political power, I focused on the human visible realm and left untouched the most superior expression of female power and authority in Africa—the female principle in the spiritual, nonvisible realm, which is made up of spiritual divinities as well as male and female functionaries who derive their political power from association with the spiritual world. A higher form of government, these goddesses, priestesses, prophetesses, spirit mediums, and diviners featured as the political heads of their communities.

In much African indigenous religious symbolism, the supreme divinity, God, creator of the world, is neither male nor female and is expressed in nongendered language. In English translation, this African creator, God, has tended to be written about as male, a handicap that owes its origins to the gender-specific nature of English as well as male-dominant religious beliefs. This section provides a corrective by presenting these supreme deities as many Africans themselves see them.

Most African societies believe that their world was created by a gender-less creator God. Among the Diola of present-day Senegambia, the genderless Great God Emitai was served by both male priests and female priestesses. The Igbo Great God, Chukwu or Chineke, was neither male nor female and was served by a slew of lesser gods and goddesses worshipped with prayers and sacrifices. The Ewe and Fon construct their creator Deity as exhibiting both male and female qualities or principles. Some societies actually regard their creator God as female. For instance, Tamarau, the creator God of the Tarakiri Ezon of the Niger Delta region of Nigeria, is considered to be female; her name means "Our Mother." She is sometimes also called Ayebau, which means "the Mother of the world." These creator Divinities rule their African worlds with the support of lesser gods and goddesses, oracles, ancestors, and masked spirits. Their decrees are proclaimed by their human helpers, mediums called to fulfill powerful and authoritative roles as interpreters of the supreme unseen world.

The matrilineal Berber peoples of North Africa place great store in the ability of human beings endowed with spiritual idiosyncrasies—especially prophets and prophetesses—to change the course of history by predicting the outcome of war or the death of an enemy. The greatest of these Berber prophetesses was Dihya, a Kahina of the Maghreb, who worked herself into a trancelike state and then predicted the future. Relatively little is known about her origins. Some sources claim that her father, Mitiya, was of Byzantine origin. She had two sons, one said to have been fathered by a Greek and the other by a Berber. We do know that Dihya ruled the Jerawa, a Berber group, and led stiff resistance to the Arabs from her stronghold in the Aures Mountains. She famously predicted, and held back, an invasion of North African Arabs pursuing gold in the eighth century CE. Her power of prophecy gave Prophetess Dihya ultimate power and authority over her people.

Prophetess Dihya's resistance was informed by religion. At the time, most Berbers had either converted to Judaism or Christianity. Therefore, as a Jewish, Christian, or indigenous religious leader, the Kahina would have opposed any advance from Arab Muslims, perceived to be barbarians—destroyers and pillagers of communities and agricultural systems. Kahina Dihya was said to have led her people in at least three successful battles against invading Arabs, but she eventually died in a battle near Tabarka, killed near the Bir el-Kahina well, thus ending her thirty-five-year rule.[19] Her military and religious authority cohered.

In the Lovedu kingdom of South Africa, the Rain Queen, Modjadji I (1800–1854), was the sovereign. Renowned throughout southern Africa, she was referred to by European observers and surrounding Africans as "She-Who-Must-Be-Obeyed." The Modjadji, a title given to all Lovedu queens, could trace her lineage to Karango (Shona immigrants from southern Zimbabwe). Authority derived from kinship, politics, economy, and religion united in her person. There have been six Rain Queens in living memory: Maselekwane Modjadji I (1800–1854); Masalanabo Modjadji II (1854–95); Khesetoane Modjadji III (1896–1959); Makoma Modjadji IV (1959–80); Mokope Modjadji V (1981–2001) and Makobo Constance Modjadji VI (2003–2005).

Modjadjis possessed the ability to transform clouds into rain, so they were referred to as *khifidolamarua daja* or "transformer of clouds." Their emotions affected the rain; if they were dissatisfied, angry, or sad, the rains might cease. Their special powers included guaranteeing the yearly seasonal cycle and fertility of crops; controlling and transforming clouds into rain; sending rainstorms and hurricanes; and withholding rain from Lovedu enemies. In 1934 or 1935, for instance, during the reign of Modjadji III, the first rains did not come until December. The resultant drought was attributed to her being upset because of her daughter's liaison with a commoner.

Rain was vitally necessary for survival in the arid Lovedu region. The rainmaking ceremony, for which the Modjadji was responsible, was one of the most important Lovedu rituals. It was held yearly at the beginning of the rainy season to appeal to the ancestors, gods, and goddesses for sufficient rain for consumption and to ensure a good harvest and adequate grazing for livestock. When rain was needed, the Lovedu sacrificed gifts to inform the Rain Queen of the "crying of people" and the need for her to protect them. The Rain Queen then gathered secret ingredients from her medicines housed in rock shelters and prepared in clay pots. The chief ingredient was the skin of a deceased queen. The Rain Queen ground various medicines, which she stirred vigorously in a pot filled with water. The pot would have to be stirred so vigorously that froth appeared on top of the pot; otherwise the medicine was not considered fully ready to use and would not create rain.[20]

Modjadji I turned the chaos of her male predecessor's reign into peace and prosperity. She was surrounded by restrictions that drove her into seclusion, fostering her conceptualization as immortal. Her fame drew many foreigners to the capital including ambassadors gathered at her court. Some brought cattle, others their daughters or sisters—gifts with which they showed homage or supplication for rain. Some queens from faraway lands came to be strengthened and fitted for their office by the Modjadji. The Zulu king, Chaka, disappointed by the failure of his mission to a great Swazi rainmaker, then supplicated the Lovedu Rain Queen as the "rain-maker of all rain-makers."[21]

Modjadji I was believed to be the living embodiment of the Lovedu rain goddess; as such, she was inaccessible and mysterious, and sacrilege incurred if anyone saw her. She governed without an official husband and was instead *female* husband to as many as forty-two wives, who tilled her fields, brewed her beer, cooked her food, kept her in domestic comfort, and traded for her. Feared for her power, and famous for her diplomacy, Modjadji I used Lovedu women to pacify intruders into her kingdom with beer and sex. She was believed to be immortal and thus could not be murdered or die of natural causes. Instead, Modjadjis were expected to take their own lives in ritual suicides, but not before choosing a successor to rule by divine right. Modjadji I committed ritual suicide in 1854, another example of self-sacrifice for the communal good.

Masalanabo Modjadji II succeeded her mother. Like her mother, she never married the father of her children and was cared for by her multiple wives. She was mainly inaccessible to her people, seldom appearing in public. She too committed ritual suicide, in 1894, after having designated her sister's daughter as heir. The sixth and last Rain Queen, Makobo Constance Modjadji VI, was crowned after the death of her grandmother, Modjadji V, on April 16, 2003. At twenty-five, she was the youngest Rain Queen in the history of the Lovedu. Makobo was the only Rain Queen with Western formal education. Her mother had been the designated successor but died two days before her own mother, Modjadji V. Makobo reluctantly accepted the crown. On the day of her coronation a slight drizzle fell, which was interpreted by the Lovedu as a good omen. However, Makobo proved to be too modern to be a Rain Queen. She wore jeans and T-shirts, visited dance clubs, watched soap operas, and chatted on her cell phone. She had a boyfriend, David Mogale, a former municipal manager. He was rumored to have moved into the Royal Compound, causing great controversy within the Royal Council, since Rain Queens were only supposed to have sex with nobles chosen by said council. The council banned him from the village, refusing to recognize their two children. On June 10, 2005, Makobo was admitted to Polokwane Medi-Clinic and died of meningitis two days later at the age of twenty-seven. Modjadji VI's death marked the probable end of the position, given that the Lovedu refuse to accept Makobo's daughter as the rightful heir to the Rain Queen crown since she was fathered by a commoner. Consequently, the two-hundred-year-old Rain Queen dynasty might have ended, along with independent female politico-religious authority among the Lovedu.[22]

In Igboland, the goddess Efuru was constructed in the mid-1850s as a savior from oppressions, raids, and other malefactions. She was created to protect and resurrect the Igbo town of Idoha, which had been depopulated by incessant slave raiding by its neighbors. The first woman dedicated to Efuru was offered as a symbol of appreciation for a victory that Efuru had helped the town attain. Her name was Eketa. Once consecrated, Eketa was renamed Eketa Nwiyi (child of Iyi [Efuru]) or Nwaefuru (Child of Efuru) for the goddess. The name Eketa means "she might survive," and survive she did. She became a wife to Efuru and gave birth to two Efuru children.

Eventually non-Idoha families, especially families from Idoha enemy populations, began to offer their daughters to Efuru in marriage as a sign that they too were entering into a peace bond with her and could therefore count on her protection. All Efuru wives were married to their goddess in a process known as *igo mma ogo*, becoming the in-law of a deity. All children born of these unions belonged to Efuru, who legitimized them by giving them her surname, Nwiyi. Efuru's protection was sought in response to the growing atmosphere of distrust and uncertainty, which had been intensified by incessant intervillage warfare. Efuru was able to build a vast and autonomous community of Efuru dedicatees/wives and their subsequent Efuru (Nwiyi) children.

The Efuru society was an autonomous and self-sufficient community in which each citizen had the rights and potential to exercise and achieve great economic and political clout. The Umuikpagu clan of Ezi Idoha community was the seat of the Efuru society, whose activities were enriched by the generosity and patronage of numerous Efuru adherents from neighboring villages. Theirs was a community of great wealth—wealth in people and wealth in Efuru gifts such as cattle, goats, chickens, and yams, which formed the bulk of the tribute presented to their protector deity. Unlike with many free-born Igbo communities, the Efuru community's sole authority was the holder of the lucrative office of high priest, Eziyi, which represented the highest political station in the commune. Tributes paid to Efuru first passed through the high priest, who received the lion's share of whatever gifts were presented. Efuru served as Umuikpagu's supreme court of arbitration, with the male chief priest acting as intermediary; cases settled in her shrine were final.

Efuru's community of wives and children worked together for the common good—to provide sustenance for members of their community. They owned large expanses of land cultivated on a communal basis. The rest of the Efuru land was divided up among individual members of the Efuru community (the majority of whom were Efuru wives). This allocation of land to Efuru wives represented a departure from Igbo laws governing land inheritance, which charged the community with land ownership.

Umuikpagu also had three markets, controlled entirely by Efuru's wives. Efuru adherents' remarkable business savvy was demonstrated in the early 1960s by their acquisition of a fleet of taxicabs and commercial buses called *oji ofo ga ana* (an upright person will not be harmed), which served not only the Efuru community but also neighboring towns. On February 18, 1988, owing to pressure from Christian adherents living in towns surrounding Idoha, the Efuru shrine was destroyed by operatives of the Anambra state government, after which Efuru's "wives and children" were expelled from her commune in Idoha. This action, however, did not put an end to the worship of the goddess Efuru, or belief in her supernatural powers. Efuru adherents created personal shrines, in a process called *ikpo Efuru* (pegging Efuru likenesses), in community members' homes.[23]

The Shona of present-day Zimbabwe venerate their ancestors as spirit mediums. They believe that the spirit of their founding prince's son, Matope, was immortal and, upon his death, entered a *mhondoro* or lion. This *mhondoro* was believed to have wandered the forests until it found a suitable medium. Each *mhondoro* had its own spirit province that could extend over one or more paramount chiefdoms. These powerful *mhondoros* ensured the well-being of entire regions, were responsible for giving advice to nations that they served, and guaranteed peace among these nations. In addition, they presided over rain-making and other important rituals. Matope's sister, Nyamhika Nehanda I, possessed supernatural powers and became a guardian spirit as well.

In 1890, the British South Africa Company began exploiting local diamond and gold mines. By 1891 Cecil Rhodes co-owned 90 percent of the world's diamond mines. British settlement of southern Africa ultimately destroyed local peoples' political, economic, and religious organizations by imposing hut taxes, introducing forced labor, suppressing religious practices, and alienating African land. This fueled southern African peoples' anger and their resistance. Between May and October of 1896, the Ndebele and Shona organized a military campaign called *chimurenga*, or war of liberation, to drive out the British, led by three *mhondoros*: Mukwati of Matabeleland, Kagubi of Western Mashonaland, and Nehanda of central and northern Mashonaland. These *mhondoros* preached that Mwari, the Great God, blamed the whites for all their suffering and expected His/Her people to drive the British away.

Regarded as the grandmother of present-day Zimbabwe, Mbuya (Mother) Nehanda and her fellow *mhondoros* employed secret messages to communicate and coordinate their efforts. However, by December 1897, the *mhondoros* had been captured, and two were charged with murder: Kagubi for the death of an African policeman, and Nehanda for the death of Native Commissioner H. H. Pollard. Both were sentenced to death by hanging. Nehanda went to her death with the defiant words, "My bones will rise again," predicting the second *chimurenga*, which culminated in the independence of present-day Zimbabwe.[24]

In eastern Africa, as far back as the 1800s, Nyamwezi women possessed an unusual degree of power and authority in ritual situations. In the kingdoms of Bunyoro and Buganda (now in Uganda), Buha, Unyamwezi, and Usukuma (in northwestern Tanzania), spirit societies were centered on groups of legendary heroes, called the Cwezi or Imandwa. As the Cwezi kingdom declined, people began to honor the spirits of their former kings. In Rwanda and Burundi, societies were dominated by spirits of the legendary heroes Ryangombe and Kiranga. These spirit mediumship societies were democratic in their inclusion of large numbers of men and women.

Spirit possession was interpreted as a sign that a spirit has chosen that person to be inhabited by him or her periodically, for the good of the community. People consulted spirit mediums on regular occasions as precautionary measures and on special occasions, when difficulties arose as a result of their neglect of the spirits. The Nyamwezi people believed that, if properly conciliated, the gods, through their spirit mediums, would ensure the health, prosperity, and fertility of their followers.

In hierarchical Nyamwezi societies women's positions depended on their status in the class system. Few upper-class women attained considerable wealth and authority. Spirit mediumship societies thus provided Nyamwezi women with great avenues for active participation in politics and religious life, including entry into a new and higher social status and supreme social group. Markers of membership in this elite social group included special regalia. Nyamwezi spirit mediums also had a secret vocabulary and esoteric knowledge, observed the food taboos of the upper classes, and viewed non-initiates as minors incapable of full participation in community affairs. Most importantly, Nyamwezi spirit mediums possessed legal immunity.

Moreover, spirit mediums operated on different social and political levels with authority over everyone from localized kinship groups to royal courts. Concerned with female activities such as fertility and agriculture, Nyamwezi spirit mediums had control over their husbands during possession. Among the Soga of eastern Uganda, for instance, spirit mediums might order a husband to get rid of a concubine during possession. Given that Nyamwezi spirit mediums were highly respected, mediumship improved female status, giving them authority and license, and access to substantial income. For instance, in Bunyoro, a typical song that the women sang during spirit mediumship initiation ceremonies included the line "You get plenty to eat as well as can put your hands in other people's purses." Spirit mediumship also offered Nyamwezi women shares in the status and prerogatives of men. For example, in Busoga, women could not ordinarily sit on stools, but during possession spirit mediums had their own skin seats and were treated as men. During Rundi ceremonies female spirit mediums wore men's ceremonial dress, sat on stools, carried spears, and had the right to judge trials. In Rwanda, the *kubandwa* spirit mediumship ceremony abolished sexual difference—all initiates, men and women, acquired the virile masculine quality called *umugabo*.[25] Once again, we see the masculinization of symbols of power and authority that, together with distinctly female articulations, asserted power and authority in society.

Conclusion

In precolonial and colonial Africa, women through the female principle could play powerful authoritative roles in the governance of their societies. Whether they operated in complementarity with their male leader counterparts, or on their own in the human political constituency as princesses, queens, queen mothers, female kings, and merchant queens, or in gerontocratic societies in which groups of elderly women and men ruled their communities, women and the female principle occupied important politico-religious roles in many African societies. They also assumed central roles in the even more powerful spiritual political constituency, wielding supernatural authority in the governance of their societies. This reminds us that gods and goddesses were the true rulers of African towns; human beings were merely the interpreters of the will of the deities. The female principle in the spiritual African political constituency ruled as the supreme genderless creator God, as goddesses (who personified natural phenomena and served in many capacities ranging from fertility gods to protectors of their communities), and as powerful and authoritative prophetesses, spirit mediums, and masked spirits. It is possible that the masculine symbolic coding of some authoritative positions held by women and the female principle evolved out of colonial reconstructions of secular and religious authority as exclusively masculine, rather than indigenous norms that governed the assertion of masculine politico-religious authority.

Notes

1. Nwando Achebe, *Farmers, Traders, Warriors, and Kings: Female Power and Authority in Northern Igboland, 1900–1960* (Portsmouth, NH: Heinemann, 2015), 54–55.

2. James Henry Breasted, *A History of the Ancient Egyptians* (New York: Charles Scribner's Sons, 1905), 217.

3. Kara Cooney, *The Woman Who Would Be King: Hatshepsut's Rise to Power in Ancient Egypt* (Danvers, MA: Broadway Books, 2015).

4. P. L. Shinnie, *Meroe: A Civilization of the Sudan* (New York: Praegar, 1967).

5. Nwando Achebe, *The Female King of Colonial Nigeria: Ahebi Ugbabe* (Bloomington: Indiana University, 2011).

6. Achebe, *Female King*.

7. Stanley B. Alpern, *Amazons of Black Sparta: The Women Warriors of Dahomey* (New York: New York University Press, 2011).

8. Robert B. Edgerton, *Warrior Women: The Amazons of Dahomey and the Nature of War* (Boulder, CO: Westview Press, 2000); Alpern, *Amazons of Black Sparta*.

9. James Greenwood, *Stirring Scenes in Savage Lands: An Account of the Manners, Customs, Habits and Recreations, Peaceful and Warlike, of the Uncivilised World* (London: Ward, Lock and Co., Warwick House, 1879), 174.

10. Edgerton, *Warrior Women*, 26; Alpern, *Amazons of Black Sparta*.

11. Edna Bay, *Wives of the Leopard: Gender, Politics, and Culture in the Kingdom of Dahomey* (Charlottesville: University of Virginia Press, 1998).

12. Beverly J. Stoeltje, "Asante Queen Mothers: A Study in Female Authority," in *Queens, Queen Mothers, Priestesses, and Power: Case Studies in African Gender*, ed. Flora S. Kaplan (New York: New York Academy of Sciences), 41–72.

13. A. Adu Boahen, *Yaa Asantewaa and the Asante-British War of 1900–1* (London: James Currey, 2003), 118.

14. Boahen, *Yaa Asantewaa*, 118.

15. Achebe, *Female King*.

16. Kamene Okonjo, "The Dual-Sex Political System in Operation: Igbo Women and Community Politics in Midwestern Nigeria," in *Women in Africa: Studies in Social and Economic Change*, ed. N. J. Hafkin and Edna G. Bay (Stanford, CA: Stanford University Press, 1976), 45–56.

17. Nwando Achebe, "'Ogidi Palaver': The 1914 Women's Market Protest," in *Shaping Our Struggles: Nigerian Women in History, Culture and Social Change*, ed. Obioma Nnaemeka and Chima Korieh (Trenton, NJ: Africa World Press, 2010), 23–51.

18. Kaplan, *Queens, Queen Mothers, Priestesses, and Power*, 8; and F. Ifeoma Ekejiuba, "Omu Okwei, the Merchant Queen of Ossomari: A Biographical Sketch," *Journal of the Historical Society of Nigeria* 3, no. 4 (1967): 633–46.

19. Van Sertima, *Black Women in Antiquity* (New York: Transaction Books, 1988).

20. E. Jensen Krige and J. D. Krige, *The Realm of a Rain Queen: A Study of the Pattern of Lovedu Society* (London: Oxford University Press, 1947).

21. Kriges, *Realm*, 10.

22. Kriges, *Realm*.

23. Nwando Achebe, "When Deities Marry: Indigenous 'Slave' Systems Expanding and Metamorphosing in the Igbo Hinterland," in *African Systems of Slavery*, ed. Stephanie Beswick and Jay Spaulding (Trenton, NJ: Africa World Press, 2010), 105–33.

24. Ruth Weiss, *The Women of Zimbabwe* (Harare: Nehanda, 1986).

25. Iris Berger, "Rebels or Status-Seekers? Women as Spirit Mediums in East Africa," in Hafkin and Bay, *Women in Africa*, 157–81.

Suggested Readings

Achebe, Nwando. *The Female King of Colonial Nigeria: Ahebi Ugbabe.* Bloomington: Indiana University Press, 2011.

Alpern, Stanley B. *Amazons of Black Sparta: The Women Warriors of Dahomey.* New York: New York University Press, 2011.

Bay, Edna. *Wives of the Leopard: Gender, Politics, and Culture in the Kingdom of Dahomey.* Charlottesville: University of Virginia Press, 1998.

Kaplan, Flora S. *Queens, Queen Mothers, Priestesses, and Power: Case Studies in African Gender.* New York: New York Academy of Sciences, 1997.

Van Sertima, Ivan. *Black Women in Antiquity.* New York: Transaction Books, 1988.

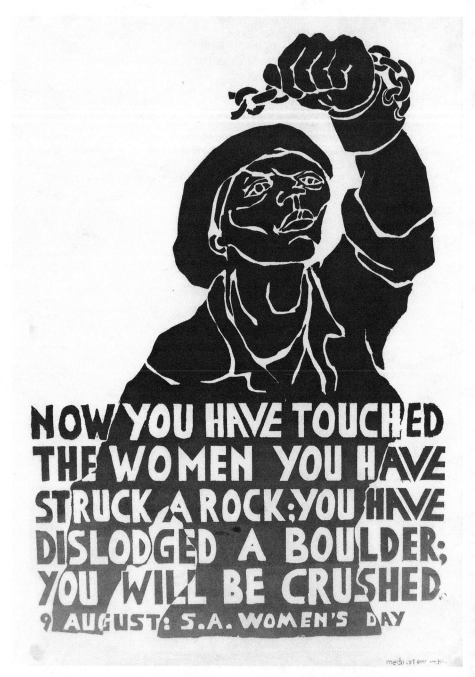

Figure 4.1 Silkscreen poster designed by Judy Seidman with Medu Art Ensemble collective. Gaborone, Botswana, 1981. Reprinted with permission by the artists.

4

COLONIALISM AND RESISTANCE

Protests and National Liberation Movements

Kathleen Sheldon

Throughout the late nineteenth and well into the twentieth century, African women responded to colonial policies that had negative impacts on their work, families, and communities. Women's precolonial political activity was generally disregarded by colonial authorities, who turned exclusively to men when establishing local political offices. Colonial actions also often had negative effects on women's work as farmers and market vendors, whether through increased taxation, attempts to control women's cultivation, or other practices that affected women's marriage and family choices. Women organized anticolonial protests using existing networks that drew on precolonial awareness of common interests. They mobilized under colonialism across wider societal and geographical areas, as colonial discrimination against women generated increased consciousness of women's shared concerns.

By the mid-twentieth century, women were involved in growing nationalist movements, in both organizations and protests that focused on women and as part of larger activities. In some cases where European settler communities resisted African independence, women played key roles in armed liberation movements. This chapter presents an overview of women's involvement in various resistance activities, with case studies illuminating women's experiences under colonial rule and their responses that included women as leaders, participants, and instigators. The role of African women in anticolonial and nationalist organizations offers evidence of vibrant communities of female activists central to the success of those movements across the continent. For nearly one hundred years, women's perspectives, contributions, and participation at all levels of anticolonial activism were essential to the eventual independence of African nations.

Africans resisted increasing controls imposed by European colonialism from its earliest years. Modern nationalist movements gained strength in the early twentieth century as organizations across the continent pushed for local African political control. Women played significant roles in anticolonial struggles and were involved in activities in every region of Africa, protesting taxation, resisting agricultural innovations that increased their already onerous labor obligations, and agitating to be included in political decision-making. In notable actions in Nigeria, Cameroon, Kenya, and South Africa, they brought women's issues to the forefront during the early years of the struggle.

Nationalist movements in most African colonies culminated in independence beginning with Egypt in 1952. By 1965 around thirty countries were independent nations, although other nations continued their liberation struggles. Women participated in nationalist movements in the 1950s and 1960s and developed new international connections as well. Women contributed to significant events and organizations, including the independence struggle in Kenya, the development of nationalism in Tanzania, the Algerian war of independence, and new political parties in West Africa and elsewhere.

Women were also crucial to later liberation movements in the Portuguese colonies, in the struggles in Namibia (then called Southwest Africa) and Southern Rhodesia (renamed Zimbabwe after independence in 1980), and in the anti-apartheid movement in South Africa. In the 1960s and 1970s, when Portugal refused to relinquish Angola, Mozambique, Guinea-Bissau, and Cape Verde, Africans initiated armed struggles, to which women contributed in a variety of capacities. Zimbabwe, Namibia, Algeria, and South Africa endured grueling armed revolts that eventually brought about majority rule despite the intransigence of white settler populations. Women were vital to the success of these resistance efforts through their work in supplying food, acting as couriers, and building alternative social orders in liberated zones. Some performed combat roles, though they faced obstacles to full acceptance and were not always rewarded later. Building on older forms of protest, they developed new ways to regain control of their family life, their work, and their villages, neighborhoods, and nations.

Women's Anticolonial Protests

Precolonial organizations managed by and for women existed across Africa (see chapter 3). Some societies in West Africa were particularly noted for systems where women had the final say in disputes over markets or agriculture, sectors where they were the primary actors. Some associations included elaborate systems of ranking, and women's groups were viewed as complementary to men's within the community, but colonial agents, nearly always men, ignored that reality.[1] The Aba Women's War in Nigeria in 1929, women's role in the Harry Thuku demonstration in Kenya in 1922, and the Anlu movement in Cameroon in the 1950s exemplify women's use of older forms of female protest against colonial intrusions into their lives.

Aba Women's War

In 1929 Igbo women in southeastern Nigeria demonstrated against extending taxation to women, a protest that came to be known as the Aba Women's War. This event is recognized as symbolic of political activities by African women protesting colonial abuses.[2] Sometimes dismissed in colonial documents as the "Aba riots," calling the region-wide protests a "women's war" focuses on women who led and organized demonstrations, while more accurately reflecting its Igbo name, Ogu Umunwanyi.[3]

The Igbo people were increasingly troubled by British actions, particularly by the British destruction of the ancient Aro shrine in 1902, and by the introduction of a system of indirect rule in which "warrant chiefs" were appointed to represent British interests in local districts. Warrant chiefs were African men who were given a document, or warrant, establishing their authority to act as agents of the British colonial government (Achebe's example, Ahebi Ugbabe, in chapter 3, was the sole female to hold the position in Nigeria). Previously there was not an extensive hierarchy of chiefs, and women had roles in local governance. Warrant chiefs, often not local in origin, had some minimal knowledge of English and frequently used their new position to exploit the local community.[4] The expansion of British rule coincided with a series of difficulties, including the 1918 influenza pandemic, which killed many Igbo and others. In 1925 a woman gave birth to a baby with an unusual deformity; though the exact issue was not clear from available evidence, it was considered a monstrous or miraculous birth and its occurrence was attributed to colonial disruptions.

Influenced by the unusual birth, women came together from across the area in November 1925 to "sweep" out polluting elements.[5] In what is sometimes called the "Dancing Women" movement, groups of women arrived at a warrant chief's compound and danced in the courtyard while sweeping it symbolically and ritually, asking that the chief clean house. They demanded a return to old customs and the rejection of British practices. African chiefs acquiesced, and in opposition to the orders of the British Divisional Officer, they helped spread the word as the dancing women requested. The dancers' efforts were not well organized enough to sustain a movement in the face of British opposition, however, and by early 1926 it had collapsed.

Since British colonies were supposed to be self-supporting, the colonial administration imposed new taxes. To organize the collection of taxes, a census of southeastern Nigeria was conducted beginning in 1927, raising many concerns. Local customs supported people counting only their own property; elders and chiefs therefore interpreted the census as an effort by British colonial agents to make people their slaves, claimed as property by those doing the counting. New taxes became even more contentious in 1929 when local chiefs began counting women as part of the census, causing many to believe that women were about to be taxed as well as men.[6] Not only had the British imposed political oppression by warrant chiefs, but they also had the effrontery to make local people pay its costs. Women had an extensive network of local authority specifically concerned with women's work in farming and trading and with protecting women with marital or other family problems. Yet British agents completely disregarded the important role of women leaders and did not include women in any way in the new colonial government.

Economically, women in southeastern Nigeria were central to the functioning of local and long-distance markets and trading networks. Palm oil and kernels were key products of their work, but in the 1920s production fell and the mechanization of oil processing increased. Thus, they were already facing threats to their livelihoods when the new danger of colonial taxation appeared. Women's economic fears were intertwined with increasing concerns about fertility and their role as mothers. Their recognized political, reproductive, and economic realms of control in precolonial Igbo society were being undermined as they lost all forms of authority.[7]

In 1929 women near the market town of Aba protested British colonial activities by using a customary method of critiquing male authority. Known as "sitting on a man," it involved singing insulting songs and otherwise ostracizing men who were not obeying proper norms of respecting women and their work. Trouble began when a government agent asked Nwanyeruwa Ojim, preparing palm oil in her compound, how many people and livestock she had. She responded, "Was your mother counted?" A scuffle ensued in which she called for help from neighboring women, who began "sitting on" the official to demonstrate their displeasure with his intrusion into women's affairs. Existing trading and kin networks under women's authority in Owerri and Calabar provinces then became a conduit for rapidly spreading news of the incident and for escalating events throughout the region. Women carrying palm branches traveled familiar market paths to report on the situation, recruiting more women to join them. They called themselves Ohandum, Women of All Towns, respecting the cooperative efforts of women from many villages.

Women demanded an end to their taxation, the removal of corrupt chiefs, and the appointment of female judges, and they voiced more general complaints about declining fertility and British practices harming women's trading. Although their grievances were related to contemporary economic and political conditions, they drew on powerful customs to express their objections, particularly the practice of censuring men who challenged women's authority and well-being, especially regarding their trading and farming livelihoods. Wearing wreathes of leaves on their heads, dressed in sackcloth, and carrying palm fronds, their appearance was designed to draw official attention to injustice. Upon arrival at British court buildings and other colonial sites, they danced and sang songs insulting men who claimed authority over them. In many cases they were nude or they raised their clothing as part of the demonstration to call attention to their womanly power over fertility, that is, survival; similar practices occurred across Africa. In this case "sitting on a man" involved women performing their anger by slapping their bellies in gestures understood locally as insulting men's manhood and courage.[8]

Although the women were clearly unarmed, the police often felt threatened. One male witness claimed during the subsequent inquiry that the women "appeared to have been seized by some evil spirit."[9] They tore down Native Court buildings and blockaded roads. One incident became a massacre when colonial police opened fire on a boisterous crowd of dancing women, killing over thirty of them, while attacks on women in other locales resulted in an official total of fifty-two deaths and fifty injuries. The actual total may never be known. No British and only one Nigerian man was killed.

The inquiry provoked by these events led the British to change some colonial policies, especially related to taxation. Taxes were not introduced in the eastern region until the 1950s. Women gained some rights to remove corrupt officials, and the warrant chief system was ended. The new policies reverted to reliance on established local male leaders, not the restoration of political or economic power to women, though the British added a few women to seats on the Native Courts.[10] Women's market grievances were not addressed, and ongoing complaints about women's loss of land rights, decreasing fertility, and diminished control over arranged marriages were ignored.[11]

Protests in Kenya in the 1920s and 1940s

Kenyan women who participated in anticolonial protests were generally less visible than men who founded and were active in organizations such as the

East African Association (EAA). One of the best-known incidents involved Mary Muthoni Nyanjiru, a political activist in Kenya in the 1920s. She worked with Harry Thuku, a labor organizer who as a mission-educated Kikuyu man was a typical leader of the EAA. The main grievances against the colonial regime were complaints about hut taxes, police repression, low wages, and coerced labor. In Kenya, men, women, and children were subjected to forced labor requirements; in some cases, women were sexually harassed and raped while working on plantations at the demand of British officials. Thuku and the EAA paid particular attention to the issue of women's forced labor and abuse, attracting support from women.

The colonial administration was increasingly aggravated by Harry Thuku's activities, and in 1922 they declared him a threat to the British colonial government, imprisoning him in the central Nairobi police station. Women mobilized, gathering in front of the station, and sang songs acknowledging his leadership and protesting his arrest. Members of the EAA went on strike to protest Harry Thuku's detention, and a crowd of seven or eight thousand assembled, including around two hundred women. Mary Nyanjiru, who had witnessed Thuku's arrest, was in the crowd. A delegation of African men met with European officials to demand Thuku's release and then returned to the demonstration, asking people to go home. The women, who initially expected men to lead the protest, became angry and began taunting the men, adding to the tension in the crowd. They sang a song and exposed their buttocks or genitals. The song claimed, "When Harry Thuku left, that is the time I started scratching my buttocks"; that is, women sought to shame those who arrested and detained their champion and the African leaders who lacked courage. The women's jeers "prevented a peaceful termination of the episode," according to an account by the British governor.

Mary Nyanjiru went to the front of the crowd, raised her skirt, and challenged the men to take her dress and give her their trousers, as they were too cowardly to act. Her intervention brought a rousing response from the women, who ululated in agreement and rushed the prison door, pushing against the armed guards and yelling, "Let's go get him!," until the guards opened fire, joined by white settler men on the verandah of the Norfolk Hotel across the street. Casualties included at least twenty-one dead, among them Nyanjiru and three other women, and twenty-eight injured. Thuku was not released then, but Nyanjiru's example was important for ensuing generations of anticolonial activists, who learned the Kikuyu political song "Kanyegenuri," which commemorated the actions of women in Nairobi in 1922.[12]

Two decades later, the British were in control of Kenyan political and economic institutions, had seized more than seven million acres of the best agricultural land, and had introduced many laws restricting Africans' freedom of
movement. Taxation and a burdensome pass system combined to control their
lives. Black Kenyan farmers were prohibited from growing profitable export
crops themselves, were paid low wages in other sectors and taxed on those
earnings, and were forced to work on British coffee and tea plantations. These
policies were designed to compel Kenyans to work for British settlers.[13]

Kikuyu areas were the hardest hit; people lost the most land and were confined to small reserves with less fertile soil that could not support the population. Land access and ownership were not simply economic issues but were
fundamental to Kikuyu family formation and social life. Young men were only
considered to be adults eligible to marry when they had land under their control, while for women adulthood involved growing food crops for their families
as a key responsibility. Land expropriation by the British damaged Kikuyu
society in the most basic ways, giving rise to intense anger and resentment.

Crowding Africans into the reserves led to land erosion and decreased soil
fertility from overuse. In the late 1940s the British introduced land management programs designed to control erosion, touting such practices as terracing
and intercropping. Trees were to be planted on hillsides so roots would help
keep soil in place. They also wanted to regulate cattle breeding by requiring
culling and vaccinations. Such agricultural requirements became women's
burden in particular, because women were responsible for growing family food
crops, though men had usually prepared the land that women then planted.
But by the late 1940s as many as half of Kikuyu men were away from their
homes doing migrant labor, meaning that women experienced increasing
demands on their time and energy. In July 1947 the Kenyan African Union
(KAU), which carried on the protests begun in early decades by the EAA,
determined that women should refuse to perform terracing mandated by colonial authorities.

In April 1948, some 2,500 women in Murang'a district, where more than
two thousand acres had already been terraced, converged on district headquarters to protest the new agricultural obligations. They sang and danced at the
local chief's household and "informed everyone that they would not take part
in soil conservation measures mainly because they felt they had enough work
to do at home." In protesting, women defied the British colonial system, widely
publicized their views, and directly confronted their exclusion from political
discussion. The district commissioner (DC) ordered their arrest for refusal to

comply with the law, but women persisted protesting, forcing the release of those who had been jailed. "A large crowd" of women came to government offices "brandishing sticks and shouting Amazonian war-cries," according to the DC. They continued their dissent until they won a minor lessening of the demands and a reduction in the terracing requirement.

Women in Murang'a rebelled again in 1951, when the colonial government began the mandatory vaccination of all cattle to control the spread of rinder-pest, a devastating disease. Women blamed the program for continued high cattle mortality, attacked inoculation centers, and chased away officials imple-menting the program. Five hundred women were arrested, and several women were injured in the resultant fracas. Women composed a song expressing their grievances:

> We women of Murang'a were arrested for refusing
> To have our cattle poisoned. And because we
> Rejected such colonial laws we were thrown into
> Prison cells and our children were wailing because
> They had no milk to drink.
> (Chorus) We beseech you, our God
> Take us away from this slavery.[14]

Such activism was foundational for women's involvement with the Land and Freedom movement in the mid-1950s in central Kenya. The British called that struggle Mau Mau and declared a government emergency when thou-sands of Kenyans took to the markets, streets, and forests to resist colonialism and fight for independence. Establishing concentration camps and turning to torture put down the rebellion; British actions resulted in more than twenty thousand Kenyan deaths, compared to the loss of fewer than one hundred British. Kenyans ultimately won their independence in 1963.[15]

The Anlu Movement in Cameroon in the 1950s

In Cameroon, adjacent to Nigeria and divided between French and British colonial control, women were also active during the nationalist struggle. In 1952 women in the French zone formed the Union Démocratique des Femmes Camerounaises (UDEFEC, Democratic Union of Cameroonian Women), the women's wing of the Union des Populations du Cameroun (UPC, Union of the Cameroon People). Their activities were strongly connected to UPC efforts to end French colonialism, though they did have some autonomy allowing them to put women's issues at the forefront. They grew more militant when French administrators introduced more stringent controls, culminating in July 1955 when the UPC, UDEFEC, and other related organizations were banned, and many male leaders were exiled, persecuted, imprisoned, and executed, resulting in more women moving into decision-making positions.

Women experienced colonial oppression in the British zone as well. New laws restricted their control over markets and agricultural work, and arrests and imprisonment disrupted family life. Increased bureaucratic regulations and fees affected market trading; women could be arrested for leaving a marketing license at home or selling goods from their houses rather than in a market. They were unhappy with their experiences of Western medicine related to pregnancy and childbirth, and there were cases where pregnant women and small children were injured or killed because of official raids against nationalist activities. Women concentrated their political efforts on supporting their work as mothers, traders, and farmers. Women organized meetings where they discussed ending French colonial rule, contributing to the spread of grassroots Cameroonian nationalism, and connecting individual complaints to the national and international anticolonial movement.

In 1958 British colonial authorities introduced agrarian reforms, including new farming methods that undercut women's authority. In July a group of Kom women in the Fon kingdom rejected new regulations calling for contoured farming. The rules had been locally introduced by a schoolteacher; women went to his school and home, singing scurrilous songs, chanting, carrying tree leaves, and dressed in trousers and rags. In November an all-women delegation marched to government offices in Bamenda, where they expressed their fears about women's loss of control over fertility and food production, waving branches and singing abusive songs that reportedly frightened those present.

The protest lasted for three years and was called *anlu*, an established method of protest used by Kom women in the Cameroon Grassfields to protect women's near-absolute authority in agriculture and to ostracize community members, male or female, who transgressed behavioral norms. Women in other regions of Cameroon were also known to hold leadership positions, as there were many queen mothers and some villages had male and female co-chiefs, and they also turned to public protest when their rights were threatened.

Although the 1958 *anlu* began as an autonomous protest focused on women and agriculture, within several months there were seven thousand members throughout the region, and demands grew to include broader political issues such as resentment about Nigerian migration into Kom areas. The women's movement was eventually affiliated with the anticolonial political party, Kameruns National Democratic Party (KNDP), which was in the midst of a dispute about Cameroon's future as part of the British or French colonial sphere. The KNDP favored unity between the French and British sectors of Cameroon; the Kameruns National Congress (KNC), the ruling party in 1958, preferred integration into a federal system in Nigeria as part of the British sphere.

The 1958 *anlu* was noted for the disruption of both colonial and traditional authority in the region when women blocked roads and obstructed the rule of the Fon, the male ruler. When the Fon palace was burned, *anlu* actions kept people from rebuilding it. During the years of protest, school attendance fell, and *anlu* participants closed markets and blocked other activities. In the end, elections held in 1961 demonstrated the influence of the women of *anlu*, since KNDP defeated the KNC party, and Cameroon remained independent of Nigeria while uniting the British and French regions.

Observers and scholars have advanced a range of interpretations since the events that marked the end of colonialism in Cameroon. It appeared that "in Kom eyes women had the right to take over Kom governance, that the women did rule Kom for three years, and that the movement's main thrust was anti-colonial in nature."[16] That is, the movement was controlled by women; they extended their right to protect their agricultural and market activities to the protection of the kingdom; and though women's rights were a factor, that was not the main thrust of *anlu*. The event was significant because of the duration of women's activism and for the outcome, which was positive for women, at least in the short term. *Anlu* clearly involved adapting older protest forms to newer nationalist goals; the shaming of men, as with Aba women sitting on a man or Mary Nyanjiru's actions, contributed to independence for Cameroon.

Women and National Political Parties

Women Mobilize in Tanzania

In the 1950s Tanzanians began organizing to end British rule in their territory. Originally a German colony known as Tanganyika or German East Africa, it was surrendered to Britain after Germany lost World War I. Most initial analyses of Tanzanian nationalism focused on Julius Nyerere, a founder of the Tanganyika African National Union (TANU) and Tanzania's first president after independence. He was an educated Christian, a status shared by many of the male TANU members. Nationalist politics was usually described as developed by Western-educated Tanzanian men until feminist historians investigated the role of Bibi Titi Mohammed (1926–2000), a Muslim woman nationalist leader in Tanzania responsible for bringing women into TANU.[17] Male TANU leaders asked Bibi Titi to develop a women's section, given the lack of female participation. Although men prompted the women, the rapid growth of the women's section can only be explained by women's existing high level of organization, which mobilized around women's interests in ending British colonialism.

Urban women's dance groups in East Africa have a long history as a widespread popular form of organization and leisure activity. Celebrating their time together, women wearing coordinated outfits performed and held competitions on a regular basis.[18] Bibi Titi was a leader of one group in Tanzania's capital, Dar es Salaam, that developed extensive contacts to organize dance competitions. Turning her efforts to TANU, she recruited women to the nationalist cause through dance groups, another example of how women used existing practices and networks to advantage in a climate of political change. Within four months of establishing the women's section of TANU, there were five thousand members, largely drawn from existing networks of activist women. Bibi Titi then extended her campaign by traveling to rural areas to recruit women. In Moshi, in northern Tanzania, existing women's clubs that focused on teaching domestic science, offering classes in child nutrition, baking scones, and home nursing, provided an entry point into local women's interests, and many joined TANU.

Lack of education was a key issue for women in Dar es Salaam, Moshi, and elsewhere. They blamed the colonial government for blocking women from having the same educational opportunities as men, while TANU promised to provide schooling for girls. Bibi Titi herself had completed Standard 4 in government schools, achieving a level of education uncommon for a Muslim woman at that time. Beyond educational goals, the women expressed a desire for respect, the ability to rule themselves, and an end to discrimination they experienced under colonialism. When Bibi Titi and her colleagues visited various women's groups and talked about TANU and its goals of independence, equality, and development, many members immediately joined because they shared those goals, especially wanting equality for themselves and their daughters.[19]

Discovering the history of Muslim women in Dar es Salaam as well as of women throughout Tanzania fundamentally changed the conventional view that the Tanzanian anticolonial movement was led solely by mission-educated men. Bibi Titi Mohammed and the women she recruited were mainly Muslim and outside the colonial educational system, but they were essential to the successful struggle to end colonialism. Without the widespread involvement of Tanzanian women, it is doubtful that TANU would have been as successful as it was, both in ending colonialism and in bringing new inclusive development policies to the country. TANU women were not alone in performing key roles in parties pushing for African independence; their counterparts can be found in Guinea and elsewhere, all pushing similar goals.

Resistance to Pass Laws in South Africa

White settler colonial governments introduced laws requiring women to carry passes in order to enter into and live in urban areas. South Africa, ruled by a white minority government, was an independent nation after 1910 and pioneered racial population control methods. British colonial officials elsewhere, such as Kenya, followed the South African example in crafting their own laws to subjugate majority African populations. While men had long been subject to pass laws, women were exempt until African men and government authorities became concerned about the numbers of women moving to urban areas. Pass laws required women seeking employment in the towns to obtain official approval from the authorities and were designed to keep women under the control of men as they moved away from the influence of male family members.

Focusing on the respect women were due because of their status as mothers, one of the earliest anti-pass demonstrations occurred in 1913 in the Orange Free State (OFS).[20] OFS authorities introduced regulations that required Africans to pay fees and obtain special permits for numerous urban services and demanded that women have permits to live in urban areas, making OFS the only province then with such requirements for women. When the Union of South Africa was formed in 1910, protestors shifted their focus from local actions in Bloemfontein to national complaints sent to parliament in Cape Town. In 1912 the OFS Native Vigilance Association joined the South African Native National Congress (SANNC; later renamed the African National Congress). The initial SANNC meeting was held in Bloemfontein, with local women present, though they primarily served food and acted as hostesses. At that meeting, African leaders from across the Union learned about the oppressive imposition of women's passes.

In the months immediately after the SANNC convention, women circulated petitions throughout the OFS calling for an end to women being forced to carry passes. Once they had collected five thousand signatures, they sent a delegation of six women to Cape Town, where they met with the minister of native affairs. He verbally agreed to remove the pass requirements for women, but he broke his promise and made no changes ending or mitigating pass laws.

When no action was taken for a year, women and their supporters turned to passive resistance to continue their protests. They decided to court arrest by refusing to carry passes. As increasing numbers of individual women were jailed for not having a pass, women called a community meeting in May 1913, where they agreed collectively to reject the passes and serve the prescribed jail term. They marched to downtown Bloemfontein and ripped up their passes in front of the police. The mayor intervened and suspended arrests for pass law violations, but two weeks later when the police arrested a woman without a pass, other women came to her aid; violence erupted, resulting in two months' imprisonment and hard labor for thirty-four women. More encouraging was that women achieved a rare positive outcome when the national government relaxed the pass requirements. In 1923 women were exempted from carrying passes throughout the Union, a step directly resulting from OFS activist women's refusal to carry passes.[21]

Anti-Apartheid Activism

A new era began in South Africa after World War II, when the 1948 election brought in a white-dominated government intent on expanding racial segregation. They enacted a set of extreme laws imposing strict segregation governed by arcane assumptions about racial categories that came to be known as *apartheid*, literally "apartness" in Afrikaans, the language of the Dutch-origin Afrikaner population. Individuals were assigned to a racial category, sometimes quite arbitrarily, depending on their appearance. Marriage, residence, and employment were strictly regulated, with any potential mixing of people of different races severely restricted and subject to punishment. People of all racial backgrounds resisted the new laws in a variety of legal and extralegal ways, including notable leadership by black women.

Women were involved in all phases of the anti-apartheid movement. In the 1950s they again protested the extension of restrictive pass laws to women. Urban women especially suffered, as they had moved into cities looking for work when they lost access to farmland (whites, comprising 13 percent of the population, took 87 percent of the land). Women responded by organizing the Federation of South African Women (FEDSAW) and sponsoring demonstrations throughout the country. FEDSAW was founded as a nonracial organization in 1954; within months there were over ten thousand members, mostly urban African women. After a number of smaller protests, FEDSAW organized the Defiance Campaign, a demonstration in 1956 where they handed in petitions opposing new pass laws. That march was their most successful action when over twenty thousand women descended on government buildings in Pretoria, chanting "You have touched the women, you have struck a rock."[22] Women's three primary objections were that passes would make difficulties for women seeking work, that women would be subject to sexual abuse by officials, and that the inevitable arrest and detention of women for pass offenses would have a negative effect on their homes and families.

Despite this massive women's demonstration, they were obliged to carry passes as government repression escalated, making it increasingly difficult for FEDSAW to organize. It ceased to be active after 1963. Though other groups formed under apartheid, including the African National Congress Women's League, they were repeatedly banned from holding meetings, and women faced immense obstacles in all aspects of their lives. Nonetheless, individual women and organizations worked tirelessly to bring about a democratic system of government based on majority rule. They finally succeeded after decades of struggle, when the first democratic elections in South African history were held in 1994, resulting in Nelson Mandela becoming president of a newly free South Africa.

Funmilayo Ransome-Kuti and the Abeokuta Women's Union in Nigeria

In Nigeria women also actively opposed British colonial rule. In one prominent example, women in the Abeokuta Ladies' Club, originally founded in 1932, ultimately got involved in broader political issues related to promoting women's rights and African political independence. The club was transformed into a vibrant political organization that fought for market women's rights and was renamed the Abeokuta Women's Union (AWU).

Funmilayo Ransome-Kuti served as president from its founding until her death in 1978. She was the first girl to enter the Abeokuta Grammar School (AGS), and she went to England for further education, later becoming a pioneering leader in women's political action and promoting girls' education. She demonstrated outspoken nationalism by wearing Yoruba dress exclusively and making all of her public speeches in Yoruba.

Before the expansion of British colonial power, women had controlled their own market work through women's councils and leaders (see chapter 3). By the 1940s, women were being increasingly taxed and had almost no representation in the government. Market women had specific complaints about burdens placed on them by the colonial administration. Market vendors were forced to accept "conditional sales," meaning that to buy sugar and other desired items for resale, they also had to buy tools and other slower-moving goods. In one of the organization's first campaigns in Abeokuta, members focused on the taxation of market women and criticized local authorities for the misuse of funds. In the mid-1940s the administration began a campaign to control perceived shortages related to World War II, confiscating rice being sold by market women. Ransome-Kuti and the Abeokuta Ladies Club contacted district officers but got no response, so they pushed local newspapers to publish reports on the marketers' situation, resulting in the immediate stoppage of government rice seizures from market women. The revolt was notable for lasting for nine months, for involving rural and urban women as well as women from different class backgrounds, and for using their local circumstances to make connections with the Nigerian nationalist movement and with women throughout the country.[23]

Following that positive result, the women's group expanded to include more market women as members and was renamed the Abeokuta Women's Union in 1946, indicating a shift to a more political stance and open membership. Although the initial impetus for the group came from Christian women, they included Muslim market women in their recruiting and subsequently welcomed women of all faiths and backgrounds. Women's groups worked with the market vendors to end onerous practices, calling for an end to government control over the markets and for no further increases in women's tax burden. The popularity of AWU among women was seen in their support; there were twenty thousand dues-paying members and as many as one hundred thousand other supporters. When women were excluded from holding government office, Ransome-Kuti and others stepped into the vacuum, fighting for women's interests.[24]

Armed Liberation Movements

African colonial governments with entrenched settler populations usually refused to negotiate independence or majority rule. Algeria was the site of one of the earliest armed liberation struggles, beginning in 1954. Although most British and French colonies became independent in the 1960s, Portugal was determined to keep its settler colonies of Angola and Mozambique, which also, like Algeria, experienced armed rebellion.

Independence War in Algeria

Located across the Mediterranean from France, Algeria became a French colony in 1820. French settlers arrived and by the early twentieth century composed almost 15 percent of the population, practicing segregation from the primarily Arab majority. While not as formalized as in Kenya or South Africa, such segregation was equally virulent when prime land was taken for settlers and economic opportunities were reserved for whites. Algerians began an armed rebellion, fighting the French in a desperate war of independence from 1954 to 1962, when whites formed about 10 percent of the population. Armed resistance to French colonialism in Algeria was based in urban areas, and women were centrally involved. The Front de Libération Nationale (FLN) incorporated thousands of women who were rarely combatants but contributed by preparing food, nursing, teaching, and sometimes performing covert tasks in communications and transportation.[25] Because many women wore Islamic dress concealing their bodies and faces, they were able for a time to move about the city of Algiers and other areas without raising French suspicions. As depicted in the classic film directed by Gillo Pontocorvo, *The Battle of Algiers* (1966), some urban women planted bombs where French settlers congregated, strategically donning or removing the veil and wearing Western clothing according to their intent. Women more commonly performed support activities for militants, such as teaching and recruiting women to the cause. Although the French introduced some new laws concerning marriage and the right to vote that were designed to emancipate women, the effects were short-lived, and most women did not experience any great advances.[26] Algeria achieved its independence in 1962 after many atrocities committed in a bitter war, whose success depended on mobilizing every sector of the population.

Nationalism in Mozambique

Portuguese African colonial rule began in the sixteenth century; though they never had large numbers of settlers, the Portuguese controlled Mozambique, Angola, Guinea Bissau, and Cape Verde through chartered companies that relied on such abuses as slavery, forced labor, oppressive taxation, and government corruption. Portugal had become a fascist dictatorship under António Salazar in 1932. By the 1950s, with the stirrings of liberation movements elsewhere, Africans began forming organizations to promote their liberation from the Portuguese. Groups such as FRELIMO (Front for Liberation of Mozambique), MPLA (People's Movement for the Liberation of Angola), and UNITA (National Union for the Total Independence of Angola) were founded, provoking strong repression from the Portuguese government. Under fascist colonialism, there were few opportunities for nationalism to grow in the Portuguese colonies as it had in other African nations.[27]

Beginning in the 1950s, Lusophone African intellectuals wrote about the abuses of colonial rule and sometimes organized groups that worked for reforms. Based in urban centers in the African colonies and in Lisbon where members had traveled for more education, such groups became part of a growing anticolonial movement. By the early 1960s nationalists in the Portuguese colonies determined that they would need to engage in armed struggle to end colonialism, since the Portuguese had made it clear that they would never voluntarily transfer power.

During the 1960s Mozambicans in the armed struggle espoused differing nationalist politics, though with the primary goal of ending Portuguese colonialism and developing Mozambican identity. FRELIMO was founded in 1962, when three earlier nationalist groups united to end Portuguese colonialism. There were fundamental differences of opinion about the character of Mozambique's oppression and consequently about what the appropriate response should be, including over women's emancipation. Those who developed a socialist consciousness became aware that women suffered particular oppression needing remedies.

Recognition of women's important role in the struggle was evident when FRELIMO's Central Committee adopted a series of resolutions in September 1962, including two important items: "to promote the unity of Mozambicans" and "to promote by all methods the social and cultural development of the Mozambican woman." The armed phase of the struggle against Portuguese colonialism began in northern Mozambique in 1964. Initially women were only marginally involved and were excluded from guerrilla training. The first women who became active were seen as role models for others; when they spoke about FRELIMO in the villages of the northern province of Cabo Delgado, other women joined. Mozambican women became known as exemplars of revolutionary spirit, promoting equality, pictured carrying arms, and embodying ideas about the possibilities for women under socialism. Women faced many obstacles to full participation in the struggle, but nonetheless their work was essential to the success of the military branch of FRELIMO.

Women's motives for joining FRELIMO were varied. Some women had experienced Portuguese brutality against themselves or family members. When husbands had not paid taxes, some wives were imprisoned, were made to do forced labor where they faced rape from the policemen in charge of their work details, and suffered torture and death at the hands of Portuguese settlers and administrators. Many women, especially younger women, joined along with their families.[28]

Mozambique was noted for the public ways in which the liberation movement incorporated policies designed to support women, despite the continued marginalization of women activists. Exhausted by seemingly endless warfare, in 1974 progressive military officers in Portugal staged a coup, ending decades of fascist government and leading to independence for Portugal's African colonies in 1975. FRELIMO became the ruling party and implemented many policies designed to support women. The liberation struggle could not have succeeded without the material contributions of women and their work; women's politcal interventions dramatically refocused the anticolonial war in a more inclusive way.

Conclusion

Women were essential to African anticolonial movements in the twentieth century. Increased colonial intrusions into their lives in the form of new taxes, pass laws, and other repressive measures motivated women's actions regarding problems they faced as individuals and in their families and communities. Women's loss of access to land and marginalization from political decisions were pivotal to the development of anticolonial sentiment. In some areas they emerged as local leaders, activists who roused their compatriots, and strategic organizers in a range of events. They relied on existing roles as marketplace managers, knowledgeable farmers, and neighborhood coordinators, always concerned with providing for their families. Movements against colonialism succeeded as a result of the important involvement of women from varied class, ethnic, religious, and other backgrounds and helped generate wider consciousness among women of common interests.

Notes

1. Kathleen Sheldon, *African Women: Early History to the 21st Century* (Bloomington: Indiana University Press, 2017), 36–61, 132–206.

2. Judith Van Allen, "'Aba Riots' or Igbo 'Women's War'? Ideology, Stratification, and the Invisibility of Women," in *Women in Africa: Studies in Social and Economic Change*, ed. Nancy J. Hafkin and Edna G. Bay (Stanford: Stanford University Press, 1976), 59–85.

3. Misty Bastian, "'Vultures of the Marketplace': Southeastern Nigerian Women and Discourses of the Ogu Umunwanyi (Women's War) of 1929," in *Women in African Colonial Histories*, ed. Jean Allman, Susan Geiger, and Nakanyike Musisi (Bloomington: Indiana University Press, 2002), 260–81.

4. Marc Matera, Misty L. Bastian, and Susan Kingsley Kent, *The Women's War of 1929: Gender and Violence in Colonial Nigeria* (London: Palgrave Macmillan, 2012), 32–39.

5. Misty Bastian, "Dancing Women and Colonial Men: The Nwaobiala of 1925," in *"Wicked" Women and the Reconfiguration of Gender in Africa*, ed. Dorothy L. Hodgson and Sheryl A. McCurdy (Portsmouth, NH: Heinemann, 2001), 109–29; A. E. Afigbo, "Revolution and Reaction in Eastern Nigeria: 1900–1929 (The Background to the Women's Riot of 1929)," *Journal of the Historical Society of Nigeria* 3, no. 3 (1966): 539–57.nnn

6. Nina Emma Mba, *Nigerian Women Mobilized: Women's Political Activity in Southern Nigeria, 1900–1965* (Berkeley: University of California Institute for International Studies, 1982), 68–97.

7. Caroline Ifeka-Moller, "Female Militancy and Colonial Revolt: The Women's War of 1929, Eastern Nigeria," in *Perceiving Women*, ed. Shirley Ardener (New York: John Wiley, 1975), 127–57.

8. Judith Van Allen, "'Sitting on a Man,' Colonialism and the Lost Political Institutions of Igbo Women," *Canadian Journal of African Studies* 6, no. 2 (1972): 165–81.

9. Ifeka-Moller, "Female Militancy," 129.

10. Nina E. Mba, "Heroines of the Women's War," in *Nigerian Women in Historical Perspective*, ed. Bolanle Awe (Lagos: Sankore, 1992), 73–88.

11. Useful overviews of this event are found in Matera, Bastian, and Kingsley Kent, *The Women's War of 1929*, and Toyin Falola and Adam Paddock, *The Women's War of 1929: A History of Anti-Colonial Resistance in Eastern Nigeria* (Durham, NC: Carolina Academic Press, 2011).

12. Material in the preceding paragraphs is drawn from Audrey Wipper, "Kikuyu Women and the Harry Thuku Disturbances: Some Uniformities of Female Militancy," *Africa* 59, no. 3 (1989): 300–337.

13. Cora Ann Presley, *Kikuyu Women, the Mau Mau Rebellion, and Social Change in Kenya* (Boulder, CO: Westview Press, 1992).

14. Songs and other quotes in this section are found in Tabitha Kanogo, "Kikuyu Women and the Politics of Protest: Mau Mau," in *Images of Women in Peace and War: Cross-Cultural and Historical Perspectives*, ed. Sharon Macdonald, Pat Holden, and Shirley Ardener (Madison: University of Wisconsin Press, 1988), 78–99.

15. Caroline M. Elkins, *Imperial Reckoning: The Untold Story of Britain's Gulag in Kenya* (New York: Henry Holt, 2005).

16. The source for preceding paragraphs is Eugenia Shanklin, "*Anlu* Remembered: The Kom Women's Rebellion of 1958–61," *Dialectical Anthropology* 15, no. 2/3 (1990): 159–81.

17. Susan Geiger, *TANU Women: Gender and Culture in the Making of Tanganyikan Nationalism, 1955–1965* (Portsmouth, NH: Heinemann, 1997).

18. Margaret Strobel, "From Lelemama to Lobbying: Women's Associations in Mombasa, Kenya," in *Women in Africa: Studies in Social and Economic Change*, ed. Nancy J. Hafkin and Edna G. Bay, 183–211 (Stanford: Stanford University Press, 1976).

19. Geiger, *TANU Women*, 42–44.

20. Julia Wells, "Why Women Rebel: A Comparative Study of South African Women's Resistance in Bloemfontein (1913) and Johannesburg (1958)," *Journal of Southern African Studies* 10, no. 1 (October 1983): 55–70.

21. Julia Wells, "Passes and Bypasses: Freedom of Movement for African Women under the Urban Areas Act of South Africa," in *African Women and the Law: Historical Perspectives*, ed. Margaret Jean Hay and Marcia Wright (Boston: Boston University African Studies Center, 1982), 126–50.

22. Cherryl Walker, *Women and Resistance in South Africa* (London: Onyx Press, 1982), 194–97.

23. Judith A. Byfield, "Taxation, Women, and the Colonial State: Egba Women's Tax Revolt," *Meridians: Feminism, Race, Transnationalism* 3, no. 2 (2003): 250–77.

24. Information in these paragraphs is drawn from Cheryl Johnson-Odim and Nina Emma Mba, *For Women and the Nation: Funmilayo Ransome-Kuti of Nigeria* (Urbana: University of Illinois Press, 1997).

25. Anne Lippert, "Algerian Women's Access to Power: 1962–1985," in *Studies in Power and Class in Africa*, ed. Irving Leonard Markovitz (New York: Oxford University Press, 1987), 209–32. Frantz Fanon also discusses women's roles in the Algerian struggle in "Algeria Unveiled," a chapter in *A Dying Colonialism*, trans. Haakon Chevalier (New York: Grove Press, 1965).

26. Ryme Seferdjeli, "French 'Reforms' and Muslim Women's Emancipation during the Algerian War," *Journal of North African Studies* 9, no. 4 (2004): 19–61.

27. Allen Isaacman and Barbara Isaacman, *Mozambique: From Colonialism to Revolution, 1900–1982* (Boulder, CO: Westview Press, 1983).

28. The preceding paragraphs are based on Kathleen Sheldon, *Pounders of Grain: A History of Women, Work, and Politics in Mozambique* (Portsmouth, NH: Heinemann, 2002), 118–29.

Suggested Readings

Geiger, Susan. *TANU Women: Gender and Culture in the Making of Tanganyikan Nationalism, 1955–1965*. Portsmouth, NH: Heinemann, 1997.

Matera, Marc, Misty L. Bastian, and Susan Kingsley Kent. *The Women's War of 1929: Gender and Violence in Colonial Nigeria*. London: Palgrave Macmillan, 2012.

Presley, Cora Ann. *Kikuyu Women, the Mau Mau Rebellion, and Social Change in Kenya*. Boulder, CO: Westview Press, 1992.

Schmidt, Elizabeth. *Mobilizing the Masses: Gender, Ethnicity, and Class in the Nationalist Movement in Guinea, 1939–1958*. Portsmouth, NH: Heinemann, 2005.

Sheldon, Kathleen. *Pounders of Grain: A History of Women, Work, and Politics in Mozambique*. Portsmouth, NH: Heinemann, 2002.

Figure 5.1. In 2016 Gambia president Yahya Jammeh ordered women workers to cover their hair in public, giving no reasons for the ban. "Gambia Orders Female Workers 'to Cover Hair,'" BBC News, January 5, 2015, http://www.bbc.com/news/world-africa-35231503.

5

RELIGIOUS FUNDAMENTALISMS AND WOMEN IN CONTEMPORARY AFRICA

Ousseina Alidou

What is meant by religious fundamentalism? Here I use Suzanne Katz's definition:

> By religious fundamentalism we do not mean religious observance, a matter of personal choice, but rather modern political movements, which we assert use religion as their attempt to win or consolidate power and extend social control. Fundamentalism appears in different and changing forms in all religions throughout the world, sometimes as a state project, sometimes in opposition to it. But at the heart of all religious fundamentalist agenda is the control of women's minds and bodies. All religious fundamentalists support the patriarchal family as central agent of such control. They view women as embodying the morals and traditional values of the family and the whole community.[1]

Moreover, religious fundamentalisms considered here are modern phenomena despite their claims to be antimodernist. While they are reacting to modern development paradigms imposed on postcolonial African countries that exacerbate inequalities, they are deeply implicated, paradoxically, in similar gendered hegemonic structures they seek to replace.[2] In addition, regardless of their sectarian differences, religious fundamentalist movements promote patriarchal or male-dominant family ideology embodied by male-headed households in which women are legal minors without authority. This ideology fosters male control of the female body and (re)production and is absolutely antagonistic toward homosexuality.[3] Nonetheless, as demonstrated here, many women have found adherence to various fundamentalisms empowering, an aspect, beyond their similarities regarding gender ideology, requiring explanation.

The end of the Cold War in the 1980s created a fertile space for a more aggressive consolidation of forces of neoliberalism across the world, often leading in Africa to multiple forms of structural violence by oppressive states and the persistently detrimental effects of economic policies of the World Bank and International Monetary Fund (IMF).[4] Neoliberal interventions, aimed at promoting corporate interests, intensified conditions of abject poverty and socioeconomic insecurity for most Africans. Fundamentalist religious movements discussed in this chapter, especially those embraced by lay people of two of the Abrahamic religions, Christianity and Islam, are partly the by-product of such conditions. Mansoor Moaddel suggests that changes in political economy are the primary stimulus for the growth of religious fundamentalisms, a view shared by Fatou Sow, who poignantly challenges human rights advocacy efforts of the Global North that do not address the inequalities produced by neoliberal globalization and its consequences on women in Africa:

> The talk of human rights heard in international fora masks the violation of citizen's rights in general—and women's rights in particular—which accompanies globalization. . . . Women experience globalisation daily when they go in search of water at the hydrants in poor neighborhoods, or when they busy themselves in thousands of other ways to fulfill the needs of their families. These are needs that men are no longer able to meet, or needs arising from the cutting of state provision for education or health services, under the constraints of structural adjustment policies. It is primarily women who pay the actual costs of the privatisation of the economy. All these factors have favoured the emergence of fundamentalist movements, in environments where religion is an integral part of culture.[5]

Religious fundamentalist leaders take full advantage of democratic space to participate in national and transnational political and other debates. Although fundamentalist leaders usually rely on lay followers who come from the lower echelons of society, it is important to highlight that leaders of contemporary religious fundamentalist movements in Africa, male or female, are in general members of the educated elite class who use religious affect to convert underclass members to their salvation theologies.[6]

Religious fundamentalist movements arise from specific historical, economic, discursive, and political contexts; within them women who embrace their patriarchal ideologies often have different motives from those of male adherents.[7] For instance, fundamentalist women leaders might use patriarchal space of piety as an opportunity to improve their social, political, and economic statuses, seizing upon a means of developing transformative female agency.[8]

Here I explore gendered understandings of religious practices, discursive and otherwise, as they relate to Muslim and Christian fundamentalisms, their implications for women, and their interaction with African "traditional" religions. I am particularly concerned with how fundamentalisms react to and engage with the state, in both nonviolent and violent ways, their impact on the education of girls and women, and their constructions of, and reactions to, witchcraft and gay culture.

Religious Fundamentalisms in Africa: Trends and Causes

Religious fundamentalism in many African contexts took strong root with the weakening of national states' power to monopolize resources for cultural production. Within expressions of democratic pluralism, religious fundamentalists are playing a major role in the public sphere in the production of new discourses defined by their readings of the scriptures, be it the Bible, the Qur'an, or oral traditions. Fundamentalisms in the African postcolonial context represent oppositional forces to weak secular states unable to address the economic needs of citizens impoverished by the effects of structural adjustment programs (SAPs) mandated by the World Bank and the International Monetary Fund and other structures of neoliberalism (see chapters 7 and 9).[9]

Through redemption and salvation theologies that use piety, fundamentalists produce their own cultures with their own symbols and rituals in opposition to both nonfundamentalist religious and secular cultures.[10] For example, the adoption in the 1990s of the Middle Eastern type veil or head covering, the hijab, by fundamentalist Muslim women in sub-Saharan Africa fits fundamentalist cultural production and women's belonging to these movements, while Muslim fundamentalist men mark their public appearance with a beard and clothing—often a pair of pants that rises three inches above the ankle and a white robe, the *jellabiya*. In *Professional Women in South African Pentecostal Charismatic Churches*, Maria Frahm-Arp demonstrates how public "power" clothing and dressing are also important signifiers for Ndebele Pentecostalist professional women used to demonstrate spiritual success, while Naomi van der Meer offers comparative insight into clothing restrictions imposed upon immigrant African women adherents to African charismatic Pentecostal churches in their attempt to mark their differences from other churches in the Dutch Reformed Church–influenced South African religious landscape.[11]

Fundamentalisms in Africa come in many forms, sometimes state sponsored or promoted. Nigeria poses a good example of how religious fundamentalism in the form of Pentecostalism and Shariatocracy (rule by Islamic *shari'a* law) became embedded in the project of state democratization with negative consequences for the lives of women and homosexuals.[12] As Ebenezer Obadare contends, the "'Pentecostalisation' of governance during the 1999 Presidential election has raised the stakes as far as the struggle to define the Nigerian public sphere is concerned, further politicizing religion, even as lip service continues to be paid to the secularity of the Nigerian state."[13] Simultaneous with this development, nine states in northern Nigeria, Zamfara being the pioneer, made *shari'a* official state law—creating a fundamentalist theocracy with all its negative gendered implications for women.[14]

At other times, religious fundamentalism comes from below as a challenge to the state. This fundamentalist challenge can take peaceful civil means, like nonparticipation in projects of the state such as voting or juries,[15] or it can resort to violent means—like Alice Lakwena's Holy Spirit and Joseph Kony's Lord's Resistance Army in Uganda, Boko Haram in Nigeria, and Al Shabab in Somalia. Even when independent of the state, a fundamentalist movement can be coopted by a state and further its interests, often to the detriment of women's rights.[16] For example, in francophone Sahelian countries such as Niger and Mali, the struggle to institute a pro–women's rights Family Code, equalizing matters of sexuality, reproductive rights, and inheritance, was compromised when politicians vying for state power decided they needed the electoral votes of large numbers of constituents under the control of fundamentalist Islamic organizations.[17] The same pattern has been observed in such countries as Kenya, Nigeria, Ghana, and Uganda, where politicians have desired the critical support of Pentecostal fundamentalist churches.[18]

Religious Fundamentalism and the State

Nowhere is religious fundamentalism in Africa more consequential than when it decides to engage the state, a contestation openly about power and authority. For instance, David Chidester describes the three ideological phases of Christian fundamentalism in South Africa, beginning with its anti-apartheid, nonmilitaristic, and nonracist theology during the 1970s, to its transformation into a pro-apartheid militaristic racist theology of the state, to its present ethno-nationalist religious fundamentalism, with global affiliations, against the democratic state. As an anti-apartheid religious movement, Christian fundamentalism in South Africa became a problem for the apartheid state, whereas in the 1980s it was an ally. South Africa entered the ethno-nationalist phase of its Christian fundamentalism in the 1990s, coinciding with the rise of religious fundamentalisms in many African countries that use religion as a means to contest the authority of the state. At this stage, in spite of South Africa's multireligious and multiracial composition, Christian fundamentalist organizations supported by U.S. Protestant fundamentalisms led by evangelicals such as Jerry Falwell began to advocate creating a "South African Christian Country" to defend the "traditional Christian family, the rights of the unborn and maintain abortion as illegal." In the 1994 election in South Africa, an advertisement of the ANC declared that "the gospel as the only framework for establishing full political inclusion and guaranteeing social justice."[19]

The rise of Christian fundamentalism stimulated the emergence of an Islamic counterfundamentalist movement known as Qibla. Like many fundamentalist organizations in other parts of Africa, it took its inspiration from the Iranian Revolution of 1979, although not Shi'a, to inscribe South Africa as a pro-Islamic fundamentalist country advocating the principles of shari'a and the teaching of the Qur'an. Gender ideology within Qibla mirrors that of South African Christian fundamentalism in its promotion of the patriarchal family with a male head of household and the denial of civil rights to homosexuals, contrary to the provisions of the democratic South African constitution.[20]

More exposed in the glare of international media has been northern Nigeria. The 1999 adoption of shari'a law in some northern Nigerian states was in the context of democratization and opening up of political space after a long experience with military dictatorship. Claiming to establish a new moral order, these shariacratic states imposed new and sometimes draconian penalties for some "sexual offenses," mainly targeting women and other gender minorities, triggering strong reactions from Nigerian women, human rights activists, and nongovernmental organizations (NGOs).[21] Included in this protest and activism were Nigerian women writers and more particularly Muslim women writers from the shari'a states, in both Hausa- and English-language novels.[22] Divisions developed in northern Nigeria between pro-shari'a and anti-shari'a groups. According to Ibrahim Jibril, a northern Nigerian human rights activist, "For the pro-Shari'a group, democracy is meaningless without religious freedom, the most important of which is the right to exercise their religion fully, which is impossible without the implementation of the Shari'a. For the anti-Shari'a group the full implementation of the Shari'a is a political transformation indicating the establishment of an Islamic State and the persecution of non-Muslims."[23]

Adopting shari'a law in both civil and criminal courts in these states can be seen as a political reassertion of Muslim identity at a time when forces of liberalization and neoliberalism had created new economic and political imbalances in the country, impoverishing populations and severely hindering the state's ability to continue subsidizing basic public services such as health, education, and youth employment.[24] Islamism and Shariatocracy were deliberate political moves by a northern Nigerian political elite that saw itself as having been pushed to the margins of political power, especially after the return of civilian rule in 1990s.

There were also many Muslims in northern and southwestern Nigeria who saw merit in embracing the *shari'a* as a way of combating pervasive corruption and disorder.[25] Like other religious dogma, Islam places great value on moral order and considers sexual offenses as one of the most prominent signs of moral decay, especially by women whose sexuality is supposed to be under male control, meaning that policing of women's sexuality became an integral component of *shari'a* law enforcement.[26] Northern Nigerian states imposed stiff penalties for what they considered to be sexual offenses such as *zina*, sexual intercourse outside marriage (e.g., adultery), pregnancy outside marriage, and homosexuality.[27] Since *shari'a* applies to all Muslims within *shari'a* states, an impression has been created that *shari'a* has been democratically established by Muslims and for Muslims. Ayesha Imam explains: "The new *Shari'a* penal codes created some new offenses in Nigerian law, mostly around *zina* and the prohibition of lesbianism. The code also recognizes stoning, retributive punishments, and blood fines. In theory, this law applies to Muslims only, thereby avoiding the charge that the Sharia Acts constitute an imposition of state religion. It remains open whether Muslims have the rights to choose to be governed by general Nigerian law without having to renounce their religious identity."[28] This religio-politicization of sex and sexuality has had implications not only for Nigeria but also for some of its neighboring nations.[29]

Although Muslim fundamentalists and Christian fundamentalists see themselves in competition, their political stands cohere concerning control of women's sexuality and reproductive health and the question of homosexuality. In this respect, some churches and mosques in Nigeria have been complicit in the widespread provocation of hostility and violence directed against homosexuals.[30] Nigerian Christian fundamentalist organizations have often been under the influence of U.S. Pentecostal churches, until the Trump/Pence election lost ground in this particular fight in their own country.[31] This new wave of violence against homosexuality has led to the emergence of activists and civil society organizations focused on combating violations of homosexuals' human rights.

Activist organizations, such as BAOBAB, have been in the forefront of challenging the violation of women's sexual and reproductive rights by religious, cultural, and state structures. They oppose the religious condemnation of women such as Safiyatu Hussain, Amina Lawal, and many others whose cases reached the international media, and the persecution of women and male prostitutes by fundamentalist morality police called *hisba*.[32] The criminalization of sex and sexuality in the name of Islam has given rise to a new generation of Muslim women writers of northern Nigeria, who in their quest for gender justice have joined the struggle to challenge political sharianization, patriarchy, and its sexual morality laws through the genius of their literary creativity. Some seek to make visible the reality of lesbianism existing within Muslim society in northern Nigeria, such as Razinat T. Mohamed in her novel *Habiba*.[33] Another writer who has championed human rights for homosexuals in Nigeria and Africa in general is the renowned Nigerian female novelist Chimamanda Adichie (see chapter 1).[34]

The latest in the switch of an African state to Islamic religious fundamentalism is the Gambia, where in December 2015 President Yahya Jammeh (now ousted) declared the Gambian nation an Islamic state in violation of the secularist mandate of the Gambian national constitution. In a television broadcast addressed to the nation, he declared, "Gambia's destiny is in the hands of the Almighty Allah." He made mandatory the wearing of the hijab for working women in particular.[35] Although Gambia's population is 90 percent Muslim, most Gambian Muslims rejected the Islamic fundamentalist populism of their theocratic head of state that attempted to divert attention away from the economic crisis facing the nation. Moreover, this Islamization of the Gambian state by its head violates citizenship rights of minority Christians and adherents of African indigenous religions by regulating all women's dress, sexuality, and freedom of movement.

Militaristic Fundamentalisms and the State

The abuse of power by heads of state who decide to push their countries down the path of religious fundamentalism through coercive violence was bound to trigger movements of counterviolence, also in the garb of fundamentalism. This is certainly part of the story of Boko Haram in Nigeria. Its leader, Abubakar Shekau, went so far as to declare that Allah ordered him to massacre more than two thousand people.[36] The majority of Boko Haram victims have been women, children, and the elderly, whose mutilated bodies are thrown into the rivers and Lake Chad on the Nigerian border with Cameroon, Chad, and Niger. The casualties of Boko Haram have taken a transnational and transborder dimension, leading ECOWAS (Economic Community of West African States) founding states Cameroon, Chad, Niger, and Ghana to call for collective military efforts to dismantle its regional hold, while its atrocities continue—using women and girls as suicide bombers in Nigeria and neighboring states, for instance. In 2018 Boko Haram militants kidnapped 110 girls from Government Girls Science Technical College but, unusually, returned 104 of them to their villages with the warning, "Don't ever put your daughters in school again!"[37]

Before Boko Haram in Nigeria, there were the Christian-based Holy Spirit Movement and the Lord's Resistance Army in Uganda, male-founded fundamentalist movements. Female-founded millennial movements in Africa have been just as important, such as the one created in the mid-1980s (1986–87) by the northern Ugandan priestess Alice Lakwena that challenged President Yoweri Museveni's National Resistance Movement (NRM) through spiritual mobilization of her Acholi adherents.[38] Priestess Alice Lakwena's new religious war with the National Resistance Army was a syncretization of Acholi indigenous spirit mediumship (see chapter 3) with Christianity.[39] According to Omara-Otunnu, "Alice Lakwena was a simple woman, less than 30 years of age, who prior to March 1987 was an insignificant member of an underground opposition group called the Uganda Peoples Democratic Movement (UPDM). . . . Alice Lakwena announced that God has sent her to oust the NRA government, rid Uganda of evil people and bring lasting peace to all Ugandans. . . . She demanded from her followers total abstinence from sex, drinking, smoking or stealing—injunctions which echo St. Paul's exhortations to Christians in his epistle to the Colossians." Lakwena gave persuasive sermons in language accessible by her followers and so inspired their submissive devotion and commitment.[40] What started as a nonviolent religious movement gradually developed into a guerrilla army fighting Museveni's government, conscripting children who had been victims of government armed forces, leading to reports that "peasants in Acholi and Lango now believe that Lakwena was sent by some devil to 'finish off all their male children.'"[41] Although Alice Lakwena's Holy Spirit army was defeated by Museveni's National Resistance Army, from its remnants arose Joseph Kony's Lord's Resistance Army.[42] Seeking to overthrow the Ugandan government, Joseph Kony, a former Catholic who kidnapped tens of thousands of children from which he drew his 104,000 soldiers, used a literal reading of the Biblical Ten Commandments to justify his atrocities.[43]

Boko Haram and the Lord's Resistance Army demonstrate the magnitude of the tragedy that can result from the transformation of a religious fundamentalist movement into an armed struggle. Because religious fundamentalist movements are guided by their own logic of divine authority, no human-made rules of war become sacrosanct. In the process, they have no boundaries on the kinds of terror they can unleash on society, with women and children as their most common victims. In February 2016, Boko Haram's lethal warfare tactics included horrific deployment of women and girls as suicide bombers camouflaged in black Islamic female dress. Three girl suicide bombers draped in black chadors were sent to attack a refugee camp of more than 50,000 persons displaced from their villages and towns in northeastern Nigeria. Two of them killed 58 people and wounded 78. The third exercised heroic agency by refusing to carry out mass killing. The agency, compliance, or coercion of female bombers in carrying out deadly missions prescribed by religious fundamentalist organizations such as Boko Haram needs further attention.[44]

Religious Fundamentalism and Female Education

Concerns about gender disparities in access to European-style secular education in Africa go back to the earliest periods of its introduction by European colonial administrations, beginning in the late nineteenth century in most places. The encounter resulted in the convergence between local male-dominant traditions and Euro-Christian Victorian values that sought to channel girls either into Euro-style domesticity as housewives for husbands who were lower-level clerks and administrators, housewifery being a previously unknown concept in Africa since most women did significant work outside the home as farmers or traders, or into domestic service for white settlers. Access to higher-level academic education was reserved for relatively few boys. Even when girls were admitted to schools, they were often encouraged to focus on vocational education in home economics. Tsitsi Dangarembga captures this reality at the beginning of her acclaimed novel, *Nervous Conditions*, where chief female protagonist Tambu's burning desire for education received little support, while her brother Nhamo's path to the mission school was facilitated.[45] Boys' access to formal education was privileged both in Christian and Islamic education, partly because religious authority structures were patriarchal, with only men becoming imams or priests. Both tended to restrict women's knowledge of the scriptures to basics that would allow them to perform the necessary rituals and initiate their young to the fundamentals of their respective faiths (see also chapter 10).

The 1990s rise of religious fundamentalism has had a major impact on girls' and women's education in the religious domain. The study by men and women alike of the Bible among Christians, on the one hand, and the Qur'an and the Hadith among Muslims, on the other, has been an integral part of the fundamentalist mission. Throughout Africa one meets women who are extremely knowledgeable, passionate, and articulate when it comes to discussing religious doctrines, be they Islamic or Christian, and who usually are fundamentalists.

A growing number of religion-based universities of Christian and Islamic orientation in several African countries have a decidedly religious mission even in their seemingly secular programs, admitting both men and women.[46] They provide women with religious credentials not easily acquired in the past. Some women even proceed abroad for further studies in religion, including Christian women theologians such as Dr. Christiana Doe Tetteh of Ghana and Nigerian women at Christian fundamentalist colleges.[47] Women sometimes form their own fundamentalist networks, allowing the followers to meet regularly, exchange educational materials and lessons for personal spiritual and entrepreneurial empowerment, and engage in proselytizing (or what is known as *da'wah* among Muslims and Christian women's fellowships.[48] In Mombasa, Kenya, for example, young women's networks calling themselves An-Nisaa (The Women) and Akhwati-l-Hudaa (The Guided Sisters), among others, engage in a wide variety of activities, from educational to philanthropic, to popularize their fundamentalist causes. Many young women members are highly educated in religious matters, some having gone as far as Al-Azhar University in Cairo.

Fundamentalism has also become a significant presence in leading African institutions of higher learning, hitherto exclusively secular, with a gendered dimension. At some universities faculty meetings usually begin with prayer in the name of Jesus or Allah. Where student organizations were once entirely secular, sometimes ethnic, today religious student organizations are more dominant and active. For example, "in September 2007 nine students, called the Ife Nine, at Obafemi Awolowo University, male and female members of a registered student organization, the Word Ablaze Fellowship, went camping at Tonkere, a village nearby, living only on bread and water, apparently in anticipation of the Rapture, which would involve their ascent to Paradise."[49]

Female students, as members and leaders, have played as large a part as males in the growth of fundamentalism on African university campuses, sometimes with the full backing of the faculty. For instance, female students engaged in the *ibadu* Islamic revivalist movement on Cheikh Anta Diop University's campus in Dakar, Senegal, use the politics of piety to transform gender relations and their daily lives by rejecting the conspicuous materialism imposed by neoliberal consumerism and developing their own alternative mode of economic empowerment.[50] As highly educated in their respective doctrines as women members of fundamentalist movements might be, in many cases their discourse seeks to justify male-dominant structures and the "religious" duty to submit to them, sometimes even under conditions that may be considered abusive. Except in a few cases of religious fundamentalism and women's empowerment discussed below, there is little evidence of critical rereadings of religious doctrinal texts to challenge patriarchal structures and relationships.

Fundamentalism and Witch-Hunting within Indigenous Religions

Adherents of African indigenous religions have often been victims of the violence of Christian and Islamic fundamentalisms. There are times, however, when followers of indigenous religions can themselves turn fundamentalist and perpetrate acts of violence against others. Furthermore, although women may enjoy equal or even high status within some indigenous African religions, there is a growing body of literature on the violation of women's rights by their adherents. In its extreme form, this fundamentalism is demonstrated especially by the case of witch-hunting, sometimes leading to the burning to death of accused women as illustrated in *The Witches of Gambaga*, a powerful documentary film directed by the Ghanaian/British filmmaker Yaba Badoe.[51] Similarly, Joshep Odhiambo, a Kenyan BBC journalist, reported the horrific lynching of women in Kisii District in western Kenya, exposing atrocities inflicted on women.[52] Accusing women, especially senior women, of being witches and burning them to death in witch-hunting rituals is one area where religious fundamentalisms of Muslim, Christian, and indigenous religions intersect.[53] Silvia Federici explains that this is accomplished with the help of desperate young male perpetrators who dispossess women. She goes on to give examples of "witch-hunting as women hunting" from Ghana, Kenya, Congo, South Africa, Zambia, and Tanzania, sometimes inspired by indigenous faith and other times by the Christian faith.[54] Older women were also the majority of the victims in the Kenyan Gusii witch-hunts of 1992–95. Men murdered there were guilty of association with suspected witches, or they were killed instead when women could not be found or they tried to protect the women.[55] In urban areas, traders are most commonly attacked, when men respond to the loss of economic security and masculine identity by discrediting prosperous women seen as threatening. Thus, in northern Ghana, female traders have been accused of gaining wealth by selling souls.[56] In Zambia those at risk are independent women, "who frequently travel as entrepreneurs and smugglers along the national highways."[57]

Women fundamentalists of all religious persuasions are among witch-hunters violating the human rights of vulnerable women and children. These include the preacher Helen Ukpabio of Calabar, Nigeria, currently based in the United Kingdom, founder and head of Liberty Foundation Gospel Ministries. She is under investigation by human rights organizations for her crusade against witches. In *Unveiling the Mysteries of Witchcraft*, she contends, "If a child under the age of two screams in the night and cries and is always feverish with deteriorating health, he or she is a servant of Satan."[58] In *Evangelical Christians in Muslim Sahel*, Barbara Cooper discusses the horrific burning of the *iya*, the senior female leader of Bori, an indigenous cult, that took place in November 2000 in Maradi, Niger, located near Zaria, Nigeria, a hotbed of Islamic fundamentalism.[59]

Fundamentalism and LGBT Rights

South Africa's post-apartheid Constitution recognizes the rights of citizens who are homosexuals or gender nonspecific, but the constitutions of most African countries do not grant equal rights to those who are lesbian, gay, bisexual, and transgender (LGBT). As a result, LGBT people have experienced a degree of support in South Africa unparalleled elsewhere on the continent. As Joanna Zimmerman observes, "the South African examples speak loud and clear: Gay rights are human rights, not Western ones, so everyone is enjoined to respect them."[60] However, South African progressive legislation is under attack by fundamentalist Christians, Muslims, and the fundamentalist followers of indigenous African religions.

In many African countries, a homophobic popular belief is that "homosexuality is a Western import" and must be fought because it undermines African morality and religious beliefs that restrict sexual acts to heterosexuality for the purpose of reproduction. Homophobic laws in some countries including Kenya, Tanzania, Uganda, Nigeria, and Ghana are forging interfaith coalitions that violate the human rights of LGBT African citizens, often leading to assaults on gay people. In the case of the brutal killing of Ugandan gay rights activist David Kato, the murderers felt vindicated by antigay laws in Uganda passed by parliament.[61] This trend has spread to many African countries, including Mauritania, where the head of state led a national antigay march and enacted laws treating homosexuality as a crime punishable by death.[62] In Zamfara state, *shari'a* law in Nigeria, which hitherto condemned only sodomy, was amended to criminalize homosexuality and lesbianism. In the Islamic Republic of Sudan, engaging in "repeated" homosexuality can bring execution.[63]

Such persecution has brought responses: *God Loves Uganda*, the documentary by African American filmmaker Roger Ross Williams, is a powerful exposé of the role of American evangelical churches in promoting antigay Christian fundamentalist extremism in Africa in general and in Uganda in particular. In Cameroon, the courageous work of feminist jurist Alice Nkom in challenging both the state penal code and the conservative Catholic Church against LGBT people is noteworthy.[64]

Religious Fundamentalism and Women's Empowerment

If religious fundamentalism often violates women's rights, then why are some women attracted to it and actively participate in it? The answer is partly that some women find that religious fundamentalism can lead to their empowerment in the form of prestige or profit. They often achieve this goal by reinterpreting sacred texts or engaging in activities in ways that open up new opportunities for women. Jane Soothill in *Gender, Social Change and Spiritual Power: Charismatic Christianity in Ghana* describes the transformation of gender politics in new Pentecostal churches in Ghana, including new forms of leadership roles for women (wives of founders of the churches or female pastor founders of the churches), as in the case of Reverend Tetteh. Women leaders of charismatic churches are referred to as "Women of God" or "first ladies" and "enjoy an independence and personal status far beyond that which their public rhetoric implies." By focusing on the spiritual egalitarian principle of charismatic churches, women leaders within these churches put greater emphasis on women's empowerment while moving away from historical biblical readings that require women to submit to patriarchal male heads of families and that demonize indigenous religions and barren women. In born-again Pentecostal churches, female "submission" in domestic relationships is tied to individual "success" on the scale of virtuous submissiveness, modeled on biblical women such as Esther and Hannah, seeking rewards in the modern form of children, status, and prosperity. However, female ministers such as Tetteh have challenged the entire edifice of female domesticity embedded in cultural, religious, and secular gender politics and exhibit affinities with feminist organizations promoting economic development for women, as shown in Tetteh's exhortation to women members: "You have looked down on yourselves for too long. You know that you have been caged. You have to come out of that cage before you can break barriers. We are afraid of so many things: the barrier of religion, the barrier of tradition, the barrier of family and the barrier of class. We are breaking it! Anything that made you afraid, I have come to tell you go for gold!"[65]

A similar experience in Pentecostalist churches can be found in Kenya. Paristau highlights the "gender paradox" at the heart of global Pentecostalism that both liberates and disempowers women in her view.[66] The Redeemed

Gospel Church has ordained women pastors, including several prominent female clergy. In Kenyan Pentecostalism, some female pastors have left their original churches to found their own churches and congregations, so that one of the most striking features of the Kenyan Pentecostal scene now is its increasingly feminized face. Many female clergy are founders, presidents, bishops, evangelists, healers, and prophetesses in new churches. Examples include Bishop Margaret Wanjiru of Jesus Is Alive Ministry (JIAM) and evangelist Teresia Wairimu of Faith Evangelistic Ministry (FEM). By 2007 Wanjiru had become sufficiently prominent to vie successfully for a seat in the Kenya Parliament, later becoming an assistant minister in President Mwai Kibaki's government.[67] She then hit international headlines when she mobilized her huge constituency to oppose the constitutional retention of the (Islamic) Kadhis Court—in spite of the fact that a large majority of its users are women seeking justice—and the legalization of same-sex marriage.[68] Reverend Judith Mbugua, founder of the Ladies Homecare Spiritual Fellowship, created a space for women's spiritual and economic empowerment through entrepreneurship within a conservative religious framework.[69]

A growing body of literature focusing on Muslim societies explains women's agency and empowering factors in their adherence and leadership roles in Islamic revivalist organizations.[70] Across West Africa, Muslim women are transforming Islamic understanding through the regendering of Islamic religious authority and opening up both secular and religious education for girls and female empowerment.[71] Muslim women demonstrate both autonomy and agency in adhering to patriarchal revivalist clerics and rejecting them when they encroach on female domains of power, as illustrated by Adeline Masquelier in *Women and Islamic Revival in a West African Town*, where senior Mawri Hausa women of Dogondoutchi, Niger, boycotted a revivalist Sufi cleric, Malam Mahamane Awal, and his *awaliyya movement* when they concluded that he was not living up to the pious ethics he preached and were turned off by his misogynist sermons. Furthermore, they disagreed with his attempt to deny them the right to secure and display their daughters' bridewealth, a special marker of womanhood in Hausa society. They remain *awaliyya* while dismissing Malam Mahamane Awal's religious authority by simply deserting his mosque.[72]

Muslim women involved in Islamic pious movements in Africa use networks for social and economic entrepreneurship to face austerity conditions engendered by neoliberal economic policies.[73] Concern for the stability of their family, especially for a devoted conjugal life, is one area where some fundamentalist women wish to reform errant husbands by using their conversion to call them to a virtuous life.[74] For example, Claire Robertson commented regarding 1990s Kenyan fundamentalist Christian women traders near Nairobi: "Women were partly attracted to fundamentalist Christianity to get their husbands to convert, stop running around with male and female friends, and pay more attention to their wives, themselves. . . . In essence, they wanted to socialize with their husbands, which was more of a middle class ideal."[75] As discussed in chapters 13 and 14, fundamentalist women are playing an important role in pushing for transformations that promote companionate marriage.

Conclusion

As a modern phenomenon, religious fundamentalism in Africa, as in other parts of the world, exists in all religions and has gendered class manifestations. Although in the early 1990s, religious fundamentalism was associated with urban women in underprivileged communities following educated male clerics, currently it involves women of all backgrounds in Africa despite their promotion of male-dominant gender ideologies that preach female subordination and advocate discrimination against women in access to jobs and formal secular education. Furthermore, extremist militant fundamentalist religions such as Boko Haram, Al-Shabab, and the Lord's Resistance Army are currently three of the deadliest religious movements employing gender-based violence. However, violence is not only advocated by extremist male fundamentalists; fundamentalist female clerics also preach sermons calling for assaults on their targets deemed demonic. Nonetheless, since the 1990s many African women have joined fundamentalist churches, mosques, and shrines of indigenous religions to seek spiritual uplift and other forms of social and economic empowerment. They are developing new forms of agency while reinterpreting their own religiosity and pious submission; some become leaders, female religious or spiritual authorities, harking back to African women's precolonial religio-political authority described in chapter 3. Examining women's economic status, autonomy, and agency is necessary for understanding their contradictory positions within fundamentalist religions.

Notes

1. Suzanne Katz, "The Rise of Religious Fundamentalism in Britain: The Experience of Women against Fundamentalism," *Gender and Development* 3, no. 1 [Culture] (February 1995): 42–44.

2. Marty Martin and Scott Appleby, eds., *Fundamentalism Comprehended* (Chicago: University of Chicago Press, 1995); Jean and John Comaroff, "Occult Economies and the Violence of Abstraction: Notes from the South African Postcolony," *American Ethnologist* 26, no. 2 (1999): 279–303; Silvia Federici, *Caliban and the Witch: Women, the Body and Primitive Accumulation* (New York: Autonomedia, 2004); Lisa Blayders and Drew A. Linzer, "The Political Economy of Women's Support for Fundamentalist Islam," *World Politics* 60, no. 4 (2008): 576–609; Barbara Cooper, *Evangelical Christians in the Muslim Sahel* (Bloomington: Indiana University Press, 2006), 23; Kalu Ogbu, *African Pentecostalism: An Introduction* (Oxford: Oxford University Press, 2008).

3. Salwa Ismail, *Political Life in Cairo's New Quarters* (Minneapolis: University of Minnesota Press, 2006); Ezra Chitando and Adriaan van Klinken, eds., *Christianity and Controversies over Homosexuality in Contemporary Africa* (London: Routledge, 2016).

4. See Federici, *Caliban*; John Mihevc, *The Market Tells Them So: The World Bank and Economic Fundamentalism in Africa* (London: Zed Books, 1995).

5. Fatou Sow, "Fundamentalisms, Globalisation and Women's Human Rights in Senegal," *Gender and Development* 11, no. 1 (May 2003): 69.

6. Comaroff and Comaroff, "Occult Economies."

7. Homa Hoodfar, *Between Marriage and the Market: Intimate Politics and Survival in Cairo* (Berkeley: University of California Press, 1997); Blaydes and Linzer, "Political Economy"; Jane Soothill, *Gender, Social Change and Spiritual Power: Charismatic Christianity in Ghana* (Amsterdam: Brill, 2008); Damaris Parsitau, "Agents of Gendered Change: Empowerment, Salvation and Gendered Transformation in Urban Kenya," in *Pentecostalism and Development: Churches, NGO and Social Change in Africa*, ed. Dena Freeman (Basingstoke: Palgrave Macmillan, 2012), 203–21; Dena Freeman, ed., *Pentecostalism and Development: Churches, NGOs and Social Change in Africa* (Basingstoke: Palgrave Macmillan, 2012).

8. Soothill, *Gender*; Paristau, "Agents of Gendered Change"; Erin Augis, "Aïcha's Sounith Hair Salon: Friendship, Profit, and Resistance in Dakar," *Islamic Africa* 5, no. 2 (2014): 199–224; Zakia Salime, *Between Feminism and Islam: Human Rights and Sharia Law in Morocco* (Minneapolis: University of Minnesota Press, 2011).

9. Comaroff and Comaroff, "Occult."

10. Cooper, *Evangelical Christians*, 31–60; Blayders and Linzer, "Political Economy."

11. Maria Frahm-Arp, *Professional Women in South African Pentecostal Charismatic Churches* (Amsterdam: Brill, 2010), 76–86; Naomi van der Meer, *Believers in the Universal Church: Processes of Self-identification among Catholic Immigrants of African Descent in the Dutch Religious Landscape* (Münster: LIT Verlag 2010).

12. Danoye Oguntola-Laguda and Adriaan van Klinken, "Uniting a Divided Nation? Nigerian Christian and Muslim Response to the Same Sex Marriage (Prohibition) Act," in *Public Religion and the Politics of Homosexuality in Africa*, ed. Adriaan van Klinken and Ezra Chitando (London: Routledge, 2016), 35–48.

13. Ebenezer Obadare, "Pentecostal Presidency? The Lagos-Ibadan 'Theocratic Class' and the Muslim 'Other,'" *Review of African Political Economy* 33, no. 110 (2006): 665–78; and Obadare, "White-Collar Fundamentalism: Interrogating Youth Religiosity on Nigerian University Campuses," *Journal of Modern African Studies* 45, no. 4 (December 2007): 517–37.

14. Ayesha Imam, "Fighting the Political (Ab)Use of Religion in Nigeria: BAO-BAB for Women's Human Rights, Allies and Others," in *Warning Signs of Fundamentalisms*, ed. Ayesha Imam, Jenny Morgan, and Nira Yuval-Davis (London: Women Living Under Muslim Laws, 2004), 125–34; Kalu Ogbu, "Sharia and Islam in Nigerian Pentecostal Rhetoric, 1970–2003," *Pneuma* 26 (2004): 242–61.

15. Ousmane Kane, *Muslim Modernity in Postcolonial Nigeria* (Amsterdam: Brill, 2003).

16. Imam, "Fighting"; Tapiwa Praise Mapuranga, "Bargaining with Patriarchy? Women Religious Leaders in Zimbabwe," *Fieldwork in Religion* 8, no. 1 (2013): 74–79.

17. Dorothea Schulz, "Political Factions, Ideological Fictions: The Controversy over the Reform of Family Law in Democratic Mali," *Islamic Law and Society* 10, no. 1 (2003): 132–64.

18. Freeman, *Pentecostalism and Development*.

19. David Chidester, *Wild Religion: Tracking the Sacred in South Africa* (Berkeley: University of California Press, 2012), 73–90.

20. Chidester, *Wild Religion*, 73–78; Farid Essack, "Three Islamic Strands in the South African Struggle for Justice," *Third World Quarterly* 10, no. 2 (1988): 473–98.

21. Imam, "Fighting."

22. Novian Whitsitt, "Islamic-Hausa Feminism and Kano Market Literature: Qur'anic Reinterpretation in the Novels of Balaraba Yakubu," *Research in African Literatures* 33, no. 2 (Summer 2002): 119–36; Abdalla Uba Adamu, "Loud Bubbles from a Silent Brook: Trends and Tendencies in Contemporary Hausa Prose Writing," *Research in African Literatures* 37, no. 3 (2007): 133–53; Shirin Edwin, *Privately Empowered: Expressing Feminism in Islam in Northern Nigerian Fiction* (Evanston, IL: Northwestern University Press, 2016); Ousseina Alidou, "Political *Shari'a* and Sexual Politics in Razinat T. Mohamed's Novel *Habiba*" (under review).

23. Gunnar J. Weimann, *Islamic Criminal Law in Northern Nigeria: Politics, Religion, Judicial Practice* (Amsterdam: Amsterdam University Press, 2010), 51.

24. Imam, "Fighting," 65–95.

25. Weimann, *Islamic Criminal Law*, 119–44; Imam, "Fighting."

26. Bakare Yusuf, "Nudity and Morality: Legislating Women's Bodies and Dress in Nigeria," in *African Sexualities: A Reader*, ed. Sylvia Tamale (Cape Town: University of Cape Town Press, 2011), 116–29; Ogbu, *African Pentecostalism*.

27. Lamido Sanusi, "Shariacracy in Nigeria: The Intellectual Roots of Islamist Discourse" (unpublished paper presented at Veranstaltungsort, Heinrich-Böll-Stiftung, Berlin, Donnerstag, February 17, 2005); Imam, "Fighting."

28. Imam, "Fighting," 73.

29. Alex Duval Smith, "Niger Border Prostitutes and the Profit of Islam," *The Independent* (Firgi, Nigeria), May 5, 2001.

30. Roland Jide Macaulay, "Homosexuality and the Churches in Nigeria," in *Other Voices, Other Worlds: The Global Church Speaks Out on Homosexuality*, ed. Terry Brown (New York: Church, 2006), 153–67; Charmaine Pereira and Jibril Ibrahim, "Le corps des femmes, terrain d'entente de l'islam et du christianisme au Nigeria," *Cahiers du Genre*, HS, no. 3 (2012/13): 89–108.

31. Chidester, *Wild Religion*.

32. Fatima L. Adamu, "Gender, *Hisba* and the Enforcement of Morality in Northern Nigeria," *Africa: Journal of the International African Institute* 78, no. 1 (2008): 136–52.

33. Alidou, "Political *Shari'a*." See Razinat T. Mohamed, *Habiba* (Ibadan: Kraft Books, 2015).

34. Chimamanda Adichie, *Half the Yellow Sun* (New York: Knopf Doubleday, 2008).

35. BBC, "Gambia Orders Female Workers 'to Cover Hair,'" January 5, 2016, http://www.bbc.com/news/world-africa-35231503.

36. Ousseina Alidou, "The Militarization of the Sahel and the Abduction of Chibok Girls in Northeastern Nigeria," *ASA Women's Caucus Newsletter*, August 29, 2014, 12–18.

37. Ali Abare Abubakar, "Militants Return 104 of 110 Girls Abducted from Nigerian School," *USA Today*, March 22, 2018, 3.

38. A. Omara-Otunnu, *The Dynamics of Conflict in Uganda: Adjustment and Revolutionary Change* (London: James Currey, 1991); Heike Behrend, *Alice Lakwena and the Holy Spirits: War in Northern Uganda, 1985–1997* (London: James Currey, 1999).

39. Behrend, *Lakwena*, 45; T. Allen, "Understanding Alice: Uganda's Holy Spirit Movement in Context," *Africa* 61, no. 3 (1991): 370–99; Seyni Moumouni, Aminatou Daouda Hainikoye, Djibo Abdoulbaki, and Ibrahim Abdoulaye Seyni Mamoudou Ali, "Étude sur la Prévention à la Radicalisation au Niger: Étude réalisée auprès des détenus présumés djihadistes" (Institut de Recherches en Sciences Humaines [IRSH] Laboratoire Religions et Sociétés [LARSO], Niamey, Niger, 2017), 1–17.

40. Omara-Otunnu, *Dynamics*, 14.

41. *The Weekly Topic* (Makere, Uganda), August 26, 1987.

42. Sverker Finnström, *Living with Bad Surroundings: War, History, and Everyday Moments in Northern Uganda* (Durham, NC: Duke University Press, 2008).

43. Martin Hitchens, as cited by Juan Cole (2014) "Boko Haram and the Lord's Resistance Army: Hunted Children and the Problem of Fundamentalism in Africa," *Informed Comment*, May 7, 2014, http://www.juancole.com/2014/05/resistance-children-fundamentalism.html.

44. Usam Sadiq Al-Amin and Dionne Searcey, "Young Bombers Kill 58 at Nigerian Camp for Those Fleeing Boko Haram," *New York Times*, February 10, 2016.

45. Tsitsi Dangarembga, *Nervous Conditions* (London: Women's Press, 1988).

46. Ousseina Alidou, *Muslim Women in Postcolonial Kenya: Leadership, Representation, and Social Change* (Madison: University of Wisconsin Press, 2013).

47. Soothill, *Gender*; Ogbu, *African Pentecostalism*.

48. Alidou, *Muslim Women*; Margot Badran, *Gender and Islam in Africa: Rights, Sexuality and Law* (Stanford, CA: Stanford University Press, 2011); Paristau, "Agents of Gendered Change."

49. Obadare, "White-Collar Fundamentalism."

50. Erin Augis, "Dakar's Sunnite Women: The Dialectic of Submission and Defiance in a Globalizing City," in *Tolerance, Democracy and Sufis in Senegal*, ed. Mamadou Diouf (New York: Columbia University Press, 2013), 73–98.

51. Yaba Badoe, director, *The Witches of Gambaga* (Fadoa Films, 2010).

52. Joseph Adhiombo, "Horror of Kenya's 'Witch' Lynchings," *BBC News*, June 26, 2009, http://news.bbc.co.uk/2/hi/africa/8119201.stm.

53. Cooper, *Evangelical Christians*; Comaroff and Comaroff, "Occult Economies"; Luise White, *Speaking with Vampires: Rumor and History in Colonial Africa* (Berkeley: University of California Press, 2000).

54. Federici, *Caliban*; Comaroff and Comaroff, "Occult Economies," 81–85; White, *Vampires*; Elom Dovlo, "Witchcraft in Contemporary Ghana," in *Imagining Evil: Witchcraft. Beliefs and Accusations in Contemporary Africa*, ed. Gerrie ter Haar (Trenton, NY: Africa World Press, 2007), 67–92; Alison Berg, "Witches in Exile," VHS, California Newsreel, 2005, www.newsreel.org.

55. Justus Ogembo, *Contemporary Witch-Hunting in Gusii, Southwestern Kenya* (Lewiston, NY: Edwin Mellen Press, 2006), 21.

56. Dovlo, "Witchcraft," 83.

57. Mark Auslander, "'Open the Wombs!': The Symbolic Politics of Modern Ngoni Witchfinding," in *Modernity and Its Malcontents: Ritual and Power in Postcolonial Africa*, ed. Jean Comaroff and John Comaroff (Chicago: University of Chicago Press, 1993), 167–92.

58. Adenike Orenuga, "Helen Ukpabio Slammed for Labelling Children 'Witches,'" *Daily Post*, April 15, 2015; Helen Ukpabio, *Unveiling the Mysteries of Witchcraft* (self-published, 2009); Chima Agazue, *The Role of a Culture of Superstition in the Proliferation of Religio-Commercial Pastors in Nigeria* (Bloomington: Author House, 2013); "Nigerian Witch Hunter Helen Ukpabio Bringing 'Gospel of Hate' to the US," International Humanist and Ethical Union, January 4, 2012, http://iheu.org/nigerian-witch-hunter -helen-ukpabio-bringing-gospel-hate-us/; Ogbu Kalu, "Gendered Charisma: Charisma and Women in African Pentecostalism," Oxford Scholarship Online, May 2008, 147– 68; "Suspected Witches Jailed," IRIN: The Inside Story on Emergencies, http://www .irinnews.org/report/92396/malawi-suspected-witches-jailed.

59. Cooper, *Evangelical Christians*, 32–53.

60. Joanna Zimmerman, "An African Epidemic of Homophobia: Harsh Anti-Gay Laws Have Been Passed in Ghana, Nigeria, Senegal and Elsewhere," *Los Angeles Times*, June 29, 2013.

61. Sylvia Tamale, "A Human Rights Impact Assessment of the Ugandan Anti-Homosexuality Bill 2009," *The Equal Rights Review* 4 (2010): 49–57.

62. Amos Sibanda, *Homosexuality: Man vs God* (Bloomington: AuthorHouse, 2016).

63. Imam, "Fighting."

64. Clár Ní Chonghaile, "Cameroonian Lawyer Urges World to Join Her in Fight against Anti-Gay Legislation," *The Guardian*, March 10, 2015; "Criminalizing Identities: Rights Abuses in Cameroon Based on Sexual Orientation and Gender Identity, *Human Rights Watch*, November 4, 2010, https://www.hrw.org/report/2010/11/04/crim inalizing-identities/rights-abuses-cameroon-based-sexual-orientation-and.

65. Soothill, *Gender*, 119, 109, 113, 116, 129–30.

66. Paristau, "Agents of Gendered Change," 209; Melissa Browning and Andrea Hollingsworth, "Your Daughters Shall Prophesy (As Long as They Submit): Pentecostalism and Gender in Global Perspective," in *Liberating Spirit: Pentecostals and Social Action in North America*, ed. Michael Wilkinson and Steven Studebaker (Eugene OR: Pickwick, 2010), 161–84.

67. Paristau, "Agents of Gendered Change," 209.

68. Jérôme Lafargue, ed., "The General Elections in Kenya, 2007," special issue of *IFRA: Institut Français de Recherche en Afrique*, no. 37 (May–August 2008); David Throup, "Politics, Religious Engagement and Extremism in Kenya," in *Religious Authority and the State in Africa*, ed. Jennifer Cooke (London: Rowman & Littlefield, 2015), 29–48.

69. Paristau, "Neo-Pentecostalism in Kenya: Its Civic and Public Roles (1970–2010)" (PhD diss., Kenyatta University, 2014).

70. Augis, "Dakar's Sunnite Women"; Erin Augis, "Religion, Religiousness and Narrative: Decoding Women's Practices in Senegalese Islamic Reform," *Journal for the Scientific Study of Religion* 51, no. 3 (September 2012): 429–41; Adeline Masquelier, *Women and Islamic Revivalism in a West African Town* (Bloomington: Indiana University Press, 2009); Alice Kang, *Bargaining for Women's Rights: Activism in an Aspiring Muslim Democracy* (Minneapolis: University of Minnesota Press, 2015); Salime, *Between Feminism and Islam*.

71. Marie Nathalie LeBlanc, "Piety, Moral Agency, and Leadership: Dynamics around the Feminization of Islamic Authority in Côte d'Ivoire," *Islamic Africa* 5 (2014): 167–98; Abdoulayed Sounaye, "Go Find the Second Half of Your Faith with the Women!," *The Muslim World* 101, no. 39 (2011): 539–54; Muriel Gomez-Perez, "Women's Islamic Activism in Burkina Faso: Toward Renegotiated Social Norms?," *Canadian Journal of African Studies* 50, no. 1 (April 22, 2016): 45–63.

72. Adeline Masquelier, *Women and Islamic Revival in West African Town* (Bloomington: Indiana University Press, 2009), ch. 8.

73. Alidou, *Modernity*, shows how Muslim women in Niger Republic use female Qur'anic schools for trade networking in female products. Augis, "Friendship"; Joseph Hill, "Entrepreneurial Discipleship: Cooking Up Women's Sufi Leadership in Dakar," in *Cultural Entrepreneurship in Africa*, ed. Ute Röschenthaler and Dorothea E. Schulz (London: Routledge, 2016), 58–80.

74. Alidou, *Muslim Women*, 145–56; Erin Augis, "Jambaar or Jumbax-out? How Sunnite Women Negotiate Power and Belief in Orthodox Islamic Femininity," in *New Perspectives on Islam in Senegal: Conversion, Migration, Wealth, Power, and Femininity*, ed. Mamadou Diouf and Mara Leitchman (New York: Palgrave Macmillan, 2009), 211–33.

75. Claire Robertson, personal communication, April 5, 2017.

Suggested Readings and Films

Agazue, Chima. *The Role of a Culture of Superstition in the Proliferation of Religio-Commercial Pastors in Nigeria*. Bloomington, IN: Author House, 2013.

Alidou, Ousseina. *Muslim Women in Postcolonial Kenya: Leadership, Representation, and Social Change*. Madison: University of Wisconsin Press, 2013.

Badoe, Yaba, director. *The Witches of Gambaga*. Fadoa Films, 2010.

Badoe, Yaba Mangela. "The Witches of Gambaga: What It Means to Be a Witch in the Northern Region of Ghana." *JENdA: A Journal of Culture and African Women Studies* 19 (2011). http://www.africaknowledgeproject.org/index.php/jenda/article/view/1211.

Davis, Jessica. *Women in Modern Terrorism: From Liberation Wars to Global Jihad and the Islamic State*. Lanham, MD: Rowman and Littlefield, 2017.

Oguntola-Laguda, Danoye, and Adriaan van Klinken. "Uniting a Divided Nation? Nigerian Christian and Muslim Response to the Same Sex Marriage (Prohibition) Act." In *Public Religion and the Politics of Homosexuality in Africa*, edited by Adriaan van Klinken and Ezra Chitando, 35–48. London: Routledge, 2016.

Soothill, Jane. *Gender, Social Change and Spiritual Power: Charismatic Christianity in Ghana*. Amsterdam: Brill, 2008.

Figure 6.1. Taking the fight for gender equality to the streets of Accra, Ghana. Photo by Alicia C. Decker, 2017.

6

AFRICAN WOMEN ORGANIZE

Alicia C. Decker and Andrea L. Arrington-Sirois

I n mid-November 2006, more than two hundred women gathered in Accra, Ghana, to participate in the first African Feminist Forum, a space where African women could celebrate and reclaim their identities as feminists, where they could push back against the deradicalization of women's movements, both within Africa and beyond.[1] The preamble to their Charter of Feminist Principles for African Feminists is bold and embraces a strong ideological position:

> We define and name ourselves publicly as feminists because we celebrate our feminist identities and politics. We recognize that the work of fighting for women's rights is deeply political, and the process of naming is political too. Choosing to name ourselves feminists places us in a clear ideological position. By naming ourselves as feminists we politicize the struggle for women's rights, we question the legitimacy of the structures that keep women subjugated, and we develop tools for transformatory analysis and action. . . . Our feminist identity is not qualified with "ifs," "buts" or "howevers." We are Feminists. Full stop.[2]

The women who participated in the forum believed that women's activism had lost much of its critical edge—that in an effort to appeal to the masses (or to donors), questions of power, privilege, and patriarchy had been watered down or abandoned. Josephine Ahikire, former dean of the School of Women and Gender Studies at Makerere University in Uganda, suggests that it is not uncommon for contemporary activists to make statements like, "I am a gender expert but I am not a feminist" or "I am a gender activist but I do not like feminism."[3] This reflects the common misconception that feminism is an import from the Global North and is therefore not relevant to African contexts. Others assume that feminism is elitist, associated with highly educated urban women who have no connection to women at the "grassroots." Whether feminism is embraced or rejected, one thing is clear—African women have a long history of collective organizing.

This chapter considers a wide variety of African women's activist movements in the late twentieth and early twenty-first centuries, focusing on the sites and strategies of collective organizing, as well as key activist issues. We begin by examining three different kinds of spaces that have facilitated collective action: nongovernmental organizations (NGOs), international conferences, and the academy. Within each of these locations, we demonstrate how women have worked together, across various axes of difference, to advocate for social change. We then analyze three significant social concerns that have served as rallying points, or sources of contention, among African women in recent years: sustainable development, female genital cutting (FGC), and the HIV/AIDS pandemic. Among many critical issues spurring women's organizing, these three are particularly salient because they are profoundly gendered, disproportionately affecting women's lives and livelihoods.

Women's Collective Organizing in NGOs

African women have been engaged in collective action for many years (see chapters 4 and 7). During the colonial era, women from all different walks of life joined political, cultural, and spiritual movements. They participated in rotating credit associations, farming groups, mutual assistance societies, dance troupes, and market associations, among others. Many were actively involved in clandestine struggles for national liberation, risking their lives by organizing secret meetings, by smuggling weapons and supplies through the bush, and by taking up arms to fight on the frontlines. Through these types of activities, African women learned to work together for justice and social change.[4] After independence, however, many women found their ability to organize significantly curtailed because of government restrictions. It was not until the 1980s, after many of the military regimes and single-party political systems of the 1960s and 1970s had collapsed, that African women were once again free to engage in collective action.

One of the earliest debates about women's organizational autonomy took place in June 1982 during a meeting of the Association of African Women for Research and Development (AAWORD). Participants questioned whether women's interests would be best served through autonomous women's organizations or through existing political parties and structures. They ultimately decided that feminism could be the basis for an alternative model of development, one that could mobilize women for political action and challenge "aspects of our cultures which discriminate, restrict and devalue women's physical, psychological and political development."[5] This meeting was significant in that it represented an emerging politicization of African women. Women were no longer seen as passive recipients of development aid but instead as political actors who thought critically about broader issues of gender and power.

The UN World Conference on Women, held in Nairobi, Kenya, in 1985, had a profound effect on African women's activism and served as the impetus for the development of many new organizations. Delegates from Uganda, for instance, created Action for Development (ACFODE), a nongovernmental organization that has promoted women's rights over the last three decades.[6] In 1988 they helped establish a Ministry of Women in Development, which served as Uganda's national machinery for women's advancement. Women's desks in other ministries soon followed, effectively mainstreaming gender within government. Three years later, they began publishing *Arise Magazine*, a periodical devoted to the promotion of women's rights, and helped establish the Department of Women's Studies at Makerere University—one of the first such programs on the continent. ACFODE is just one of many organizations working to empower Ugandan women. Similar organizations exist throughout the continent, which speaks to the tremendous strength of women's collective activism in Africa today.

Regional organizations are also important vehicles for women's empowerment. Because they work across national borders, they have a much broader focus. Women in Law and Development in Africa (WiLDAF), for example, is a network of five hundred different organizations spread across twenty-seven African countries.[7] Established in 1990 with the goal of promoting strategies that would link law and development to women's empowerment, WiLDAF has been instrumental in garnering international attention and support for women's rights. In March 1995, they held a meeting in Lomé, Togo, calling for the development of a protocol that would integrate women's rights into the African Charter on Human and People's Rights. Adopted by the Organization of African Unity (OAU) in June 1981, the charter served to neutralize gender by implying that women and men understood and experienced rights and violations in the same way. In fact, Article 18(3) was the only article that referred specifically to women, and it did so by bundling women's rights with other so-called vulnerable groups, such as the disabled, children, and the elderly. By not specifying how the state would eliminate discrimination against women or how they would ensure the protection of their rights, the charter made it virtually impossible for women to hold their governments accountable.[8] WiLDAF argued that by not addressing the specific needs of African women, the charter failed to support their rights.

Three months after the Lomé meeting, the General Assembly of the OAU mandated that the African Commission on Human and People's Rights develop such a protocol. Eight years later, on July 11, 2003, the African Union, the successor body to the OAU, met in Maputo, Mozambique, to adopt the Protocol to the African Charter on Human and People's Rights on the Rights of Women in Africa. The Maputo Protocol, as it is popularly known, entered into force on November 25, 2005, after being ratified by fifteen member states. Without the activist efforts of WiLDAF and other women's rights organizations in Africa, this important protocol might never have become part of international law.

Women's Conferences

International conferences have also served as important sites and sources of activism for African women. Many of these meetings were organized by international bodies, such as the United Nations or the African Union, and utilized a formal bureaucratic approach to social networking. Others evolved more organically out of social movements, thus allowing participants to frame their own agendas. Both strategies have provided opportunities for African women to discuss (and oftentimes heatedly debate) issues that are most pressing in their lives. One of the first such meetings in Africa was the third World Conference on Women, which took place in Nairobi, Kenya, in July 1985. Although African women had been actively involved in both previous world conferences, this was the largest gathering of women in the history of the United Nations. Many of the more than sixteen thousand women who attended the conference and the parallel NGO forum were African. For this reason, it served as a catalyst for women's mobilization throughout the continent.[9]

Another significant forum for African women is the Feminist Dialogue, which first convened in December 2004 during the third African Social Forum in Lusaka, Zambia.[10] Frustrated with the "grim state of gender representation," as well as the hierarchical and nonparticipatory plenary sessions and panel discussions, approximately forty women from across the continent decided to craft an alternative space where they could "remake power" in a different kind of way.[11] In the dialogue, women discussed and offered critiques of power, feminisms, and mobilization. They even organized their chairs in a circular fashion so that everyone had an opportunity to participate. At the conclusion of the event, participants decided to create an email discussion list so that they could continue to communicate and share feminist literature. Through such actions, they believed they would be able to "wrest feminist dialogue back from the predominantly white and Northern/Western academic spaces which have coopted and subsequently come to define—and confine—debate."[12] It is unclear whether there have been additional Feminist Dialogues held at subsequent African Social Forums. However, we know that African women were actively involved in the third International Feminist Dialogue that took place in 2007 in conjunction with the World Social Forum in Nairobi.[13] This clearly suggests that these Feminist Dialogues, both African and International versions, are perceived as important spaces for women's activism.

The African Feminist Forum (AFF) is yet another important space of activism for African women. In November 2006, numerous self-identified African feminists gathered in Accra, Ghana, for four days to debate strategies of the African women's movement. According to one of the participants, Ayesha M. Imam,

> The (formal and informal) objectives of the AFF are to develop an independent, self-directed, self-controlled arena where we can analyze our realties, develop our own priorities and strategies, and speak for ourselves. Autonomy and self-definition are integral to feminism, as a right and need in itself, and vis-à-vis patriarchal definitions and control. In the case of the AFF it is also a defense: against the pressures of external definitions (primarily from feminists in the global North who, although themselves discriminated against, generally have more "voice" and better access to publishing, research, grants and other resources than do feminists in Africa); against externally defined agendas (primarily through donor conditionalities—who even when supportive have their own agenda and constituencies to answer to); and, against accusations of imitating foreigners (primarily from conservative forces as a means of delegitimizing feminism in Africa).[14]

The African Women's Development Fund hosted the event. Their aim was not to be representative but instead "to bring together the most influential and interesting activists and thinkers of the African women's movement."[15] The forum included plenaries and workshops, as well as artistic presentations, mock debates, and various self-care services such as massage, sexuality workshops, and African dance aerobics. Key outcomes included the following: (a) a historical timeline of the African women's movement, (b) a preliminary database of self-defined African feminists, (c) a summary of conference discussions, and (d) the adoption of a Charter of Principles for African Feminists, based on principles of human rights, choice, nondiscrimination, and individual and collective accountability. Despite these accomplishments, the forum received criticism for its lack of diversity and inclusion, particularly in terms of lesbians and transgender persons, as well as young people more generally. It was also criticized for being out of touch with the needs or problems of less educated or poor women.[16] Nonetheless, the AFF has continued to be an important space for self-identified feminists in Africa. Additional meetings have since been held in Kampala, Uganda (2008), Dakar, Senegal (2010), and Harare, Zimbabwe (2016). A series of national feminist forums have also taken place in a number of countries including Uganda, Nigeria, Ghana, Senegal, and Congo-Brazzaville.[17] These important meetings clearly demonstrate that African women have found creative ways to work together, across difference, for justice and social change.

Intellectual Activism

Some of the most exciting forms of activism have taken place within the academy. Over the last forty years, African women have developed feminist scholarly networks that have significantly challenged traditional forms of knowledge production and dissemination. One of the first was the Association of African Women for Research and Development (AAWORD), which was established in Dakar, Senegal, in 1977 to promote research, advocacy, and training efforts that would improve the status of women and transform gender relations in Africa. More specifically, the association sought to produce scholarship that was by and for African women—research that would enable them to "claim their own agenda" and "define their [own] research priorities and methodological tools."[18] This was an important objective because most research about women in Africa, at least up until that point, had been produced by Western and/or male scholars and did not reflect African women's realities. The intellectual activism that spurred the creation of AAWORD continues today, as evidenced by their impressive portfolio of research, training, and advocacy activities.

Another significant feminist network that emerged around this time was the Women's Research and Documentation Project in Dar es Salaam, Tanzania. In 1978 a small group of women got together to discuss informally "the women's question." Within two years, they had grown to nearly twenty members and had affiliated with the Institute of Development Studies at the University of Dar es Salaam. Soon, however, the women decided to sever their ties with the institute because of disagreements with male leaders over resources and policy making. Fed up with "male supremacist relations of all kinds and at all levels," the women chose instead to create an autonomous space where they could conduct research and share information about the struggle for women's liberation.[19] Like AAWORD, this organization served as a model for later projects that emerged on the continent, and it remains an important site for African feminist research and publishing.

Ideas about women's empowerment spread throughout the continent not only through research and documentation centers but also through the classroom. In 1979 the Department of Sociology at Ahmadu Bello University in Nigeria offered its first course in women's studies, focusing on "Women in Society."[20] By the early 1980s, a number of different universities in South Africa had also begun teaching courses on women and gender issues from various theoretical perspectives.[21] It would be nearly a decade, however, before African women's studies had become a discipline in its own right. One of the first and most prominent programs is located at Makerere University in Uganda. Following the 1985 World Conference on Women in Nairobi, female scholars and development practitioners discussed how they might implement the "Nairobi Forward-Looking Strategies for the Advancement of Women" at home. In addition to founding ACFODE, described above, the delegates were determined to create an academic department within the university that would enable them to conduct research and teach about the status of women.[22] In July 1987, representatives from ACFODE and the Uganda Association of University Women submitted a proposal to the university's Donor Conference calling for the creation of a women's studies program. The proposal received tremendous support, and planning for the new program was soon underway. Although the University Council formally approved the program in July 1989, the Department of Women's Studies did not become operational for another two years because of funding delays.[23] In 1991 they began offering a two-year master's degree, as well as short-term evening courses for local politicians and development practitioners. Several years later, in 1999, they introduced a three-year undergraduate course, in addition to a research-intensive PhD program. As the department grew, it became increasingly obvious that gender training was relevant to all students across campus. To accommodate curricular needs, the university administration elevated the department to the School of Women and Gender Studies in 2011—the first of its kind in Africa.

Another hub of feminist intellectual activism is the African Gender Institute at the University of Cape Town in South Africa, established in 1996 as a means of "challenging the imbalances resulting from persistent gender discrimination and inequality, and exacerbated by racism in higher education institutions in Africa."[24] From the beginning, its mandate was "to provide a safe space where women in the academy could develop their intellectual and leadership capacities; where African women writers, researchers, policy-makers and practitioners would be given new opportunities; [and] where Africa-centric applied knowledges of gender, transformation, and democratic practice could be developed and propagated." In addition to undergraduate and graduate degree programs, the institute designs and implements projects that enhance research, networking, capacity building, and knowledge creation throughout much of the continent. Since 2002, they have published a peer-reviewed scholarly journal called *Feminist Africa*. This journal, like all of the institute's activities, fosters critical consciousness among African women and men so that they can better contribute to Africa's transformation.

Women and gender studies is also firmly embedded within various universities in North Africa. In April 1998, a number of Moroccan female professors launched the first two women's centers in the region—the Centre for Studies and Research on Women, located at the Université Sidi Mohamed Ben Abdellah in Fes, and the Center of Women's Studies at Mohammed V University in Rabat.[25] According to Fatima Sadiqi, the coordinator of the center in Fes, the main objective of these centers was "to invigorate the liberal arts curricula by redesigning courses that would reflect the scholarship on women."[26] They also served as a springboard for the country's first postgraduate units in women and gender studies, which began admitting students in 2003. Students in these graduate programs learn to critique deeply rooted cultural constructs, such as the idea that books by and about women are not scholarly and worthy of investigation. In addition, the programs teach students that knowledge is never objective and that it comes from research *and* lived experience. This linking of theory to practice is imperative, as the Ministry of Higher Education requires all postgraduate courses to produce knowledge that is beneficial to the larger community. Indeed, this is why intellectual work is such a crucial form of activism.

Case Study #1: Sustainable Development

African women's economic activism is closely connected to their critical roles in the economy, which have been affected by changing development policies governed by international donors (see chapters 4 and 8). In the 1960s and 1970s, newly independent countries, having enjoyed an initial period of relative stability, began to face major economic crises—a product of both internal and external circumstances. Development programming, which emerged from this context, largely excluded women, profoundly affecting their status and experiences in the last half of the twentieth century.

The history of African development has been riddled with conflict and failure, in large part because the people tasked with determining its goals and policies are largely from the Global North. The disconnect between what works and is valued in the Global North and what works and is valued in individual, unique countries in the Global South complicates strategies for development and "progress." For many decades, the World Bank and the International Monetary Fund did a poor job of listening to the ideas of the very people they were supposed to help. They have also struggled to understand how women fit into the development equation. Since the 1970s and 1980s, there have been at least four major approaches to "the woman question" within African development: women *in* development (WID), women *and* development (WAD), gender *and* development (GAD), and gender mainstreaming.

The WID approach, which was associated with "Westernization" and "industrialization," often ignored women's economic importance in the informal sector and assumed that women's waged employment in the formal sector would improve women's status.[27] Subsequent approaches framed African women as active players in the development process. WAD practitioners, for example, recognized that women's labor was essential to local and state economies, and they demanded that development policies account for this. The GAD approach, with roots in "Third World feminism," promoted women as *agents* of development rather than as simply passive *recipients*. This approach "situates gender domination within broader socioeconomic relations and seeks to restructure local, national, and international institutions in dramatic ways."[28] It acknowledges historical and cultural variations in gender relations and looks at specific gender and class ideologies. Importantly, GAD programming incorporates the voices of women that a development plan will affect, a significant departure from the WID and WAD models. A more recent approach is gender mainstreaming, which seeks seamless integration considerations of women and gender into the design of development programming. It focuses not simply on women's economic opportunities, but instead on broader social, cultural, and political spheres. While gender mainstreaming may produce more comprehensive development planning, it fails to consider one fundamental question: Does development ever really empower African women?

Morocco serves as an example of the ineffective integration of women into development policy. Following a neoliberal approach to development, the country underwent a push for modernization. In 1983 Morocco initiated a structural adjustment program that ultimately harmed women. Through "state feminism," an official government policy meant to address women's conditions and promote gender equality, women's status was undermined. According to Moha Ennaji, "the economic reforms . . . which fostered economic liberalization and free trade, led to a reduction of state feminism. The relative retreat of the State from the economic scene as the main agent of change undermined its commitment to gender equality. In general, it is working-class women who have suffered most from these unfair economic and social reforms."[29] This reality is not unique to Morocco. All too often, international development programs have relieved governments of their duty to advocate for women's rights, which creates greater obstacles to gender equality.

Nonetheless, African women are not simply victims of development. In 2002, for instance, hundreds of Nigerian women staged two separate "take-overs" of a U.S.-owned Chevron Texaco oil subsidiary called Escravos, located in the Niger Delta.[30] The profits from the region's abundant oil are mainly exported, leaving the region extremely underdeveloped and impoverished. On July 8, an estimated 150 women took over the refinery, holding several thousand oil company employees and managers hostage and halting oil production. Women wanted the company to provide their communities with electricity, schools, water systems, health clinics, and other infrastructure that would raise their standard of living. They also demanded jobs for their unemployed sons and pensions for people over age sixty. The company verbally capitulated to their demands on July 17. The following day, another takeover occurred at four more facilities located fifty miles to the east. Echoing the demands made by the first group of protestors, these women also insisted that Chevron officials visit their village to see their impoverished living conditions. The protestors also charged the company with environmental damage resulting from natural gas flare-ups. The type of economic development that Chevron was bringing to the nation was not the kind that women needed for their communities. Women used the only resources they had—their bodies— to resist a global superpower. Twelve days after the second protest began, Chevron agreed to the women's demands.

Another example can be found in the Gambia, where local women resisted an environmental development scheme concocted in the Global North based on the problematic assumption that African women have a "natural" connection to the earth and are therefore effective stewards of the land. Melissa Leach's work demonstrates how African women resisted these assumptions and refused to participate in a tree-planting program that would produce fruit their husbands could then sell. Likewise, in Kenya, grassroots women pushed back against development programs that expected them to be the sole defenders against soil erosion and depletion. As Leach explains, "Women's groups in Kenya digging soil conservation terraces did so to secure the patron-client relations which might bring them famine relief food from the agencies concerned, not because (as those agencies stated at the time) they felt close to nature or even had much interest in conservation."[31] Although women re-mained burdened with an increased labor expectation, they engaged in the work on their own terms and did not buy into the development model and stereotypes pushed on them by the development agencies (see chapter 8).

Case Study #2: Female Genital Cutting

Our second case study focuses on one of the most divisive and sensitive activist concerns—that of female genital cutting (FGC). Also known as female circumcision or genital mutilation, FGC is hotly contested at local, national, and global levels as scholars, journalists, medical practitioners, politicians, community leaders, and activists, many of them African women, weigh in on the practices. African woman have organized in diverse ways around the issue, which serves as a reminder that African women do not all share the same perspectives (see also chapter 16).

Just as African women are not a monolithic group, FGC is not one practice with only one meaning. Instead, it is a variety of practices with different symbolisms depending on societal context. The most radical procedure is called infibulation and involves cutting off the clitoris and the external labia, then sewing together the vaginal opening, leaving a small hole the size of a pencil to allow for expulsion of menses and urine. It is done when a girl has attained puberty, or even when an infant. Infibulation can have serious health consequences, such as infections and fistulas, and can result in painful sexual intercourse and (sometimes deadly) childbirth. Given the high possibility of dire consequences, many question why such a practice was implemented and what functions it still serves. Infibulation seems to have been created as a method of controlling women's sexuality by curtailing sexual pleasure and desire. Women were deemed "clean" and "pure" if they had undergone the procedure, thus making them preferable to uncut women, who were perceived as more likely to engage in extramarital affairs.

More geographically widespread but rapidly diminishing in Africa is clitoridectomy, which can involve the complete or partial removal of the clitoris, or a symbolic nick of it. It is usually part of girls' puberty rites and symbolizes the complementarity of the sexes (i.e., boys get circumcised, as do girls, hence the term "female circumcision"). Like their male counterparts, girls are supposed to demonstrate bravery, enduring the procedure in silence. Consequently, the practice is regarded as an important rite of passage and not one that can be easily eliminated or replaced.[32] That said, FGC is in decline in some places because education has brought greater understanding of the health consequences. Increased urbanization has also led to the elimination of some rites of passage or the reform of puberty rites to exclude it. Sometimes it has declined because of high expenditures connected to the ceremonies.[33]

Criticism of FGC began when early twentieth-century Europeans colonizing Africa became increasingly aware of, and horrified by, such practices. Colonial administrators, missionaries, and Western health-care providers regarded all forms of FGC as barbaric and wanted to stop them. Some colonial governments attempted to ban such practices, but resistance was strong and enforcement difficult.[34] European settlers tried to discourage such practices through educational campaigns and the medicalization of childbirth and reproductive care. Often those campaigns were unsuccessful in changing African opinion and sparked further distrust between Europeans and Africans, further documented in chapter 16.

By the 1950s and 1960s, health-care providers and African women opposed to genital cutting began speaking out publicly, provoking discussions within communities, often among those who were more educated. The World Health Organization (WHO) and other global bodies also began examining the issue more closely. In 1979 they organized a conference in Sudan where they officially condemned such practices and recommended that governments eradicate them. Within five years, the Inter-African Committee on Traditional Practices Affecting the Health of Women and Children (IAC) was formed, with a primary focus on FGC and its harmful consequences. It was formed by a group of African delegates who attended a UN-sponsored workshop on developing programs and policies to end FGC and determined "there was a critical need for an African regional voice in an international campaign against FGM."[35] Crucially, this group of African anti-FGC activists developed an agenda that not only worked to end FGC and other harmful customs but also aimed to "promote and support those traditional practices that improve and contribute to the health, human development and rights of women and children." The IAC was one of the first African-sponsored organizations to combat FGC, with an early focus on education, network building among larger NGOs and global bodies, and bringing African governments into the conversation. In recent years, they have shifted their focus to the community level by involving grassroots politicians, medical practitioners, and religious leaders.

While the international community established official recommendations and some African activists began promoting their platforms, a wider global audience also began taking an interest in the issue. In 1992 Alice Walker published *Possessing the Secret of Joy: A Novel*, thus bringing FGC to a broader audience. One year later, Walker and Pratibha Parmar published *Warrior*

Marks: Female Genital Mutilation, a companion piece to their film *Warrior Marks*.[36] Their stinging indictment of infibulation was highly problematic. Not only did they reduce FGC to infibulation and suggest that that was widely practiced throughout the continent but they also framed it as an inherently violent, immutable, and unjustifiable cultural tradition. FGC thus became more widely known among American and European audiences, inciting many to advocate its abolition. Highlighting the deep divides within this debate, many African scholars spoke out against the involvement of outsiders, even if they opposed the practice. In a pointed critique, Seble Dawit and Salem Mekuria wrote, "We are African women who have been working to abolish the ancient practice of female genital mutilation. . . . But we take great exception to the recent Western focus on female genital mutilation in Africa, most notably by the novelist Alice Walker. . . . As is common in Western depictions of Africa, Walker and her collaborator, Pratibha Parmar, portray the continent as a monolith. African women and children are the props and the village the background against which Alice Walker, heroine-savior, comes to articulate their pain and condemn those who inflict it."[37] Dawit and Mekuria challenged the legitimacy of non-Africans engaging in the anti-FGC movement and recentered African women's initiatives as most appropriate and most likely to succeed. They described groups within Africa working to end the practices:

> Some are working with ministries of health and education. Others work in villages to move traditional circumcisers away from their trade and teach villagers about the physical and psychological harm of the practice. Still others work with doctors and other health-care providers to make them more responsive to the women's needs and work with powerful religious leaders and village elders to make them advocate against the practice. . . . Westerners and those of us living in the West who wish to work on this issue must forge partnerships with the hundreds of African women on the continent who are working to eradicate the practice.[38]

Dawit and Mekuria reveal the numerous ways that African women, both academics and activists, are fighting against such practices.

By the late 1990s, numerous grassroots and national organizations were opposed to the practice. While transnational organizations like the IAC and global bodies like the WHO and the United Nations Development Fund for Women (UNIFEM) continued to support campaigns against FGC, African women developed stronger organizations and devised multidimensional plans to publicize their cause and to change national legislation and local practices. Although external financial support is helpful (and oftentimes required), there is a balancing act between African women who are working "on the ground" and allies from the Global North who want to "help." Today we can see a number of global networks that are promoting African-led movements to end FGC. A recent iteration of this approach is The Girl Generation, a "social change communications initiative" that seeks to develop intra-African networks that empower grassroots groups to organize against FGC. According to Leyla Hussein, an activist against gender-based violence,

> The Girl Generation will bring together campaigners from all over the world to push for change more effectively. The campaign will support advocacy work to drive social and behavioral change in ten African countries, starting in Kenya, Burkina Faso, and Nigeria. Stories of change will be brought to a global audience, and media campaigns will be launched. The Girl Generation will also work with the African Diaspora to support efforts to end FGM in their countries of origin. The movement to end FGM urgently needs an increase in financial commitments, and the Girl Generation will mobilize resources to end FGM in a generation.[39]

This campaign foregrounds global collaborative supportive efforts while acknowledging that African women lead the movement.

An increasing number of activists and grassroots organizations are also organizing local efforts to eradicate the practice. They highlight the health risks of FGC and encourage communities to think of new, non-invasive initiation ceremonies to mark the transition from girl to woman. Dr. Heli Bathija of WHO explains that the involvement of community members in pushing the anti-FGC message is crucial, with "positive results in many places, for instance in Kenya, Uganda and Egypt. In Senegal women have taught other women about human rights, health and sanitation, which prompted them to see female genital mutilation as unnecessary."[40] Often, community activists link ending FGC to expanded opportunities for women, education, improved health, and lower maternal and infant mortality rates. Nurses and teachers in some countries have been empowered to incorporate anti-FGC messages in their community work, bolstering efforts of grassroots organizers.

Local efforts to end FGC often take advantage of resources that come from national and international bodies. This allows activists to respond directly to the unique challenges of each locality. This model of grassroots organization follows the Community Empowerment Program approach to FGC eradication and community development advocated by the Tostan organization. Tostan began in Senegal with the mission of empowering communities to seek change through local initiatives. It follows a rights-based ideology that highlights expanding women's rights and opportunities, assuming that eventually communities with empowered women will decide to end the practice of FGC. The Tostan model has been implemented in numerous African countries and is often employed in NGO efforts to reduce FGC.[41] In Sudan, for example, anthropologist Ellen Gruenbaum identified the Tostan model as an important part of ending FGC:

> Feminist leaders and humanitarian organizations, in their eagerness to move rapidly on the change agenda, have turned to the idea of women's empowerment as the key element of the successful Tostan model (from Senegal originally) for ending FGC practices. The Tostan model engages women and girls in building their own capacities to change their lives and communities. The assumption is that when they have the conditions that allow them to make choices—and when they decide the time is ripe, as Nawal El Saadawi said—they will end FGC on their own, without it being the explicit goal of the program.[42]

Communities most successful in decreasing FGC are those that decide for themselves that such practices are no longer desirable or necessary. Activists, scholars, feminists, midwives, nurses, teachers, and community organizers are finding ways to work together and with local communities to provide resources, knowledge, and space for open discourse to eradicate controversial practices.

Case Study #3: The HIV/AIDS Crisis

Our third case study concerns the HIV/AIDS crisis and the critical role that African women play in the struggle. While there is a large body of literature examining international responses to the pandemic, the work of African women who advocate for expanded access to quality health care and support for those affected is often overlooked. While outside forces influence these health-care advocates and grassroots activists, quite often their focus is on applying homegrown solutions to the immediate problems their community members face. African women are a driving force behind such mobilization efforts.

Unfortunately, there is a significant disjuncture between the incredible amount of money funneled into African countries to address the pandemic and the lack of notable results.[43] According to policy analyst Hakan Seckinelgin, "existing intervention channels and actors have not been as productive as expected or assumed," and resources are not "reaching people who are in need."[44] This disconnect between funding and relief has driven communities and individuals to develop strategies to care for the ill, with African women at the forefront of such efforts. Community organizer Ngozi Iwere argues, "The fact that health care systems are practically overwhelmed and that terminally ill people in this region are nursed at home and in the community implies that African women have an especially heavy burden as women, as poor people and as traditional caregivers."[45] Women have been on the frontlines of this crisis and have mobilized to provide relief and education to their communities.

There is growing awareness that African women's grassroots organizations have developed successful strategies to help their communities cope with the HIV/AIDS crisis. In countries with extensive external funding and international NGOs working with governments, more attention goes toward community-led initiatives. One of the ways donor organizations and governmental agencies and parastatals try to bridge the gap between funding and outreach is by working with grassroots organizations. In South Africa, for instance, an NGO called Gender AIDS Forum (GAF) offered a training workshop in 2004 to women from KwaZulu-Natal who were offering support to HIV/AIDS patients in their area. The program's theme was "Inside-OUT," and it "aimed, firstly, to raise women leaders' consciousness of what [Patricia] Hill-Collins calls the intersectionality of gender, race and class, and how these intersected personal dimensions connect with HIV and AIDS. Secondly, the programme aimed to empower women to confront oppression in their lives and to become effective leaders in their communities."[46] The women who attended the training returned to their communities with more information about HIV/AIDS and continued the frontline work they were doing with their own education, testing, and treatment campaigns, albeit with more connections to donors and government agencies aiding them in their work.

Faith-based groups also offer women a space to organize. Orphans and widows/widowers often have little to no resources and face heavy stigmas in their communities after parents and spouses die from AIDS. They benefit from faith-based groups, such as Children in Distress (CINDI Kitwe) in Zambia, started by Catholic women who joined with other religious women's groups to provide resources and support to orphans. CINDI now provides food, shelter, and education for orphans of AIDS victims, nutritional support to impoverished members of the community, and a holistic support system for HIV/AIDS patients that includes acquiring antiretroviral drugs (ARVs), securing appropriate nourishment for patients on ARV regimens, and providing psychosocial services to AIDS patients and their families. The scope of CINDI projects is vast and locally driven. The organization's leaders focus on the unique needs of local communities and design outreach to match those specific challenges.

CINDI Kitwe is but one example of the countless community-led initiatives found throughout Africa that demonstrate the ways that African women have mobilized in response to the HIV/AIDS crisis. Community members turned activists did not sit idly by when HIV/AIDS took its toll on their neighborhoods. Instead, they found ways to organize and reach out to those infected in ways that international NGOs could not. The fact that so many leaders of these local movements are women is not without critique, however. Some feminists argue that women, already burdened with gender and class oppression, are further entrenching themselves in stereotypical and disempowering roles as caregivers and nurturers, while making it easier for governments and international donors to disengage. Women are rising to the challenges presented by the HIV/AIDS crisis, and yet their responses stem from necessity and may not feel like genuine empowerment. Nonetheless, the women who respond to the devastating impact of HIV/AIDS in their communities show how powerful grassroots movements can be and how much change they can effect.

Conclusion

Campaigns to promote sustainable development, to end FGC, and to respond to the HIV/AIDS crisis offer three examples of the types of issues around which women organize, while also revealing some of the ways in which they carry out this important work. Women have also actively participated in grassroots campaigns related to domestic violence, divorce and inheritance laws, girls' education, human trafficking, agricultural reform, and peacebuilding, among others. As this chapter shows, African women are not simply inserting themselves into existing frameworks but instead are mobilizing when they see a need and devising strategies that work for their specific communities. They situate their work in and across multiple spaces, including international bodies, universities, national governments and parastatals, NGOs, and community-based grassroots organizations. In twenty-first-century Africa, activists benefit from the ever-increasing connectivity of the modern world, using social media, digital databases, and improved transportation and communications technology to connect with others, to spread awareness, and to access information and resources to advance their own causes. Clearly, they are combining the old with the new to bring about robust social change. As such, they are an example to the rest of the world.

Notes

1. Josephine Ahikire, "African Feminism in Context: Reflections on the Legitimation Battles, Victories and Reversals," *Feminist Africa* 19 (2014): 7–23.

2. African Feminist Forum, Preamble to the Charter of Feminist Principles for African Feminists, accessed February 21, 2018, http://www.africanfeministforum.com/feminist-charter-preamble/.

3. Josephine Ahikire, 2007, quoted in Ahikire, "African Feminism in Context," 17.

4. For an excellent historical discussion of African women's collective action, see Aili Mari Tripp, Isabel Casimiro, Joy Kwesiga, and Alice Mungwa, *African Women's Movements: Changing Political Landscapes* (New York: Cambridge University Press, 2009), chapter 2.

5. AAWORD Declaration 1982, quoted in Tripp et al., *African Women's Movements*, 55.

6. Action for Development (ACFODE), accessed February 21, 2018, "About ACFODE: Background," http://acfode.org/background/.

7. WiLDAF, "About Us: History," accessed March 26, 2017, http://wildaf-ao.org/index.php/en/about-us/history.

8. Irene Mukumu Wairimu, "The Maputo Protocol: Evaluating Women's Rights," *Pambazuka News*, June 11, 2015.

9. Tripp et al., *African Women's Movements*, 152.

10. The first International Feminist Dialogues (IFD) took place in January 2004 in Mumbai, India, prior to the opening of the World Social Forum. It was meant to oppose not only neoliberalism but also oppression and discrimination on the basis of gender, race, ethnicity, class, caste, nationality, and sexual orientation. The Feminist Dialogue in Lusaka was undoubtedly inspired by the Mumbai event. Additional IFD took place in Porto Alegra, Brazil, in 2005 and in Nairobi, Kenya, in 2007.

11. Amanda Alexander, "The African Social Forum Feminist Dialogue: Power, Feminisms and Mobilization," *Feminist Africa* 4 (2005): 1.

12. Alexander, "The African Social Forum," 2–3.

13. Janet Conway, "Reflections on the 3rd International Feminist Dialogues: Notes from a Newcomer," *Journal of International Women's Studies* 8, no. 3 (April 2007): 211–13.

14. Ayesha M. Imam, "Birthing and Growing the African Feminist Forum," *Development* 52, no. 2 (2009): 167.

15. L. Muthoni Wanyeki, "The African Feminist Forum: Beginnings," *Women in Action* 1 (2007): 36.

16. Conway, "Reflections," 212.

17. For additional information on the African Feminist Forum, see http://www.africanfeministforum.com.

18. AAWORD, "History," accessed August 26, 2015, http://www.afard.org/presentationang.php?id=histo.

19. Ruth Meena and Marjorie Mbilinyi, "Women's Research and Documentation Project (Tanzania)," *Signs: Journal of Women in Culture and Society* 16, no. 4 (Summer 1991): 853.

20. Bolanle Awe and Nina Mba, "Women's Research and Documentation Center (Nigeria)," *Signs: Journal of Women in Culture and Society* 16, no. 4 (Summer 1991): 860.

21. Debby Bonnin, "Women's Studies in South Africa," *Women's Studies Quarterly* 24, no. 1–2 (Spring–Summer 1996): 381.

22. Department of Women and Gender Studies, Makerere University, *Celebrating 10 Years of Existence* (Kampala: Transmedia Uganda, 2002), 10–12.

23. E. Maxine Ankrah and Peninah D. Bizimana, "Women's Studies Program for Uganda," *Signs: Journal of Women in Culture and Society* 16, no. 4 (Summer 1991): 866.

24. African Gender Institute, "About AGI: History," accessed February 21, 2018, http://www.agi.ac.za/agi/about/history.

25. Fatima Sadiqi, "Facing Challenges and Pioneering Feminist and Gender Studies: Women in Post-Colonial and Today's Maghrib," *African and Asian Studies* 7 (2008): 464.

26. Sadiqi, "Facing Challenges," 465.

27. Eva M. Rathgeber, "WID, WAD, GAD: Trends in Research and Practice," *Journal of Developing Areas* 24, no. 4 (July 1990): 490–91.

28. Frances Vavrus and Lisa Ann Richey, "Women and Development: Rethinking Policy and Reconceptualizing Practice," *Women's Studies Quarterly* 31, no. 3–4 (Fall 2003): 10.

29. Moha Ennaji, "Steps to the Integration of Moroccan Women in Development," *British Journal of Middle Eastern Studies* 35, no. 3 (Dec. 2008): 341.

30. Monica Moorehead, "Nigerian Women Take Over Chevron Texaco," *Worker's World*, August 1, 2002.

31. Melissa Leach, "Earth Mother Myths and Other Ecofeminist Fables: How a Strategic Notion Rose and Fell," in *Gender Myths and Feminist Fables: The Struggle for Interpretive Power in Gender and Development*, ed. A. Cornwall, E. Harrison, and A. Whitehead (Malden, MA: Blackwell, 2008), 72.

32. Elizabeth Heger Boyle, *Female Genital Cutting: Cultural Conflict in the Global Community* (Baltimore: Johns Hopkins University Press, 2002), 24–29.

33. Stanlie M. James and Claire C. Robertson, "Re-Imaging Transnational Sisterhood," in *Genital Cutting and Transnational Sisterhood: Disputing U.S. Polemics*, ed. Stanlie M. James and Claire C. Robertson (Urbana: University of Illinois Press, 2002), 5–16.

34. Frances A. Althaus, "Female Circumcision: Rite of Passage or Violation of Rights?," *International Family Planning Perspectives* 23, no. 3 (September 1997): 132.

35. Inter-African Committee on Traditional Practices (IAC), "About IAC," accessed February 21, 2018, http://iac-ciaf.net/about-iac/.

36. Walker, Alice, and Pratibha Parmar, *Warrior Marks: Female Genital Mutilation* (New York: Harcourt Brace, 1993), Pratibha Parmar, dir., *Warrior Marks* (New York: Women Make Movies, 1993).

37. Seble Dawit and Salem Mekuria, "Bad Marks for 'Warrior Marks,'" *Off Our Backs* 24, no. 2 (February 1994): 25.

38. Dawit and Mekuria, "Bad Marks."

39. Leyla Hussein, "The Girl Generation—Let's End FGM Once and for All," *Huffington Post UK*, December 12, 2014, http://www.huffingtonpost.co.uk/leyla-hussein/the-girl-generation-lets-_b_5972410.html.

40. Judith Mandelbaum-Schmid, "Mali Takes Grassroots Approach to Ending Female Genital Mutilation," *Bulletin of the World Health Organization* 82, no. 2 (February 2004): 153–54.

41. Tostan, "About Us: Mission & History" and "Areas of Impact," accessed February 21, 2018, http://www.tostan.org.

42. Ellen Gruenbaum, "Feminist Activism for the Abolition of FGC in Sudan," *Journal of Middle East Women's Studies* 1, no. 2 (Spring 2005): 104.

43. For a concise overview of the response to the HIV/AIDS crisis and its failings, see Hazel R. Barrett, "Too Little, Too Late: Responses to the HIV/AIDS Epidemics in Sub-Saharan Africa," *Geography* 92, no. 2 (Summer 2007): 87–96.

44. Hakan Seckinelgin, "Who Can Help People with HIV/AIDS in Africa? Governance of HIV/AIDS and Civil Society," *Voluntas: International Journal of Voluntary and Nonprofit Organizations* 15, no. 3 (September 2004): 288.

45. Ngozi Iwere, "Community-Level Interventions against HIV/AIDS from a Gender Perspective," presented at the Expert Group Meeting on "The HIV/AIDS Pandemic and Its Gender Implications," Windhoek, Namibia, November 2000, http://www.un.org/womenwatch/daw/csw/hivaids/Iwere.html.

46. Shirley Mthethwa-Sommers, "In the Frontlines of the AIDS Inferno: Women Leaders' Contributions," *Agenda: Empowering Women for Gender Equity* 65 (2005): 40.

Suggested Readings

Badri, Balghis, and Aili Mari Tripp, eds. *Women's Activism in Africa*. London: Zed Books, 2017.

Gbowee, Leymah, with Carol Mithers. *Mighty Be Our Powers: How Sisterhood, Prayer and Sex Changed a Nation at War*. New York: Beast Books, 2011.

Maathai, Wangari. *Unbowed: A Memoir*. New York: Anchor Books, 2007.

Ntleko, Abegail. *Empty Hands, a Memoir: One Woman's Journey to Save Children Orphaned by AIDS in South Africa*. Berkeley, CA: North Atlantic Books, 2015.

Tripp, Aili Mari, Isabel Casimiro, Joy Kwesiga, and Alice Mungwa. *African Women's Movements: Transforming Political Landscapes*. Cambridge: Cambridge University Press, 2009.

7

WOMEN AND POLITICS IN AFRICA

Aili Mari Tripp

W omen historically played important governing roles in many parts of Africa (see chapter 3) but were often sidelined with the spread of Islam, Christianity, and colonialism. However, since the mid-1990s there has been a new ascendance of women leaders in Africa at all levels, from representation in the local government to the national legislature and involvement in the executive. This chapter provides a brief overview of women's roles in various political configurations prior to colonialism, during colonialism, and after independence and then describes more recent increases in women's political leadership, explaining the rise by four interrelated factors: (1) the expansion of political rights and civil liberties, particularly with shifts from authoritarian to semi-authoritarian/democratic "hybrid" regimes; (2) the emergence of autonomous women's movements that accompanied this opening; (3) pressures from international actors such as UN agencies, regional organizations, donors, and other external actors; and (4) the decline of conflict in Africa, which increased rates of change in countries exiting conflict.

Political power, formal and informal, is important to women. In the modern context, access to power means having control over basic decisions affecting one's life, from land rights to access to education and protections against violence. It affects how resources are distributed within a society, human rights, and equity in policy. Justice and fairness demand that all citizens have equitable access to influence processes that affect their daily lives.

Women's Political Participation in History:
Changes and Continuities

In precolonial Africa women exerted political control in a variety of ways, although their impact varied from region to region, nation to nation. In some parts of Africa women ruled kingdoms, founded cities and states, and launched military conquests of territory. In addition to women leaders mentioned by Nwando Achebe (chapter 3), famed women military leaders included Queen Amina Sarauniya of Zazzau (today Zaria) in Nigeria (ca. 1533–1610), who expanded Zazzau to its largest size and became famous for popularizing the building of earthen city wall military fortifications, which came to be known as "Amina walls." Seh-Dong-Hong-Beh in Abomey (Benin) led an army of six thousand women against the Egba (Yoruba) fortress of Abeokuta in 1851. Queen Nzinga's (1623–63) accomplishments in Angola and parts of Congo included leading armies against the Portuguese, creating alliances to secure slave trading routes, complete reconstruction of a kingdom while fighting the Portuguese, assigning women to key offices, and, notably, including women in the army at all levels.[1]

In some cases women ruled as *sole rulers* (Mbundu, Madagascar, Ethiopia). Sometimes they reigned as regents until their sons or other young heirs to the throne were old enough to rule. There was a continuous line of queens in Madagascar from 1828 to 1897, including Queen Ranavalona I, Queen Rasoherina, Queen Ranavalona II, and Queen Ranavalona III. Ethiopia's ancient and modern history is replete with women leaders going back 6,500 years. The legendary Queen of Sheba (born in 1020 BC), known as Makeda in Ethiopia, is considered, together with King Solomon of Israel, to be the founder of the Solomonic dynasty. Other famous women leaders include tenth-century Queen Yodit, who attacked the ruling Axumite dynasty and leveled Axum, usurping the throne, reigned for forty years, and started the Zagwe dynasty that held power between the ninth and twelfth centuries. Her mythologized brutality is still recounted to this day. Queen Zauditu (1876–1930) was the first woman head of a modern state in Africa. She was preoccupied with the religion of the Ethiopian Orthodox church for much of her reign, but she presided over Ethiopia's entry into the League of Nations and the abolition of slavery under the direction of her successor Ras Tafari Makonnen (Haile Selassie). Madam Yoko (1878–1908) of Kpaa Mende and Seneghum in modern-day Sierra Leone was known for her brilliance and ambition. She used a British alliance to gain control of Kpaa Mende and then employed diplomacy and conquest to bring fourteen chiefdoms under her rule. The British made her paramount chief of their protectorate from 1898 to 1906, but her British ties cost her the support of many of her subjects.[2]

More commonly in the second type of power arrangement, a female (mother or sister of the king) *ruled jointly* with a king or chief (e.g., among the Banyarwanda, Bamileke, Lunda, and Chamba peoples). A variant of this involves a *dual-sex governance system* discussed by Achebe (chapter 3) that was common among the Igbo and Yoruba in Nigeria, in which female leaders controlled the economic, political, cultural, and moral affairs of women, and male leaders did the same for the men in the community.[3] Dual-sex governance has persisted to this day in the form of women's councils in eastern Nigeria such as the Igbo Ikporo-Onitsha and in the persistence of the authority of Asante queen mothers in Ghana.[4] In Swaziland there were at least seven women joint rulers from 1875 to the present.[5] A third configuration involved a *tripartite sharing of power* between the king, mother, and sister as in Buganda, Kitara, and Ankole in Uganda.[6]

In kinship-based decentralized political systems in precolonial Africa, women's leadership was not institutionalized as it was in the kingdoms. When women assumed leadership of their communities, it was generally in the absence of a male heir upon the death of a father or husband.[7] For some groups, authority was organized along the lines of age and even age sets or associations. Each age set carried its own responsibilities, and ritual obligations and age conferred not only authority but also respect, since younger people would seek advice from the elders. Since experience, rather than formal education, was the major source of knowledge and elders were approaching death, they were closer to joining venerated ancestors. Men gained authority as elders of a community, as did women past childbearing age. In some societies, elders had mixed-gender associations; in others associations were separated by gender, with women having greater powers than men including sanctioning particular men, especially for offenses committed against women.

The spread of Islam and Christianity undermined the political importance of women leaders, whose political authority was further eroded by colonialists, who dealt primarily with local male authorities as they did in their home countries. For example, the key royal female positions of queen mother (*namasole*) and queen sister (*lubuga*) in Buganda were undermined when Uganda became a protectorate of Great Britain in 1894. Previously, of the three individuals who could be addressed as *kabaka* or king, two were women, including the queen mother and the queen sister. The *namasole* had her own courts and estates and exercised powers that resembled those of the king.[8] She was the most important woman in Buganda.[9] The *lubuga* was the other woman held in highest regard and became the official "wife" of the king, although he was forbidden from having sexual relations with her, nor could she have any children. She shared the throne with him and had the same powers he had, controlling estates in each district and presiding over her own courts and chiefs whose ranks were equivalent to those of the king's chiefs.[10] Under British rule both women were ignored, while the influence of the *kabaka* and clan leaders was also weakened when senior chiefs gained power.[11]

However, even in societies where women's direct political power diminished, they continued to exert pressure through indirect means, such as by influencing public opinion and male leaders.[12] Women's role as spiritual and moral leaders, although not recognized by colonial authorities, remained important in many communities (see chapter 3). Women also continued to exert influence through their involvement in various types of organizations formed around age groups, agricultural production, trade, market sales, mutual aid, and control of initiation and other rituals, using them to protest colonial impositions. It is not surprising, then, that women played leadership and other crucial roles in many nationalist anticolonial movements, as shown by Kathleen Sheldon (chapter 4).

Women's Political Participation in the Postcolonial Period

After independence, women found their leadership curtailed again, this time by constraints imposed by newly independent regimes led by single parties or military leaders, who increasingly limited women's leadership to their state- or party-led women's organizations. Nationally, women's activities were to be channeled through women's organizations and wings affiliated with the ruling party, which used these organizations as sources of funds, votes, and entertainment.[13] The relationship between the ruling party and women's organizations was sometimes solidified by placing them under the control of the wife of the head of state. By the late 1980s such relationships had been created, for example, between Umoja wa Wanawake wa Tanzania and the ruling party Chama cha Mapinduzi in Tanzania, Maendeleo ya Wanawake and the dominant Kenya African National Union, and in Sierra Leone between the Women's Wing and the All People's Congress. Cooptation effectively marginalized women's leadership and channeled women into mobilizing around a narrow set of concerns, generally apolitical, involving cultural and income-generating activities. Another impetus for women's mobilization around economic issues was the decline of formal sector employment in economies after the 1980s (see chapter 6), due partly to effects of the imposition of structural adjustment programs by the International Monetary Fund and the World Bank.

Women's political participation was also limited by their lack of educational and employment opportunities relative to those of men; time constraints that kept them tied to domestic duties; cultural and religious prohibitions on women's public activities; and objections from male public officials and politicians. These limitations varied according to a woman's age, marital status, class, region, and religion.

Explaining Women's New Political Representation

Women's political participation, nevertheless, began to expand after the 1990s because of four major factors: (1) political liberalization and democratization; (2) the expansion of autonomous women's movements and coalitions; (3) new international pressures from donors, the United Nations, and other international and regional organizations; and (4) the decline of conflict, which opened the door to new political actors in the states involved.

Women's Movements and Political Liberalization

As the economic crisis deepened in the 1980s, financially strapped governments in Africa began loosening their restrictions on autonomous associations and started to liberalize politically, especially after the 1990s. These associations increasingly had independent resources, their own leadership autonomous from the ruling party, and devised their own strategies and agendas. In a country like Niger, virtually the only women's group to operate since independence was the Association des Femmes du Niger, formed in 1973. After the loosening of restrictions on associations in 1984, new women's groups emerged such as the Association des Femmes Commerçants et Entrepreneurs du Niger, Union des Femmes Enseignant du Niger, and the Association des Femmes Juristes du Niger. In Tanzania, the opening came in the late 1980s, after which groups such as the Tanzania Media Women's Association, Tanzania Women Lawyers Association, and the Tanzania Gender Networking Program emerged and began to lobby for women's rights reforms. This newfound autonomy also allowed women's organizations to press for greater political representation of women.

In Senegal the campaign for gender parity was spearheaded by the Conseil Sénégalais des Femmes (COSEF), formed in 1995 to bring women politicians together with the women's movement. In 1998 they began raising the issue of quotas (preferential political candidacy for women) with various political parties, which promised to implement them. But after the 1998 elections it was evident that the parties' commitment was insufficient, and women's groups decided that they needed a legal means to enforce parity. Abdoulaye Wade, who had made campaign promises regarding gender parity in representation, became president in 2000. COSEF then seized this moment to advance the issue. In 2004, under Wade, Senegal signed the African Union Protocol to the African Charter on Human and Peoples' Rights on the Rights of Women in Africa, also known as the Maputo Protocol (see also chapter 6), which includes a provision supporting gender parity.

COSEF then launched the "Together, let's strengthen democracy with gender parity!" campaign in 2005. They received input from various legal and constitutional experts and worked together with the Ministry of Women to get parity introduced into parliamentary elections. Leaders of the movement such as COSEF president Fatou Kiné Diop stated that their independence from the ministry gave them added leverage. They worked with women from the parties and held a demonstration on March 27, 2007, in which women, dressed in white, got the parties to support their campaign. As a result, the gender parity law was adopted in 2012, mandating that candidate lists include both male and female candidates in equal numbers. Since Senegal has a mixed electoral system, these provisions apply to both proportional representation party lists and the seats contested through the plurality system in multimember constituencies. As a result, in a constituency with five seats, two would have to be filled by a woman. A Committee on Gender Parity was to oversee the implementation of the parity law.[14] Due to these reforms, Senegal today has a parliament where 42 percent of the seats are held by women, one of the highest rates in Africa and the world (see table 7.1).

TABLE 7.1. Women's legislative representation in Africa and quota adoption

Country	Percentage of women in parliament	Type of quota
Rwanda	61	Legislated candidate quota
Namibia	46	Voluntary political party quotas
Senegal	42	Legislated candidate quota
South Africa	42	Voluntary political party quotas
Mozambique	40	Voluntary political party quotas
Ethiopia	39	Voluntary political party quotas
Tanzania	37	Reserved seats legislated, voluntary party quotas
Burundi	36	Reserved seats legislated
Uganda	34	Reserved seats legislated
Angola	31	Legislated candidate quota

Sources: Inter-Parliamentary Union, "Women in National Parliaments," accessed August 6, 2018, http://www.ipu.org/wmn-e/classif.htm; International IDEA, Gender Quotas Database, accessed August 6, 2018, https://www.idea.int/data-tools/data/gender-quotas.

In contrast, the lack of a vibrant women's movement in Botswana has resulted in setbacks. In Botswana's long-standing democracy, women parliamentarians have lost support and hold only 8 percent of the seats, a drop from a high of 18 percent with the 1999 election. At the local level, according to the Botswana Association of Local Authorities, women account for only 19 percent of leadership positions. In the 1980s and 1990s, women's organizations mobilized and were briefly able to push for increased political representation, the creation of a women's policy agency, reform of discriminatory laws, and the passing of progressive legislation.[15] By the early twenty-first century, however, the Botswana women's movement had lost momentum and had become anemic due to a drop in donor funding, internal difficulties, and the hemorrhaging of NGO leaders to government positions.[16] The two opposition parties, the Botswana National Front (BNF) and the Botswana Congress Party (BCP), adopted 30 percent quotas for female candidates in 1999 but did not ensure that quotas were met.[17] Commentators pointed to a fierce culture in Botswana that discourages women from public engagement. As Ntibinyane Ntibinyane explained, there are "Tswana sayings—such as '*Ga di nke di e etelelwa pele ke manamagadi pele*' (loosely translated, 'women would never lead'),'' expressing common beliefs that create additional obstacles for women.[18]

The example of Botswana, already a democracy by the early 1990s, suggests that it was not democracy itself that was key to claims to political power by new actors, including women. Rather, it was the *process of political opening* and liberalization that energized new constituencies such as women to demand political representation. The contrast between Botswana and Senegal also illustrates the importance of having a mobilized interest group of women, generally in coalition with political parties, civil society groups, and UN agencies, to press for women's leadership.

International Influences

External donor funds often facilitated the expansion of new women's organizations and coalitions, particularly urban-based nongovernment organizations, which often went hand in hand with pressures from United Nations agencies, the African Union (AU), and other international and regional actors, which pressed state governments to comply with international norms and treaties promoting women's rights, such as the Convention on the Elimination of Discrimination against Women (CEDAW) or the AU's Maputo Protocol. The 1985 UN Conference on Women in Nairobi, attended by 15,000 women from 140 countries, served as a catalyst for women's mobilization across the continent, as did the 1995 UN Beijing conference attended by 35,000 (see chapter 6).

The African Union and regional bodies such as the Southern African Development Community (SADC) subsequently initiated efforts to expand women's representation within their member states, setting a target of 30 percent in 1997 and 50 percent in 2010. Thus, in 2015 SADC countries had higher rates of representation (24 percent) than non-SADC countries (17 percent).

Postconflict Influences

Finally, postconflict trends played an increasingly important role after 1990 in influencing women's political representation. This was not true after earlier conflicts, but by the 1990s international and regional norms and actors had changed political expectations regarding women's rights in a way that influenced constitutional and legislative outcomes. In general, postconflict countries have double the rates of representation for women in parliament compared to non-postconflict countries. In Rwanda, which experienced major genocide and conflict in 1994, women hold 61.3 percent of the legislative seats. Not only is this the highest rate in the world, but also Rwanda is the only country with more than half of its legislature made up of women. Likewise, in Algeria, women's proportion of legislative representation jumped from 2 percent in 1987 prior to the conflict between the government and the Islamists (1991–2002) to 32 percent after the 2012 elections. Except for Tanzania and Senegal, the countries with the highest rates of female legislative representation in Africa today have emerged from major conflict.

It is no accident that the first elected female president in Africa came from a postconflict context. Ellen Johnson Sirleaf was elected after years of conflict in Liberia and emerged as a strong advocate of women's rights. Postconflict countries are passing more legislation entailing women's rights and including more women's rights provisions in their constitutions. These developments are tied to societal transformations that took place during war. The decline in conflict after the mid-1990s established new institutions through which women could assert their interests. Peacekeeping negotiations allowed women to insert their demands; they did so in Africa more than in other continents. Women's organizations influenced constitution-making processes and were able to include more woman-friendly provisions than constitutions revised simultaneously in countries without civil wars. Women's rights activists also saw to it that electoral rules were amended in ways that supported their goals. At the local level, conflicts transformed gender relations and roles, especially where women played roles as peacemakers.[19]

Changing Patterns of Political Representation

Parliamentary Leadership

African countries have some of the world's highest rates of female political representation. Across the continent, numbers of women in parliament tripled between 1990 and 2010. We are now seeing a diffusion of these sub-Saharan trends into northern Africa and especially the Maghrib, where women parliamentarians in Tunisia hold 31 percent of the parliamentary seats, 25 percent of the seats in Mauritania, and 21 percent in Morocco, mainly as a result of the adoption of electoral quotas. These trends in the Maghrib are distinct from what we see in other parts of the Middle East, where the rates of female legislative representation are generally much lower. (In the United States, women hold only 20 percent of the legislative seats in the Senate and House.) There are female speakers of the house in one-fifth of African parliaments, higher than the world average of 14 percent.

The gradual increase of female representation in Scandinavia used to be the model when Nordic countries were alone in enjoying high rates of female representation. This older pattern has been replaced by what Danish political scientist Drude Dahlerup has dubbed the new "fast track" model, evident in African countries that have experienced dramatic jumps in female parliamentary representation primarily through the adoption of electoral quotas.[20] Such quotas became especially popular after 1995, the year of the UN Fourth Conference on Women in Beijing, which adopted a Platform of Action that encouraged member states to promote the leadership of women in all spheres. In the decades leading up to 1995, only six countries in sub-Saharan Africa had adopted quotas while today 65 percent of all African countries have adopted gender quotas.

In countries with quotas, women claim 25 percent of parliamentary seats, while in countries without quotas women claim an average of 14 percent of the seats. Three types of quotas have generally been adopted; on average they have been equally successful in terms of the extent to which they increase female representation. Reserved seats or women's lists, mandated by constitutions or legislation or both, set aside seats for which only women can compete. These guarantee from the outset, prior to the election, that a predetermined percentage of seats will be held by women. In a second arrangement, parties themselves voluntarily adopt a quota, regardless of whether there was a constitutional or legal mandate. These are often, although not always, successful because parties themselves have voluntarily decided to take steps to ensure greater female representation. Finally, a third arrangement involves compulsory quotas, where legislation requires that all parties include a certain percentage of women on their candidate lists. They generally do not mandate where they should be placed on the list, which is crucial to the success of such a provision.

In Africa, there is little difference in regime type between countries with the highest rates of representation. On average, women in democracies hold 24 percent of the seats, while in hybrid regimes with a mix of authoritarian and democratic tendencies and in authoritarian regimes they hold 19 percent and 21 percent of the seats, respectively. Authoritarian regimes and democracies are equally likely to adopt quotas, although hybrid regimes are slightly less likely to do so. There is no statistically significant correlation between regime type and levels of female representation, nor is there a relationship between adoption of quotas and regime type.

Executive Leadership

African parliamentary patterns are evident in other areas of leadership as well. Prior to 2000, only nine women had run as presidential candidates in Africa, and only three had served as heads of state (see table 7.2). Carmen Pereira was briefly acting head of state in Guinea Bissau (1984); Ruth Perry served as the chairperson of the Council of State of Liberia in 1996; and Sylvie Kinigi served as president briefly in Burundi (1993–94). Between 2000 and 2015, at least fifty-three women ran as presidential candidates in Africa. The majority of women presidential candidates polled less than 1 percent of the vote (22 out of 27, or 81.5 percent).[21] The majority of women running as presidential candidates come from countries that have a very low percentage of women in legislatures, with a heavy preponderance in West and Central Africa. Most served only for short periods of time often in an interim capacity, suggesting that women have an easier time entering positions of power in times of uncertainty, unrest, and transition.

Since 1975 there have been twelve female vice presidents, of whom Specioza Wandira Kazibwe in Uganda served the longest, for a period of ten years (see table 7.3). Since 1993, there have also been eleven prime ministers, of whom Luísa Días Diogo of Mozambique held the position the longest (six years) (see table 7.4). As with the presidency, many filled the prime ministerial position only briefly or in an acting capacity because the country was going through a transition.

Women are taking over key ministerial positions in defense, finance, and foreign affairs, a departure from when they primarily held ministerial positions in the so-called softer ministries of education, community development, sports,

TABLE 7.2. Female heads of state

1984	Carmen Pereira	Guinea Bissau
1993–94	Sylvie Kinigi	Burundi
1996–97	Ruth Perry, chairperson of the Council of State	Liberia
2004	Elizabeth Alpha Lavalie	Sierra Leone
2006–18	Ellen Johnson Sirleaf	Liberia
2012–14	Joyce Banda	Malawi
2012–15	Monique Agnès Ohsan-Bellepeau	Mauritius
2014–16	Catherine Samba-Panza (acting head of state)	Central African Republic
2015–18	Ameenah Gurib-Fakim	Mauritius

Source: Worldwide Guide to Women in Leadership, http://www.guide2womenleaders.com.

TABLE 7.3. Female vice presidents

1975–76	Élisabeth Domitien	Central African Republic
1980–91	Alda Neves da Graça do Espirito Santo	Sao Tomé e Principe
1994–2003	Dr. Specioza Wandira Kazibwe	Uganda
1997–2017	Aisatou N'Jie Saidy	The Gambia
2004–14	Joyce Mujuru	Zimbabwe
2005–8	Phumzile Mlambo-Ngcuka	South Africa
2005–6	Alice Nzomukunda	Burundi
2006–7	Marina Barampama	Burundi
2008–9	Baleka Mbete	South Africa
2009–12	Joyce Banda	Malawi
2010–12	Monique Agnès Ohsan-Bellepeau	Mauritius
2015–	Inonge Wina	Zambia

Source: Worldwide Guide to Women in Leadership, http://www.guide2womenleaders.com.

and youth. Today, for example, South Africa has a female defense minister, Nosiviwe Mapisa-Nqakula; Mariam Mahmat Nour is Chad's minister of planning and international cooperation; and Nialé Kaba is Côte d'Ivoire's minister of economy and finance. Women hold close to or more than 40 percent of ministerial positions in South Africa, Cape Verde, Burundi, and Uganda. Of the ten countries with the highest percentage of women in the cabinet, six are

Table 7.4. Female prime ministers

1993–94	Agathe Uwilingiyimana	Rwanda
1993–94	Sylvie Kinigi	Burundi
2001–2	Mame Madior Boye	Senegal
2002–4	Maria das Neves Ceita Batista de Sousa	Republic of São Tomé e Príncipe
2004–10	Luísa Días Diogo	Mozambique
2005–6	Maria do Carmo Trovoada Pires de Carvalho Silveira	São Tomé e Princípe
2009	Cécile Manorohanta	Madagascar
2011–12	Cissé Mariam Kaïdama Sidibé	Mali
2012	(Acting) Adiatu Djaló Nandigna	Guinea Bissau
2013–14	Aminata Touré	Senegal
2015–	Saara Kuugongelwa-Amadhila	Namibia

Source: Worldwide Guide to Women in Leadership, http://www.guide2womenleaders.com.

postconflict countries, once again suggesting that postconflict dynamics influence women's leadership in distinct ways.

Regional Leadership

Women are visible in regional bodies as well. They make up 50 percent of the African Union parliament, and in July 2012 South Africa's Nkosazana Dhlamini-Zuma took over the leadership of the African Union Commission. From 2004 to 2009, Gertrude Mongella of Tanzania chaired the AU's Pan-African Parliament as the first president of that body. Fatoumatta Ceesay from Gambia heads up the parliament of the Economic Community of West African States (ECOWAS), which is made up of fifteen member states, and Margaret Nantongo Zziwa is speaker of the East African Legislative Assembly. One sees similar changes in the judiciary, with women magistrates advancing to top levels. African women judges are even making it into the international arena with Fatou Bensouda from Gambia as the chief prosecutor in the International Criminal Court. All but one of the current five African judges on the International Criminal Court are women.

Local-Level Leadership

Even at the local level, women hold almost 60 percent of local government positions in Lesotho; they represent 43 percent of the members of local councils or municipal assemblies in Namibia; and they make up over one-third of local government seats in Mauritania, Mozambique, Tanzania, and Uganda.

Electoral Participation

Changes in the electorate are less striking than changes in leadership, which suggests that it is easier to change institutions than popular attitudes. In general, men seem to vote at slightly higher rates than women: roughly 3 percent more men than women vote on average in countries surveyed by Afrobarometer in Round 6 of a survey (2014/2015) (see table 7.5). In Botswana, Lesotho, and South Africa more women than men have voted consistently since 1999, and the gender gap has lessened in Malawi since 1999 so that now more women vote than men. A similar pattern is evident in Swaziland after 2011. There have been elections in Cape Verde, Egypt, Ghana, Togo, Morocco, Namibia, Senegal, and Zimbabwe where more women than men voted, according to Afrobarometer surveys, but, in general, it appears that southern Africa as a region has consistently seen more women than men voting, perhaps as a result of the SADC influence. In Botswana in 2009, some 403,000 women registered to vote compared to 320,000 men, even though they elected few women leaders.[22] Given the limited number of countries for which there is data, it is difficult to generalize for the whole continent.

Constraints on Women Politicians

Women candidates face particular constraints, including cultural attitudes, lack of financial support, and even violence. In countries such as Lesotho, Madagascar, Mali, and Nigeria, only half the men believe that women should have a chance to be elected. Women have significantly higher rates of support for women as leaders in most countries surveyed, however. Table 7.6 reflects positive responses to the statement, "Women should have the same chance of being elected to political office as men."

Some have argued that cultural attitudes on gender equity influence women's political leadership the world over.[23] However, with regard to women's representation, the various institutional factors, particularly the introduction of quotas, tend to override cultural constraints. Some argue that Islam has dampened support for women's rights. This may be true in terms of attitudes, but the introduction of quotas minimizes the importance of such factors. In Africa, many countries with the highest rates of female representation have significant Muslim populations, such as Algeria, Tunisia, Mauritania, Niger, Senegal, Eritrea, Sudan, Somalia, and Tanzania. They adopted quotas and increased rates of representation because there were concerns that attitudes might pose

TABLE 7.5. Voting frequency by gender

	2014–15		2011–13		2005–6		1999–2000	
	Male (%)	Female (%)	Male (%)	Female (%)	Male (%)	Female (%)	Male (%)	Female (%)
Total	71.30	67.70	75.70	71.00	77.40	72.10	75.50	69.20
Algeria	46.80	47.00	52.10	46.10				
Benin	78.40	73.80	92.00	84.20	91.00	87.00		
Botswana	58.40	61.50	60.90	62.80	65.60	69.10	51.30	56.20
Cape Verde	68.50	72.30	79.70	79.50	67.30	65.60		
Egypt	67.60	67.80	83.40	75.70				
Ghana	78.20	78.10	77.60	72.90	85.60	88.70	89.60	87.40
Kenya	82.50	78.60	75.90	70.90	73.10	55.60		
Lesotho	72.00	73.90	73.70	73.30	71.10	70.70	69.60	67.80
Madagascar	76.40	68.70	72.10	57.70	80.70	72.40		
Malawi	68.90	70.10	79.00	78.20	79.50	79.00	90.00	87.20
Mali	76.60	72.30	68.90	63.70	83.90	72.50	77.60	6.004
Morocco	41.90	43.80	56.50	48.20				
Namibia	67.10	62.20	69.10	69.40	81.70	76.10	66.50	62.40
Nigeria			78.30	77.10	74.60	62.60	75.10	57.20
South Africa			71.60	75.50	76.60	78.10	81.60	83.00
Tanzania	69.30	62.90	84.90	77.50	84.80	77.30	90.60	84.20
Tunisia	62.10	51.40	72.50	65.80				
Uganda			85.10	81.50	81.20	76.40	82.40	74.20
Zambia	65.70	55.80	68.50	62.20	63.80	56.60	52.90	45.60
Zimbabwe	73.50	69.80	68.70	62.30	75.90	72.80	43.00	45.70

Note: Shaded areas indicate more women than men.
Source: Afrobarometer Survey, www.afrobarometer.org.

TABLE 7.6. Opinion survey on support for women as leaders (2014–15)

	Men (%)	Women (%)	All (%)
Algeria	23	51	35
Botswana	79	86	83
Burundi	69	78	73
Cameroon	64	74	69
Cape Verde	89	94	91
Benin	64	82	73
Ghana	62	78	70
Côte d'Ivoire	70	88	79
Egypt	34	55	40
Kenya	70	82	76
Lesotho	47	67	57
Madagascar	51	70	61
Malawi	61	60	61
Mali	53	62	57
Mauritius	69	88	78
Morocco	50	83	63
Namibia	73	86	79
Nigeria	47	54	50
Senegal	52	78	65
Zimbabwe	57	79	68
Swaziland	71	86	78
Togo	83	92	88
Tanzania	59	78	68
Tunisia	59	66	61
Zambia	69	75	72
Total	63	77	70

Source: Afrobarometer Survey, www.afrobarometer.org.

particular constraints for women attempting to run for office. Nonetheless, predominantly Muslim Senegal has one of the highest rates of female representation in the world, with 43 percent of its parliamentary seats held by women.

Cultural constraints do affect women in other ways. One particular constraint for women in patrilineal societies is finding a constituency in which to run. If women run in their natal constituency, they are often seen as not identifying sufficiently with their husband's family since wives are supposed to leave the natal home at marriage. However, those who run in the constituency of their husbands often say they are not accepted since they are considered outsiders, which coheres with African ideas about lineage families, that is, all those descended from a common ancestor. Hence, women marrying into patrilineal families are seen as outsiders (see chapter 13).

There may be cultural prohibitions on women speaking and campaigning in public places. Husbands may forbid their wives' entry into politics because of how it may reflect on them and the gossip it might generate. For this reason, one often finds that women who run for office are disproportionately single, divorced, or widowed. Part of the stigma may have to do with the perception that women politicians are loose women, that they are bad mothers and wives, or that they are not adequately fulfilling their marital obligations.

Women may also fear politics because it is considered dirty and dangerous, a game only fit for men. As Kenyan women's rights activist Dr. Maria Nzomo put it: "Women are still afraid of power . . . we need to realize that politics does not make itself dirty, people make it dirty and that we can't continue to say it is dirty and sit on the sidelines. We need to jump in and change politics. We have to deal with it."[24] Even then, the hurdles may be too high. I interviewed women politicians in Kenya in 2014 after the 2013 elections. Violence perpetrated by militias hired by politicians has marred Kenyan elections. As newcomers to politics, women find that the violence creates strong disincentives to run for office. In the run-up to the 2013 parliamentary elections, one woman candidate reported that she had had her dress pulled up over her head in public; she was ready for the attack and had worn long pants underneath her dress. She went on to win, but only after she was beaten by fifty young men in her office during the nomination process and hospitalized after her hair was pulled. Another woman candidate's five-year-old son was killed, and she fled the country. Violence against women in Kenya more generally is endemic and virulent, rooted in masculine beliefs that women are men's property (see chapter 15).

Some Kenyan attacks are aimed at undermining the female candidates' integrity. An opponent of a female candidate had fliers distributed in her constituency claiming she was a devil worshipper and had sworn to kill a thousand women and children; she was greedy with her family; she was not supported by her husband, who was allegedly backing another candidate; and she was an exhibitionist who had removed her blouse and told men to suckle her breasts for the next five years. The last statement was regarded as especially vulgar and repulsive in the Kenyan context. Her husband, who did support her, ended up hospitalized, partly due to the stress of her running. She remained undaunted and ran anyway.

Many women interviewed were told to withdraw from the race by elders, clan members, male rivals, and family members because it was unbecoming for a woman to run, women cannot lead men, or it was against Islam for women to run. Unsupportive families significantly added to challenges female aspirants faced. One woman parliamentary candidate's husband gave her money and moral support, but his mother vocally opposed her candidacy, even send-ing a family delegation to dissuade her. As a result, she could not run in the husband's constituency; she ran in her natal constituency, where other obsta-cles existed.

Kenyan single women were attacked for not being married, and others were called too old, while male candidates were not criticized for the same attributes. Misinformation spread that women could vie only for the county women rep-resentative seats (reserved only for female candidates) rather than for open seats for which either men or women could run. Parties also sometimes pressed women not to seek open seats. Such pressures, not faced by men, discourage women from even attempting to run for office. Jacqueline Adhiambo Oduol aptly summarized the toll this took on women politicians: "Systemic gender dominance (through methods such as making women invisible, making women ridiculous, burdening women with guilt and shame, double punishment of women and withholding information from women) persists with limiting beliefs, which claw back on gains made as expectations within and outside established networks reinforce discrimination against women."[25]

Finally, the internal culture of a legislative body, for example, can be hostile to women. Gendered divisions of labor place burdens on women, with women bearing heavier responsibilities in households and communities. Meetings running late into the night pose challenges for women in terms of safety and child care that men do not generally face. Some find that the financial costs of running and remaining in office are onerous. Women tend to be economically disadvantaged, which imposes additional constraints on them, particularly with regard to patronage-related expectations.

As women become more accustomed to holding elective office and as others become used to seeing them there, many such concerns fade, but sometimes disparaging treatment and remarks have to be dealt with head on. Given the large number of women in the Rwandan parliament (6.3 percent), Claire Devlin and Robert Elgie found that parliamentarians reported that the pres-ence of women had affected the culture of the body, making women feel more at home in the parliament and increasingly confident, participating more than men, who had historically dominated the chamber.[26] One of the consequences of having so many women in parliament has been increased pressures to pass legislation regarding women's rights. The Forum for Women Parliamentarians has led initiatives to pass legislation affecting women relating, for example, to inheritance, gender-based violence, and the rights of pregnant and breast-feeding mothers. They also helped get a provision into the 2003 constitution regarding gender quotas.

Despite attitudes hostile to women as leaders, the overwhelming majority of people in countries surveyed by Afrobarometer supported women leaders to varying degrees, with women consistently more supportive than men. The introduction of quotas helped ameliorate some of the cultural constraints women politicians face.

Conclusion

Precolonial women's leadership was usually based on hereditary position, age, or ability, as it was for men, with women rulers sometimes assuming the garb and authority more commonly conferred on men (see chapter 3). Their military exploits were often notable. Thus, colonial and early post-independent governments in a perverse way, by discriminating against women, raised consciousness among African women and fostered gender awareness that undergirds women's claims to political authority today.

Women's representation in African legislatures increased threefold between 1990 and 2010, and women made considerable gains in leadership of the executive, local government, and the judiciary. Many such changes can be explained by three developments. Political opening (i.e., the shift to multiparty elections, and greater freedom of assembly and speech) in the 1990s allowed for the emergence of women's movements, even where those openings were limited. Political liberalization allowed women to seek their own sources of funding, pursue their own agendas, and select their own leaders. This was a big change from the earlier postcolonial period when women's leadership was limited to organizations tied to the ruling party or state financially, as well as through their agendas and leadership. Women's organizations and coalitions began to engage issues of women's political leadership with reform agendas that took them well beyond the development-oriented goals of the early postcolonial period, which focused on handicrafts, homemaking, and income generation. UN agencies, African regional organizations, international and regional women's organizations, as well as foreign donors supported domestic women's organizations' strategies to influence states. They provided a new normative environment that helped governments set new goals regarding women's rights.

Finally, countries affected by major conflict experienced major disruptions in gender relations, forcing women to play greater roles in their households, communities, and nations. Ending conflicts opened up new space for women's rights activists to influence peace treaties and constitutions and led to the creation of new institutional rules and bodies that allowed for greater female leadership. All these factors combined help explain why Africa today is providing important leadership globally in the area of women's political representation.

Notes

1. Edna G. Bay, *Wives of the Leopard: Gender, Politics, and Culture in the Kingdom of Dahomey* (Charlottesville: University of Virginia Press, 1998); A. Adu Boahen and Emmanuel Kwaku Akyeampong, *Yaa Asantewaa and the Asante-British War of 1900–1* (Accra, Ghana: Sub-Saharan Publishers, 2003); Linda M. Heywood, *Njinga of Angola: Africa's Warrior Queen* (Cambridge, MA: Harvard University Press, 2017).

2. Carol Hoffer, "Mende and Sherbro Women in High Offices," *Canadian Journal of African Studies* 6, no. 2 (1972): 151–64.

3. Kamene Okonjo, "The Dual-Sex Political System in Operation: Igbo Women and Community Politics in Midwestern Nigeria," in *Women in Africa: Studies in Social Economic Change*, ed. Nancy J. Hafkin and Edna G. Bay (Stanford, CA: Stanford University Press, 1976), 45–58; Judith Van Allen, "'Aba Riots' or Igbo 'Women's War'? Ideology, Stratification, and the Invisibility of Women," in Hafkin and Bay, *Women in Africa*, 59–86; Bolanle Awe, "The Iyalode in the Traditional Yoruba Political System," in *Sexual Stratification: A Cross-Cultural View*, ed. Alice Schlegel (New York: Columbia University Press, 1977), 144–59.

4. Nkiru Nzegwu, "Recovering Igbo Traditions: A Case for Indigenous Women's Organizations in Development," in *Women, Culture and Development: A Study of Human Capabilities*, ed. Martha C. Nussbaum and Jonathan Glover (Oxford: Clarendon Press, 1995), 444–65.

5. "Current Women Leaders," Worldwide Guide to Women in Leadership, accessed February 19, 2017, http://www.guide2womenleaders.com/Current-Women -Leaders.htm.

6. Annie M. D. Lebeuf, "The Role of Women in the Political Organization of African Societies," in *Women of Tropical Africa*, ed. Denise Paulme (Berkeley: University of California Press, 1963), 93–119; Beverly J. Stoeltje, "Asante Queen Mothers," *Annals of the New York Academy of Sciences* 810, no. 1 (1997): 41–71.

7. Lebeuf, "Role of Women," 93–119.

8. John Milner Gray, "Early History of Buganda," *Uganda Journal* 2, no. 4 (1934): 259–70.

9. Laurence D. Schiller, "The Royal Women of Buganda," *International Journal of African Historical Studies* 23, no. 3 (1990): 455–73.

10. Nakanyike B. Musisi, "Women, 'Elite Polygyny,' and Buganda State Formation," *Signs* 16, no. 4 (1991): 757–86; John Roscoe, *The Baganda: An Account of Their Native Customs and Beliefs* (London: Macmillan, 1911).

11. Susan Diduk, "Women's Agricultural Production and Political Action in the Cameroon Grassfields," *Africa: Journal of the International African Institute* 59, no. 3 (1989): 338–55; David E. Apter, *The Political Kingdom in Uganda* (Princeton, NJ: Princeton University Press, 1961).

12. Jean O'Barr, "African Women in Politics," in *African Women South of the Sahara*, ed. Margaret Jean Hay and Sharon Stichter (London: Longman, 1984).

13. Filomina Steady, *Female Power in African Politics: The National Congress of Sierra Leone Women* (Pasadena: Munger Africana Library, California Institute of Technology, 1975); Kathleen Staudt, "Women's Political Consciousness in Africa: A Framework for Analysis," in *Women as Food Producers in Developing Countries*, ed. Jamie Monson and Marion Kalb (Los Angeles: UCLA African Studies Center, 1985).

14. Nathalie Bissonnette, "Senegal, Governance Gets a Make Over," Uniterra, Ottawa, Canada: World University Service of Canada (WUSC) and Centre for International Studies and Cooperation (CECI), 2013.

15. Gretchen Bauer, "Update on the Women's Movement in Botswana: Have Women Stopped Talking?" *African Studies Review* 54, no. 2 (2011): 23–46.

16. Zitha Mokomane, "Civil Society," in *Transparency, Accountability and Corruption in Botswana*, ed. Zibani Maundeni (Rosebank, Cape Town: Made Plain Communications, 2008); David Sebudubudu and Bertha Zimba Osei Hwedie, *Democratic Consolidation in SADC: Botswana's 2004 Election* (Johannesburg: Electoral Institute for Sustainable Democracy in Africa, 2005).

17. B. M. Kethusegile-Juru, *Intra-Party Democracy and the Inclusion of Women* (Johannesburg: EISA Research Report, 2002), 8.

18. Ntibinyane Ntibinyane, "Where Are Botswana's Women Politicians?," OSISA: Open Society Initiative for Southern Africa, November 29, 2011, http://www.osisa .org/womens-rights/blog/where-are-botswanas-women-politicians.

19. Aili Mari Tripp, *Women and Power in Postconflict Africa* (New York: Cambridge University Press, 2015).

20. Drude Dahlerup and Lenita Freidenvall, "Quotas as a Fast Track to Equal Representation for Women," *International Feminist Journal of Politics* 7, no 1 (March 2005): 26–48.

21. Melinda Adams, "Liberia's Election of Ellen Johnson-Sirleaf and Women's Executive Leadership in Africa," *Politics and Gender* 43, no. 3 (2008): 475–84.

22. Ntibinyane, "Botswana's Women Politicians."

23. Ronald Inglehart, Pippa Norris, and Chris Welzel, "Gender Equality and Democracy," *Comparative Sociology* 1, no. 3–4 (2002): 321–45; Ronald Inglehart and Pippa Norris, *Rising Tide: Gender Equality and Cultural Change around the World* (Cambridge: Cambridge University Press, 2003).

24. Maria Nzomo, "Women and Politics in Kenya" (presentation to USAID Gender and Democracy in Africa Workshop, Washington, DC, July 28, 1995).

25. Jacqueline Adhiambo Oduol, "Challenging Patriarchy: New Spaces and Strategies for Advancing Gender Equality in Africa," *State Interventions and Gender Equality in Kenya*, virtual workshop hosted by the Heinrich Boll Stiftung, 2013.

26. Claire Devlin and Robert Elgie, "The Effect of Increased Women's Representation in Parliament: The Case of Rwanda," *Parliamentary Affairs* 61, no. 2 (2008): 237–54.

Suggested Readings

Bauer, Gretchen, and Jennie E. Burnet. "Gender Quotas, Democracy, and Women's Representation in Africa: Some Insights from Democratic Botswana and Autocratic Rwanda." *Women's Studies International Forum* 41, no. 2 (2013): 103–12.

Cherif, Nedra. "Tunisian Women in Politics: From Constitution Makers to Electoral Contenders." FRIDE Policy Brief, no. 189, November 2014. http://fride.org/down load/PB_189_Tunisian_women_in_politics.pdf.

Johnson Sirleaf, Ellen. *This Child Will Be Great: Memoir of Africa's First Woman President.* New York: Harper, 2010.

Kabira, Wanjiku Mukabi. *Time for Harvest: Women and Constitution Making in Kenya.* Nairobi: University of Nairobi Press, 2012.

Tripp, Aili Mari. *Women and Power in Postconflict Africa.* New York: Cambridge University Press, 2015.

PART III

ECONOMY AND SOCIETY

Figure 8.1. Selling "European" vegetables grown in Ghana (Tafo market, Kumasi).
Photo by Gracia Clark.

8

AFRICAN WOMEN IN THE REAL ECONOMY

Prehistoric, Precolonial, Colonial, and
Contemporary Transitions

Gracia Clark

The central economic role women have taken in the survival and prosperity of their communities dates from the earliest human origins in Africa and continues unabated through recent global transformations. While now elite men, often non-African executives, control the national and multinational corporate sectors and many recognized public institutions, the quantity and strategic importance of the work women do assure that their efforts remain central to sustaining ongoing forms of production, including wage labor and self-employment. Factors that impair their effectiveness, such as inadequate control of resources, an unequal gender division of household labor, and ideological constraints or penalties, hamper those contributions to the detriment of the general welfare.

The widespread stereotype of African women as passive victims crumbles in the face of African women's incessant efforts to survive and prosper. Analysts have adopted the concept of livelihood to do justice to the closely interwoven paid and unpaid activities that together sustain individuals and communities over the long term. This is a struggle some people shirk and many do not win, but it has left a legacy of experimentation and innovation in every part of the continent. A diverse repertoire of choices for work and family arrangements provides flexibility—the best preparation for an unpredictable future.[1]

Gendered material relations and ideological assumptions about gender permeate various African economic systems in their multifaceted historical specificity. The complex of socioeconomic factors supporting production, reproduction, and stratification draws upon gender in its expressions, inflected by gender, class, race, age, ethnicity, nationality, and other cross-cutting principles of inequality. While such intersections often have significantly reinforced the inequalities generated by each, they can also provide significant leverage for social change. Material and symbolic gender relations mutually construct (together with these others) the vital building blocks that any society uses to maintain, reproduce, and transform economic life.[2]

Much current research on economic issues relies on categorizations that obscure women's economic activities and dismiss them as trivial or nonproductive. Some sets of categories impose artificial divisions: production from reproduction; public from private; local from global; formal from informal sectors; legal from illegal activities or cash from subsistence crops. Other sets assume an evolutionary trajectory: "primitive," "traditional," or "modern/Western" values; "tribal," "peasant," or state societies, local, national, or transnational relations; even superstition, religion, or science. However, economic processes commonly straddle these divisions. Far from weakening African economies, processes bridging and contradicting such categories create cohesive and flexible systems that withstand many challenging circumstances.

Conventional U.S. economic analysis makes a sharp distinction between work and family, confining the economy to work for wages or profits and measuring it primarily through recorded monetary transactions, as gross domestic product (GDP). Official statistics miss much production for sale to local consumers, self-employment, subsistence production, and unpaid family labor. Attempts to estimate this "unofficial," "informal," or "second" economy generally find that it represents much national production, not only in African countries. Domestic and cultural work that keeps a family or community healthy and working together receives even less attention, from cooking and cleaning to maintaining cultural values and social institutions. This brief overview uses conventional economic terminology, while acknowledging its limitations and the colonial and male-dominant baggage it carries. Fluidity in practices that bridge such divisions highlights how actual conditions contradict binary categories that assume separation. The intersections of categories presumed separate often reinforce inequalities but also provide leverage for social change.

Foraging

Few Africans today base their livelihood primarily on gathering and hunting, although foraging contributes valuable nutritional variety to contemporary farmers and herders. Gathering, performed mostly by women, not only provided more reliable nutrition for past societies wholly dependent on them but is critical for the survival of endangered populations today. Wild plants provide scarce vitamins and minerals and mature over a longer part of the year than domesticated crops, reducing the hungry season. Gathering nuts and seeds, fishing, and collecting small animals such as snails or turtles can provide significant protein. When land pressures or climate change reduce access to wild foods, the resulting malnutrition confirms their historical importance in the diet. In times of war, drought, or famine, gathering wild foods remains a critical survival skill; refugees who can identify wild foods survive when others starve. During recent famines in Darfur, Sudan, adults turned to gathering wild berries used as a grain substitute, both for personal consumption and sale in local markets.[3] Many early commodities traded long distances in precolonial Africa came from foraging, including ivory, kola nuts, palm oil, and shea butter. Panning for gold and smoking fish, snails, and game yielded other high-value commodities. Basic tools such as digging sticks developed for gathering are still widely used by farmers, along with containers for carrying, cooking, and storing food made from netting, gourds, or clay.

Farming

Women farmers feature prominently in the long history of African economies and still play leading parts in farming at every level of technology from hand tools to factory farms. Africans domesticated a number of plant species, including indigenous strains of rice, millet, and yams in West Africa and teff, coffee, and beans in Ethiopia. Women's preeminent role in seed selection and preservation for today's local varieties suggests that historically they were pioneers in African agricultural innovations as an extension of their gathering and food preparation responsibilities. Advanced agricultural methods originated in Africa centuries before European contact. Sophisticated irrigation systems in ancient Egypt and Sudan anchored empires all along the Nile Valley that harnessed its annual flood. Sudanese in Upper Nubia (350 BCE–350 CE) tapped ground water to plant three crops per year, inventing an animal-powered water wheel still used today.[4] West African women in coastal Gambia, Casamance, and Liberia managed complex irrigation systems by modifying natural swamps to control water levels and prevent salt buildup.[5]

Most farming systems in precolonial Africa, particularly south of the Sahara, featured shifting cultivation. Farmers cleared new plots of land every year or two, burning the existing vegetation as fertilizer before planting. Each plot then had to lie fallow for as long as twenty years to renew its fertility. These long-fallow farming systems, adjusted to the local ecology, yielded well and were ecologically stable for long periods, until colonial authorities restricted freedom of movement.[6]

African farmers still generally rely on diversification of plants to reduce important risks. Using several different staple crops varies their diet seasonally and reduces the need for crop storage, a major source of post-harvest losses. Staggered harvest seasons for different crops also reduce important labor bottlenecks in weeding, harvesting, and processing, usually performed by women. Rainfall variations that damage one crop may leave another unscathed or even favor it, reducing the likelihood of catastrophic harvest failures due to drought, flood, insects, or disease. Planting multiple crops within the same field (intercropping) also protects fragile tropical soils with a continual variety of vegetation.

African cultures combined gender, age, and marital status in many ingenious patterns to divide the agricultural workload and effectively coordinate the efforts of different family members.[7] One common system still used designates certain crops as men's crops and others as women's crops, often grown in separate fields. For example, Liberian women plant swamp rice in the dry season while Cameroonian women plant cassava in fields not suitable for men's yams or millet. Elsewhere women and men grow different crops in the same field. Ghanaian Konkomba and Nigerian Igbo consider yams a men's crop because they require heavy work building ridges or mounds for planting. Women plant soup vegetables on the sides of the yam mounds, protecting them from erosion and weeding both crops at once. Yams belong to men who build the mounds (or hire it done), while vegetables not consumed in family meals belong to women who weed them.

In grain-growing areas, men and women typically complete different tasks on the same crop. Men clear and plant the fields, while women weed throughout the growing season. Children scare birds away from the ripening grain, a critical task. It must be harvested promptly, creating a peak labor demand. Women and girls do most of the extensive post-harvest processing of grain, including threshing, drying, seed selection, storage, and grinding into flour, along with cooking meals and rationing grain supplies to last until the next harvest. In some complex farming systems women work on their own crops and also on men's crops. In Hausa households in Nigeria and Niger, a single grain species can be grown both on the personal fields of men and women and in joint household fields on which both genders work. Land tenure, crop ownership, and use rights are specific to each type of field.[8] In Cameroon, women grow most of the cassava themselves while also performing gender-specific tasks on men's yam fields.

In some cultures, farming itself is identified with either women or men. In the Cameroonian grassfields, the Nso liken farming and beer brewing to pregnancy and consider them "naturally" female. All three are long, complex processes requiring diligence and knowledge but with uncertain outcomes.[9] The Nigerian Yoruba find it equally "natural" that men farm and women trade.[10] Mursi men of Ethiopia take cattle to distant pastures in the rainy season while women plant crops. Men without farmland have trouble keeping wives and founding households.

African women farmers continually innovate and experiment, rather than repeat blindly what their mothers taught them. In the last few centuries, they have welcomed new crops and adapted processing techniques from other continents, fitting newcomers into their farming systems alongside established crops, while developing new varieties of the old crops. For example, cassava, plantain, and bananas all use a distinctive replanting technique, with the harvester immediately replanting fresh cuttings from the old plant. They also require less weeding than indigenous grains or yams, reducing pressure on women's labor. Predominantly male tasks, especially land clearing, are more often mechanized, while such recent improvements as hybrid seed and fertilizer require increased weeding.

American corn (maize) arrived in the seventeenth century with Portuguese traders and colonists and spread widely in the West African grasslands. Its cultivation was required by British colonial authorities to feed forced labor cheaply, and so it came to dominate grain production in eastern and southern Africa, where it remains the staple food. Maize was more disruptive than cassava to local farming systems because it needs a longer growing season than indigenous millets and sorghums, more precisely timed rains, and more careful weeding. Corn yields vary more sharply from year to year, and the crop exhausts soil more rapidly. Farm women developed and preserved local seed varieties in many places that mitigated these risks and labor demands, selecting for drought and pest resistance and large grain size, which reduces storage losses and eases hand grinding.

Livestock

Pastoralism or herding supports many African communities, although it is less common than farming. Africans raise a wide variety of domesticated livestock, each with particular needs for forage and water and commercial opportunities, which shape their migration patterns. Forested areas and swamps breed tsetse flies that carry a disease lethal to camels and cattle, which require savannah or prairie climates. Dusty or damp conditions give chickens respiratory diseases. In very wet conditions, only pigs and ducks thrive. Camels survive in the harshest desert climates, since they can browse off shrubs and small trees.

Because they only need water every three or four days, they can travel farther for food and survive droughts. Gabra women in northern Kenya consider them a more reliable source of milk than cattle for this reason.[11] However, since camels reproduce quite slowly, they recover slowly from losses due to disease, war, or drought. Goats multiply rapidly under good conditions, with two or three births a year, while sheep bear lambs once a year, with some multiple births.[12] Goats also eat almost any kind of vegetation, need more water than cattle, and more commonly overgraze vegetation. Steers are in steady demand for larger cities and for export. Goats and sheep are more often slaughtered for meat or sold locally to meet cash needs but are rarely milked.

A division of labor by gender and age allows pastoral communities to manage their diverse labor demands. One such system associates men with herding and women with farming, as noted for Mursi people of Ethiopia and the Sotho of southern Africa, whose semi-arid territories straddle the boundary between arable and non-arable land. Young men take cattle off to distant pastures during the rainy season, while women settle seasonally on land suitable for farming small grains such as millet, sorghum, and fonio. Another common division of labor puts women in charge of dairy production, trading milk, yogurt, and other milk products for grain with adjacent farming communities that need the protein. Women keep dairy cows near their customers while young men take other cattle farther away during the dry season.

Women's expertise in the exacting techniques of dairy processing are vital to ensuring the consistent quality of these products on which their communities' health and grain supply depend. Milking itself takes considerable skill in handling and maintaining a cooperative relationship with the animal mother. Without converting milk into less perishable fermented forms or cheeses, much surplus would be wasted. Women must delicately balance various demands for milk, judging how much to retain for calves, how much to give young children, and how much to sell. As custodians of cows and calves, women become expert in the veterinary care of young animals and birthing mothers, as well as supervising children who herd goats and sheep.

The respect and symbolic value given cattle explains their importance to both male and female gender roles. A Wodaabe or Nuer young man took his nickname from that of his beloved steer given him by his father, decorated it, and composed praise songs for it as a symbol of male beauty. A young Nuer bride negotiated the size of her bridewealth, a dairy herd, with her new husband's family, stopping at every stream to demand more cows on the way to his home. These cows and their offspring could not be sold without her permission, fed her children, and insured having bridewealth for future sons.

Bridewealth made her the "cattle-linked sister" to the brother who used them to marry and become a "bull."[13] She could invoke this to claim a home with him in case of widowhood or divorce. When twentieth-century Ngoni men paid bridewealth in cash with their wages from South African mines, they referred to the money as "cattle without legs."[14]

Cattle herders depend on a complex network of overlapping rights in cattle and land to help them overcome the challenges of erratic rainfall and livestock epidemics. Rather than owning permanent pastures, they need access to different locations during the rainy and dry seasons and to transit routes with watering stations between them. Loans and gifts of cattle cement relations between friends and kin, linking each family to a broad network of relationships that share information on where rain has fallen and spread the risk of loss from raiders, drought, or disease outbreaks in any one herd.

Fisheries

Fishing, an ancient way of life for Africans since the Sahara Desert was a lake, continues as an important source of income for shore dwellers. Like pastoralism, it has become a specialty of certain ethnic groups, in addition to being a supplemental practice for foragers or within farming communities. Women are particularly active in shallow-water fishing with nets and traps and in collecting shellfish.[15] One interesting example of women initiating technical advances in a river fishery comes from the Volta River estuary in Ghana. Ada women harvested many clams from this area to sell fresh or smoked in nearby towns. However, the Volta Dam, built to generate electricity in the 1960s, dramatically changed the flow pattern of the river, sweeping newly hatched clams out to sea before they could attach themselves to the riverbed. Noting the shrinking yield of adult clams, local women developed successful methods for restoring clam beds, gathering baby clams from the main channels and reseeding them by hand.

In fishing communities the gender division of labor commonly leaves canoe and other artisanal fishing to men. Women sell fresh fish to neighboring communities and process considerable quantities of fish locally through drying, smoking, and fermentation. They then market these more durable fish products far inland through indigenous marketing networks, also predominantly staffed by women traders. Near Accra, Ghana, women have developed better fish smokers successfully promulgated through appropriate technology projects. Prosperous women traders or smokers might invest in small boats and nets. Much of the small-boat catch from the East African Great Lakes moves on ice to urban consumers as far away as Nairobi.

Women Undermined

Changes in all these productive activities during colonial rule and after independence sidelined women's property rights and locally processed products, such as edible oils, soap, preserved fish, and dried vegetables, which provided them with important income. A large proportion of the financial investment, legal protection, and policy support provided by governments and international assistance goes to industrial export production. Factories rarely employ significant numbers of women as entrepreneurs or skilled workers, while governments divert natural resources and funds away from sectors where women historically exercised more control.

Ocean fishing has now become highly industrialized. African businessmen operate fleets of large motorized vessels, landing catches in the large modern ports with cold-storage facilities along African coastlines. These fish are then sold fresh or frozen through the national formal sector. Multinational corporate-owned factory ships use male wage laborers, who cannot pass on a share of the catch to their female relatives for processing. In Ghana and elsewhere along the Atlantic coast, consumer preference for smoked fish diverts part of these larger catches to fish smokers who buy from the cold stores. These large cannery ships operating offshore, sometimes illegally close to the East and West African coasts, significantly reduce the catch available for local fishermen using canoes and small motor boats, hence to local female-dominated processing and marketing chains, and contribute substantially to overfishing the oceans. The large ships are designed to bypass national ports, and their catch is exported directly to the global market in cans or frozen packaging. A few local men get jobs on these floating factories, but women do not.

Pastoralist women faced especially drastic exclusion when colonial authorities generally oversimplified complex overlapping rights to cattle. Loans, bridewealth, and cattle designated for specific wives were ignored by British officials in Kenya, for instance. When setting up cattle dips to prevent disease, they registered cattle to the person bringing them in, usually a young man. Official cattle markets established at the same locations could more easily buy beef cattle if they only recognized individual ownership. Market authorities attributed Maasai reluctance to sell at these markets to a primitivist reverence for cattle or ignorance of the idea of commerce. Meanwhile, officials in more remote northern districts were complaining that "their" Maasai only too readily sold cattle to itinerant Somali traders frequenting their seasonal camps.[16]

Development projects aimed at helping pastoralists also often disregard women's rights and income linked to dairy production. In dry grassland areas

such as inland Kenya, the British promoted new breeds for increased beef production, not milk. Dairying projects featured stall-fed cows in agricultural
communities where grass could be cut and carried, usually by women and children. Such labor-intensive care yields more milk, but that is sold to industrial
dairies, not processed for local consumption. Goats, sheep, and other smaller
animals more often kept by women generally receive proportionately less aid
and other support than cattle raising.[17]

Fierce competition for land between farmers and herders often arises when
land scarcity pushes farming communities farther onto marginal lands, while
drought simultaneously pushes herders into farming districts to find pasture
and water. Fighting breaks out sporadically in northern Cameroon and northern Ghana between Fulbe herders and neighboring farmers, especially when
animals destroy crops or farmers bar herds from local water sources. During
long droughts, herds' survival depends on access to river valleys or swampy
areas not usually considered pasture. These are the most likely sites for irrigation projects and other permanent improvements, which would be destroyed
by such occasional use.

Most African women farm, meaning that their main concerns are access
to land and control of the crops they raise. With shifting cultivation, factors
that restrict farmers' rotation capacity can lead rapidly to falling yields and soil
erosion. Large tracts of land were taken out of the land pool for white settlers'
commercial plantations in Algeria, eastern Africa, and southern Africa. Africans were forced onto the remaining land and had to keep planting the same
small fields. Many governments still outlaw field burning in favor of modern
methods of permanent land use that require expensive fertilizers. The threat
of arrest induces farmers to burn during the dry season, when they can plausi-
bly blame wildfires, rather than to burn more efficiently and safely after the
first rains, just before planting.

West, East, and Central African colonial policies pressured Africans to grow
export crops on their own land, while in Algeria, eastern Africa, and southern
Africa officials openly appropriated farmland for European settlers. In South
Africa only 13 percent of the land was left for "natives" (who comprised 87
percent of the population), while British officials in Zimbabwe, Kenya, and
Zambia reserved the most fertile land for their smaller settler populations. Mass
evictions drastically disrupted the cultural and economic continuity of affected
African communities and made self-sufficient farming virtually impossible.

Where lineages or communities manage land allocation, leaders often
believe women need less land or give the more desirable plots (more fertile
or closer to roads) to men, who are believed more capable of taking advantage

of them. The matrilineal Asante have some women cocoa farmers, but they are fewer in number and have smaller farms than men.[18] Without wives or daughters-in law to provide free labor, Asante women may have only adolescent boys and girls at their command, reducing the acreage they can cultivate. In patrilineal societies, women may lose the right to use lineage land at marriage or lose marital land access with divorce or widowhood.

Programs that register land titles to individuals rarely institutionalize women's use rights, even where men historically also had only use rights. In mountainous districts around Mount Meru, Mount Kilimanjaro, and elsewhere, plots at different altitudes provided microclimates suited to different crops. Land tenure reform consolidated individual land rights into a single large plot, eliminating this strategy.[19] In Zambia's Gwembe Valley, otherwise patrilineal Tonga women passed valuable floodplain plots from mother to daughter, while men herded cattle on higher land. A colonial dam on this river completely submerged women's lands; their informal land rights merited no compensation. Men were allocated grazing land elsewhere in the country, though of inferior quality.[20]

Reinterpretations of "African tradition" frequently deny women land rights even when these existed within living memory. Near Arusha in Tanzania, elderly women reported that both men and women had been entitled to own land. Women had owned about 30 percent of plots, but local men insisted their tradition said women could not own land.[21] In Gambia, women managed irrigated rice fields unchallenged before a development project improved them and allocated the improved plots to men. Once this happened, men claimed within a few decades that solely male ownership was "our tradition."[22]

Even where enough land is available, labor migration can seriously disrupt farming. Demand for cash to pay taxes and the disruption and displacement of nonfarming activities based in the countryside increase the pressure for seasonal or longer-term migration. Young men, the most likely to migrate during the dry season, would otherwise be preparing new land in advance of the seasonal rains. Without them, those family members left in the village may be forced to reuse plots that are easier to clear. Women's time constraints for weeding then frequently limit the acreage under cultivation.

Female-headed households and those with absent male heads manage farming differently than older types of joint households. Parts of southern Africa with high male migration can see up to 63 percent de facto female-headed households, including not only divorced, widowed, or never married women, but also those whose husbands have lost contact or stopped providing assistance.[23] Female farm managers take full responsibility for decision making about farm production, performing both male and female tasks. Since land is commonly registered to a sole male owner, a woman farmer can have difficulty accessing credit, markets, or extension advice.

African women farmers grapple with gender discrimination compounded by their structural position within agriculture. Research, training, and credit often neglect food crops, women's crops, and smaller farms. Scientists select varieties for qualities demanded by the world market, not those suited to local conditions and consumers. Most women grow local foodstuffs, while government and donor agriculture programs promote export crops grown on a larger scale by "modern" male farmers who monocrop. In Zimbabwe before independence, official price supports targeted hybrid maize and so only benefited expatriate landowners who could afford to purchase imported seeds plus fertilizer and insecticide these plants required. When price supports were extended after independence to small farmers of millet and sorghum, African women's response outstripped government storage capacity. Rather than expanding a successful program, they scrapped it.[24]

By combining export crops with food crops for local consumption or sale, African farmers offset significant risks tied to export crops. Government credit for seed, fertilizers, and pesticides may arrive at the wrong time, locking farmers into a cycle of debt.[25] Volatile world prices for commodities such as coffee and corn bring boom or bust cycles based on global demand or global yields, with little reference to local conditions or investments. Permanent commitment to world market production is hard to reverse once land has been planted with long maturation tree crops such as cocoa, tea, and coffee.

Contract farming also locks farmers into multiple years of monocropping through long-term commitment to a single corporate buyer of, for example, sugar cane or pineapples. Recruitment criteria often designate a male landowner whose wife and immediate family furnish unpaid labor. The contract specifies not only crop choice but planting techniques, timing of applications of insecticide and fertilizer, and even the number of weedings. All risk of crop or market failure rests with the farm family, since inputs are extended on credit and deducted from sales proceeds regardless of yield.[26] Corporate buyers also can easily manipulate quality standards when global demand fails to meet their expectations. For example, when BUD Senegal could not sell all the green beans for which it had contracted from Senegalese farmers, it rejected a higher proportion of beans, forcing the dumping of the rest on local markets.[27]

Few African rural communities survive on farming alone. Wage labor, craft production, trading, and other nonfarm activities by both men and women provide income needed to stabilize the rural population. North Africa, with its long Mediterranean coastline, developed centuries-old rural crafts such as women's rug weaving and men's sword making that brought wealth and reputation. Where the crop-growing season is short, as in the dry Sahel bordering the Sahara, nonfarming activities were part of an older annual cycle. Today they have grown in importance under pressure of drought and desertification.[28]

Trade

Production for sale long predates European colonization of Africa. Trade crossed the Sahara to the Mediterranean and also came up the Nile from pharaonic times. Yemeni traders colonized the eastern coast, settling on nearby islands as they crossed the Indian Ocean. On Zanzibar they established plantations with enslaved labor to supply spices such as cloves to a consumer market extending to China and northern Europe. A unique Swahili culture arose from this meeting of Arab and African peoples, dominating the coast and spreading far inland along caravan routes stretching to the African Great Lakes region and probably to Great Zimbabwe.

During the early caravan trade chroniclers rarely reported women traders undertaking long journeys by water or by land. They also constituted a minority of porters in forested areas, either as free or enslaved labor. Instead, women participated by supplying the local goods caravans needed, including the major export commodities of palm oil, salt, gold, and kola. They made and sold baskets, leather goods, and pottery used for transport, and they also intensified production of foodstuffs and cooked food for sale to the caravans.

Rural trade in foodstuffs between neighboring ecological zones, by contrast, is often associated with women. Pastoralist women exchanged dairy produce for grain, and fishing communities relied on local women traders to bring essential inland farm produce in return for smoked fish. While covering short distances compared to the caravans, coastal women walked for days circulating between village markets.[29] Local markets were widespread across the African continent, usually sponsored, protected, and taxed by local chiefs or other indigenous authorities.

Where African societies had strong central governance, the control and regulation of long-distance trade often anchored them economically and politically. Ancient kingdoms managed trade and exchange fundamental to their wealth up and down the Nile. In West Africa, a series of Sahelian empires arose based economically on their control of trade routes through present-day Mali, Niger, and Chad. Less centralized coastal societies also hosted important trading networks, with wealthy merchants negotiating on fairly equal terms with European ship captains in the sixteenth through late nineteenth centuries.

Descriptions of these leading merchants include women as well as men. The seventeenth and eighteenth centuries saw the peak of the Atlantic slave trade, which drained vital labor from remote rural communities with more land than labor. Women's role in farming and reproduction made enslaved women more valuable to African communities as subordinated workers and wives, in contrast to the transatlantic demand for men (see chapter 9). Wealthy magnates in Nigerian Igbo trading towns also expanded their households and labor forces through purchase.[30]

At first, coastal West African towns had relatively small nonfarming populations to feed including European traders and residents, wealthy African traders and officials, and Africans employed as storekeepers, porters, and crewmen. Such occupations were almost exclusively male, while African women traders already dominated most food supply networks. Reprovisioning European ships provided another important market for foodstuffs. West African women supplied specialized items that remained edible on long sea voyages, such as hard tack and salted meat or fish. Ships also stopped for fresh supplies at Africa's southern tip on the way to the East Indies. The sparse indigenous population offered little agricultural surplus, but Dutch settlers enslaved local Africans of both genders as farm laborers in the Cape Colony they established in the 1600s.

European colonial rulers increasingly sought to control African territory from the 1700s through the 1900s, disrupting active control of trading by local rulers and elites and favoring local branches of European firms. European firms moved away from dealing with independent African merchants, hired fewer Africans as storekeepers and agents, and brought in more European employees. Such practices discouraged the continued participation of ambitious West African men, some of whom had tried ordering shipments directly from European factories. Retail trading in imports such as cloth became closely associated there with women through the passbook system, which tied women wholesalers to a single expatriate firm.[31] In East Africa, the British disrupted Swahili and Somali trade with the interior and forbade Africans from keeping retail shops, licensing only immigrants from India. Mercantile colonialism forbade trade across new artificial colonial borders, labeling even established routes as illegal smuggling so their participants risked arrest.

Urban centers and their nonfarming populations (both African and European) grew rapidly in the twentieth century, so African women's urban food supply function grew proportionately in scale and complexity. In Kumasi, Ghana, the city's daily market had been relatively small before conquest because many residents lived in chiefly households with farming estates. The ring of weekly markets in nearby villages still operates today, but weekly bulking markets on main roads through the surrounding regions supplied much more farm produce from the 1930s on. Networks of long-distance traders and Kumasi wholesalers developed that shifted seasonally to draw supplies from every corner of Ghana. The trading network supplying Ibadan, Nigeria, saw successive geographical expansions that added new ethnic intermediaries.[32] In Kenya, African women fed growing Nairobi by expanding their trade in beans, grains, and vegetables, with the tacit consent of British authorities, who exempted them from carrying passes controlling men's movements.[33]

Regional variations in configurations of trade in food and consumer goods reflected the degree of colonial disruption of preexisting trade networks. Without white settlers, West African trade networks survived colonial conquest in the hands of women traders, who responded with enthusiasm to the expansion of urban commerce and dominated wholesaling of food and consumer goods. Meanwhile, Asante men moved out of market trading into more lucrative opportunities growing cocoa and other export crops.[34] Women gari (cassava flour) traders in Ibadan also accumulated substantial financial and social capital.[35]

Wholesale trade in food and consumer goods remained in men's hands in southern and eastern Africa. Unlike in West Africa, Nairobi women traders did not pass businesses on to daughters, so they did not develop skills and capital; wholesalers were, and are, primarily African men.[36] In southern Africa, women's presence in the cities remained largely illegal until majority rule; elaborate distribution networks were too conspicuous. Whites deliberately dispossessed Africans of lands judged to have commercial agricultural potential.[37] Numerous female food retailers serving the African population in Harare, Zimbabwe, bought their supplies from a small set of European or Lebanese wholesalers.[38] The enforced exclusion of black South Africans from all-white urban centers left them with relatively little commercial experience or property to draw upon when legal barriers were lifted after majority rule.

The Official Economy, or "Formal Sector"

Private and public wage employment in most African countries remains deeply marked by its foundations in colonial rule, when pervasive protection and promotion of expatriate-led enterprises blurred the distinction between private and public sectors. Local colonial officials and chiefs proved their competence by fulfilling quotas for recruiting forced laborers, military draftees, and wage workers for mines or other European-sponsored sectors. Economic opportunities in areas designated as labor reserves were deliberately stifled, while head taxes enforced by jail and flogging pressed young men to earn cash to protect their family elders as well as themselves. Cocoa, coffee, sugar, and other export crops were marketed through monopolistic European firms or government marketing boards, not local marketplaces. In French West Africa taxes could only be paid in cotton or groundnuts, because revenues from these exports funded the colonial state. North Africa, particularly Egypt, had a more developed corporate sector than most of sub-Saharan Africa, but the vast majority of its craft exports, food, and consumer goods still come from small workshops and outdoor marketplaces.

Expatriate settlers or companies enjoyed the cheap labor of landless African men and women on their plantations and in rural light industry. Massive official intervention created and enforced poor working conditions for female coffee pickers in Kenya or domestic workers in South Africa. Piece rates, irregular seasonal schedules, and arbitrary discipline contrasted sharply with the more formal wage labor contracts given to male miners or railwaymen. After independence, many national governments relied on revenues from the same corporate multinational industries. Socialist regimes in Ghana, Mozambique, and Tanzania took over these large-scale, export-oriented enterprises as state farms or factories.[39] In new export industries, such as floriculture in Kenya and Ethiopia, multinational enterprises enjoy subsidized infrastructure and tax breaks that bolster their relative advantage over smaller local enterprises.[40]

White-collar work expanded rapidly for educated African men in the civil service, teaching, and health professions shortly before independence. Educational opportunities for African women were relatively few and largely inappropriate to either these newly Africanized occupations or to women in farming, trading, and domestic service. Some educated women managed to commercialize lessons intended to prepare them for housewifery and domestic service, becoming caterers, bakers, hoteliers, dressmakers, and knitters. Gender discrimination and sexual harassment in the formal workplace, also prevalent in the Western world, further discouraged many educated African women from attempting white-collar careers. They filtered only gradually into occupations considered appropriate for European women, such as teaching, nursing, and clerical work (see chapter 10). In the 1980s, when structural adjustment programs mandated drastic cutbacks in public employment and shrank local industry, African women employees had less seniority than men and suffered disproportionate layoffs.

The Unofficial Economy, or "Informal" Sector

The association of the corporate and public sectors of Africa's official economies with men injects strong gendered content into the material and ideological conflicts between them and the much larger unofficial economy. The explosive growth of unofficial sectors of the economy belies government claims that only the formal sector has the potential to expand and diversify to meet the needs of future generations. Overflowing open-air markets, street traders, and roadside workshops display the extent to which governments, whether neoliberal or socialist, fail to govern economic life. Yet they cannot acknowledge their dependence upon the so-called informal sector to meet the subsistence needs of their populations and satisfy growing consumer aspirations. The vitality and ingenuity of small-scale traders and producers keep the hope of survival alive, but only because of their poverty.

As employers, colonial and independent governments wanted to keep African wages low, while their legitimacy depended on delivering a rising standard of living. The British Gold Coast authorities attempted food price controls during World Wars I and II, when shortages fueled demands for increased wages and raised the cost of feeding local military personnel and jail inmates. The British blamed market women, while nationalist activists blamed collusion and abusive practices of expatriate firms. Political support from market women helped achieve independence for Ghana, but their elected leaders promptly turned to scapegoating them the same way.

The vast majority of Africans seek income and consumer goods outside the official economy, which cannot deliver the reliable livelihoods it promises. During economic and political crises, rigid systems of official production and distribution easily break down, leaving the informal sector the better organized side of economic life. Even formal sector employees regularly supplement their incomes with unofficial side enterprises. Lower-level wage workers do so to make ends meet, while higher-level functionaries take advantage of their positions to accumulate wealth from illicit contracts or diverted goods. From the 1990s on, many young men leaving school entered trading because prospects of obtaining salaried or even blue-collar jobs seemed remote.

Gendering this work female makes its low incomes and profit margins more tolerable, while also veiling its economic importance. Formal sector workers felt their incomes should remain substantially higher than those of market traders by virtue of their education and gender, but inflation rapidly dissolved their real wages after 1970. The denunciation of successful traders as "greedy women" was amplified by its resonance with complaints about wives who made "unreasonable" demands for child support or, even worse, wives who now earned more than their husbands.

Tensions over control of women's labor and sexuality in the family easily inflame efforts to control unofficial economic domains coded female. Hostility and repression particularly target "those women" in a highly moralistic discourse. Street clearance campaigns in the name of civic beautification or private property often turn violent. In 1970s and 1980s Ghana, women market traders faced extralegal price control raids, floggings, evictions, and confiscations—a few were even shot by soldiers. Meanwhile, men working as carpenters, shoemakers, or roadside fitters negotiated for approved price levels and relocation. Raids that cleared the streets of Harare, Zimbabwe, before international conferences or state visits throughout the 1980s swept up women without formal marriage certificates and deported them to rural areas, while repeated police attacks on Nairobi hawkers in the 1980s and 1990s continued colonial forms of oppression.[41]

Conclusion

African women today work within economies with many interwoven layers. Ancient patterns of trade and production persist, but only because people transformed them drastically in response to subsequent conditions. Ancient farming practices are viable today precisely because contemporary strategies of warfare and development reinforce their usefulness. Rural communities now have been impoverished and destabilized by resource constraints and competition from imports that undermine both farming and nonfarming activities. Globalization reaches into remote villages through emigration, taxation, and violence, while health and education services remain inaccessible.

However, women have not remained passive in the face of harmful changes. They have taken active roles in protecting farmlands from climate change and pollution. In Kenya, Dr. Wangari Maathai organized the Green Belt Movement to combat soil erosion through reforestation campaigns. It also targets government complicity in clear-cutting forests and allocating marginal lands to displaced farmers while selling large tracts to officials and wealthy patrons. Dr. Maathai was beaten by government thugs, ran for president, and received the Nobel Peace Prize.[42] In southern Algeria, rural women and children led by teacher Fatiha Touni demonstrated in 2015 against water pollution caused by Halliburton's fracking, despite tear gas and beatings from the police and army.[43] Igbo women in Nigeria repeatedly occupied corporate oil facilities, protesting against the lack of local hiring and land and water pollution (see chapters 4, 6, and 7).[44]

Urbanization has multiplied needs for food, housing, and safety, creating new opportunities and pressures in gaping spaces left by a precarious and irresponsible formal sector combined with the privatization of public services and assets. High-value real estate in central urban commercial districts is coveted by developers for office and retail complexes, leading to violent clashes with market or street traders. Meanwhile, flexible employment practices in the multinational corporate economy spread across rich and poor countries, tarnishing the formal sector's reputation for order and stability. Legal protections hard won by workers in wealthy countries no longer apply to most of them, and still fewer apply to illegal immigrants in their neighborhoods or to workers in developing countries, especially women in the informal sector.

The distinction between formal and informal sectors has been reified in a way that reinscribes gender, racial, and ethnic stratification of access to economic resources. The ideology of "modernization and development" assumes that the corporate sector has more potential for growth, and hence deserves the bulk of national budgets and donor assistance, while women and poor, racialized, or ethnicized people fall into the "backward" informal sector, which justifies diverting resources from those historically subordinated and excluded. Lower assessment of the needs and entitlements of those who work in the informal sector veils its continuing subsidy of the corporate sector. Their poverty is attributed to their reluctance to abandon cultural values incompatible with economic rationality, masking the history of dispossession and appropriation of resources once available to them. Perversely, neoliberal policies romanticize the informal sector, assuming its infinite absorptive capacity can meet any need disavowed by the corporate or public sectors with no additional capital or policy support. This fiction of its autonomy distorts both its actual continuities and its frenetic innovations.

The intricate web of economic linkages and interdependencies unfortunately has not resulted in a harmonious global community with a strong commitment to mutual support. Multiple principles of inequality thrive and generate increasing polarization at every level. Yet these same complex interconnections also provide the leverage with which African women contest their economic subordination, openly or tacitly. Constantly weaving together old and new skills and resources, some women succeed in overcoming barriers and achieve wealth, education, or political power, although often unrecognized or unremembered. For most, their achievements lie in sustaining their families or communities despite daunting threats. When the dominant economic model devalues or ignores their contributions and disavows any responsibility for their well-being, survival qualifies as a personal victory.

Notes

1. Jane Guyer, *Marginal Gains: Monetary Transactions in Atlantic Africa* (Chicago: University of Chicago Press, 2004).

2. For further discussion see my introduction to *Gender at Work in Economic Life*, ed. Gracia Clark (Walnut Creek, CA: Altamira Press, 2003), ix–xvii.

3. Alex de Waal, *Famine That Kills: Darfur, Sudan* (Oxford: Oxford University Press, 1995).

4. Debra L. Martin, George J. Armelagos, and Kay A. Henderson, "The Persistence of Nutritional Stress in Northeastern African (Sudanese Nubian) Populations," in *African Food Systems in Crisis: Part One: Microperspectives*, ed. Rebecca Huss-Ashmore and Solomon Katz (Langhorn, PA: Gordon and Breach 1989), 163–88.

5. Jennie Dey, *Irrigated Rice-Farming Systems* (Rome: Food and Agriculture Organization, 1985).

6. Audrey Richards, *Land, Labour and Diet in Northern Rhodesia* (Oxford: Oxford University Press, 1940); Melissa Leach, *Rainforest Relations: Gender and Resource Use among the Mende of Gola, Sierra Leone* (Edinburgh: Edinburgh University Press, 1994); Henrietta Moore and Megan Vaughn, *Cutting Down Trees: Gender, Nutrition and Agricultural Change in the Northern Province of Zambia* (Portsmouth, NH: Heinemann, 1994).

7. Jane Guyer, "Female Farming in Anthropology and African History," in *Gender at the Crossroads of Knowledge: Feminist Anthropology in the Postmodern Era*, ed. Michaela Di Leonardo (Berkeley: University of California Press, 1991), 257–77.

8. Polly Hill, *Rural Hausa* (Cambridge: Cambridge University Press, 1972).

9. Miriam Goheen, *Men Own the Fields, Women Own the Crops: Gender and Power in the Cameroon Grassfields* (Madison: University of Wisconsin Press, 1996).

10. Niara Sudarkasa, *Where Women Work: A Study of Yoruba Women in the Marketplace and in the Home* (Ann Arbor: University of Michigan Press, 1973).

11. Asmarom Legesse, "Adaptation, Drought, and Development: Boran and Gabra Pastoralists of Northern Kenya," in Huss-Ashmore and Katz, *African Food Systems*, 261–80.

12. Constance M. McCorkle, Michael F. Nolan, Keith Jamtgaard, and Jere L. Gilles, "Social Research in International Agricultural R&D: Lessons from the Small Ruminant CRSP," *Agriculture and Human Values* 6, no. 3 (1989): 42–51.

13. E. E. Evans-Pritchard, *The Nuer* (Oxford: Clarendon Press, 1947).

14. John and Jean Comaroff, "Goodly Beasts, Beastly Goods: Cattle and Commodities in a South African Context," *American Ethnologist* 17 (1990): 195–216.

15. Peter Randall, *Women in Fish Production* (Accra, Ghana: FAO Regional Office for Africa, 1984).

16. Dorothy Hodgson, *Once Intrepid Warriors: Gender, Ethnicity and the Cultural Politics of Maasai Development* (Bloomington: Indiana University Press, 2001).

17. McCorkle et al., *Small Ruminant CRSP*.

18. Christine Okali, *Cocoa and Kinship in Ghana: The Matrilineal Akan of Ghana* (London: Kegan Paul, 1983); Gwendolyn Mikell, *Cocoa and Chaos in Ghana* (New York: Paragon, 1989).

19. Anne Fleuret, "Indigenous Taita Responses to Drought," in Huss-Ashmore and Katz, *African Food Systems*, 221–38.

20. Lisa Cliggett, *Grains from Grass: Aging, Gender and Famine in Rural Africa* (Ithaca, NY: Cornell University Press, 2005).

21. Els Upperman, "Gender Relations in a Traditional Irrigation Scheme in Northern Tanzania," in *Gender, Family and Work in Tanzania*, ed. Colin Creighton and C. K. Omari (Burlington, VT: Ashgate. 2000), 357–79.

22. Judith Carney, "Struggles over Land and Crops in an Irrigated Rice Scheme." in *Agriculture, Women and Land: The African Experience*, ed. Jean Davison (Boulder, CO: Westview Press, 1988), 59–78.

23. Jennie Dey, *Women in Rice Farming Systems* (Rome: Food and Agriculture Organization, 1984); Constantina Safilios-Rothschild, *Women in Sheep and Goat Production in the Third World* (Rome: FAO Expert Consultation on Women in Food Production, December 1983).

24. Safilios-Rothschild, *Women*.

25. John I. Curry, "Occupation and Drought Vulnerability," in Huss-Ashmore and Katz, *African Food Systems*, 239–60.

26. Peter D. Little and Michael J. Watts, eds., *Living under Contract: Contract Farming and Agrarian Transformation in Sub-Saharan Africa* (Madison: University of Wisconsin Press, 1994).

27. Maureen Macintosh, *Gender, Class and Rural Transition: Agribusiness and the Food Crisis in Senegal* (London: Zed, 1989).

28. Curry, "Occupation"; A. de Waal, *Famine*.

29. Pieter De Marees, *Chronicle of the Gold Coast of Guinea* (1602), trans. A. Van Dantzig and Adam Smith (Oxford: Oxford University Press, 1985).

30. De Marees, *Chronicle*; Felicia Ekejiuba, "Omo Okwei, the Merchant Queen of Ossomari," *Journal of the Historical Society of Nigeria* 3, no. 4 (1967): 633–46.

31. Margaret Priestley, *West African Trade and Coastal Society: Family Study* (Oxford: Oxford University Press, 1969).

32. Jane Guyer, "Feeding Yaounde: Capital of Cameroon," in *Feeding African Cities: Studies in Regional Social History*, ed. Jane Guyer (Manchester: Manchester University Press, 1987), 112–54.

33. Claire C. Robertson, *Trouble Showed the Way: Women, Men, and Trade in the Nairobi Area, 1890–1990* (Bloomington: Indiana University Press, 1997).

34. Gracia Clark, *Onions Are My Husband: Survival and Accumulation by West African Market Women* (Chicago: University of Chicago Press, 1994).

35. Mimi Wan, "Secrets of Success: Uncertainty, Profits and Prosperity in the 'Gari' Economy of Ibadan, 1992–1994," *Africa* 7, no. 1 (2001): 225–52.

36. Robertson, *Trouble*.

37. Maud Shimwaayi Muntemba, "Women and Agricultural Change in the Railway Region of Zambia," in *Women and Work in Africa*, ed. Edna Bay (Boulder, CO: Westview Press, 1983), 83–103.

38. Nancy E. Horn, "Women's Fresh Produce Marketing in Harare, Zimbabwe: Motivations for Women's Participation and Implications for Development," in *African Market Women and Economic Power: The Role of Women in African Economic Development*, ed. Felix K. Ekechi and Bessie House-Midamba (Westport, CT: Greenwood Press, 1995), 141–55; Mary Johnson Osirim, *Enterprising Women in Urban Zimbabwe: Gender, Microbusiness, and Globalization* (Bloomington: Indiana University Press, 2009).

39. Aili Tripp, *Changing the Rules: The Politics of Liberalization and the Urban Informal Economy in Tanzania* (Berkeley: University of California Press, 1997); Kathleen Sheldon,

"Sewing Clothes and Sorting Cashews: Factories, Families and Women in Beira, Mozambique," *Women's Studies International Forum* 14 (1991): 27–35.

40. Tizita Abate Beyene, "Socio-economic Opportunities and Implications of Cut Flower Industries in Ethiopia: The Case of Flower Farms in the Rift Valley and Sebeta" (master's thesis, Norwegian University of Life Sciences, Ås, Norway, 2014).

41. Robertson, *Trouble*; Ilda Lindell, "Introduction: The Changing Politics of Informality—Collective Organizing, Alliances and Scales of Engagement," in *Africa's Informal Workers: Collective Agency, Alliances and Transnational Organizing in Urban Africa*, ed. Ilda Lindell (London: Zed Books, 2010), 1–32.

42. Wangari Maathai, *The Green Belt Movement: Sharing the Approach and the Experience*, rev. ed. (New York: Lantern Press, 2006).

43. Borzou Daragahi, "Environmental Movement Blocks Fracking in Algeria's Remote South," *Financial Times*, March 9, 2015, https://www.ft.com/content/db622d4c-c0f6-11e4-88ca-00144feab7de.

44. Amnesty International, *Nigeria: Repression of Women's Protests in Oil-Producing Delta Region* (London: Amnesty International, 2003).

Suggested Readings

Chalfin, Brenda. *Shea Butter Republic: State Power, Global Markets, and the Making of an Indigenous Commodity*. New York: Routledge, 2004.

Early, Evelyn. *Baladi Women of Cairo: Playing with an Egg and a Stone*. Boulder, CO: Lynne Rienner, 1993.

Leach, Melissa. *Rainforest Relations: Gender and Resource Use among the Mende of Gola, Sierra Leone*. Edinburgh: Edinburgh University Press, 1994.

Moore, Henrietta L., and Megan Vaughan. *Cutting Down Trees: Gender, Nutrition, and Agricultural Change in the Northern Province of Zambia, 1880–1990*. New York: Heinemann, 1994.

Schmidt, Elizabeth. *Peasants, Traders, and Wives: Shona Women in the History of Zimbabwe, 1870–1939*. New York: Heinemann, 1993.

Figure 9.1. An evolution of women in mini-sculptures? Photo by Edward Robertson.

9

WOMEN AND SLAVERY

Changes and Continuities

Claire Robertson

I n precolonial Africa, more women were kept as slaves than men, the implications of which scholars have explored for some thirty years.[1] I summar-
ize explanations for this phenomenon by analyzing the importance of women,
free and enslaved, while contrasting the gendered implications of different
systems. In contemporary gendered analyses, scholars usually consider how
oppressions deriving from different sources intersect to intensify their impact.
Thus, in the United States, Britain, or France, which practiced white settler
colonialism and racialized chattel slavery, the enslaved were usually of African descent and enslaved women experienced multiple oppressions related to
their gender, class, race, age, and sometimes ethnicity (some slave owners dis-
criminated against or preferred certain slaves based on ethnic stereotypes). In
sixteenth- or seventeenth-century Africa, white settlers in some areas (South
Africa, Angola, Mozambique), racialized chattel slavery, but in most of Africa
it was class status, ethnicity, language, or nationality that differentiated slaves
from their owners. For African societies practicing slavery (most did not), the
goal was to assimilate the slaves ultimately into their owners' societies with
high variations in degrees of assimilation, with women and girls seen as most
assimilable.

This chapter examines precolonial African lineage or assimilative versus
chattel slavery; gradations of servitude for women; the work of bondwomen;
the impact of the transatlantic slave trade on African slavery; degrees of slave
assimilation in various societies; the rights of enslaved women, especially
regarding property ownership; and the roles of free and enslaved women as
slave owners. Colonialism's impact on women's slavery is considered along with
women's difficulties seeking emancipation. Lastly, I consider how colonialism
and multinational corporations fostered Africa's disadvantaged position in the

world capitalist economy and weakened the position of women to help create new forms of slavery.

Chattel versus Assimilative Slavery

Studying women and slavery in Africa has undermined many inaccurate stereotypes about slavery and women. Until the 1980s the scholarly literature about slavery was dominated by assumptions that chattel plantation slavery in the United States and the Caribbean, enforced by whites, was typical and defined slavery as a whole.[2] Such stereotypes have been overturned by many African historians, including those who established that sex ratios predominating in the Atlantic slave trade, in which normally two-thirds of those exported from Africa were male, were determined primarily by socioeconomic conditions in Africa, where demand was higher for female slaves. Although European traders preferred purchasing male slaves because of assumptions about men's higher capacity for agricultural labor, the sex ratio among the slaves exported depended mainly on that among those supplied by certain African states and traders. There were several substantial export slave trades affecting Africa, each with differing sex ratios for the enslaved, with more women exported than men across the Sahara, to the Middle East and possibly into the Mediterranean and Indian Ocean trades, while more men were exported in the transatlantic trade.[3]

Slavery is better understood as a continuum of statuses rather than one condition, abandoning the dominance of chattel slavery as definitional of all slavery.[4] Chattel slaves have no property rights but are property themselves, have no personhood before the law, and have been removed from natal kin relations. Notwithstanding, studies of chattel slavery have for some time questioned aspects of this definition, given evidence of chattel slaves reconstituting kin relationships fictively or biologically and securing limited property rights, for instance. Among Africa's highly varied precolonial economic structures were a few where chattel slavery was practiced: the Sahel (rarely), on Arab-owned Zanzibar clove plantations, and southern Nigerian nineteenth-century European-owned palm oil plantations, instigated by industrializing Europe's heightened demand for lubricants, as well as in early areas of colonial southern Africa white settlement mentioned above.

However, more slavery systems can be termed lineage, or assimilative, in Africa. Less onerous forms of lineage or assimilative slavery reflected a general goal of increasing numbers of free members of a society through biological reproduction and assimilation of members acquired first by enslavement, unlike chattel systems aimed at creating a permanent underclass supplying cheap labor. The common practice of lineage or assimilative slavery is key to the high valuation of women slaves in much of Africa since they also had value for expanding numbers of lineage members, especially in situations of low population exacerbated by the Atlantic slave trade and within patrilineal systems, where assimilation as junior wives or concubines was easier than in matrilineal ones. Moreover, women were more vulnerable to enslavement than men because of liabilities within socioeconomic structures. Lastly, colonial emancipation favored men since women were more likely to have been assimilated within lineages, their slave status masked as relatives.[5]

The continuum of disadvantaged statuses within African societies included at the less oppressive end pawnship, whereby junior members of debtor lineages, usually female, were lent to a creditor's household, their labor securing the loan by paying the interest. With loan repayment they were supposed to return to their lineages, but in practice they often married their creditor or a member of his or her lineage. Forgiveness of the debt served as the customary bridewealth payment to her lineage. Also at the less oppressive end of the continuum were (usually male) clients who technically were unfree before customary law but who had complete freedom of movement to marry and own property (even slaves) themselves, in exchange for a form of sharecropping or a monthly or yearly payment to the owner.[6]

Precolonial slavery in Africa, then, often did not conform to a typical chattel slavery model but was highly varied, especially for women. Male dominance was common in many, not all, African societies so that "free" women often did not have full rights. Gradations in statuses existed such that free, junior wife, concubine, freed, pawn, indentured, maidservant, dependent, and slave shaded into each other or represented different stages in a woman's life or of assimilation into a new society. Often the status of a nominally "free" but junior female was in practice indistinguishable from that of a female slave, at least in terms of their work. Given that even during early colonialism (for most countries the late nineteenth and early twentieth centuries), age was more important than gender in determining authority and privileges,[7] the assertions of those enslaved as children that they were treated like free persons make sense. While aging served to disadvantage slaves in chattel systems where the capacity for work served as the chief criterion of a slave's value, in assimilative systems slaves could acquire more rights and respect with age.

The Importance of Enslaved Women's Work

There were more female slaves held in Africa than male primarily because of their high reproductive (defined as domestic work) and productive (for

commodity production) labor value and secondarily for their biological reproductive function. Women slaves' labor replaced the extensive labor expected
of free women, who consequently often were the primary users, supervisors,
and owners of women slaves.[8] The work of female slaves in both domestic and
commercial production has usually been underestimated. Domestic work often
has not been considered to be work. Some have assumed that all women's work
was (is) domestic, with no economic value, applying the housewifery model
irrelevant for African women. Therefore, women's slavery has not been seen
as a labor system but rather as a method of recruiting concubines or of increasing the influence of lineages. However, understanding the economics of African social systems has been substantially furthered by the study of women and
slavery and in turn influenced the breaking of stereotypes in the study of slavery elsewhere.

There was high variation in types of work done by women slaves, from mining gold in the Gold Coast and Madagascar or processing cloves on Zanzibar,
to many routinized labor-intensive horticultural tasks such as weeding, sow-
ing, and harvesting, to trading independently or as helpers for women traders,
making thread for male weavers, and highly diversified household tasks involved in processing and cooking food, carrying firewood, doing laundry,
cleaning, child and elder care, and, often, compulsory sexual relations (e.g.,
sex work). Some owners farmed out slaves as prostitutes, gave them away as
booty to loyal soldiers, profited from their involvement in trade, or used them
as bridewealth to secure wives. Along with their function as pawns, all of these
were economic uses, although they were also valued socially to a greater or
lesser extent depending on the society. The high value of women's work meant
that women slaves cost more in African markets than male slaves, and that
their emancipation was fought in many cases.[9]

Wealth in precolonial Africa usually depended on how much labor a person
or lineage controlled, and therefore was counted in people: family, depen-
dents, clients, slaves, wives, children. Land ownership was not usually private
(Ethiopia's feudal system was an exception) but depended on capacity to use
it. Most precolonial labor-intensive horticultural labor was done by women, as
well as most household tasks (see chapter 8).[10] Slave women's labor replaced
or supplemented the labor of free women, which was considerable and essential
to societal survival, especially in dominantly Muslim societies where seclusion
of free women was practiced. Slave women had no honor to protect and therefore could move about and work outside their homes. A sex-segregated division of labor made women slaves primarily the helpers of women owners or
supervisors.

Slavery is a labor system above all, not mitigated by the sexual uses of slaves but intensified by them. For women, slavery often involved sex work, not only as prostitutes, although that was relatively common in urban chattel slavery. It is widely recognized that compulsory sexual relations were characteristic of most forms of slavery for women. Enslaved women and girls were frequently raped. Forced or asymmetrically consensual, the sexual relations of women slaves could be a route to advancement, as when they bore children to the owner or a member of his lineage and were assimilated by becoming a junior wife or concubine.[11]

Paradoxically, given the usual sexualized Euro-American stereotype that slave women, especially in harems, were primarily valued for sex and biological reproduction, one situation where a slave woman's sexuality might not have been valued was in harems. In North Africa, Dahomey, and Kano, Nigeria, secluded slave women were more likely to be household drudges than sex slaves, protected by their seclusion, or sex segregation and the ruler's authority, along with their free cohorts, from random sexual impositions.[12] The North African Barbary Coast pirate slave trade that largely coincided with the Atlantic slave trade enslaved perhaps a million Europeans over its history and provided some concubines to royal harems, but narratives of enslavement from such women suggest that most performed domestic rather than sex work.[13] In general, slavery in Muslim nations involved a wide range of statuses for male slaves, ranging from royal adviser to galley slave, but was less varied for females. In sub-Saharan Africa, most enslaved Muslim women did agricultural labor, as did non-Muslims.

Women and Assimilative/Lineage Slavery

Differing social structures were largely determinant of assimilative processes in lineage slavery. Eighteenth- and nineteenth-century West African empires such as Asante, Dahomey, and the Sokoto Caliphate practiced large-scale slavery as a core element of their society and exported many slaves. They established slave villages, effectively segregating many slaves from freed persons. However, many coastal and decentralized societies had small-scale lineage slavery dominantly intended to incorporate more people into their society. Both matrilineal societies and patrilineal societies often found women slaves easier to assimilate, structurally and socially. Girls' socialization to be obedient to their elders made them easier to control. In patrilineal societies, slave women became junior wives, usually freed once they had borne a child to the owner or a member of his family. That child was free, taking the status of the father; freed slaves and their children expanded the numbers of lineage members. Among precolonial African societies practicing slavery, most had no second-generation slavery. In some societies, descendants of slaves bore a permanent stigma, but just as often they did not. In Kano and Dahomey, some slave women bore heirs to the throne, achieving freedom, eminence, and power in so doing.[14] In matrilineal societies, free women determined descent and lineal affiliation, but male dominance was a factor, and men might opportunistically take slave wives to create de facto patrilineages to their own advantage, since slave women usually lost their lineage affiliation with enslavement. This successful strategy could give a man control not only over his sisters' sons but also over his slave wives' children. The malleability of kin connections in Africa could maximize the desirability of owning women slaves.

There were, however, structural limitations to assimilative advantages in many cases for women slaves. Records show that slave women in East and West Africa often had aspirations to achieve respectability by making legal marriages in which bridewealth was paid, but they had no natal lineage members to receive it. Full assimilation would have meant that the owner's lineage would receive it, but since a bondwoman's partner normally belonged to that lineage, it could not accept bridewealth, given issues of incest. Mombasa slave women tried to achieve freedom and respectability by arranging their own marriages, while Bwanikwa, an East African slave, felt that only emancipation would bring full assimilation. In Accra, capital of the Gold Coast colony, Adukwe, a woman enslaved as a child after British abolition, tried most of her life and failed to have a legal marriage confirmed by bridewealth being given to the lineage that acquired and assimilated her.[15] The increasing literature that focuses on enslaved women's experiences and agency allows better understanding of such gendered impacts.[16]

Slaves' Rights in African Systems

An astonishing aspect of women and slavery in Africa for those wedded to Western stereotypical notions of chattel slavery is that in many African lineage systems slaves, including women, could own property. West, Central, and certain Muslim African women were more likely than those in eastern and southern Africa, however, to exercise power through property ownership since precolonial eastern and southern kinship systems were more likely than North, Central, and West African systems to treat women as male property. In West Africa some free women not only owned slaves but traded them, and occasionally slave women owned slaves, as in coastal Senegal, the Gold Coast, Bissau, southern Nigeria, and Dahomey, including Madam Yoko (see chapter 7).[17] These women were successful in achieving social mobility by buying slaves rather than purchasing their own freedom. Before and after British abolition of slavery in the Gold Coast (1874), some women expanded their slave ownership, buying young girls used for domestic and trade purposes.[18] In dominantly Muslim countries, elite women could own slaves.[19] Some North African privileged slave concubines owned slaves.[20] Class differences are evident among women slaves in Benguela in Angola, where elite concubines commanded the labor of poor domestic slaves, who were more likely to be subjected to sexual violence.[21]

The cosmopolitan hierarchical societies of precolonial coastal West Africa produced highly varied social arrangements that allowed some women of slave origin to assume power. In coastal Senegal, as well as elsewhere in West Africa, urban women, some enslaved, made alliances with foreign traders resulting in mixed-race offspring including daughters, some of whom became powerful in local politics and society. Some traded slaves, and all relied in the nineteenth century on slave women's household labor. In Eweland in the Gold Coast, strangers formed such alliances with locals, including slaves, to form powerful lineages.[22] In such situations, clearly class was more important than gender or slave status for women's capacity to own slaves. Fenda Lawrence, Gambian slave trader and wife of a British trader, for instance, traveled to Georgia as a free woman to settle and defend her property rights once her husband was no longer around; to do so she had to obtain a deposition proving that she was free.[23]

The institution of "woman-to-woman" marriage, widespread in Africa, allowed some prosperous women, including King Ahebi (see chapter 3), to become "husbands," taking junior women as wives by paying bridewealth or buying a female slave, thereby creating a de facto matrilineage within a patrilineal system, or raising children who belonged to their deceased husband's lineage. Clearly, African kinship and legal variations, especially with regard to women and slavery, do not follow the chattel slave model, both in the types of work women did and in their mutable status. That could vary over their lifetimes from enslavement in youth to childbearing and freedom in maturity, and occasionally to wealth when elite status or trading brought the ownership of slaves.

Cultural Influences of Enslaved Women

African women slaves assimilated into owners' societies could have substantial cultural influence. That influence as well as their capacity to develop an autonomous slave culture depended on such factors as their housing, numbers, and positions within a society; the nature of their work activities and cultural attitudes; and their degree of assimilation and autonomy of action. In general, chattel slaves were less able to influence wider society. For instance, chattel slavery as practiced in South Africa by white settlers against local peoples varied from place to place depending on whether slaves were involved in domestic tasks or agricultural labor. Their cultural impact on white society was severely limited by racism. Autonomy for women chattel slaves at the Cape of Good Hope was strongly circumscribed because, housed separately at their owners' residences, they mostly did domestic work and had no opportunity based on separate space to organize collective resistance or develop or maintain a specific material culture.[24]

Assimilative slavery could diminish the possibility of forming a separate slave culture or increase slave women's cultural influence, depending on the situation. For example, coastal West and Central African women who were or had been slaves, and achieved business success and therefore slave owning themselves, often founded new lineages with stranger men, who ultimately became influential as cultural intermediaries with the outside world.[25] The few slave women in the Dahomean royal palace who rose to be concubines and sometimes queen mothers when their sons became rulers presided over a community with much cultural diversity due to the presence of women slaves of different ethnicities and nationalities, while cross-ethnic marriages could also have a strong political impact through alliances.[26]

At a less exalted level, inland slave women exported to East African coastal households influenced their Arabized owners culturally; in Mombasa slave women formed dance groups and tried to overcome their status through assimilative behavior and hypergamy.[27] In Sudan, under the Condominium government, slave women and their descendants were culturally and politically important to government efforts to establish colonies in underpopulated areas.[28] In Mali, slave women made essential contributions to preserving oral traditions and to cultural production as *griottes*, women bards.[29]

Assimilative Slavery Was Still Slavery

If assimilative slavery could carry more advantages for the enslaved than chattel slavery, realistic assessment of its processes and consequences for African women, as well as changes over time including the impact of the Atlantic slave trade, in particular, are still necessary. The process of enslavement usually entailed brutal treatment of those sold into the trade, whatever form of slavery they eventually experienced. Typical of the treatment of an enslaved woman while in the trade might have been the harrowing experiences involving rape, pregnancy, and abortion forced upon a Circassian slave girl taken to

Cairo by slave dealers in the mid-nineteenth century.[30] Missionary accounts and court records provide documentation for South Africa, in particular, of extreme maltreatment of female chattel slaves.[31] The perils of European captivity for Sara Baartman, a woman whose body was exhibited in Britain and France while she was alive and (against her wishes) after she died at a relatively young age, have been well documented (see chapter 2).[32] Slaves who eventually assimilated into their owners' societies usually fared better than chattel slaves, their treatment generally reflecting their degree of assimilation, the limits of assimilation within a society, and the progress of assimilation over their lifetime (i.e., age-related status).

While it is often assumed that women slaves in assimilative systems were better treated, and some did achieve power and wealth, that assumption has been questioned. For instance, in late nineteenth-century Nigeria, Yoruba women traders were particularly vulnerable to being kidnapped into slavery and encountered competition from many male Hausa slaves who entered into trade and industry. Violence was exercised against both free and enslaved women, including their sexual exploitation. Consequently, many women fled to missions or to Lagos when the cost of redemption increased as well as their vulnerability to re-enslavement if they had managed to achieve manumission.[33] Freed women and children in nineteenth-century East Africa experienced many perils that often ended in re-enslavement, including an ex-slave named Swema. Swema, along with many others, experienced liminality induced by slave ancestry (lack of protection by a free lineage), famine, and economic crisis, all of which made some women and children especially likely to be enslaved and re-enslaved.[34] The youth of many female slaves, even in systems most advantageous to them, could factor into maltreatment from a contemporary perspective, given that beating children was routine in some societies (including Europe and the United States at the time).

The Impact of the Transatlantic Slave Trade

Any societal practice involving systematic subjugation of individuals even temporarily deprived of rights is liable to corruption by more oppressive systems that may enslave them permanently. The transatlantic slave trade affected local societies such that some began slaving who had not had slavery before. Sometimes women had to do more men's work, and polygyny could intensify with the absence of more men, but more often slave raiders took most of the able-bodied adults in villages. The absence of able-bodied adults reduced cultivated areas and a society's capacity to survive. Lineage or assimilative slavery became more like chattel slavery in Angola, for instance.[35]

Ritualized forms of service to the gods could become more oppressive and did in Igboland. Under pressure of the Atlantic slave trade, the Aro oracle condemned more persons to slavery for minor infractions and profit.[36] The chaos created by the Angolan Atlantic slave trade helped cause Nbena, a free woman, to be enslaved through another enslaved woman's trickery, sold by an Angolan owner, and paradoxically freed under the Portuguese concept of "original freedom."[37] More generally, females who were supposed to be pawns sometimes ended up as trade slaves, contrary to legal custom, and were exiled permanently from their own people. The Atlantic slave trade therefore changed forms of slavery practiced within societies, modifying customary laws and moving assimilative slavery toward chattel practices.

Abolition for Enslaved Colonial African Women?

One of the primary British justifications for the imposition of colonial rule was to end slavery. They abolished the slave trade in 1807 and slavery in 1834–37 and used their navy to prevent slave shipments from West Africa, in particular. Often the first ordinance the British promulgated with the establishment of colonial rule in the late nineteenth century outlawed slavery. Racism inflected their abolition movement so that slaves freed from impounded ships were normally not allowed to return home but were sent to be converted by missionaries in Sierra Leone, hence Freetown's name.[38] However, their efforts regarding female slaves fell far short of their goal, vitiated both by local resistance in the form of claims that women slaves were relatives like junior wives or concubines when they tried to achieve freedom by complaining to colonial courts, and by colonial officers' reluctance to interfere in "domestic arrangements," which they normally left to the local courts in indirect rule. In Sudan, colonial shari'a courts tended to deny slave women's manumission efforts, given the valuable productive and reproductive roles of women slaves; this was also the case in Mauritania.[39] Abina, a Gold Coast woman, was enslaved after the imposition of colonial rule but then sought and achieved her freedom through the court.[40] According to German East African court records, many women slaves in the late nineteenth century fled to missions or used the courts to claim their freedom.[41] Despite a supposed commitment to abolition of slavery, British officials in northern Nigeria collaborated with local influential men to continue women's enslavement into at least the 1920s, probably in exchange for male cooperation in indirect rule. So-called domestic slavery was not outlawed until 1937, more than a hundred years after British general abolition of slavery.[42]

Women slaves also encountered problems with emancipation precisely because of assimilative tendencies within many societies or male-dominant customary social arrangements. Women had more difficulty getting money to achieve self-emancipation, were reluctant to leave their children, and did more of the labor-intensive unskilled work while men secured more skilled wage labor. Their free children usually belonged to their free fathers, often owners. In the French West African Sahel after emancipation, thousands of male slaves abandoned their owners for urban migration or to return home, but females usually stayed where they were. In the later days of precolonial slavery, mostly young girls were enslaved; many did not remember their homes or have the means to return. Many freed women, successfully integrated into their owners' societies, did not return to their natal societies. Cases were common where slave owners claimed ownership of "freed" women's children as a mechanism to keep the women and expand their lineages, a claim more often than not accepted by the courts and also made in chattel slavery areas. In the Western Cape in South Africa, both slaves and owners saw slavery through the lens of gender relations, which shaped slaves' access to freedom and did not favor female emancipation.[43] The main area of contestation between slave owners and women slaves in early twentieth-century Mombasa, Kenya, was the right to arrange their own marriages; the courts did not recognize that right for at least twenty years after the 1907 British proclamation abolishing slavery.[44]

Nonetheless, some women fled with their children to Christian mission stations, where their stories were sometimes recorded. In Eweland the emancipation of a couple resulting from Christian conversion at a mission station ended with the husband freeing the wife and his other slaves.[45] However, in East Africa the mid to late nineteenth-century conditions of widespread raiding and warfare meant that it sometimes was better to belong to an owner capable of defending the household rather than be a "free" person without a patron for protection. Escaped or freed slaves were routinely captured and re-enslaved by others. If in West Africa some enslaved women like Dahomean "Amazons" could even be soldiers, nineteenth-century East African women's vulnerability to enslavement and re-enslavement demonstrates that emancipation could worsen the situation of both high- and low-status free women.[46]

Slavery for women continued partly because of colonialist actions beyond simply refusing requests in court for emancipation, such as refusal to recognize the authority of female rulers, weakening the status of all women in some societies, while imposing Victorian laws that made women male property. Such policies in some cases created male dominance where it was unknown or insignificant before colonialism, and in others reinforced precolonial male-dominant structures. The freeing of some women slaves through appeals to colonial courts was exceptional.

Colonial furthering of cash crop production upped the demand for women's agricultural labor. In southern Niger after emancipation the absence of women slaves' labor meant that many men pressured their wives to do more horticultural work and looked for mechanisms to increase and enforce wives' labor obligations to their husbands. Sometimes an increase in domestic violence against women resulted.[47] Most colonial powers required forced labor of their African subjects to a greater or lesser extent, building roads and other infrastructure or cultivating cash crops. In the case of King Leopold's Congo with the forced cultivation of rubber, Belgians unapologetically and openly practiced chattel slavery. Emancipation of slaves did not work as it should have in Africa and could even worsen free women's status; colonialism, despite its claims, did not abolish slavery.

The World Capitalist Economy and New Forms of Slavery

Colonialism, with its failure to abolish slavery for women and girls in particular, forced labor, diminution of women's power and authority, and pioneering role in spreading negative effects of the world capitalist economy, helped create and expand forms of contemporary slavery, especially for women.[48] Older forms of servitude in Africa now have generally disappeared, with occasional exceptions like the shrine slaves, *trokosi*, in Ghana, young girls serving priests of local gods. Given by their families to the shrine priests in hopes of securing benefits like helping members escape punishment for crimes, they provide sex and domestic work. This institution violates Ghana's constitution and various international conventions outlawing slavery but is widely condoned.[49] Other modern forms of slavery in Africa have ancient roots; for example, Kano household slavery laid the foundation for enslaving modern domestic workers. Africa now, like the rest of the world but at a higher rate, has sexual and ritual slavery and forced labor, with various estimates of its extent, one of the highest being 6.4 million slaves now held in Africa, including some 800,000 in North Africa.[50]

Women's systemic social and economic liabilities inflicted by male dominance were worsened by colonialism and are furthered by neocolonialism, in which political "independence" is undermined by continuing and worsening economic domination by multinational corporations.[51] Women more than men are likely to be enslaved in new ways, especially by the global trafficking in women.[52] Contemporary slavery for African women and others usually entails employment in factory, sex, or domestic work around the world. The physical mobility of African women improved with colonial rule (within new borders) due to suppression of raiding and local warfare, enabling some women to become long-distance traders, for instance. Currently, women (and men) frequently leave home in search of better economic opportunities. Enslavement of African women has resulted from crossing the Sahara to go to Europe; kidnapping from Senegal into Mauritania, which now has the highest numbers of slaves in Africa, estimated variously from one twenty-fifth to one-fifth of the population; or East Africans enslaved as servants in Indian Ocean societies. Some have found themselves in the United States without passports or legal recourse when employers abuse them (the United States now has an estimated sixty thousand slaves).[53]

The main cause of slavery that links the precolonial status of African women to the contemporary situation is women's systematic lack of access to key resources and their lower status and lack of opportunities in some societies, a situation that was spread across Africa by colonialism and encouraged by multinational corporations paying women less than men.[54] Now, in order to attract corporate investment, some countries advertise the availability of cheap female labor. Like the economies of most African countries, women's vulnerabilities make them targets for the downside of the world market economy, unable to protect themselves from the depredations of multinational corporations and their local clients. They do not have to be quiet, however (see chapters 6 and 12). In New York some escape in the hopes that, despite their illegal immigrant status (strict immigration laws enable the continuation of slavery), the authorities will help them, but then they risk deportation, a process applied especially to women of color. Women resist new forms of enslavement however they can.

How can contemporary slavery be defined? Inflected strongly by male dominance, enabled by illegality and rapid transport, created by increasingly impoverished neocolonial economies within multinational corporate dominance, slaves are disposable people, without rights, removed from kin links and mostly female.[55] Slaves, as in chattel slavery, have no rights, but their work is their punishment, their sale being illegal. Poverty helps to perpetuate contemporary slavery in supporting high population growth due to high infant mortality, need for child labor and support in old age, and lineage family ideology (see chapter 13).[56] Employers have no investment in their survival, given they were not bought, and their replacement is easy when poor working conditions and poverty destroy their health. Unlike in most past forms of slavery, often victims are lured into precarious situations voluntarily, although sometimes impoverished families sell daughters. Male dominance is key in supporting all forms of contemporary slavery, just as an increasingly intrusive world capitalist economy has been instrumental in creating new forms of slavery.

The typical slave now is female, including in new forms of wage slavery where mainly female factory workers, often immigrants, are paid nominal wages and forced to meet quotas. Their captivity includes being locked down at work and in dormitories, like U.S. prison workers, and farmed out to businesses at substandard wages.

The literature on contemporary slavery, although acknowledging its disproportionately female victims, often fails to consider the gendered implications of this fact. Slavery is condoned in many ways and places, including by multinational corporations that purposefully ignore slavery practiced by local contractors while insisting on strict profitability requirements. Slavery is now more often than not gendered female worldwide, including in Africa.

Conclusion

It is not surprising, given African women's historically high economic importance (see chapter 8), that most slaves kept in Africa were and are female. Slavery in precolonial Africa valued women more than men primarily for their labor and secondarily for expanding numbers of lineage members. Forms of slavery practiced in most African societies with slavery were assimilative, aimed at expanding societal membership, rather than creating a permanent enslaved underclass as in chattel slavery practiced by Europeans in Africa and elsewhere. Slaves in most of Africa had rights to marry, own property, and keep profits, for instance, and some enslaved women ended up as successful slave traders and rulers. Free women, whose labor was replaced by that of women slaves in sex-segregated labor systems, profited most from highly varied forms of enslaved women's labor. Mainly because of assimilation into owners' societies and structural vulnerabilities, women had more difficulties in achieving manumission than men, including under colonial rule, which promised to abolish slavery but in many cases abetted its continuation for women.

Precolonial structures that made women in some areas more likely than men to be enslaved in Africa, plus colonial rule that generalized male dominance and deprived women of rights helped cause the postcolonial rise in slavery fostered by increasing geographical mobility and multinational corporate dominance. New forms of slavery in Africa are often characterized by victims placing themselves at risk while seeking economic opportunities, which for women are linked to survival. Survivors find it difficult to achieve legal manumission when slavery itself is illegal and authorities are compromised by corruption and racism. The result is that slavery and slave trafficking are increasing in Africa and the world, with women and girls as main objects, sought for their labor value, not assimilation, to supply a world market.

Notes

1. The photo in this chapter depicts, from left to right and from oldest to newest (1970–present), a two-inch-tall Ghanaian gold weight, a Nigerian wood carving, an Angolan clay sculpture, and a twelve-inch-tall wood carving of unknown origin. Such statues were made primarily for the tourist trade; none are signed.

2. Claire Robertson and Marsha Robinson, "Re-Modeling Slavery as If Women Mattered," in *Women and Slavery*, vol. 2, *The Modern Atlantic*, ed. Gwyn Campbell, Suzanne Miers, and Joseph C. Miller (Athens: Ohio University Press, 2008), 253–83.

3. Paul Lovejoy, "Internal Markets or an Atlantic-Sahara Divide? How Women Fit into the Slave Trade of West Africa," in *Women and Slavery*, vol. 1, *Africa, the Indian Ocean World, and the Medieval North Atlantic*, ed. Gwyn Campbell, Suzanne Miers, and Joseph C. Miller (Athens: Ohio University Press, 2007), 259–79; G. Ugo Nwokeji, "African Conceptions of Gender and the Slave Traffic," *William and Mary Quarterly* 58, no. 1 (2001): 47–67.

4. Igor Kopytoff and Suzanne Miers, "African Slavery as an Institution of Marginality," in *Slavery in Africa: Historical and Anthropological Perspectives*, ed. Suzanne Miers and Igor Kopytoff (Madison: University of Wisconsin Press, 1977), 1–59.

5. Claire C. Robertson and Martin A. Klein, "Women's Importance in African Slave Systems," in *Women and Slavery in Africa*, ed. Claire C. Robertson and Martin A. Klein (Madison: University of Wisconsin Press, 1983), 3–25.

6. Suzanne Miers and Igor Kopytoff, eds., *Slavery in Africa: Historical and Anthropological Perspectives* (Madison: University of Wisconsin Press, 1977).

7. Claire C. Robertson, *Sharing the Same Bowl: A Socioeconomic History of Women and Class in Accra, Ghana* (Bloomington: Indiana University Press, 1984).

8. Robertson and Klein, "Women's Importance."

9. Gareth Austin, "Human Pawning in Asante, 1800–1950: Markets and Coercion, Gender and Cocoa," in *Pawnship in Africa: Debt Bondage in Historical Perspective*, ed. Toyin Falola and Paul E. Lovejoy (Boulder, CO: Westview, 1994), 119–59; Emily Burrill and Richard Roberts, "Domestic Violence, Colonial Courts, and the End of Slavery in French Soudan, 1905–1912," in *Domestic Violence and the Law in Colonial and Postcolonial Africa*, ed. Emily Burrill, Richard Roberts, and Elizabeth Thornberry (Athens: Ohio University Press, 2010), 33–53.

10. Susan Martin, "Slaves, Igbo Women and Palm Oil in the Nineteenth Century," in *From Slave Trade to "Legitimate" Commerce: The Commercial Transition in Nineteenth-Century West Africa*, ed. Robin Law (Cambridge: Cambridge University Press, 1995), 172–95; Robin Law, "'Legitimate' Trade and Gender Relations in Yorubaland and Dahomey," in Law, *From Slave Trade to "Legitimate" Commerce*, 195–214.

11. Paul Lovejoy, *Slavery, Commerce and Production in West Africa: Slave Society in the Sokoto Caliphate* (Trenton, NJ: Africa World Press, 2005).

12. Heidi Nast, *Concubines and Power: Five Hundred Years in a Northern Nigerian Palace* (Minneapolis: University of Minnesota Press, 2005); Mohammed Ennaji, *Serving the Master: Slavery and Society in Nineteenth-Century Morocco*, trans. Seth Graebner (New York: St. Martin's Press, 1999); Martin A. Klein, "Sex, Power, and Family Life in the Harem: A Comparative Study," in Campbell, Miers, and Miller, *Women and Slavery*, 1:63–81.

13. Paul Baepler, *White Slaves, African Masters* (Chicago: University of Chicago Press, 1999); Robert C. Davis, *Christian Slaves, Muslim Masters: White Slavery in the Mediterranean, the Barbary Coast, and Italy, 1500–1800* (New York: Palgrave Macmillan, 2003).

14. Nast, *Concubines*; Edna G. Bay, *Wives of the Leopard: Gender, Politics, and Culture in the Kingdom of Dahomey* (Charlottesville: University Press of Virginia, 1998); Beverly B. Mack, "Service and Status: Slaves and Concubines in Kano, Nigeria," in *At Work in Homes: Household Workers in World Perspective*, ed. Roger Sanjek and Shellee Colen (Washington, DC: American Anthropological Association, 1990), 14–34.

15. Marcia Wright, "Bwanikwa: Consciousness and Protest among Slave Women in Central Africa, 1886–1911," in Robertson and Klein, *Women and Slavery*, 246–67; Wright, *Strategies of Slaves and Women: Life-Stories from East/Central Africa* (New York: Lilian Barber Press, 1983); Margaret Strobel, *Muslim Women in Mombasa* (New Haven, CT: Yale University Press, 1979); Claire C. Robertson, "Post-Proclamation Slavery in Accra: A Female Affair?," in Robertson and Klein, *Women and Slavery*, 220–45.

16. Alice Ballagamba, Sandra E. Greene, and Martin A. Klein, eds., *African Voices on Slavery and the Slave Trade* (Cambridge: Cambridge University Press, 2013); E. Ann McDougall, "A Sense of Self: The Life of Fatma Barka," *Canadian Journal of African Studies* 12, no. 2 (1998): 395–412.

17. George E. Brooks, "The *Signares* of Saint-Louis and Gorée: Women Entrepreneurs in Eighteenth-Century Senegal," in *Women in Africa: Studies in Social and Economic Change*, ed. N. J. Hafkin and E. G. Bay (Stanford: Stanford University Press, 1976), 19–44; Brooks, "A Nhara of the Guinea-Bissau Region: Mãe Aurélia Correia," in Robertson and Klein, *Women and Slavery*, 295–319; Philip Havik, "From Pariahs to Patriots: Women Slavers in Nineteenth-Century 'Portuguese' Guinea," in Campbell, Miers, and Miller, *Women and Slavery*, 1: 309–33; Bay, *Wives*.

18. Kwabena Adu-Boahen, "Abolition, Economic Transition, Gender and Slavery: The Expansion of Women's Slaveholding in Ghana, 1807–1874," *Slavery and Abolition* 31, no. 1 (2010): 117–36; Adu-Boahen, *Post-Abolition Slaveholding in the Gold Coast: Slave Mistresses of Coastal Fante, 1807–1874* (Saarbrucken: Lambert Academy, 2011); Adu-Boahen, "Post-Emancipation Slave Commerce: Increasing Child Slave Trafficking and Women's Agency in Late Nineteenth-Century Ghana," *Lagos Historical Review* 9 (2009).

19. Eugenia Rodrigues, "Female Slavery, Domestic Economy and Social Status in the Zambezi *Prazos* during the Eighteenth Century," in *Women in the Portuguese Colonial Empire: The Theatre of Shadows*, ed. Clara Sarmento (Newcastle-upon-Tyne: Cambridge Scholars, 2008), 31–50.

20. Eve Trout Powell, *Tell This in My Memory: Stories of Enslavement from Egypt, Sudan, and the Ottoman Empire* (Stanford: Stanford University Press, 2012).

21. Mariana P. Candido, "Concubinage and Slavery in Benguela, c. 1750–1850," in *Slavery in Africa and the Caribbean: A History of the Enslavement and Identity since the Eighteenth Century*, ed. Olatunji Ojo and Nadine Hunt (New York: I.B. Tauris), 65–83.

22. Hilary Jones, *The Métis of Senegal Urban Life and Politics in French West Africa* (Bloomington: Indiana University Press, 2013); Sandra E. Greene, *Gender, Ethnicity and Social Change on the Upper Slave Coast: A History of the Anlo-Ewe* (Portsmouth, NH: Heinemann, 1996).

23. Lillian Ashcraft-Eason, "'She Voluntarily Hath Come': A Gambian Woman Trader in Colonial Georgia in the Eighteenth Century," in *Identity in the Shadow of Slavery*, ed. Paul Lovejoy (New York: Continuum, 2009), 202–21.

24. Wendy Woodward, "Contradictory Tongues: Torture and the Testimony of Two Slave Women in the Eastern Cape Courts in 1833 and 1834," in *Deep Histories: Gender and Colonialism in Southern Africa*, ed. Wendy Woodward, Patricia Hayes, and Gary Minkley (Amsterdam: Rodopi, 2002), 55–83.

25. Brooks, "*Signares*"; Brooks, "Nhara"; Bruce L. Mouser, "Women Slavers of Guinea-Conakry," in Robertson and Klein, *Women and Slavery*, 320–39; Sandra E. Greene, "Crossing Boundaries/Changing Identities: Female Slaves, Male Strangers, and Their Descendants in Nineteenth- and Twentieth-Century Anlo," in *Gendered Encounters: Challenging Cultural Boundaries and Social Hierarchies in Africa*, ed. Maria Grosz-Ngaté and Omari H. Kokole (New York: Routledge, 1997), 23–41; Candido, "Concubinage"; Carol P. MacCormack, "Slaves, Slave Owners, and Slave Dealers: Sherbro Coast and Hinterland," in Robertson and Klein, *Women and Slavery*, 271–94.

26. Boniface Obichere, "Women and Slavery in the Kingdom of Dahomey," *Revue d'histoire d'outre-mer* 66 (1978): 5–20; Bay, *Wives*.

27. Carol Eastman, "Women, Slaves and Foreigners: African Cultural Influences and Group Processes in the Formation of Northern Swahili Coastal Society," *International Journal of African Historical Studies* 21, no. 1 (1987): 1–20; Strobel, *Muslim Women*.

28. Susan Kenyon, "Zainab's Story: Slavery, Women and Community in Colonial Sudan," *Urban Anthropology and Studies of Cultural Systems and World Economic Development* 38, no. 1 (2009): 245–66.

29. Mamadou Diawara, "Women, Servitude and History: The Oral Historical Tradition of Women of Servile Condition in the Kingdom of Jaara (Mali) from the Fifteenth to the Mid-Nineteenth Century," in *Discourse and Its Disguises: The Interpretation of African Oral Texts*, ed. Karin Barber and P. F. de Moraes Farias (Birmingham: Institute of African Studies, 1989), 109–37.

30. Ehud Toledano, "Slave Dealers, Women, Pregnancy and Abortion: The Story of a Circassian Slave Girl in Mid-Nineteenth Century Cairo," *Slavery and Abolition* 2, no. 1 (1981): 53–68.

31. Pamela Scully, *Liberating the Family? Gender and British Slave Emancipation in the Rural Western Cape, South Africa, 1823–1853* (Portsmouth, NH: Heinemann, 1997); Woodward, "Tongues."

32. Yvette Abrahams, "Disempowered to Consent: Sara Bartman and Khoisan Slavery in the Nineteenth Century Cape Colony and Britain," *South African Historical Journal* 35 (1996): 89–114.

33. Francine Shields, "Those Who Remained Behind: Women Slaves in Nineteenth-Century Yorubaland," in *Identity in the Shadow of Slavery*, ed. Paul Lovejoy (New York: Continuum, 2009), 164–83.

34. Edward A. Alpers, "The Story of Swema: Female Vulnerability in Nineteenth Century East Africa," in Robertson and Klein, *Women and Slavery*, 185–219; Wright, *Strategies*.

35. Patrick Manning, "The Enslavement of Africans: A Demographic Model," *Canadian Journal of African Studies* 15, no. 3 (1981): 499–526; John Thornton, "Sexual

Demography: The Impact of the Slave Trade on Family Structure," in Robertson and Klein, *Women and Slavery in Africa*, 39–48; Joseph C. Miller, *Way of Death: Merchant Capitalism and the Angolan Slave Trade, 1730–1830* (Madison: University of Wisconsin Press, 1988).

36. F. I. Ekejiuba, "The Aro Trade System in the Nineteenth Century," *Ikenga Journal of African Studies* 1, no. 1 (1972): 11–26. Nwando Achebe questions whether or not certain ritualized services were originally forms of slavery. Nwando Achebe, "When Deities Marry: Indigenous 'Slave' Systems Expanding and Metamorphosing in the Igbo Hinterland," in *African Systems of Slavery*, ed. Stephanie Beswick and Jay Spaulding (Trenton, NJ: Africa World Press, 2010), 105–33.

37. Jose C. Curto, "The Story of Nbena, 1817–1820: Unlawful Enslavement and the Concept of 'Original Freedom' in Angola," in *Trans-Atlantic Dimensions of Ethnicity in the African Diaspora*, ed. Paul E. Lovejoy and David V. Trotman (London: Continuum, 2003), 43–64.

38. Claire Robertson, "Racism, the Military, and Abolitionism in the Late Eighteenth- and Early Nineteenth-Century Caribbean," *Journal of Military History* 77, no. 2 (2013): 433–62.

39. Ahmad A. Sikainga, "Shari'a Courts and the Manumission of Female Slaves in the Sudan," *International Journal of African Historical Studies* 28, no. 1 (1995): 1–23; E. Ann McDougall, "Dilemmas in the Practice of *Rachat* in French West Africa," in *Buying Freedom: The Ethics and Economics of Slave Redemption*, ed. Kwame Anthony Appiah and Martin Bunzl (Princeton, NJ: Princeton University Press, 2007), 158–78; Urs Peter Ruf, *Ending Slavery: Hierarchy, Dependency and Gender in Central Mauritania* (Bielefeld: Transcript Verlag, 1999).

40. Trevor R. Getz and Liz Clarke, *Abina and the Important Men: A Graphic History* (Oxford: Oxford University Press, 2011).

41. Jan-Georg Deutsch, "Prices for Female Slaves and Changes in Their Life Cycle Evidence from German East Africa," in Campbell, Miers, and Miller, *Women and Slavery*, 1:129–44.

42. Paul Lovejoy, "Concubinage and the Status of Women Slaves in Early Colonial Northern Nigeria," *Journal of African History* 29 (1988): 245–66.

43. Scully, *Liberating*.

44. Strobel, *Muslim Women*.

45. Sandra Greene, *West African Narratives of Slavery Texts from Late Nineteenth- and Early Twentieth-Century Ghana* (Bloomington: Indiana University Press, 2011).

46. Bay, *Wives*.

47. Richard L. Roberts, "Women's Work and Women's Property: Household Social Relations in the Maraka Textile Industry of the Nineteenth Century," *Comparative Studies in Society and History* 26, no. 2 (1984): 229–50; Barbara A. Cooper, *Marriage in Maradi: Gender and Culture in a Hausa Society in Niger, 1900–1989* (Portsmouth, NH: Heinemann, 1997); Burrill and Roberts, "Domestic Violence."

48. The Wikipedia article "Slavery in Contemporary Africa" assumes that the colonialists abolished slavery. For a regionally focused look at the roots of contemporary African slavery, see Claire Robertson, "We Must Overcome: Genealogy and Evolution of Female Slavery in West Africa," *Journal of West African History* 1, no. 1 (Spring 2015): 59–92.

49. Abayie B. Boateng, *The Trokosi System in Ghana: African Women and Children* (Westport, CT: Praeger, 2001); Hilary Amesika Gbedemah, "*Trokosi*: Twentieth Century Female Bondage—A Ghanaian Case Study," in *Voices of African Women: Women's Rights in Ghana*, ed. Johanna Bond (Durham, NC: Carolina Academic Press, 2005), 83–95; Sarah C. Aird, "Ghana's Slaves to the Gods," *Human Rights Brief* 7, no. 1 (1999): 6–8, 26.

50. *Global Slavery Index* (November 2014). Reliable estimates of numbers of precolonial slaves held across Africa are impossible given the lack of documentation, while estimates of those exported in the historical transatlantic trade to the Americas between circa 1450 and the nineteenth century hover around 11 to 13 million persons.

51. Stephanie Beswick and Jay Spaulding, eds., *African Systems of Slavery* (Trenton, NJ: Africa World Press, 2010); Mack, "Service"; Richard Roberts and Benjamin N. Lawrance, eds., *Trafficking in Slavery's Wake: Law and the Experience of Women and Children in Africa* (Athens: Ohio University Press, 2012).

52. A. Adepoju, "Review of Research and Data on Human Trafficking in Sub-Saharan Africa," *International Migration* 43, no. 1–2 (2005): 75–98; Kevin G. Bales, *Disposable People: New Slavery in the Global Economy* (Berkeley: University of California Press, 1999); M. Gramegra, "Trafficking in Human Beings in Sub-Saharan Africa: The Case of Nigeria" (paper presented at International Conference on New Frontiers of Crime: Trafficking in Human Beings and New Forms of Slavery, Verona, Italy, October 22–23, 1999).

53. Max Fisher, "This Map Shows Where the World's 30 million Slaves Live. There Are 60,000 in the U.S.," *Washington Post*, October 17, 2013.

54. Roberts and Lawrance, *Trafficking*.

55. Bales, *Disposable People*.

56. A 2016 estimate of African population growth by the UN Population Division noted that Africa's population is increasing when that of all other continents is decreasing, that by 2050 Africa alone will account for 54 percent of world population growth, with African women on average bearing 4.7 children compared to 2.5 globally in 2016. Joseph J. Bish, "Population Growth in Africa: Grasping the Scale of the Challenge," *The Guardian*, January 11, 2016.

Suggested Readings

Ballagamba, Alice, Sandra E. Greene, and Martin A. Klein, eds. *African Voices on Slavery and the Slave Trade.* Cambridge: Cambridge University Press, 2013.

Campbell, Gwyn, Suzanne Miers, and Joseph C. Miller, eds. *Women and Slavery.* Vol. 1, *Africa, the Indian Ocean, and the Medieval North Atlantic.* Vol. 2, *The Modern Atlantic.* Athens: Ohio University Press, 2007.

Olatunji, Ojo, and Nadine Hunt, eds. *Slavery in Africa and the Caribbean: A History of Enslavement and Identity.* London: I. B. Tauris, 2012.

Roberts, Richard, and Benjamin N. Lawrance, eds. *Trafficking in Slavery's Wake Law and the Experience of Women and Children in Africa.* Athens: Ohio University Press, 2012.

Robertson, Claire C., and Martin A. Klein, eds. *Women and Slavery in Africa.* Madison: University of Wisconsin Press, 1983.

Figure 10.1 Secondary school girls at the end of a school day, Freetown, Sierra Leone, 2017. Photo by Ernest Beoku-Betts.

10

EDUCATION FOR AFRICAN GIRLS

Still Striving for Equality

Josephine Beoku-Betts

Since the 1990s, education of women and girls has been a heightened priority in international and national development policy discourses. At the International Conference on Education for All in 1990, underrepresentation of girls in education was highlighted as "the most urgent priority" if gender disparities in education at the primary and secondary levels were to be eliminated by 2015 and girls' access to good basic education realized through formal and non-formal education programs.[1] Also, the second and third priorities among the conference's 2000 Millennium Development Goals emphasized gender equity and the eradication of disparities between boys and girls in formal education for achievement of universal primary education by 2015.[2] As a result of these and other policy initiatives, various international donor organizations, national governments, and nongovernment agencies (NGOs) increased funding and introduced innovative programs to increase access and equality in educational opportunities and outcomes, particularly for women and girls. A 2011 UNESCO report, *Financing Education in Sub-Saharan Africa*, for example, states that international donors provided $2.6 billion in 2008 for education in Africa and that many African countries increased their real expenditure on education by more than 6 percent each year between 2000 and 2011. This report notes that since then the number of children in primary school in the region has risen by 48 percent from 87 million to 129 million, and that enrollment in preprimary, secondary, and tertiary education grew by more than 60 percent from 2000 to 2008.[3] Furthermore, at both primary and secondary school levels, the enrollment rate for girls has increased faster compared to boys. In general, educational systems that receive strong financial support produce higher enrollments and a narrower gender gap.[4] While such reports show evidence of gender parity and increasing enrollments in most sub-Saharan Africa (SSA) educational systems, this is not commensurate with the overall quality of education, which has declined. For example, in many countries, the number of students per teacher has increased, and shorter school days have been introduced to accommodate morning and afternoon school sessions.

Despite this significant progress, the African region, particularly SSA, is of critical concern to international organizations and scholars because, compared to other world regions, including North Africa, gender parity in education at all levels continues to lag. For example, the 2012 UNESCO *World Atlas of Gender Equality in Education* reports that globally SSA has the lowest proportion of countries reaching gender parity in education at both primary and secondary levels. Although the number of girls out of school is declining due to greater implementation of universal primary educational policies, girls are more likely to drop out of school and have lower achievement levels.[5]

This chapter examines gender disparities in formal education in SSA, focusing on primary and secondary education. While recognizing that North African countries such as Algeria, Tunisia, Egypt, Libya, and Morocco share the same continental space, a common colonial history, and political, social, and economic development challenges with the rest of Africa, SSA has the highest income inequality and poverty levels at all stages of development worldwide. Furthermore, North African countries are usually categorized with Middle East Arab states (as MENA, Middle East and North Africa) in UN development data. Although there are wide disparities among these countries (e.g., oil- and non-oil-producing economies) this has led to significant differences in the achievements of the Africa and MENA regions. The MENA countries have made significant strides in education in such areas as increased financial investment and student enrollment at all levels. For instance, in Morocco, a country not endowed with oil resources, current development efforts include government provision of elementary school education for all children, even in the remotest villages.

This chapter questions why progress in gender equality in education has been slow despite efforts to address the problem and identifies conceptual and policy issues shaping the opportunity structure and lived experiences of girls in African educational institutions. Some scholars argue that, while national and international efforts to provide greater access to education for girls have been progressive, they fail to consider complex social, political, and economic processes that shape structures of social equality in local contexts.[6] In other words, even when opportunities are presented for girls to access and take maximum advantage of the education provided, complex and intersecting factors foster gender inequality (e.g., social class, regional disparities, age, religion, sexuality, and ethnicity) and interact with local and global economic processes to frame meanings and understandings of gender role norms, values, attitudes, and practices. These factors are exacerbated by the HIV/AIDS and Ebola epidemics in Africa, the increasingly powerful role of fundamentalist religions that oppose formal education for girls, with resultant attacks on schoolgirls, as with Boko Haram in northern Nigeria, or the criminalization of homosexuality in Uganda and Cameroon, to name a few (see chapters 5, 14, and 16).

Therefore, simply to prioritize gender parity as determined by measures of improved access to schooling for girls will be limited without adequate consideration of how broader issues of structural inequality, lack of rights, and enforcement of social justice also impact the lived experiences of girls in school, household, and community contexts. As stated by Joan Dejaeghere and Frances Vavrus, "gendered relations of power in cultural, economic, and political domains are not easily rectified through schooling."[7] I argue, therefore, that in examining educational outcomes of girls in African schools, gender parity as defined by access and achievement must be examined in relation to gender equality as defined by issues of structural inequality and power relations governing gender norms and values and ways in which these impact gender inequalities in expectations and outcomes of girls.

The first section discusses some trends in girls' education at the primary and secondary levels in various SSA countries. Data analysis is drawn from available gender statistics from the World Bank, UNESCO Institute for Statistics, and UNESCO World Atlas of Gender Equality in Education. Descriptive statistics presented in tables 2 through 5 are based on currently published global development data or estimates compiled by the World Bank for 1990, 2000, 2005, 2010, and 2013–14. Although much of the data is disaggregated by gender, it is incomplete or missing for many countries. Only broad conclusions are drawn from this data, although they do reveal some similarities and differences in rates of access, achievement, and completion. This data also does not provide in-depth evidence to explain structural factors impacting girls' experiences of schooling and what they conceive or expect of their particular educational contexts. For example, a study on perspectives of Tanzanian secondary school girls found there was a need to equip these girls with relevant training for future employment. It revealed a disconnect between their expressed aspirations and realization of those goals after graduation.[8]

The second section employs qualitative evidence drawn from secondary sources to examine the complex interconnections of local, global, and other contextual factors that shape gender disparities in the educational outcomes of African girls in primary and secondary schools. I analyze ways in which scholars have critiqued conceptual, policy, and programmatic interventions designed to improve gender equality and girls' agency in schools. Issues examined in this section include rural and urban disparities, socioeconomic disparities, religion, sexual violence and harassment in schools, and children with special needs such as refugees and the internally displaced from armed conflict. The final section discusses emerging studies on gender and education that are giving voice to female students in terms of how they make sense of their lived experiences in school environments and their aspirations for the future.

Investment, Enrollment, and Completion Trends in Primary and Secondary Education

Primary Education

Although the effort to eradicate gender disparities in education and achieve universal primary education by 2015 did not succeed, significant advances in growth of the school-age populations can be seen worldwide, and particularly for SSA. In this region, the school-age population has a projected growth rate of 24.2 percent between 2010 and 2020 as compared to 8.9 percent in Arab states and 0.7 percent in North America and Western Europe.[9] Partly this reflects almost full enrollments already achieved in the latter areas. Within SSA, there are variations among countries. For example, Mauritius has a negative growth of 3.7 percent while Niger has a projected growth rate of 52 percent. Education in many SSA countries is heavily supported by international donors with at least a quarter of public education budgets in countries such as Mali funded through such sources.[10]

The number of mandated years set by a government for compulsory education of its children indicates commitment to the idea of education as a human right. Table 10.1 shows that in general, the majority of SSA countries require compulsory education for between seven to fourteen years, although in comparison to other regions worldwide, SSA accounts for 40 percent of countries providing compulsory education for only five to six years. Ethiopia requires no education for its future citizens.

Among schoolchildren fortunate enough to receive a primary school education, there is steady growth in the percentage of girls enrolled relative to boys, although in most countries they are not yet at parity. Table 10.2 shows the percentage distribution of girls enrolled in primary school from 1990 to 2013/14 in selected countries with available data.

Most of these countries show a steady increase in girls' access to school between 1990 and 2013–14. Indeed, some countries, such as Senegal, Uganda,

Table 10.1. Required amount of primary and middle school education in SSA by country, 2009

Years of required Education	Number of Countries	Countries
None	1	Ethiopia
5 to 6 years	9	Equatorial Guinea, Madagascar (5); Cameroon, Benin, Gambia, Guinea-Bissau, Senegal, Sierra Leone (6).
10 to 14 years	15	Botswana, Central African Republic, Côte d'Ivoire, Democratic Republic of the Congo, Ghana, Guinea, Namibia, Seychelles, Togo (10); Burkina Faso, Cape Verde, Congo, Gabon, Liberia (11); Mauritius (12).
Total	40 Countries	

Source: UNESCO Institute for Statistics, 2012.

Rwanda, Sierra Leone, and The Gambia, now have slightly higher primary enrollment of girls than boys. There are also countries, such as Benin, Burkina Faso, and Guinea, where the percentage of girls in primary school has increased by 10 to 15 percent between 1990 and 2013/14.

Dropout Rates

Though there has been an increase in the number of girls attending primary school, the transition between primary and secondary school is associated with extremely high dropout rates for both male and female students in SSA countries. According to a 2012 UNESCO report, nearly two-thirds of SSA countries have a dropout rate greater than 30 percent as compared to 13 percent in other regions of the world. In SSA, the highest school wastage is found in Chad, where over 70 percent of children do not complete primary school. The report also states that a substantial proportion of children who drop out of school are girls, although there are similar rates for boys in some countries. For example, more boys than girls drop out of school in Lesotho, Namibia, Zambia, and Sudan, whereas more girls than boys drop out of school in most countries.[11]

The persistent problem of high dropout rates in African primary schools is mainly due to poverty. Based on a minimum income of $1.25 a day, the percentage of the SSA population in poverty in 2011 was 46.8 percent.[12] The burden many poor SSA countries face in meeting neoliberal economic policies imposed

TABLE 10.2. Primary education enrollment (% female pupils)

Country	1990	2000	2005	2010	2013/2014
Benin	33.9	40.17	43.55	46.46	47.34 **
Botswana	51.6	49.67	49.29	NA	48.82 *
Burkina Faso	37.98	40.81	43.71	46.77	48.43 **
Cameroon	45.95	45.74	45.24	46	46.75 **
Central African Rep.	38.79	NA	41.07	41.87	NA
Congo, Dem. Rep. of	41.29	NA	NA	46.28	47.28 **
Congo, Rep. of	48.03	47.77	47.91	48.32	NA
Côte d'Ivoire	41.58	42.7	NA	NA	46.36 **
Equatorial Guinea	NA	44.93	48.69	49.1	NA
Ethiopia	39.47	39.2	45.07	47.47	47.36 **
Gambia	NA	46.41	50.41	50.28	50.94 **
Ghana	44.86	47.16	47.92	48.95	48.96 **
Guinea	30.93	39.82	44.08	44.75	45.49 **
Kenya	48.9	49.38	48.71	NA	49.78 **
Liberia	NA	41.91	NA	NA	46.92 **
Madagascar	48.81	48.99	48.9	49.42	49.66 **
Mauritius	49.41	49.19	49.23	49.18	49.51 **
Namibia	52	50.02	49.81	49.26	49.05 *
Nigeria	43.19	43.93	44.88	46.66	NA
Rwanda	50.06	49.57	50.89	50.74	50.75 **
Senegal	41.76	45.99	48.63	50.9	51.56 **
Seychelles	NA	49.31	48.34	49.74	49.26 **
Sierra Leone	40.92	48.37	NA	NA	50.08 *
South Africa	49.61	48.57	48.73	48.63	48.56 **
Togo	39.28	43.82	45.94	47.36	48.4 **
Uganda	44.37	48.23	49.57	50.09	50.12 *

*Available 2013 data
**Available 2014 data
Source: Gender Statistics, World Bank (2015).

by the International Monetary Fund (IMF) and World Bank, such as structural adjustment programs in the 1980s and Poverty Reduction Strategy programs in the 1990s, have imposed difficult demands such as deregulation, decentralization, and privatization, which increased debt and led many countries to reduce expenditure on social services such as education. As a result of these policies, many countries are not sufficiently economically secure to build or maintain good schools, train good teachers, and pay teachers an adequate salary. Even if primary school education is free, many parents cannot afford to provide school supplies for their children and often have to pull their children out of school to care for sick family members, assist with daily economic activities to support the family, or prepare them for early marriage. These problems are exacerbated in countries that are experiencing high adult mortality resulting from health epidemics such as HIV/AIDS or Ebola or dealing with civil unrest, which in some cases directly affects the education of girls. Overall, girls are especially susceptible to dropping out of school in countries where differences between the sexes in access to schooling and mortality rates are high.[13]

Socioeconomic and rural-urban differences are also pertinent to understanding dropout and completion rates by gender in primary schools. Children from rural low-income households are more likely to drop out of school than their peers from relatively higher income and urban areas regardless of gender. However, compared to boys, girls are especially disadvantaged in countries with wide income and regional differences and with very low primary school attendance rates.[14]

Table 10.3 shows primary school completion rates for boys and girls, respectively, in the last year of primary school as a percentage of the relevant age group between 1995 and 2014. With the exception of Mauritius and Botswana, there was a significant gap between boys and girls in most countries in completion rates between 1995 and 2005. For example, in Benin, Guinea, and Togo in 1995, there was a significant gap in primary completion rates for girls as compared to boys. Since 2005 more girls of primary school age have been able to complete school and in many cases have more than doubled their percentage distribution within their gender category since the mid-1990s. Notwithstanding, the percentage of girls completing primary school is lower than that for boys, although the gap is substantially smaller in the 2013 and 2014 period. While countries such as Ghana and Kenya show that girls complete primary school at a rate similar to that of boys, others such as Botswana, Madagascar, and Rwanda show that in recent years, girls are more likely to complete primary school than boys.

Secondary Education

The preceding section shows that access to primary education has made much progress for boys and girls in SSA, primarily because of universal primary education policies, which in many countries have been supported through increased government expenditure and funding from international donors. While there has been steady progress in the proportion of girls enrolled in secondary school, there is greater gender disparity in this category than at the primary level, especially widening between the lower and upper secondary levels.[15] Also, dropout rates for girls are significantly higher in the transition

TABLE 10.3. Primary completion rate, male and female (% of relevant age group)

COUNTRY	1995 Girls	1995 Boys	2005 Girls	2005 Boys	2010 Girls	2010 Boys	2013/2014 Girls	2013/2014 Boys
Benin	19.02	41	NA	NA	55.96	73.66	70.19 **	82.42 **
Botswana	95.87	84.57	98.66	90.89	NA	NA	101.22 *	98.11 *
Burkina Faso	15.28	21.8	27.47	35.87	44.16	49.88	62.98 **	59.02 **
Cameroon	NA	NA	NA	NA	64.29	75.34	67.76 **	76.51 **
Central African Rep.	NA	NA	19.6	33.32	29.5	51.28	NA	NA
Congo, Dem. Rep. of	NA	NA	NA	NA	52.28	69.21	59.98 *	73.48 *
Ethiopia	11.28	16.54	35.98	50.58	55.74	59.88	53.26 **	54.04 **
Gambia	33.51	48.59	70.42	72.77	74.67	72.28	68.96 **	65.68 **
Ghana	NA	NA	71.52	77.28	NA	NA	100.72	101.46
Guinea	9.58	28.91	43.4	64.74	47.19	67.65	55.62 **	67.76 **
Kenya	NA	NA	89.92	92.01	NA	NA	104.12 **	102.89 **
Liberia	NA	NA	NA	NA	NA	NA	54.03 **	63.45 **
Madagascar	30.65	31.32	57.62	57.92	71.21	69.88	70.77 **	66.79 **
Mauritius	95.96	95.74	97.97	97.01	99.5	99.02	98.57 **	96.41 **
Namibia	NA	NA	88.95	81.64	84.49	77.69	89.18 *	83.81 *
Nigeria	NA	NA	74.94	89.98	71.56	80.31	NA	NA
Rwanda	NA	NA	NA	NA	74.01	65.07	72.13 *	60.94 *
Senegal	NA	NA	47.53	55.09	57.63	55.33	62.73 *	55.33 *
Sierra Leone	NA	NA	NA	NA	NA	NA	67.57 *	71.47 *
Togo	26.1	54.61	61.31	85.62	61.12	79.78	78.93 **	91.24 **
Uganda	NA	NA	54.05	60.59	56.25	57.23	55.28 *	55.93 *

*Available 2013 data
**Available 2014 data
Source: Gender Statistics, World Bank (2015).

from lower to upper levels of secondary school, particularly where girls are over the age range for their cohort because of repetition.[16]

Most countries around the world now have full enrollment for both sexes at the secondary school level. However, often less than half of male and female students are able to attend secondary school in SSA. Drawing on World Bank Gender Statistics for selected countries with available and relatively consistent data for the time periods used in this study, table 10.4 shows changes in the percentage of girls enrolled in secondary schools between 1990 and 2015. Overall, there has been a modest increase in girls attending secondary school, with most countries now in the 40 percentile range. Some exceptions are South Africa, Botswana, Rwanda, Mauritius, and Madagascar, which are almost at or above 50 percent. In Rwanda, South Africa, and Botswana, there are more girls relative to boys enrolled in secondary school.[17]

Table 10.5 presents lower secondary school completion rates for boys and girls, respectively, in the final year of school as a percentage of the relevant age group for selected countries with available and consistent data between 1995

TABLE 10.4. Secondary education (% female pupils)

COUNTRY	1990	2000	2005	2010	2013/2014/2015
Benin	NA	31.16	35.42	NA	40.22 **
Botswana	52.52	51.37	50.49	0	51 *
Burkina Faso	NA	38.95	40.73	42.49	45.73 **
Cameroon	40.5	NA	43.83	NA	45.68 **
Congo, Dem. Rep. of	NA	NA	NA	36.4	38.15 **
Ethiopia	NA	39.99	37.26	44.86	NA
Gambia	32.23	NA	NA	48.78	NA
Ghana	39.05	43.99	44.51	NA	47.35 **
Guinea	24.52	NA	32.9	NA	39.12 **
Liberia	NA	41.65	NA	NA	43 **
Madagascar	48.51	NA	48.95	NA	49.52 **
Mauritius	49.67	48.51	48.85	50.55	49.69 **
Nigeria	42.87	44.88	44.61	45.83	NA
Rwanda	45.44	49.1	47.21	50.67	52.49 **
Senegal	33.5	39.24	42.45	46.29	NA
Seychelles	NA	51.31	50.29	49.44	49.24 **
Sierra Leone	34.71	NA	NA	NA	46.67 *
South Africa	53.77	52.4	51.35	51.14	50.9 **
Uganda	36.35	43.38	44.3	46.04	46.36 *

*Available 2013 data
**Available 2014 data
Source: Gender Statistics, World Bank (2015).

and 2014. Lower secondary school is a critical stage that determines future prospects for a student in terms of tracking into academic or vocational streams or for school completion to join the labor market and family businesses, or, in the case of many girls, to prepare for marriage. Girls less often complete secondary school at any level in SSA than boys. This table shows nonetheless that some countries, such as Botswana and Mauritius, display relatively high completion rates for girls and boys, and this has been a consistent trend over the past twenty years. Other countries, such as Burkina Faso, Ethiopia, Guinea, and Togo, show low overall rates for boys and girls. Although there is progress toward both groups completing lower secondary school, a higher percentage of boys graduate relative to girls.

Several factors explain why girls generally lag behind boys in accessing and completing secondary school. Secondary school is not free, and parents find themselves deciding whether to invest in educating sons or daughters. Given male-dominant cultures in many African countries, and narrow gender role expectations for girls, girls are disproportionately denied access to secondary education because schooling is perceived as offering relatively low returns for girls, and girls are not expected to hold wage jobs. Girls are also more likely to face sexual abuse and harassment from male peers, male school teachers, and older men in their communities. Security issues promoted by lack of bathrooms and adequate sanitary facilities, as well as long walks from home to school, contribute to constraints girls face at each stage of their education experience. Teachers, who bear prime responsibility for communicating to students societal expectations of proper gender roles, influence students' interests, aspirations, and performance in secondary schools. For example, both male and female teachers expect boys to outperform girls in science disciplines.[18] Dropping out due to the high demand for domestic labor, pregnancy, or discrimination is common for girls. These and other sociocultural and economic factors discussed later lead to disproportionately high repetition and attrition rates for girls.

Conceptual and Policy Discourses

Here I examine conceptual and policy discourses that impact educational programs to explain why providing girls with greater access to schooling will not necessarily solve the problem of inequality in educational opportunities or outcomes, arguing that broader societal issues of rights and social justice should be factored into policy and program agendas. Formal education in the Global South operates within gendered social systems influenced by male-dominant norms that reinforce gender role expectations and marginalize women and

TABLE 10.5. Lower secondary completion rate, male and female (% of relevant age group)

COUNTRY	1995		2005		2010		2013/2014/2015	
	Girls	Boys	Girls	Boys	Girls	Boys	Girls	Boys
Botswana	88.46	75.46	87.5	80.53	NA	NA	87.23 *	86.28 *
Burkina Faso	NA	NA	8.15	11.58	14.6	18.2	23.06 **	26.36 **
Ethiopia	9.55	13	13.5	24.14	24.86	32.13	27.94 **	30.77 **
Gambia	NA	NA	57.24	75.93	57.96	62.24	61.88 **	61.20 **
Ghana	NA	NA	51.61	61.77	NA	NA	75.23	79.69
Guinea	NA	NA	14.77	31.37	27.53	43.39	27.85 **	42.13 **
Madagascar	NA	NA	17.52	18.14	27.64	29.52	36.77 **	37.32 **
Mauritius	79.25	70.35	84.74	76.38	87.51	76.51	89.77 **	80.02 **
Namibia	NA	NA	64.09	57.79	62.64	53.85	62.70 *	55.72 *
Senegal	NA	NA	17.74	22.12	27.94	32.57	40.05 **	40.51 **
Togo	8.25	23.42	26.05	51.39	24.35	45.88	29.21 **	46.60 **
Uganda	7.42	12.37	NA	NA	25.49	29.99	27.57 *	31.13 *

*Available 2013 data
**Available 2014 data
Source: Gender Statistics, World Bank (2015).

girls.[19] Conceptual and policy approaches used to explain the impact of these systems on gender inequalities in education are largely informed by Western perspectives, which leads to incomplete distorted evidence that impacts policies and programs designed to foster gender equality in schooling.[20]

Western analyses of gender and education largely derive from neoliberal international agendas for economic development and poverty reduction in the Global South. Funded by powerful agencies such as the World Bank, UNESCO, and other international donor agencies, these studies use neoliberal economic paradigms that position individuals at the center of analysis, making them accountable for overcoming their marginalization. For example, human capital theory is widely known for its impact on educational policies and programs of the World Bank and other international development agencies. It assumes that education will provide the tools to achieve economic growth and social development by producing skilled workers for the market economy and emphasizes individual attributes such as personal values and attitudes used by rational individuals to maximize educational and career goals. As a conceptual framework for formulating educational policies and programs to promote gender equality in schooling, human capital theory lacks adequate explanations for how gender, race, class, ethnicity, and other intersecting factors produce and reinforce unequal educational outcomes. Regarding women, human capital theory emphasizes "modernization" of the family by women improving their maternal and family-supportive roles.[21] Accordingly, international funding for educating women and girls has mainly invested in primary education as a tool to reduce poverty, lower family size, delay marriages, and produce healthy educated children, with less attention from funding agencies on increasing numbers of women and girls in secondary and tertiary education.[22]

In contrast, the rights-based approach to gender equality in education aims at full equality between women and men and the full participation of women in development, informed by the gender and development (GAD) theoretical framework (see chapter 6) that allows for attention to issues regarding educational access, as well as gender-coded practices within schools and on gendered outcomes of schooling. UNESCO was a major proponent of the rights-based approach and launched many programs such as those raising awareness about gender stereotypes and prejudices in educational materials and promoting equality in vocational and technical training leading to employment for women.[23] The "Education for All" campaign launched collaboratively by UNESCO, the World Bank, and UNICEF in 1990 and the Millennium Development Goals (MDGs) are examples of the rights-based approach put into practice and demonstrate that one overarching theory does not control all education funding.

Naila Kabeer, a feminist scholar of economic development, has argued that the rhetoric of women's equality and empowerment embedded in the rights-based perspective is controversial and difficult to translate into policy because it critically examines content, process, and outcomes and advocates redistribution of power and resources.[24] Findings from the Global Monitoring Report of the "Education for All" campaign reveal that using enrollment and completion statistics to assess gender parity under this model is inadequate because these statistics only reveal minimum information, some of which could be fabricated.[25] Elaine Unterhalter and Amy North provide the example of Ghana where the number of children attending school and recorded in attendance registers is inflated by over 100 percent because schools receive funding according to enrollment numbers; the Ghanaian government is aware of the unreliability of these statistics.[26]

The intersectionality perspective on gender and education in the Global South more closely interrogates interconnections between local and global economic and political forces that shape the nature of gender relations in schools. Intersectional oppressions based on class, race, caste, gender, and sexuality impact the experiences of girls in schools.[27] This postcolonial or poststructuralist feminist approach aims to produce knowledge useful for understanding the connections between gendered power relationships and educational experiences in schools,[28] and it centers the voices of Global South scholars in the debate on gender and education, while taking into account empowerment, gender equality, and social justice issues, producing more nuanced understandings of education and gender inequality that are linked to the struggle for socioeconomic justice. New diaspora (see chapter 12) scholars from the Global South such as Chandra Mohanty, Oyèrónkẹ́ Oyěwùmí, and Obioma Nnameka provide related analytical frameworks that investigate the complex political, economic, and cultural understandings of objectifying and silencing Southern women and girls in Western feminist scholarship. They emphasize the need to understand historical and contemporary contexts of colonial, neoliberal, and local patriarchal encounters in knowledge construction.[29] Scholars in the gender and education field who go beyond numbers and apply this approach include Joan Dejaeghere, Frances Vavrus, N'Dri Assié-Lumumba, and Pholoho Morojele.[30]

Societal Factors

A variety of societal factors shape gendered experiences such as poverty, neoliberal economic development policies, religion, and male-dominant cultures that intersect with gender, class, sexuality, and geographical location to marginalize girls despite their increasing enrollment rates in school. Here I also look at ways in which girls make sense of their lived experiences and construct alternative aspirations and visions of their future.

Rural/Urban Disparities

Although much progress has been made in increasing girls' access to school in sub-Saharan Africa, rural girls encounter many difficulties with attending schools, a fact often overlooked when emphasizing statistical data to measure gender parity.[31] For example, only 12 percent of girls in rural areas are able to attend school among the Hausa in Nigeria. In northern Ghana, women and girls are more disadvantaged in access to education because of historical legacies of colonialism, whose missionaries did not build schools there because of Muslim resistance to enforced conversion to Christianity of students and colonial goals to ensure availability of unskilled labor for the mines and plantations in the south.[32]

A related problem for girls in rural areas are the long distances between their homes and schools due to few schools being available. Proximity to school has a direct impact on girls' access and performance because of safety issues related to long commutes. Parents are often reluctant to send girls to school if they have to walk long distances to school unaccompanied. A study of secondary schoolgirls in rural Masaka District, Uganda, found that it took several girls at least five hours a day to complete a sixteen-mile walk to and from school, often through desolate areas. Resultant problems arising for such girls included not only lack of homework time and exhaustion but also vulnerability to sexual harassment from schoolboys and men. One student stated, "The biggest problem is these men who disturb us, begging for sex."[33]

Then there is the issue of the unequal gender division of labor in household chores. Girls' many domestic chores must be completed at home before leaving for school or after returning home late in the evening, which affects their school attendance record and ability to complete homework. Lateness arriving at school is often punished. While some schoolboys might ride bikes to school and so shorten their commute, in rural areas in Buganda, girls are not permitted to ride bicycles. In general, the rate of success in exams is lower in rural than urban schools because of lack of resources to equip schools. Given the challenges girls face, as discussed above, their exam performance is usually lower than boys'. Although much effort has been put into developing rural schools in SSA, examination certificates and results from rural schools are also often valued less than those for urban schools in many countries, Zimbabwe in particular.[34]

Another factor affecting rural educational systems is that wage employment opportunities are not widely available in rural areas, particularly for women. A 2008 Ghanaian study found that 27 percent of all men between the ages of fifteen and sixty-four were in wage employment compared to 8.9 percent for women, while women in wage employment usually occupy lower civil service occupational ranks such as secretaries and receptionists.[35] In southern African countries such as Lesotho and Zimbabwe there is a high rate of male migration from rural areas to urban or mining areas for school leavers. Boys tend to leave earlier because of family responsibilities to herd cattle, plus other employment opportunities that favor men with limited education in mining and cash crop farming. Educational policies that do not address the employment needs of girls in rural regions ultimately perpetuate gender imbalances in labor force participation rates. From their parents' perspective, since most girls in rural areas farm and will continue to farm, it makes more sense for girls to be trained by their parents, especially their mothers, rather than making their way, sometimes hazardously, to distant schools.

Socioeconomic Background

The socioeconomic background of parents is critical to educational opportunities available to children. Research in SSA shows that children from financially stable families are more likely to be in school or to stay in school than those from families with few financial resources. Better-off parents are more likely to provide school supplies such as uniforms, books, and school fees and rely less on child labor to assist with household chores and other economic activities. They are usually more educated and upwardly mobile, employed in the formal sector, and more likely to understand the value of good formal education for children's futures.[36] Research in some West African countries also shows that girls have better chances to obtain more education when mothers have attained at least secondary-level education since those mothers will have stronger bargaining power within families to invest in their children's education, especially their daughters'.[37] However, girls from impoverished families farmed out as domestic servants or enslaved normally receive no schooling (see chapter 9).

Sexual Violence and Sexual Harassment

Sexual violence and sexual harassment are endemic problems damaging the education of girls in SSA (see chapter 15). A 2014 Human Rights Watch report points out that girls' education is shortchanged due to their vulnerability to physical and psychological abuse from rape and sexual assaults perpetrated by classmates, teachers, and other school officials.[38] A community member responded to an interview about girls' education in rural Kenya: "the girl child is an endangered species in the Inka community since their childhood is often cut short by expectations to engage in sexual behavior at a young age." Girls are socialized to comply with societal norms about femininity and expected gender roles in their communities, making them susceptible to sexual violence in the schools, while male-dominant ideas support boys' exerting power over girls in conformity with established systems of hegemonic masculinity. These values are reinforced in schools through peer pressure and coercion of girls to perform sexual favors and "sexual patronage," the latter involving transactional sex for money or other items.[39] Human Rights Watch reports that in Zambia most sexual abuses by teachers go unreported, and they are not held accountable or penalized for abusive behavior. In fact, parents in some cases were willing to arrange a marriage between their daughter and the abuser.[40]

Such attitudes and actions often result in girls' pregnancies, for which schoolgirls are usually expelled, but men and boys are not held accountable for sexual impositions, including rapes. Most recently in Sierra Leone, as a result of the Ebola epidemic that left schools closed for over eight months, the government prohibited pregnant schoolgirls from attending school and taking exams. Media reports note that during this health crisis, sexual violence increased, and many young girls engaged in transactional sex in order to help support their families.[41] Poverty and the cost of a secondary school education contribute to schoolgirls engaging in transactional sex to cover school fees, school supplies, and other school-related financial commitments, sometimes with the encouragement of parents.

Discourse on female sexuality in Africa has received very little attention in the literature on gender and education. In 1996 Amina Mama pointed out, "Considering that sexuality has been a major area of interest within women's studies internationally, the first question one asks in surveying African women's studies is, why there are so few studies on sexuality?"[42] This is still a pressing issue for lesbian, gay, bisexual, and transgender (LGBT) students in African schools today (see chapter 14). Human Rights Watch reports that in South Africa, girls who are LGBT are bullied, harassed, and threatened by peers and teachers in spite of strong legislation that prohibits discrimination and intolerance in schools. Failure by school authorities to enforce such laws and educational policies perpetuates and reinforces discrimination against these students and prevents them from achieving educational goals.[43]

Health

Many schoolgirls in SSA end up missing school because of lack of clean water and sanitation either at home or in school, particularly when menstruating. When clean water is not available, girls are susceptible to discrimination from peers and teachers because they do not have access to sanitary napkins and water for washing. Unsafe toilets also make them vulnerable to sexual violence at school. Malaria and HIV/AIDS are prevalent in many countries and negatively affect the attendance record of girls in school, especially when they come from poor families and cannot afford to go to modern hospitals for treatment. According to the UN Millennium Project, about three-quarters of young people aged fifteen to twenty-four infected with HIV/AIDS in SSA are women and girls.[44] In sum, when the health and hygiene of young girls are compromised as a result of these factors, girls are likely to miss school and perform poorly on exams.[45]

Religion

Although school enrollment figures might portray a bright picture for gender parity in primary and to some extent secondary schools in SSA, there are families who for religious or moral reasons do not want their daughters to attend school. In Muslim households, especially those with fundamentalist beliefs (see chapter 5), girls are particularly vulnerable, largely because parents feel that educational institutions are influenced by westernization and Christianity and that they will interfere with Muslim religious beliefs. A prominent example is the case of 276 girls at a government secondary school in Borno State in northern Nigeria, who were abducted from their dormitories in the dead of night by Boko Haram militants on April 14, 2014. Several organizations have been established to campaign against this heinous crime, including "Bringbackourgirls," formed by a group of educated Nigerian women. Boko Haram strictly observes *shari'a* law, which requires the practice of female seclusion, including for girls who have reached the age of puberty. This cultural and religious practice encourages early or forced marriage of girls and deprives them of their right to an education. The indigenous religious practice of *trokosi*, discussed in chapter 9, also prevents some Ghanaian girls from obtaining an education, while subjecting them to sexual abuse by shrine priests.[46]

Women Refugees and Displaced Girls

Civil conflicts in African states such as the Democratic Republic of Congo, Liberia, Sierra Leone, Angola, and Somalia since the 1990s have further dismantled the infrastructure of already weak economies and disrupted the capacity of governments to provide quality education for their citizens (see chapter 15). The forced displacement of girls is of particular concern because these armed conflicts undermine existing educational achievements. In conflict situations, girls are usually expected to care for younger siblings while their mothers are at work supporting their families. Young girls are susceptible to kidnapping, sexual violence, and sexual exploitation, as well as forced labor. Even when makeshift schools are available for refugees or the internally displaced, parents are hesitant to have daughters take advantage of such opportunities because of security issues. In many SSA countries recovering from armed conflict, civil society organizations funded by international agencies, charities, and school alumni organizations in the new diaspora have stepped in to provide resources to sustain crumbling school systems.

Promising Voices

As shown, various efforts to eliminate discriminatory practices that perpetuate gender inequality in school environments are difficult to implement because of gender role norms and values instilled in the wider community. Some argue that the school is actually a microcosm of this process and that girls internalize their expected roles by maintaining a "culture of silence" that marginalizes their engagement with society.[47] Emerging studies on gender and education are increasingly giving voice to female students in order to understand how they make sense of their lived experiences in school environments and how the complex processes that govern their lives in and out of school impact their educational performance and aspirations for the future. A case study of Tanzanian girls' perceptions of the value of a secondary school education shows that their aspirations are not just based on the formal credentials and employment opportunities that education will bring, but that they fully understand that school equips them with the tools to transform their lives for the better in the future.[48] Meanwhile, girls' and boys' experiences of gender roles in rural primary schools in Lesotho warn us not to make assumptions about girls' conformity to stereotypical hegemonic feminine gender roles. There was evidence of policing and sanctioning of girls by teachers who expressed intolerance when girls asked questions in class, played and fought with boys, or displayed questionable sexual conduct. Notwithstanding, girls developed inventive ways to subvert and challenge dominant gender roles.[49] These examples show the importance of incorporating the knowledge and perspectives of students in formulating and implementing policies to best serve the goals of promoting gender equality and girls' empowerment in African educational systems.

Conclusion

This chapter examines gender disparities in formal education in sub-Saharan Africa, focusing on primary and secondary education. While there are significant improvements in the number of girls enrolled in primary school in some countries, in most countries girls have not reached parity with boys. Progress was largely due to government-mandated policies to promote compulsory primary education and financial support from international donors and agencies. Although there are substantial numbers of girls completing primary school and enrolling in secondary school, there are fewer girls than boys, and there are extremely high rates of attrition for girls in the transition between primary and secondary school and completion of lower secondary school.

I argue that to understand the experiences of girls in SSA educational systems, we must go beyond the numbers to examine contextual factors such as power relations governing gender norms and values in the wider community and their impact on the school environment. A review of the literature shows that neoliberal conceptual and policy approaches used to address persistent gender inequalities in African educational systems have reinforced existing gender inequalities in these societies. Recent feminist approaches such as intersectional theory used to explain gender inequality in African educational systems provide more nuanced understandings of local and global processes that shape political, economic, and sociocultural contexts governing patterns of gender inequality and the struggle for social justice. Successful approaches put the voices of students at the center of analysis and deconstruct essentialized notions of gender by examining ways in which girls resist and subvert expected norms and values in their cultural environments. They add valuable perspectives to our understanding of the more material aspects of girls' disadvantages with respect to education.

African schoolgirls encounter many problems ranging from long commutes to school, lack of water and sanitation at home and in school, safety issues stemming from sexual violence and sexual harassment, sexual identity issues, lack of schools and alternatives to agricultural employment in rural areas, displacement from armed conflict, unequal gender roles assigning most domestic chores to girls, and discriminatory religious practices. Breaking down these barriers will require restructuring educational systems, economies, and institutional environments in transformative ways that go beyond numbers and neoliberal policies and that take into account girls' perspectives on education, allowing for the empowerment of African girls through schooling.

Notes

I would like to thank Deorajhee Judy Mahabir for providing research assistance in preparing the tables. I also thank the coeditors and reviewers for their thoughtful feedback.

1. Rosie Peppin Vaughan, "Girls' and Women's Education within UNESCO and the World Bank, 1945–2000," *Compare* 40, no. 4 (2010): 405; Fiona Leach, *Practising Gender Analysis in Education* (Oxford: Oxfam GB, 2003), 5.

2. Shelley Kathleen Jones, "Girls' Secondary Education in Uganda: Assessing Policy within the Women's Empowerment Framework," *Gender and Education* 23, no. 4 (2011): 385.

3. UNESCO, Institute for Statistics, *Financing Education in Sub-Saharan Africa: Meeting the Challenges of Expansion, Equity, and Quality* (Montreal: UNESCO, 2011), accessed October 26, 2015, http://uis.unesco.org/sites/default/files/documents/financing-education-in-sub-saharan-africameeting-the-challenges-of-expansion-equity-and-quality-en_0.pdf.

4. UNESCO, *World Atlas of Gender Equality in Education* (UNESCO Publishing: Paris, 2012), accessed October 26, 2015, http://uis.unesco.org/sites/default/files/documents/world-atlas-of-gender-equality-in-education-2012-en.pdf.

5. UNESCO, *World Atlas*; Leach, *Practising Gender Analysis*, 5.

6. Elaine Unterhalter and Amy North, "Girls' Schooling, Gender Equity, and the Global Education and Development Agenda: Conceptual Disconnections, Political Struggles, and the Difficulties of Practice," *Feminist Formations* 23, no. 3 (2011): 4.

7. Joan Dejaeghere and Frances Vavrus, "Educational Formations: Gendered Experiences of Schooling in Local Contexts," *Feminist Formations* 23, no. 3 (2011): viii.

8. Hanna Posti-Pahokas and Paivi Palojoki, "Navigating Transitions to Adulthood through Secondary Education: Aspirations and the Value of Education for Tanzanian Girls," *Journal of Youth Studies* 17, no. 5 (2014): 664–81.

9. UNESCO, *World Atlas*.

10. UNESCO Press, "Financing Education for All," Education for All Global Monitoring Report 2012, accessed November 4, 2015, http://www.unesco.org/new/fileadmin/MULTIMEDIA/HQ/ED/pdf/gmr2012-report-ch2.pdf.

11. UNESCO, *World Atlas*, 46; Leach, *Practising Gender Analysis*, 5.

12. World Bank, "Gender Statistics 2015," accessed November 15, 2015, http://data.worldbank.org/data-catalog/gender-statistics.

13. Leach, *Practising Gender Analysis*, 5, 7.

14. UNESCO, *World Atlas*, 57.

15. UNESCO, *World Atlas*, 57.

16. Hanna Posti-Ahokas and Elina Lehtomaki, "The Significance of Student Voice: Female Students' Interpretations of Failure in Tanzanian Secondary Education," *Gender and Education* 26, no. 4 (2014): 339.

17. World Bank, "Gender Statistics."

18. Josephine Beoku-Betts, "Gender and Formal Education in Africa: An Exploration of the Opportunity Structure at the Secondary and Tertiary Levels," in *Women and Education in Sub-Saharan Africa: Power, Opportunities, and Constraints*, ed. M. Bloch, J. Beoku-Betts, and B. R. Tabachnik (Boulder, CO: Lynne Rienner, 1998), 177.

19. Dejaeghere and Vavrus, "Educational Formations," vii–xvi; Rosie Peppin Vaughn, "Girls' and Women's Education within UNESCO and the World Bank, 1945–2000," *Compare* 40, no. 4 (2010): 405–23.

20. Shailaja Fennell and Madeline Arnot, "Decentering Hegemonic Gender Theory: The Implications for Educational Research," *Compare* 38, no. 5 (2008): 526.

21. Peppin Vaughn, "Girls' and Women's Education," 411.

22. Unterhalter and North, "Girls' Schooling," 5.

23. Peppin Vaughn, "Girls' and Women's Education," 414–15.

24. Naila Kabeer, *Reversed Realities: Gender Hierarchies in Development Thought* (London: Verso, 1994).

25. UNESCO, *Education for All: Is the World on Track*, EFA Global Monitoring Report (Paris: UNESCO, 2002).

26. Unterhalter and North, "Girls' Schooling," 5.

27. Dejaeghere and Vavrus, "Educational Formations," ix.

28. Fennell and Arnot, "Decentering," 525–38; H. B. Holmarsdottir, I. B. Moler Ekne, and H. L. Augestad, "The Dialectic between Global Gender Goals and Local Empowerment: Girls' Education in Southern Sudan and South Africa," *Research in Comparative and International Education* 6, no. 1 (2011): 14–26.

29. Chandra T. Mohanty, "Under Western Eyes: Feminist Scholarship and Colonial Discourses," *Feminist Review* 30 (1988); Oyeronke Oyewumi, ed., *African Women and Feminism: Reflecting the Politics of Sisterhood* (Trenton, NJ; Africa World Press, 2003); Obioma Nnaemeka, "Nego-Feminism: Theorizing, Practicing, and Pruning Africa's Way," *Signs: Journal of Women in Culture and Society* 29, 2 (2004): 357–85; Amina Mama, "Critical Capacities: Facing the Challenges of Intellectual Development in Africa," Inaugural Lecture Prince Claus Chair in Development and Equity, Institute of Social Studies, The Hague, April 28, 2004, http://princeclauschair.nl/inaugural-address -mama/; F. Steady, "Race and Gender in the Neoliberal Paradigm of Globalization," in *African Women and Globalization: Dawn of the 21st Century*, ed. J. R. Chepyator-Thompson (Trenton: NJ: Africa World Press, 2005), 19–42.

30. Dejaeghere and Vavrus, "Educational Formations"; N'Dri Assié-Lumumba, ed., *Women and Higher Education in Africa* (Abidjan, Cote D'Ivoire: CEPARRED, 2007); Pholoho Morojele, "What Does It Mean to Be a Girl? Implications of Girls' and Boys' Experiences of Gender Roles in Rural Lesotho Primary Schools," *Education as Change* 15, no. 1 (2011): 133–47.

31. Lizzi Milligan, "'They Are Not Serious like the Boys': Gender Norms and Contradictions for Girls in Rural Kenya," *Gender and Education* 26, no. 5 (2014): 466.

32. A. K. Darkwah, "Education: Pathway to Empowerment for Ghanaian Women?" in *Feminisms, Empowerment and Development*, ed. A. Cornwall and J. Edwards (London: Zed Books), 89.

33. Jones, "Girls' Secondary Education," 385–413, 393.

34. Nicola Ansell, "Secondary Education in Lesotho and Zimbabwe and the Needs of Rural Girls: Pronouncements, Policy, and Practice" *Comparative Education* 38, no. 1 (2002): 92.

35. Darkwah, "Education," 90.

36. A. Kazeem, L. Jensen, and C. Shannon Stokes, "School Attendance in Nigeria: Understanding the Impact and Intersection of Gender, Urban-Rural Residence, and Socio-Economic Status," *Comparative Education Review* 54, no. 2 (2010): 305.

37. P. Glick and D. E. Sahn, "Schooling for Girls and Boys in a West African Coun-try: The Effects of Parental Education, Income, and Household Structure," *Economics of Education Review* 19, no. 1 (2000): 63–87.

38. Human Rights Watch, "General Recommendation on Girls'/Women's Right to Education," June 23, 2014, https://www.hrw.org/news/2014/06/23/human-rights-watch -submission-general-recommendation-girls/womens-right-education.

39. Milligan, 'They Are Not Serious,'" 469–70.

40. Human Rights Watch, "General Recommendation on Girls'/Women's Right to Education," June 23, 2014.

41. Laura Angela Bagnetto, "Pregnant School Girls Barred from School and a Right to Education," RFI, March 29, 2015, http://en.rfi.fr/africa/20150329-sierra-leone-preg nant-girls-barred-school-human-rights-education-ebola-education.

42. Amina Mama, "Women's Studies and Studies of Women in Africa during the 1990s," *CODESRIA Working Paper Series* 5 (1996): 39.

43. Human Rights Watch, "General Recommendation," 6–7.

44. U.N. Millennium Project Task Force on Education and Gender Equality 2005, *Taking Action: Achieving Gender Equality and Empowering Women* (London: Earthscan, 2005), 56.

45. Human Rights Watch, "General Recommendation," 8; for examples of hygiene problems girls face due to lack of clean water and sanitation, see Jones, "Girls' Second-ary Education," 396.

46. Theresa Tuwor and Marie-Antoinette Sossou, "Gender Discrimination and Education in West Africa: Strategies for Maintaining Girls in School," *International Journal of Inclusive Education* 12, no. 4 (2008): 368.

47. Benedicta Egbo, "Women's Education and Social Development in Africa," in *Issues of African Education: Sociological Perspectives*, ed. A. A. Abdi and A. Cleghorn (New York: Palgrave Macmillan, 2005), 114–58.

48. Posti-Ahokas and Palojoki, "Navigating Transitions," 664–81.

49. Morojele, "What Does It Mean?," 133–47.

Suggested Readings

Jones, Shelley Kathleen. "Girls Secondary Education in Uganda: Assessing Policy with the Women's Empowerment Framework." *Gender and Education* 23, no. 4 (2011): 385–413.

Morojele, Pholoho. "What Does It Mean to Be a Girl? Implications of Girls' and Boys' Experiences of Gender Roles in Rural Lesotho Primary Schools." *Education as Change* 15, no. 1 (2011): 133–47.

Posti-Ahokas, Hanna, and Elina Lehtomaki. "The Significance of Student Voice: Female Students' Interpretation of Failure in Tanzanian Secondary Education." *Gender and Education* 26, no. 4 (2014): 338–55.

UNESCO. "Gender Review." Global Education Monitoring Report 2016. http://gem -report-2016.unesco.org/en/gender-review/.

Varvus, Frances. "Uncoupling the Articulation between Girls' Education and Tradi-tion in Tanzania." *Gender and Education* 14, no. 4 (2002): 367–89.

MISSIONS AFRICAINES, 150, COURS GAMBETTA, LYON.
COTE-D'OR - Procession à Salt-Pont.

Figure 11.1. Procession of Christian women, Salt Pond, Gold Coast, ca. 1920. Missions Postcard Collection, Yale Divinity School Library.

URBANIZING WOMEN

Merging the Personal, Political, and Spatial

Teresa Barnes

Dakar, Johannesburg, Lagos, Dar es Salaam, Nairobi, Libreville, Kinshasa, Cairo, Harare. Histories of African women in these cities have generally been written in one of two ways. Since the 1980s, scholars have generally traced the ups and downs of women's social and economic status while they were living in towns and cities but have said little about the land-, sound-, and streetscapes of those same cities. But as Egyptian activist Nawal El Saadawi wryly observed about Cairo, "I've travelled all over the world, but I have never seen the likes of Egyptians for exerting the same pressure with their hands on the car horns as they do with their feet on the accelerator. My flat is on the fifth floor, but the car horns still sound like screams, like a continuous wailing."[1] Histories of urban women in Africa rarely integrate the noise, heat, dust, and the smells of roasting meat, perfume, and sewage into narratives about the rise and fall of gendered political influence. In many urban histories the city itself is often, paradoxically, largely invisible.

Also problematically, works on urban African geography relate the built environment to race and class but less often to women and gender.[2] How have women experienced life in African cities? For example, when churchwomen in their starched whites marched smartly down a street in colonial Accra, as in the photo opposite, how did the women in the foreground relate to the men in the background? How did their presence alter the life of the street that day? As Julia Clancy-Smith wrote about nineteenth-century Tunis, the "meaning of streets and other public domains was structured by gender first and foremost, more so than race, class or ethnicity."[3]

Bridging the personal, political, and spatial aspects of African cities will be the task of the next generation of Africa's urban gender specialists. They will heed warnings about portraying the African city—nothing if not vibrant—as one-dimensional.[4] And they will be following in the footsteps of Africa's novelists, whose evocation of the many dimensions of gendered urban life has often been breathtaking.[5]

Another cleavage to track in the study of urban Africa is the very concept of gender itself. By implying both unchanging, reproductively based differentiation and necessary structural contestation between male and female, mechanistic applications of U.S.- and European-derived gender theory to African history has been shown to do violence to African concepts and practices, which have been both discursively situational and corporeally fluid.[6] Gender has literally been made and remade through urban clashes and compromises. If, for example, learning to manipulate and negotiate colonial restrictions meant that female migrants to colonial Harare discovered that to be a woman was to become permanently, structurally dependent on men; if gender was remade in colonial Libreville in fluid processes of "urban becoming"; or if the "city girls" of Dar es Salaam in the 1970s, sporting miniskirts and Afros, resembled both African American women in Los Angeles and the more modest women of rural Tanzania, then historians and social scientists can map those changes over time.[7]

Another challenge in discussing African urbanization is to bring all urban women into a single interpretative frame. On a continent where in the colonial period race almost always correlated directly with class, separate historiographies could almost lead one to believe that white, brown, and black women lived in completely different cities. Women of European descent have largely had a separate historiography in African studies; women of Asian descent have been virtually invisible.[8] In this chapter, unless otherwise noted, the terms "African women" and "women" refer to women who spoke one or more indigenous African languages as their first language.

African cities have a long and varied history. The great African medieval cities such as Meroë, Alexandria, and Timbuktu and old cities of the North and East African coasts such as Cairo, Tunis, and Mombasa predate many European cities. In the twenty-first century, African urban spaces range from sprawling capital cities to dusty provincial administrative towns; from grimy inner cities to calm green suburbs; from ramshackle shanty settlements dotted with market women's stalls to skyscraping apartment blocks and glittering shopping malls. This diversity presents a challenge to simplistic generalizations.[9]

The first two sections of this chapter deal with demographics and the impact of colonialism on women's urban migrations. The third section looks at the intertwining of the personal and the economic in families, marriages, and markets, leading to a section that deals with the many ways that women tried to secure improvements in their livelihoods in the early independence and liberation eras, years of mainly unkept official promises. The persistence of women as performers of domestic labor is taken up in the next section. The following section briefly considers women's recreational and leisurely urban activities. The last section suggests that modern urban planning practices have largely ignored women's histories and concerns.

Demographics

Urbanization has a very long history on the African continent.[10] Some towns have roots in precolonial city-states such as the Sokoto Caliphate in modern-day northern Nigeria.[11] Some cities are very old centers of trade and/or learning (Alexandria, Fez, Timbuktu, Mombasa). Not simply big villages (of which there were many), precolonial African towns and cities exhibited economic and social differentiation, specialized craftsmanship in many fields, large architecturally designed buildings, and the centering of political power (often expressed in military terms). Examples of these were Great Zimbabwe in Zimbabwe and Mpanza of the Kongo in Angola. Starting in the fifteenth century, the Portuguese, Dutch, French, and British set up coastal settlements, some of which stayed at the level of simple fortifications to defend their slave and produce trading, but others grew slowly to be complex urban spaces. Chinese explorers recorded that Kilwa, a trading city on the East African coast, had two- and three-story houses in the fifteenth century. Cape Town, at the southernmost tip of the continent, had a population of 1,450 in the 1720s, and approximately 20,000 a hundred years later.[12] Africa's current metropolitan areas often began or grew substantially with colonial economic expansion: as trading ports (Dakar, Lagos, Durban, Accra, Maputo), mining camps (Johannesburg, Enugu), or railway termini (Nairobi, Port Harcourt, Kampala). Others had their genesis in the long struggle against the Atlantic slave trade (Monrovia, Freetown, Libreville).

Until the late twentieth century, the majority of Africa's population was overwhelmingly rural (see chapter 8), living in family homesteads in small or large villages surrounded by combinations of extensive fields, pastures, forests, or deserts, or pursuing patterns of seasonal migration. As late as 1970 only 10 percent of Africa's population lived in towns larger than 100,000 people; but these were on steep upward trajectories. The population of Kinshasa, Congo, grew from 34,000 in 1930 to 402,000 twenty years later.[13] Similarly, Bamako's population grew from 76,000 in 1958 to 675,000 in 1983.[14] The population of Dar es Salaam quadrupled between 1948 and 1967.[15] Overall, from 1950 to 1990, the annual urban growth rate of francophone West Africa was 7.8 percent, one of the highest in the world, while for all of sub-Saharan Africa from 1975 to 1990 it was 4.4 percent, the highest in the developing world.[16] Demographers have debated how to account for these high growth rates, since traditional urbanization theory holds that economic growth is the main pull factor that draws labor and families from rural to urban areas.[17] African urban growth rates have skyrocketed even though for most of their new residents, city streets have turned out to be paved with mud or sand rather than gold.[18]

From "African Women in Towns" to "'Wicked' Women"

Beginning in the early 1970s, Anglophone scholars of urbanization began to chronicle the presence of African women in urban areas. Building on a few urban case studies and the modernization perspectives provided by sociologists of urban Africa, these works were set in a problematic "emerging Africa" paradigm in which cities were "modern" and rural areas were "traditional." One focus of scholarship of Africa's "emergence" was the extent to which women were integrated into the political, domestic, and cultural lives of African cities. They generally agreed that women followed men to the cities, implying that at some point Africa's cities had been virtually male-only settlements. Works written in this vein considered topics like migrancy, kinship, prostitution, and political involvement largely as ways of tracking the transformation of a supposedly stable "traditional" rural Africa into one that more closely resembled the hustle and bustle of the urbanized West, ignoring Africa's many historically long-established urban populations.[19]

One of the first groups to draw feminist scholarly attention were women traders and market vendors and their centuries-old traditions of entrepreneurism, which have been especially prevalent in West and Central Africa (see chapters 3, 6, and 8).[20] In places, the pressures of colonialism detached women's trading traditions from their moorings in more collective understandings and practices of economic activity.[21] In others, colonial restrictions resulted in women banding together to demand rights and concessions.[22] As opportunities for formal employment waned with the economic fortunes of postindependence Africa, vending and market work has become a common strategy. There is considerable variation across the continent. In Accra, for example, where women's market trade is old and well established, some successful traders live lavishly. They can be virtual one-woman supermarkets, providing goods, services and credit to customers and family members alike. As one market woman/moneylender in Accra confided to Claire Robertson in the 1970s, she lent money to her clients, "at 50 percent interest [per month], but for my husband, only 30 percent."[23]

But in other cities, women's relatively new involvement in trade has not rescued them from domestic or financial stresses.[24] These women sell from makeshift stalls when licensed trading in legal markets is unaffordable. Out in the sun or shaded by an umbrella, they display piles of firewood on the street, festoon their bodies with yard goods for sale, walk along balancing trays on their heads piled high with foodstuffs, and, as Nancy Horn put it, "cultivate customers."[25]

African women have also had a long-established presence in the formal urban wage labor force. The relative decline since the 1990s of the once-vital field of African labor history, however, means that few studies exist on women workers in urban manufacturing and processing factories.[26] The focus of much labor history is wage work, but the access of many African women to wage work from the colonial period onward was restricted by their relative lack of education in comparison to men; their salaries have historically been at least 50 percent lower than those of their male counterparts.[27] In colonial Harare, spotty statistics indicate that, at most, only a quarter of the African women living in the city ever had formal, waged employment. Interestingly, when most urban women were servants in white households, factory work such as tobacco processing attracted women whose English skills could not cope with the demands of communicating about domestic work with their employers. Women factory workers earned less than domestic workers.[28]

A great deal of research also remains to be undertaken on women in formal urban employment in the postcolonial era. For example, Gunilla Andrae's study of a non-unionized textile plant in Lagos in the 1990s noted that the working conditions were often condemned as "slavery" by the women workers. Andrae described the economic life of a textile factory worker named Gloria, characterized by multitasking in addition to her full-time job:

> Gloria does a little trading on the side. She sells clothes to supplement her income. She buys goods from traders, mainly clothes, but also other things like recently a wall clock. Her main supplier is a friend in her church and her customers are her co-workers and others, who pay by instalments. She takes some interest for herself and passes on the customers' instalment payments to her suppliers. . . . Her husband also has a fridge and sells soft drinks. She would like to have one of her own. Finally, she buys things for her children to sell on their way to school in order to earn what little they can.[29]

In the 1980s most historians reached consensus that, although in most pre-colonial African societies women had independent access to resources and varying degrees of authority over the use of their own assets, their status generally declined in the colonial period. European colonialists almost universally considered women to be legally and mentally on a par with children or the property of husbands, fathers, or brothers. Left out of the dubious limelight of colonial efforts to transform African educational, political, and economic life, African women found that they were not considered when new socio-economic rules were formulated and the crumbs of colonialism distributed.

In colonial Zimbabwe, African women learned that their access to social power and economic resources would have to be mediated entirely through men. Thus, being an African woman in town meant learning how to meet myriad responsibilities—health, food, housing, reproduction, and child care—largely without access to the perks of legal adulthood from which they were barred. Women, forced to become adept at cultivating symbiotic relationships with men who did have above-board access to resources, thus became purveyors of alcohol, recreation, and sex, which were in high demand in urban spaces.[30] Thirty years ago scholar Luise White memorably chronicled how urban colonial Nairobi women provided men with the "comforts of home." White's work was pivotal in lifting urban African women into the analytical limelight while discarding colonial-era discourses emphasizing their character flaws and moral weakness. Rather, rural women who came to Nairobi in the early years of the twentieth century carved out spaces for themselves in economically rational ways. Some put down roots in the city and pursued strategies of capital accumulation. Others did not look to acquire permanent assets such as land and housing in town but made urban visits to earn money to send as remittances back to rural kin.[31] In colonial Dar es Salaam, where the ratio of African women to men in 1948 was 140:100, women were largely barred from formal employment but survived by cobbling together combinations of cooking, hawking, cleaning homes, doing laundry, brewing alcohol, and selling sex.[32]

Women's status as legal minors was not without its ironies, however. Without formal rights to independent housing, education, or employment, their physical mobility was generally unregulated by colonial administrators who considered them to be beneath notice. Many rural authorities around the continent in the colonial era bewailed that young women either relocated themselves to towns, defying the wishes of their fathers, brothers, and husbands along the way, or were infected in their homesteads with new dress codes and a seemingly insatiable lust for the bright lights. That these anxieties were overstated paradoxically pointed to the pivotal role of African women in both rural and urban economies. Nonetheless, the loud chorus of African patriarchal complaint that issued from across the continent about "wicked" and "uncontrollable women" by the late colonial era is a prime example of the actual invention of social standards of women's subservience and obedience.[33] Generally speaking, it was not until the patriarchal complaints began to register in settler colonial government offices that those officials belatedly began to pay attention to the fact that significant numbers of African women had long settled into many urban niches.[34]

There was not a homogeneous group of "urban African women," even within the confines of any one particular town or city. Some owned or had access to more material wealth than others and could keep their noses well above waters that threatened to overwhelm poorer women. Scholarly insight recognizing degrees of differentiation among urban women led to the development of an influential subset of urban studies that focused not only on African class formation but also on the growth of the elusive ideology of respectability. These studies showed that by the end of the colonial period, achieving respectability was predicated on the possession of domestic skills, material goods, a "correct" marriage, and often membership in religious organizations.[35] For example, in colonial Lagos an influential subset of respectable, and highly respected, professional African women, some holding law, medicine or social science degrees from Western universities, worked tirelessly for women's empowerment.[36] Perhaps urban women's single-minded striving for respectability was a measure of the depths to which colonialism had pushed them. What they worked for, above all, was a recognizable dignity that could not be violated without sanction. Colonial era indignities like mandatory tests for venereal diseases were thus particularly loathed.[37]

Women made a definite impact on Africa's cities in the realms of dress and performance culture. As Karen Tranberg Hansen has written, "widespread cultural sensibilities about gender, sexuality, age, and status converge on the dressed body, weighing on women's bodies much more heavily than on men's."[38] In the early colonial period, the conjoining of the concepts of "cloth, cash and capitalism" meant that over time more and more women adopted woven cloth and elaborate clothing emphasizing bodily coverage as acceptable alternatives to earlier styles utilizing beads, skins, leaves, and minimalist cloth-based garments.[39] Towns and cities provided additional stages for new articulations of corporeal beauty, respectability, and fashion.[40] According to Terence Ranger, in colonial Bulawayo, "In the 1930s township girls wore no shoes and went about dowdily. . . . But in the late 1940s and 1950s all that changed. . . . There emerged in the towns of Rhodesia 'an altogether new class of African woman: young, vital, emancipated and fashion-conscious.'" He quoted the reminiscences of one such 1950s diva: "With your 'Stiff' [starched white petticoat] on, and flared there just like a peacock what more could you want? One would walk confidently with one's head high, proud and confident. Those were good old days, I tell you, so wonderful that if one was getting on a bus wearing a 'Stiff' one was really seen!! I mean seen!!"[41] Pushing the boundaries of acceptable behavior in work and dress, African women have given its cities some of their most recognizable characteristics.

Families and Alliances

Personal relationships between African women and men can be portrayed as static, calculated transactions where financial gain is the motivating factor and entrenched gender discord the primary dynamic.[42] Works written in these traditions have often not heeded Oyèrónké Oyěwùmí's admonition about the error of overlaying Western definitions of gender as intrinsically adversarial onto social systems that have operated with very different assumptions.[43] Cynical Western interpretations of the widespread practice of exchanging bridewealth at the time of marriage as "buying a wife" are perhaps to blame for this. As the historiography of emotions gains traction in African studies, however, scholars are beginning to acknowledge that African people have had hearts as well as wallets.[44] Studies of African urban family life and commercialized sex—which could be seen as "sexual politics"—are also starting to take cognizance of people's complex identities and motivations.[45]

Marriage strategies in colonial Libreville, Gabon, for example, were the means to the end of constructing relationships of affinity—"parenthood, emotional attachment, care in times of illness, allegiance and trust" between old and new family members (see chapter 13). Rachel Jean-Baptiste relates a 1944 court case that illustrated how marriage bonds, survival, and the urban landscape were intimately intertwined. The case was brought when fights broke out between a wife, Pauline, her husband, Fidèle, some of his countrymen, and Pauline's employer, Goyo, and his wife over sexual compensation.

> Pauline testified that, with the consent of Fidèle, she had worked for one month as a cook for the Fang guard named Goyo. Over the course of her employment, she had sex with Goyo five times, in secret, in locations where no one saw them. She had not asked her husband, Fidèle, for consent to have sex with Goyo. When Goyo terminated her employment, he paid her wages of 25 francs for cooking meals. But he did not compensate her for her sexual work. Pauline

confessed to Fidèle that she had sex with Goyo and that Goyo had not compensated her. Fidèle beat her . . . and commanded that they go to Goyo's house to request the adultery fee. Pauline, Fidèle, and some Bandjabi male friends arrived at Goyo's house to request that Goyo compensate Fidèle for sexual access to Pauline. . . . Goyo denied that he had sex with Pauline. Furthermore, Goyo's wife took her by the arm, led her to the side, rebuked her for causing such scandal in the wee hours of the night, and told them to leave.[46]

Libreville itself enabled this arrangement. Economically, the well-being of Pauline and Fidèle's marriage required her to work for another man; the landscape gave Pauline and Goyo places to meet clandestinely. All parties struggled to remake meaningful relationships in which their responsibilities and desires could be met. What it meant to be a proper woman and wife and a proper man and husband were literally being made and remade in these urban circumstances.[47]

Sexuality in Africa has not always meant heterosexuality (see chapters 5 and 14). Cities and towns have provided spaces to explore and develop diverse sexual cultures.[48] African histories and cultures of sexuality have transcended rigid Western norms, and it may be more accurate to say that it is homophobia—rather than varied forms of homosexuality—that has been the West's export to Africa.[49]

Overall, in the larger picture of gender and colonialism, the relegation of African women to the sidelines and to the status of "other" had important repercussions as African households and communities began to face new political and economic challenges at the onset of the era of Africa's independence. Women had to fight their way "in."

Promises, Promises

Africans in many colonies achieved majority rule and independence through protracted military campaigns against settlers of European descent fighting in partnership with their respective metropoles (see chapter 4). In Algeria, Guinea-Bissau, Angola, Mozambique, Zimbabwe, South Africa, Kenya, and Namibia the dynamics of armed struggle often transformed women's status—at least temporarily—because they were needed in new roles. Women earned jobs as soldiers, drivers, leaders and fighters in armies that desperately needed new recruits. Often borrowing from the emancipatory discourses of Communist-led Second World liberation forces in these colonies promised women that national liberation would result in the dignity women craved and the improvements in material life that they needed (see chapters 4 and 7).[50] However, most colonies in Africa achieved majority rule without resort to military force. Even so, nationalist parties pressing settlers and metropolitan administrations and civil servants to "quit" also enlisted and accepted the energies of urban African women.[51] To these women, too, were made promises of material improvements following takeovers of political power.

Urban areas were prime settings for individual and national anxieties about gender and politics. African independence movements, almost universally located in cities, were apt to describe themselves, when stymied or outmaneuvered by colonialism, as "emasculated."[52] Independence parties and armed liberation movements tended to include and attract women supporters and occasionally leaders, but rarely prioritized women's concerns regarding reproductive rights, housing, work, education, and child care.[53]

The record of independent African nations in relation to women was mixed. Independence brought distinct advances; by and large urban African women gained increased access to social services such as education (see chapter 10) and to formal employment outside the sector of domestic service. But legal emancipation and women's elevation to the status of legal adults on paper was often not accompanied by corresponding changes in actual practice. Initial official emphasis on discourses of emancipation often quickly faltered. Women were targeted and punished when they attempted to exercise the liberation and independence they believed they had sacrificed for and had been promised. In many instances, the gendered anxieties of African men about reversing supposed colonial era "emasculation" was expressed in well-publicized attempts to curb the lifestyles of urban women. Thus, in Dar es Salaam in 1970–71, Operation Vijana tried to prevent urban "indecency" by forbidding women to wear miniskirts; women were assaulted by mobs of young men and charged in the courts for showing their legs in defiance of a newly proclaimed and prohibitive "national culture."[54] Similarly, gendered anxieties bubbled to the surface in Zimbabwe in 1983 when Operation Clean-Up randomly rounded up women from the streets of Harare, Bulawayo, and Gweru and charged them with indecency and prostitution.[55] In more recent years, Tunisian, Algerian, Egyptian, and Libyan women of the "Arab Spring" movement across North Africa have also seen their urban public activism attacked by male "revolutionaries," who have not been able to contemplate gender equality as a real priority.[56]

Who Will Wash the Dishes, the Clothes, and the Floors?

In Africa, human hands generally do the work that domestic appliances do in the West. Domestic work historically marked a racial boundary between colonizers and colonized, as settlers and missionaries exercised self-appointed authority to teach Africans that "cleanliness is next to Godliness."[57] European settlers mostly did not do their own domestic work, instead hiring cooks, gardeners, babysitters, and cleaners from the African populace. The gender of urban Africa's legions of scrubbers and sweepers has not always been a foregone conclusion, however. In the early colonial period, domestic workers were usually African men, who found domestic employment a reasonable alternative to farm, mining, and factory work, and who were more likely to have learned a colonial language. Adult African men who performed domestic work were called "houseboys" and "garden boys." When colonial economies started to grow after World War II, many men moved to better-paying jobs, and women became domestic servants. Settler anxieties about the proximity of African men to settler women in intimate spaces also fueled this shift.

In the postcolonial era, although urban Africa has a reputation for dirt and grime, even when city streets and alleys are full of mud and unmentionables, home interiors are almost always kept scrubbed, swept, and as spotless—and often as well decorated—as humanly possible.[58] As an enduring marker of class status and aspirations, African women with access to resources almost always employ other African women to do such domestic labor. When the woman of the house herself has a waged job (and sometimes even when she does not), the menial work in her home must still be done—rather than let dust accumulate! For example, a 1980s study of women workers in a garment factory in Beira, Mozambique, showed that they employed or recruited relatives as domestic workers to clean, cook, and feed children; their long working days made it impossible to wait in line at a communal faucet to collect water or to find three hours a day to scrub the family's clothes.[59] These arrangements built on enduring traditions of gendered and generational in-family care and service as well as colonial traditions of domestic work.[60]

Studies of urban southern Africa in particular have shown the close link between racialized domestic labor and urban landscapes. In South Africa and colonial Zimbabwe, for example, behind the main house of the white family, or sweltering on the roofs of high rises, shed-like rooms housed "live-in" African domestic workers. Usually lacking modern amenities, such tiny dwellings were positioned so that their occupants were simultaneously near enough to employers to be constantly on call but also discreetly out of sight.[61] These workers were not robots, however. As Rebecca Ginsburg has shown, they helped each other learn the transportation and law enforcement codes of the city, and sometimes they covertly transgressed "house rules" that kept them subservient to employers. Subtle power plays between white families and their domestic workers echoed larger confrontational dynamics between white and black. The ways that employers and employees lived together in these intimate spaces gave the most ironic possible lies both to the public ideology of "apartheid" (which literally meant separation) and to the rationale for exploitation that servants were part of the family.[62]

Although domestic work is almost always low paid, it can have differing impacts on the lives of the workers. Thus, one young rural migrant doing domestic work in Dar es Salaam reported, "My intention was to study and do my own business. But this is the second year in Dar es Salaam and I do not have any hopes to realize my goals." Another reported, however, "I am better placed than I was in the village. My life has improved a little."[63]

In some cases the market for domestic labor in urban Africa has contributed to child trafficking (see chapter 9) when poor young girls from rural areas come to the city to earn cash by scrubbing and cooking. In Nairobi, one young rural migrant said,

> I am the firstborn . . . of four children. My mother was single by the time she died. I do not know who my father is and where he stays. . . . [S]he used to work as a bar attendant in Kisumu. When she died, we all came home to live with our grandmother who is aging and sickly. We all experienced hunger, and my siblings always suffered from malaria. Dani [grandmother] asked Auntie [current employer] to take me to Nairobi to stay with her so that I can get some money to support my siblings.[64]

In Accra in the late 1970s, elite families regularly employed rural teenage girls under the guise of claimed but fictional relationships and justification of paying their school fees. But the girls often worked without schooling or proper housing, with their earnings sent without consultation back to rural parents, while boys in such situations were indeed relatives and had their school fees paid.[65]

Domestic work in contemporary Africa is slowly being officially recognized as a significant factor in urban life. In order to remedy often deplorable conditions, in the twenty-first century there are moves to unionize Africa's domestic workers. The 2013 summit of domestic workers' organizations in Africa drew representatives from seventeen African countries.[66]

Bright Lights

It is important to remember that Africans have emotional lives and like to enjoy themselves: listening, for example, to Uum Kulthum in Egypt or Miriam

Makeba in South Africa—singers whose unforgettable voices symbolized both nationalism and urban life for millions of their countrymen and women. Women's participation in religious and political organizations has been a prominent feature of urban life on the continent (see chapters 4 and 14). We have gotten glimpses into ways that African cities have offered their residents access to recreation such as sports matches and musical concerts both as performers and spectators.[67] For example, Africa's passionate love affair with the sport of football (soccer) is shared by female citizens; national women's teams and even, sometimes, competition leagues in the larger cities are becoming more common.[68]

As Phyllis Martin pointed out, daily urban life for women has meant "sitting around in a compound, chatting while the evening meal is being prepared; . . . tying their hair and exchanging news; playing cards; strolling with friends in the evening and buying doughnuts from fast-food sellers who sit with lanterns at the roadside; or, in Brazzaville, watching the thundering rapids of the Congo River."[69] While formal activities have always been race- and class-based, and the urban poor have often been barred from participation, more leisure and recreational activities are available to urban women, as opposed to their rural counterparts.

New Cities, Old Problems?

A new city, financed by Nigerian and international capital, is rising on ten square kilometers of land reclaimed from the sea on the outskirts of Lagos. Eko Atlantic is being planned on a scale to rival Dubai. Whereas bustling, vibrant, decrepit Lagos has a population of 18 million, ultra-modern Eko Atlantic is projected to house 250,000 people living in steel-and-glass skyscrapers with every modern technological amenity—and private security. It is projected that 150,000 people will commute into Eko Atlantic every day.[70] But how will the gleaming new city deal with the political and economic issues that confront the residents of nearby Lagos, which also continues to grow? Will the women of Eko Atlantic be more gainfully employed, safer, and happier as a result of living there? Is there a gendered component to the planning of this metropolis? As Mary Njeri Kinyanjui perceptively notes about Nairobi, "[African] urbanization is complicated by planning ideologies that exclude rather than include. [The] city was never really meant for all."[71]

On the other side of the continent from Eko Atlantic and at the other end of the spectrum of Africa's urban areas lie the three connected towns of Wadi Halfa, new Wadi Halfa, and New Halfa in the Sudan, which perhaps more typically exemplify African urban dynamics. Wadi Halfa was an ancient town in northern Sudan until 1964, when it was submerged sixty meters in the Nile due to construction of the Aswan High Dam in Egypt. New Wadi Halfa grew haphazardly on the shores of the resulting lake, while New Halfa was started hundreds of kilometers away to the south as a resettlement scheme for displaced residents of the old town. New Halfa had to develop new commerce, administration, transport, and service functions for the town's fifty thousand residents and provide services for the half-million people of surrounding subsistence farming areas and agricultural schemes. Fifty years later the water supply is uncertain and buildings built in the 1960s with asbestos roofs are crumbling, with predictable health and safety implications for townspeople. It is unclear that the particular needs of female residents received any attention among various city planning efforts.[72]

Conclusion

There is nothing more ubiquitous than a woman on a hot, noisy street in an African city hawking food to busy passersby. Perhaps her tray is piled with boiled eggs, ripe red tomatoes, or skewers of pineapple. Behind these offerings lie complex urban histories, geographies, and sociologies; so we must regard our seller with distinct respect for the vast amount of territorial and social savvy that she carries along with her foodstuffs. Perhaps her labors are witnessed by an impeccably dressed and coiffed woman driving by in an air-conditioned four-wheel-drive vehicle on her way to a meeting of the national parliament. In financial, housing, and educational terms, her worlds are miles away from those of the street hawker. But from another perspective, they are both African women on the street, strategizing about ways to meet family, personal, community, and national objectives in an environment where opportunities are mixed with distinct hazards. Their personal, political, and spatial worlds intersect at many points; indeed, the trader might be the mother of the member of parliament.

This chapter has surveyed complex histories of women and urbanization in Africa. Africa's diverse urban areas have all been spaces where the cultural meanings of gender have been and are being constantly made and remade. Women established footholds in these cities from their earliest days, and even when relegated to its most insecure economic and social spaces, they have become individual and collective forces demanding respect. These urban spaces have increasingly offered more opportunities for women with the disappearance of colonialism; but they paradoxically have also created new and perilous forms of autonomy.

Notes

1. Nawal El Saadawi, *Memoirs from the Women's Prison* (Berkeley: University of California Press, 1986), 2.

2. Abdou Maliq Simone and Adbeighani Abouhani, eds., *Urban Africa: Changing Contours of Survival in the City* (Dakar: Codesria, 2005); Garth Myers, *African Cities: Alternative Visions of Urban Theory and Practice* (London: Zed Books, 2011); Noellen Murray, Nick Shepherd, and Martin Hall, *Desire Lines: Space, Memory and Identity in the Post-Apartheid City* (New York: Routledge, 2007).

3. Julia Clancy-Smith, "Gender in the City: Women, Migration and Contested Spaces in Tunis, c. 1830–81," in *Africa's Urban Past*, ed. David Anderson and Richard Rathbone (Portsmouth, NH: Heinemann, 2000), 198.

4. Ntone Edjabe and Edgar Pieterse, preface to *The African Cities Reader: Pan-African Practices* (Vlaeberg, South Africa: Chimurenga: African Centre for Cities, 2010), 5.

5. Doris Lessing, *The Grass Is Singing* (London: Grafton, 1950); Cyprian Ekwensi, *People of the City* (1954; repr., Trenton, NJ: Africa World Press, 2004); Marjorie Macgoye, *Coming to Birth* (New York: Feminist Press, 2000); N'gugi wa Thiong'o, *Wizard of the Crow* (New York: Anchor Books, 2007); Phaswane Mpe, *Welcome to Our Hillbrow* (Athens: Ohio University Press, 2011).

6. Oyeronke Oyewumi, "Conceptualising Gender in African Studies," in *The Study of Africa*, ed. Paul Tiyambe Zeleza, vol. 1, *Disciplinary and Interdisciplinary Encounters* (Dakar: Codesria, 2006), 314–17.

7. Teresa Barnes, *We Women Worked So Hard: Gender, Urbanization and Social Reproduction in Colonial Harare, Zimbabwe, 1930–1956* (Portsmouth, NH: Heinemann, 1999); Rachel Jean Baptiste, *Conjugal Rights: Marriage, Sexuality, and Urban Life in Colonial Libreville, Gabon* (Athens: Ohio University Press, 2014); Andrew Ivaska, "In the 'Age of Minis': Women, Work and Masculinity Downtown," in *Dar es Salaam: Histories from an Emerging African Metropolis*, ed. James Brennan, Andrew Burton, and Usuf Lawi (Dar es Salaam: Mkuki wa Nyota, 2007), 213–31.

8. Hilary Jones, *The Métis of Senegal: Urban Life and Politics in French West Africa* (Bloomington: Indiana University Press, 2013); Ushewhedu Kufakurinani, "White Women and Domesticity in Colonial Zimbabwe, 1890 to 1980" (PhD diss., Department of Economic History, University of Zimbabwe, 2015); Nupur Chaudhuri and Margaret Strobel, eds. *Western Women and Imperialism: Complicity and Resistance* (Bloomington: Indiana University Press, 1992); Fay Chung, *Re-living the Second Chimurenga: Memories from the Liberation Struggle in Zimbabwe* (Uppsala: Nordic Africa Institute, 2006).

9. See, for example, Samer Bagaeen and Ola Uduka, eds., *Gated Communities: Social Sustainability in Contemporary and Historical Gated Developments* (London: Earthscan, 2010).

10. Anderson and Rathbone, *Africa's Urban Past*; Bill Freund, *The African City* (Cambridge: Cambridge University Press, 2007), 1–64.

11. Mark DeLancey, "Moving East, Facing West: Islam as an Intercultural Mediator in Urban Planning in the Sokoto Empire," in *African Urban Spaces in Historical Perspective*, ed. Steven Salm and Toyin Falola (Rochester: University of Rochester Press, 2005), 3–21.

12. Catherine Coquery-Vidrovitch, *The History of African Cities South of the Sahara* (1993; repr., Princeton: Markus Wiener, 2008), 20, 131, 311.

13. Kenneth Little, *African Women in Towns* (Cambridge: Cambridge University Press, 1973), 8, 12, 13.

14. Mariken Vaa, "Paths to the City: Migration Histories of Poor Women in Bamako," in *Small Town Africa: Studies in Rural-Urban Interaction*, ed. Jonathan Baker (Uppsala: Scandinavian Institute of African Studies, 1990), 173.

15. Ivaska, "Age of Minis," 214.

16. Cris Beauchemin and Phillipe Bocquier, "Migration and Urbanisation in Francophone West Africa: An Overview of the Recent Empirical Evidence," *Urban Studies* 41, no. 11 (2004): 2245.

17. Sean Fox, "Urbanization as a Global Historical Process: Theory and Evidence from Sub-Saharan Africa," *Population and Development Review* 38, no. 2 (2012): 285–86.

18. Deborah Potts, "Whatever Happened to Africa's Rapid Urbanization?," *World Economics* 13, no. 2 (2012): 17–29.

19. Vaa, "Paths to the City," 174.

20. Claire Robertson, "Ga Women and Socioeconomic Change," in *Women in Africa*, ed. Nancy Hafkin and Edna Bay (Stanford: Stanford University Press, 1976), 113–14; Gracia Clark, *Onions Are My Husband: Survival and Accumulation by West African Market Women* (Chicago: University of Chicago Press, 1994).

21. Barbara Lewis, "The Limitations of Group Action among Entrepreneurs: The Market Women of Abidjan, Ivory Coast," in Hafkin and Bay, *Women in Africa*, 135–56.

22. Judith Van Allen, "Sitting on a Man: Colonialism and the Lost Political Institutions of Igbo Women," *Canadian Journal of African Studies* 6, no. 2 (1972): 165–81.

23. Robertson, "Ga Women," 125.

24. Claire Robertson, *Trouble Showed the Way: Women, Men and Trade in the Nairobi Area, 1890–1990* (Bloomington: Indiana University Press, 1997).

25. Nancy Horn, *Cultivating Customers: Market Women in Harare, Zimbabwe* (Boulder, CO: Lynne Rienner, 1994).

26. South African women have received the lion's share of attention in labor history. See Iris Berger, *Threads of Solidarity: Women in South African Industry, 1900–1980* (Bloomington: Indiana University Press, 1992); Ray Alexander Simons, *All My Life and All My Strength* (Cape Town: STE, 2004); Emma Mashinini, *Strikes Have Followed Me All My Life: A South African Autobiography* (New York: Routledge, 1991); Laura Phillips and Deborah James, "Labour, Lodging and Linkages: Migrant Women's Experience in South Africa," *African Studies* 73, no. 3 (2014): 410–31.

27. Catherine Coquery-Vidrovitch, *African Women: A Modern History* (Boulder, CO: Westview Press, 1997), 232.

28. Barnes, *We Women Worked So Hard*, 35–42.

29. Gunilla Andrae, "A Woman Worker in a Lagos Factory: Her Power Base in Family, Community, Labour Market and Union," in *Transforming Female Identities: Women's Organizational Forms in West Africa*, ed. Eva Evers Rosander (Uppsala: Nordiska Afrikainstitutet, 1997), 72–73.

30. Elizabeth Schmidt, *Peasants, Traders and Wives: Shona Women in the History of Zimbabwe, 1870–1939* (Portsmouth, NH: Heinemann, 1992); Barnes, *We Women Worked So Hard*; Teresa Barnes, "Virgin Territory? Travel and Migration by African

Women in Twentieth-Century Southern Africa," in *Women in African Colonial Histories*, ed. Jean Allman, Susan Geiger, and Nakanyike Musisi (Bloomington: Indiana University Press, 2002), 164–90; Tsuneo Yoshikuni, *Elizabeth Musodzi and the Birth of African Feminism in Early Colonial Zimbabwe* (Harare: Weaver Press, 2008).

31. Luise White, *The Comforts of Home: Prostitution in colonial Nairobi* (Chicago: University of Chicago Press, 1990).

32. Ivaska, "Age of Minis," 214–15.

33. Dorothy Hodgson and Sheryl McCurdy, eds., *"Wicked" Women and the Reconfiguration of Gender in Africa* (Portsmouth, NH: Heinemann, 2001), 11–13; Eric Hobsbawm and Terence Ranger, *Invention of Tradition* (Cambridge: Cambridge University Press, 1983).

34. Teresa Barnes, "'To Raise a Hornet's Nest': The Effect of Early Resistance to Passes for Women in South Africa on the Pass Laws in Colonial Zimbabwe," *Agenda: Empowering Women for Gender Equity* 5 (1989): 40–52.

35. Karen Hansen, ed. *African Encounters with Domesticity* (New Brunswick, NJ: Rutgers University Press, 1992); Elaine Salo, "Respectable Mothers, Tough Men and Good Daughters: Producing Persons in Manenberg Township, South Africa" (PhD diss., Emory University, 2004).

36. Saheed Aderinto, *When Sex Threatened the State: Illicit Sexuality, Nationalism, and Politics in Colonial Nigeria, 1900–1958* (Urbana: University of Illinois Press, 2014), 32–34, 47.

37. Lynette Jackson, "'When in the White Man's Town': Zimbabwean Women Remember *Chibeura*," in Allman, Geiger, and Musisi, *Women in Colonial African Histories*, 191–218.

38. Hansen, "Dressing Dangerously," 166.

39. Jean Allman, "'Let Your Fashion Be in Line with Our Ghanaian Costume': Nation, Gender and the Politics of Clothing in Nkrumah's Ghana," in *Fashioning Africa: Power and the Politics of Dress*, ed. Allman (Bloomington: Indiana University Press, 2004), 145–47.

40. Timothy Burke, *Lifebuoy Men, Lux Women: Commodification, Consumption and Cleanliness in Modern Zimbabwe* (Durham, NC: Duke University Press, 1996).

41. Terence Ranger, *Bulawayo Burning: The Social History of a Southern African City, 1893–1960* (Rochester, NY: James Currey, 2010), 178–79.

42. Anne Lewinson, "Love in the City: Navigating Multiple Relationships in Dar es Salaam, Tanzania," *City and Society* 18, no. 1 (2006): 90–115; Jennifer Cole and Lynn Thomas, eds., *Love in Africa* (Chicago: University of Chicago Press, 2009).

43. Oyewumi, "Conceptualising Gender in African Studies."

44. Nancy Rose Hunt, "The Affective, the Intellectual, and Gender History," *Journal of African History* 55, no. 3 (2014): 331–45; Saheed Aderinto, "Modernizing Love: Gender, Romantic Passion and Youth Literary Culture in Colonial Nigeria," *Africa* 85, no. 3 (2015): 478–500.

45. Saheed Aderinto, "Of Gender, Race and Class: The Politics of Prostitution in Lagos, Nigeria, 1923–1954," *Frontiers: A Journal of Women's Studies* 33, no. 3 (2012): 71–92.

46. Jean-Baptiste, *Conjugal Rights*, 132, 162–63.

47. Claire Robertson, *Sharing the Same Bowl: A Socioeconomic History of Women and Class in Accra, Ghana* (Bloomington: Indiana University Press, 1984).

48. Heike Ingeborg Schmidt, "Colonial Intimacy: The Rechenberg Scandal and Homosexuality in German East Africa," *Journal of the History of Sexuality* 17, no. 1 (2008): 25–59.

49. Babacar M'Baye, "The Origins of Senegalese Homophobia: Discourses on Homosexuals and Transgender People in Colonial and Postcolonial Senegal," *African Studies Review* 56, no. 2 (2013): 109–28.

50. Josephine Nhongo-Simbanegavi, *For Better or Worse? Women and ZANLA in Zimbabwe's Liberation Struggle* (Harare, Zimbabwe: Weaver Press, 2000); Wambui Waiyaki Otieno, with Cora Ann Presley, *Mau Mau's Daughter: A Life History* (Boulder, CO: Lynne Rienner, 1998); Chung, *Re-living the Second Chimurenga*; Maitseo Bolaane, "Cross-Border Lives, Warfare and Rape in Independence-Era Botswana," *Journal of Southern African Studies* 39, no. 3 (2013): 557–76; Stephanie Urdang, *And Still They Dance: Women, War and the Struggle for Change in Mozambique* (New York: Monthly Review Press, 1989).

51. Susan Geiger, *TANU Women: Gender and Culture in the Making of Tanganyikan Nationalism, 1955–1965* (Portsmouth, NH: Heinemann, 1997).

52. Natasha Erlank, "Gender and Masculinity in South African Nationalist Discourse, 1912–50," *Feminist Studies* 29, no. 3 (2003): 653–71; Daniel Mekonnen and Mirjam van Reisen, "The Role of Women in Post-Conflict Transformation in the Horn of Africa: A Case Study of Eritrea," *African Journal of Business and Economic Research* 8, no. 1 (2013): 83–108.

53. Teresa Barnes, "'Not until Zimbabwe Is Free Can We Stop to Think about It': The Zimbabwe African National Union and Radical Women's Health Activists in the United States, 1979," *Radical History Review* 119 (2014): 53–71.

54. Ivaska, "Age of Minis," 217–28; see also Karen Tranberg Hansen, "Dressing Dangerously: Miniskirts, Gender Relations, and Sexuality in Zambia," in Allman, *Fashioning Africa*, 166, 182n2.

55. Gay Seidman, "Women in Zimbabwe: Post-Independence Struggles," *Feminist Studies* 10, no. 3 (1984): 419–40; E. Sisulu and M. Mwalo, *Women in Zimbabwe* (Harare: SAPES Trust, 1989).

56. Fatuma Ahmed Ali and Hannah Muthoni Macharia, "Women, Youth, and the Egyptian Arab Spring," *Peace Review: A Journal of Social Justice* 25 (2013): 359–66; Elisabeth Johansson-Nogues, "Gendering the Arab Spring? Rights and (In)security of Tunisian, Egyptian and Libyan Women," *Security Dialogue* 44, no. 5–6 (2013).

57. Burke, *Lifebuoy Men, Lux Women*.

58. Craig Fraser, *Shack Chic: Art and Innovation in South African Shack-Lands* (Cape Town: Quivertree, 2003).

59. Kathleen Sheldon, "Sewing Clothes and Sorting Cashew Nuts: Factories, Families, and Women in Beira, Mozambique," *Women's Studies International Forum* 14, no. 1/2 (1991): 32.

60. Janet Henshall Momsen, ed., *Gender, Migration, and Domestic Service* (London: Routledge, 1999), 183–94, 195–213; Janet Bujra, *Serving Class: Masculinity and the Feminisation of Domestic Service in Tanzania* (Edinburgh: Edinburgh University Press, 2000).

61. Jacklyn Cock, *Maids and Madams: Domestic Workers under Apartheid* (New York: Women's Press, 1990); John Pape, "Still Serving the Tea: Domestic Workers in Zimbabwe, 1980–1990," *Journal of Southern African Studies* 19, no. 3 (1993): 387–404.

62. Rebecca Ginsburg, *At Home with Apartheid: The Hidden Landscapes of Domestic Service in Johannesburg* (Charlottesville: University of Virginia Press, 2011).

63. Esther W. Dungumaro, "Consequences of Female Migration for Families in Tanzania," *African Review of Economics and Finance* 5, no. 1 (2013): 52.

64. Kennedy Nyabuti Ondimu, "Determinants of Rural to Urban Migration of Domestic Workers in Nairobi, Kenya," *International Journal of Contemporary Sociology* 44, no. 2 (2007): 244.

65. Robertson, *Sharing the Same Bowl.*

66. Jacklyn Cock, "Challenging the Invisibility of Domestic Workers," *South African Review of Sociology* 42, no. 2 (2011), accessed July 19, 2015, http://wiego.org/infor mal-economy/declaration-african-regional-domestic-workers-conference.

67. Joyce Jenje Makwenda, *Zimbabwe Township Music* (Harare, Zimbabwe: Storyville, 2005); Chuka Onwumechili and Gerard Akindes, eds., *Identity and Nation in African Football: Fans, Community and Clubs* (London: Palgrave Macmillan, 2014).

68. Jimoh Shehu, ed., *Gender, Sport and Development in Africa: Cross-Cultural Perspectives on Patterns of Representations and Marginalizations* (Dakar: CODESRIA, 2010).

69. Phyllis Martin, *Leisure and Society in Colonial Brazzaville* (Cambridge: Cambridge University Press, 2002), 10–11; see also Paul Tiyambe Zeleza and Cassandra Veney, eds., *Leisure in Urban Africa* (Trenton, NJ: Africa World Press, 2003).

70. "Nigeria: Africa's First Smart City," *Africa Research Bulletin: Economic, Financial and Technical Series* 50, no. 2 (2013): 19883A–19884B.

71. Mary Njeri Kinyanjui, *Women and the Informal Economy in Urban Africa: From the Margins to the Centre* (London: Zed Books, 2014), 117.

72. Adil Mustafa Ahmad and Mohammed El Hadi Abu Sin, "Urban Development in a Rural Context: The Case of New Halfa, Sudan," in Baker, *Small Town Africa,* 247–63; Adil Mustafa Ahmad et al., "Reviving Wadi Halfa: A Tale of Three Towns" (unpublished paper, n.d. but likely 2011), accessed August 17, 2015, https://www.slide share.net/bakrimusa/reviving-wadi-halfa-a-tale-of-three-cities.

Suggested Readings

Aderinto, Saheed. *When Sex Threatened the State: Illicit Sexuality, Nationalism, and Politics in Colonial Nigeria, 1900–1958.* Urbana: University of Illinois Press, 2015.

Anderson, David, and Richard Rathbone, eds. *Africa's Urban Past.* Portsmouth, NH: Heinemann, 2000.

Ginsburg, Rebecca. *At Home with Apartheid: The Hidden Landscapes of Domestic Service in Johannesburg.* Charlottesville: University of Virginia Press, 2011.

Sheldon, Kathleen. *African Women: Early History to the 21st Century.* Bloomington: Indiana University Press, 2017.

Simone, Abdou Maliq. *For the City Yet to Come: Changing African Life in Four Cities.* Durham, NC: Duke University Press, 2004.

Figure 12.1. Weini Yemana, an Eritrean asylum seeker with daughter, Kisana. Photo by Paul Jeffrey.

12

WOMEN AND THE
NEW AFRICAN DIASPORA

Cassandra Veney

The Euro-American slave trade created much of the historic African diaspora in the Americas. When slavery was outlawed in the United States in 1864, four million people of African descent gained their freedom. The country's historic African diaspora was also made up of free persons of African descent who had migrated to the United States, such as Cape Verdeans who first came to work in the whaling industry in the eighteenth century.[1] Others came from the Caribbean and Latin America.

Because of strict racist immigration policies, the numbers of Africans and people of African descent who migrated to the United States in the twentieth century remained low, only rising with late twentieth-century legal reforms. This chapter provides an overview of the women who make up the new African diaspora in the United States. Often immigrants and refugees are viewed as faceless and genderless. However, the experiences of women and men as immigrants and refugees are gendered. Here I look at the national origins of women in the new African diaspora and their participation and engagement in the economy and their communities, analyzing the intersectionality of gender, race, class, and immigrant status by examining how women in the new African diaspora negotiate these signifying markers that often determine their status in their homes, communities, and the workplace. What, if any, new identities have these women formed as they define, shape, and create new spaces for community and transnational agency and empowerment? The answers indicate that identities and skills arising from their African origins often contribute to success in the U.S. context, despite the many obstacles posed by discrimination.

On the one hand, many new diaspora African women entered the United States at a time when their civil rights were protected with the passage of the Civil Rights Act of 1964 and the Voting Rights Act of 1965. On the other hand, gender and racial discrimination are still rampant, and many African diasporic women face individual and group discrimination in the workforce and classroom, on the street, and in communities where they live. This discrimination is based on stereotypes or the fear of increasing competition for jobs, college admissions, housing, contracts, and affirmative action opportunities.[2] Nonetheless, I demonstrate that women from the old and new African diasporas have forged partnerships and linkages that transcend nationality, ethnicity, immigration/citizenship status, and class and that continue, in essence, the kinds of activism of African women discussed in chapter 6.

Legalities of Immigration:
Refugees versus Immigrants and Asylum Seekers

Refugees and immigrants have to undergo strict medical and security clearances, often taking years, now complicated further by a xenophobic U.S. president.[3] Furthermore, their encounters with the government are vastly different, as refugees are automatically entitled to certain governmental benefits. Refugees have sponsors assigned to them before they enter the country. The sponsor or Voluntary Agency (Volag) provides ninety days of assistance in the form of clothing, food, housing, employment, and medical care and helps refugees navigate state governmental agencies to ensure that children are immunized and enrolled in schools, drivers' licenses are obtained, and welfare benefits are accessed. Following the terrorist attacks of September 11, 2001, refugees and people granted asylum must apply for legal permanent residence after one year of arrival in the country; they can apply for citizenship after another five years.[4] It is important to note also that some new diasporan African women came to the United States not directly from Africa but were educated and worked in Europe, Canada, or Australia and then migrated to the United States.[5] Others were born in Caribbean or Latin American countries. In addition, immigrants who have been granted temporary protection status (discussed below) are authorized to work and travel in and out of the country.

The Arrival of African Women Refugees and
Immigrants; Legalities Redux

Restrictive racist immigration laws precluded the entry of large numbers of Africans and people of African descent into the United States prior to the 1960s. It was not just these laws that barred their entry. Most Africans and African-descent people, especially in the Caribbean, were under European colonial rule until the 1960s and 1970s.[6] Despite colonial rule, African students traveled to the United States for university training with the understanding that they would return home after they graduated. The importance of African development for most postindependence leaders was the overriding goal; therefore most students, but not all of them, returned home. However, changes in immigration laws enabled thousands of Africans and those of African descent to resettle in the United States beginning with the passage of the 1965 Hart-Cellar Act that abolished hemispheric quotas benefiting immigrants from Europe. It had provisions for the inclusion of skilled labor, along with providing preferences for family reunification—many African women could now legally migrate to join their husbands—and humanitarian cases. It is important to note that the push for a change in immigration law became a part of the civil rights struggle as members of the historic African diaspora promoted an inclusive immigration policy as part of their agenda.[7]

The Immigration and Nationality Act of 1980 was passed after most African countries had gained their independence. However, the nationalist goals of development and democracy for Africa did not come to fruition for many countries and their citizens. By the 1980s, many African countries experienced political, economic, and social turmoil that ranged from civil wars or military coups to economic collapse.[8] These factors drove thousands of Africans from their countries of origin; many ended up in the United States.

Also, the economic crises spearheaded by the two oil shocks of the 1970s put many African economies on a downward spiral. Many African countries had borrowed heavily during the 1970s from the International Monetary Fund (IMF) and the World Bank, but their domestic savings and favorable prices for commodities such as copper, oil, coffee, cocoa, and tea allowed them to meet their debt repayments. This became increasingly more difficult by the 1980s when the IMF and World Bank imposed structural adjustment programs (SAPs) on most African economies. The neoliberal market-oriented agenda called for the rolling back of the state in terms of social services, education, and employment.[9] Education on all levels was negatively affected as states reduced funding for this critical sector contributing to Africa's development (see chapter 10). Thousands of African academics left African careers and went to Europe and Canada before finding their way to the United States. Others came directly to the United States.

The 1980 Immigration and Nationality Act was followed by the Immigration Control and Reform Act of 1986 (IRCA), which allowed thousands to apply for amnesty and remain in the country if they had entered illegally or had overstayed their visas. To qualify for amnesty, individuals had to meet certain criteria and go through a two-phase process. In order to change status from illegal to legal temporary resident, a person had to apply for the program between May 5, 1987, and May 4, 1988. Applicants had to prove that they had continuously and unlawfully resided in the country since January 1, 1982, and had not committed any felonies. Legal temporary resident status remained in effect for eighteen months, during which period there was no eligibility for welfare benefits. After it ended, immigrants were able to adjust their status to be lawfully admitted permanent residents and obtain the coveted "green card."

However, in order to receive the green card, one had to obtain a level of English competency along with competency in U.S. civics. In the end, approximately 2.7 million people were granted amnesty under this law.[10] Thirty thousand Africans applied to adjust their status under IRCA; although this number represents a small percentage of those who gained legal resident status, it is important to emphasize that these Africans later could apply for permanent resident status and then move on to citizenship.[11] Their move from illegal to legal to citizenship provided new economic and educational opportunities for themselves and their families—they could now sponsor their relatives for resettlement. The Extended Voluntary Departure (EVD) program also allowed some Africans, especially those from Ethiopia and Uganda, to remain in the country during the 1980s. The U.S. attorney general identified certain African nationalities for inclusion in the program because their lives might have been threatened if they returned home. Therefore, they were allowed to remain in the country regardless of their visa status.[12] Even after the EVD was lifted many who remained in the country became a part of the new African diaspora. Many had come to the country as students, but with the imposition of SAPs, corruption, and the slow pace of democratization, they realized that future careers in Africa did not look promising.

More recent African immigrants such as Liberians, Somalis, Sudanese (later South Sudanese), Rwandans, and Burundians have been granted permission to remain in the country under the same circumstances after 1999. After 1999, EVD ended as a program designated by the president, and instead Temporary Protection Status (TPS) is granted to nationals of certain countries identified by Congress, although this is changing with Trump-initiated restrictions.[13] Conditions in immigrants' countries of origin considered to be life-threatening, therefore warranting TPS, include natural disasters and other humanitarian crises. Everyone does not automatically qualify for TPS; it is only available to those who were in the United States when Congress made the designation. Those with felony convictions or two misdemeanors or who are considered a threat to national security do not qualify.

The Immigration and Nationality Act (INA) of 1990 established the Diversity Immigrant Visa Program, better known as the "green card" lottery, as a means to increase the number of immigrants from underrepresented regions.[14] This allowed thousands of Africans to obtain legal permanent residency and later to apply for citizenship. The top winners of the diversity visa lottery have come from Nigeria, Ethiopia, Egypt, and Kenya. Winners of the lottery must have a high school degree or must demonstrate that they have two years of vocational work experience.[15]

National Origins of Refugees

Refugees from Africa began to be admitted in small numbers in the 1980s as a result of instability and conflict in Somalia and Ethiopia. In 1980, the first African refugees (955) were admitted.[16] In the 1990s, the numbers of African refugees admitted for resettlement began to increase a little, but they never reached the numbers of Vietnamese or Russians. African refugees processed for third country resettlement came from Sudan, Burundi, Somalia, Rwanda, Ethiopia, and the Democratic Republic of the Congo. In 2000, there were 17,561 refugees admitted from Africa; by 2001, the number had increased to 19,020, but after the terrorist attacks of September 11, 2001, the number of refugees admitted from Africa plummeted to 2,551. By 2005 the number rebounded to 20,745 and increased to 22,472 by 2015.[17] Most Africans of the new diaspora arrived in the United States after 2000. Earlier arrivals that make up the more established groups came from Egypt, Cape Verde, South Africa, and Algeria. There are more men than women who make up this population, but that varies by countries of origin.

African Women as Refugees:
Legalities, Geographic Dispersal, and Occupations

African women refugees are admitted into the country on a case-by-case basis, like men, when they have applied for asylum, which they might get—if they have demonstrated a well-founded fear of persecution based on gender, race, religion, nationality, or membership in a political or social group, and they are unable and unwilling to return to their country of origin or habitual residence. They can also be admitted as part of a relative's application or if they have an anchor relative in the United States who can apply for them. If an anchor relative sponsors them, they do not have to demonstrate a well-founded fear of persecution.

The granting of refugee status and legal immigration normally does not take women's status into consideration unless conventional gender roles are at issue—a woman who is a legal immigrant's wife. Women and girls who have undergone female genital cutting have a higher chance of being granted asylum as opposed to those who make a plea based on the threat of female genital cutting. Even for those who are granted refugee status based on this well-founded fear of persecution, it is a traumatizing experience. This is because the asylum seeker must provide detailed forensic evidence that she has undergone the procedure. This is not done in one interview, but rather these details must be repeated throughout the asylum proceedings.[18]

Refugees and migrants have not been studied enough in terms of their gender. We can only get a full in-depth understanding of any diaspora when we provide a gendered analysis. The old way of viewing an immigrant or refugee family as one headed by a male with a wife and children lacks accuracy when applied to Africans who make up the new diaspora in the United States.[19] It is important to note that the high proportion of women among recent African migrants to the United States has been characterized as the feminization of African international migration.[20] In fact, a sizeable number of young, single, unmarried, and educated women represent the new African diaspora in the United States.[21] The reality of this new immigrant population sheds light on the importance of the 2013 National Defense Authorization Act signed by President Obama. An amendment to the act was added to address the concern that some African immigrants under the age of eighteen were being transported back to various countries during their vacation breaks to undergo female genital cutting. The act stipulates that a parent or guardian who is found guilty of transporting a female immigrant can receive a five-year prison sentence because it is a felony crime.[22]

The thousands of African women who now make the United States their home are not dispersed evenly across the country. Rather, they are concentrated in several states and in certain metropolitan areas, including New York (Brooklyn, Long Island, Manhattan), Virginia (northern Virginia), Texas (Houston and Dallas-Ft. Worth), Minnesota (St. Paul-Minneapolis), Pennsylvania (Philadelphia), Washington, DC/Maryland, Georgia (Atlanta), Illinois (Chicago), New Jersey (Hackensack, Teaneck, Englewood, Patterson), California (Los Angeles, San Francisco, Oakland), Ohio (Columbus), and Massachusetts (Boston, Quincy, Cambridge).[23]

Regardless of their status as immigrants or refugees, African women have high rates of participation in the workforce, as in Africa. This is especially true for the women who are single, divorced, or widowed. Still, women who are married also participate in the workforce at significant rates. It is important to make a distinction between labor participation in the formal and informal sector. This is because the formal sector is regulated by the government, is based on the rule of law, provides certain benefits, and usually provides women with a minimum level of protection against racial, sexual, and gender discrimination. The informal sector does not have to provide any of these protections, it is not regulated by the government, and women are often "paid under the table," where taxes and benefits are not provided by the employer. If they are self-employed in the informal sector, they will have to provide for their own social security, health care, and so forth. Women who are refugees, permanent legal residents, or citizens will have better opportunities to secure employment in the formal sector since IRCA imposes sanctions on employers who hire undocumented workers.

African women are found in a variety of occupations and sectors of the U.S. economy: health care, child care, sales/retail, administrative support, education, management, business, finance, law, and the media. In the health-care industry African women are nurses—both registered and licensed practical nurses, doctors, laboratory technicians, and administrators. In business and finance, African women are accountants, bankers, financial advisers, marketers, and entrepreneurs. African women are represented in the educational sector as teachers on all levels, including the tertiary level, as researchers, students, staff, and administrators.[24]

African women work for federal, state, and local governments in various capacities and in the nonprofit sector from large philanthropic organizations to community development and service organizations. All of these represent work in the formal sector available to women who are documented immigrants. Those who are undocumented are often forced to work in the informal sector in such jobs as hair braiding, cooking, serving, cleaning and washing dishes in restaurants, cleaning homes and offices, domestic service, and street vending (clothes, jewelry, food, carvings, etc.).[25]

Because most women in the new African diaspora in the United States live in urban areas, these have sizeable numbers of immigrants (documented and undocumented) and refugees from all over the world, often living in "ethnic" enclaves that cater to people's countries of origin in terms of food, music, clothes, and beauty products.[26] Many African women have taken advantage of this and have entered the informal sector as entrepreneurs, opening stores and shops that sell books, clothes, DVDs, jewelry, and cosmetics. African braiding salons can be found in most urban areas from Waterbury, Connecticut, to the hundreds located in Chicago, New York, Atlanta, and Los Angeles.

It is not just immigrant women's status that pushes them into the informal sector; there are other challenges and problems that such women must overcome. For example, language barriers prevent many from fully participating in the formal sector, especially women from countries where English is not widely spoken. Women from countries such as Guinea, Mozambique, Algeria, Angola, Senegal, Somalia, or Côte d'Ivoire, for instance, may have higher participation rates in the informal sector than women from anglophone Ghana, Nigeria, Sierra Leone, Liberia, Kenya, Zimbabwe, and South Africa. In addition, many women worked in the informal sector before arriving in the United States—trading, for instance, an experience that is difficult to translate into a formal economy job. To sell legally they need licenses, available only to documented immigrants. To obtain licenses they must be able, or get someone else, to fill out paperwork and navigate the bureaucracy in cities such as Atlanta, Houston, Chicago, and New York.

Another large stumbling block to opening a business is obtaining capital. Without savings, helpful relatives, a husband/partner, or an inheritance, they must seek funds from a bank or other lending institution, where language may be a barrier, and where illegal status, discrimination, lack of collateral, or an absent or low credit rating might prevent them from obtaining a loan. Banks and lending institutions often ask about previous business experience, work experience, and the possession of collateral such as a house to guarantee the loan. Access to any of these may be predicated on having legal status.

Class and Workforce Experience

Class status for African women of the new diaspora who are entrepreneurs, work in businesses established by other African migrants, or work in the informal sector, retail sales, or support positions in health care and administration might disadvantage them in comparison to other women migrants. It is a defining characteristic for those in the new African diaspora, where advantages accrue to those with higher education and professional qualifications, fluency in English, longer periods of time lived in the United States, and social capital. In other words, new African diaspora women cannot be lumped into one category. There is a significant difference between a Somali woman who arrives in St. Paul, Minnesota, alone after spending several years in a refugee camp in Kenya and a woman from Ghana who has a college degree or two years of vocational training and immigrated legally as the result of the Diversity Visa Lottery. Furthermore, women professors who arrive in the country from Canada, the United Kingdom, Germany, or France and who are hired to teach in the United States will have a different experience from those who came into the country on student visas that expired, putting them in undocumented status. Even within families statuses can vary. For instance, in the 1990s a Ghanaian man, his wife and two children came to the United States on his student visa, only to have his wife deported because, prohibited from getting a green card, she took a job as a nurse's aide to supplement their meager income. She then joined the legions of those working illegally in the United States who are regularly repatriated.

However, professional women, fluent in English and middle or upper middle class, still have problems and face particular challenges as African women migrants. First, regardless of the advantages mentioned above, they are still viewed first as black and then as black women by the larger society, just as lesser-skilled African women are. The same racist discrimination experienced by African women of the historic diaspora will be exercised against them, racialized as the Other, the undeserving, welfare queens, affirmative action hires, or admitted students, along with the infamous labels such as domineering matriarchs, mammies, jezebels, and sapphires.[27] African women migrants unaware of the racial and gender history of the United States will have more difficulties navigating hostile educational, corporate, medical, legal, and business environments.

Unless these women acquired U.S. degrees and certifications, they will have to go through a protracted process of getting recertified to meet U.S. qualifications. Many of them do not have the time, money, or resources to do so. Therefore, women who might have been doctors, accountants, engineers, and lawyers in their home countries end up not being able to secure employment in these professions or reenter their professions at a lower level. For example, someone who is a Kenyan registered nurse might become a licensed practical nurse because those qualifications are less time-consuming and cheaper to obtain. After migrating to the United States, a woman who worked as a certified public accountant (CPA) in Nigeria might work for an accounting company, but not as a CPA since she is without the time or resources to take classes preparing her to pass the required examination. Even when new African diaspora professional women obtain positions due to their qualifications, they are often scrutinized and denied opportunities to advance in their careers due to racially inflected and gendered discrimination.

Regardless of whether women work in professional, unskilled, or low-skilled jobs, or in the informal or formal sector, their economic activities in the United States are tied to their homelands in various ways. As women, they are still responsible for and expected to contribute financially to their families and communities back home for occasions such as weddings, burials, school fees, medical costs, and other family emergencies. Remittances are an important mechanism for new African diaspora women to remain in contact and to play a role in their homelands. Women from across Africa have contributed to the development of their homelands through investing in schools, hospitals, businesses, and housing construction.

Participation in Cultural Institutions and Community Activism

It is widely believed that women, especially as mothers and the backbone of families and communities, are responsible for maintaining and passing on cultural traditions and customs. Indeed, new African diaspora women in the United States negotiate and renegotiate their identities as African women and mothers, drawing on strong African roots to do so. Among the most important cultural institutions for women of the new African diaspora are churches and mosques.[28] Some African immigrant communities have established their own churches while others join and attend predominantly African American churches and predominantly white churches. When African immigrant communities have established their own churches, women often serve as pastors, assistant pastors, ushers, first ladies of the church, choir members, deaconesses, and members of various committees such as the missionary board and usher board. They are involved in all aspects of the churches as Sunday school and Bible school teachers, fund-raisers, endowers and receivers of scholarships, and sustainers of all aspects of religious institutions because these provide spaces for spiritual sustenance and rites of passage such as marriages, blessings or baptisms of children and adults, and funerals.

Churches and mosques established by African immigrants often serve the same functions they continue to do for the historic African diaspora. They provide and allow their members to develop leadership, organizational, financial, and communication skills. They serve as outlets for information on politics, employment, housing, scholarships, immigration, and other information that is pertinent to the various communities. The many African immigrant women who join and attend African American churches, with plenty to choose from in any major urban area, are welcomed because the historic diaspora established their own churches when they were not welcomed at the white churches. Membership in an African American church offers participation in a number of boards and committees, networking, and other advantages. Since major metropolitan areas where most African immigrants have settled are also home to many members of the historic African diaspora, the newcomers can easily find a welcoming religious institution to join. Where mosques do not already exist, migrant women have played roles in establishing them.

Women of the new African diaspora are also engaged in their communities through participation in various ethnic associations established in most metropolitan communities with sizeable communities of African migrants. Ethnically based associations help African migrants in the United States and members' families in the homeland by ensuring in times of a crisis or emergency that financial and other forms of support are provided, especially when there is a death. Immigrants who lose a family member are often responsible for paying for a funeral in their homeland. Regardless of the length of their U.S. residence, African migrants who die in the United States are usually buried in their homeland. Members of the migrant community contribute money for transportation costs to the homeland and other financial expenses. Members of the historic African diaspora who are acquainted with the deceased through work, the church, the mosque, school, or marriage often visit their home with contributions of money and food.

Racial discrimination spurs community activism. Regardless of how new African diaspora women view themselves or identify in terms of national origin or ethnicity, they must cope in the United States with being lumped into one racial bloc defined by skin color, "black" as opposed to "white." They, along with their children, are likely to experience individual and institutional racism and discrimination as did those from the historic African diaspora. Experiences of racism in the workforce and by their children in schools have impelled new African diaspora women to engage in civic activities, form community organizations, and become leaders in their communities.

Africans as Model Minorities?

Studies have documented the disparate educational outcomes in U.S. schools for African American and Latino students in terms of who is singled out for special education classes, gifted and talented classes, advanced placement classes, and disciplinary actions.[29] Some argue that children of immigrants from Africa and the Caribbean have better educational outcomes than African Americans from the historic diaspora and that many Ivy League colleges and other highly competitive predominantly white colleges and universities admit by preference African American students of African and Caribbean descent to demonstrate that race is not an impediment to their educational attainment.[30] Certainly many students from the new African diaspora do well in school and go on to be accepted by prestigious colleges and universities, often reflecting the high priority placed on getting a good education by their highly educated parents. However, many others do not.

The model minority myth assigned to students of Asian origin has also been assigned to students from the new African diaspora, but it would be misleading for both groups if this myth were accepted at face value.[31] African migrant women, mothers of new diaspora students, are forced to face reality when they grapple with individual and institutional racism experienced by their children in schools across the United States. Not only do they have to deal with negative racial stereotyping assuming African American intellectual and educational inferiority, with lower expectations of students of African descent and harsh disciplinary measures such as school expulsions and detentions, but they also soon discover that schools vary highly in terms of courses offered, teacher qualifications, gifted and talented programs, after-school programs, fine arts programs, and numbers of students who graduate on time and go on to attend college.

Women's Activism in Improving Education, Girls' Identity Crises

Faced with this reality, African women have formed community organizations and engaged in civic activities for the benefit of all children disadvantaged by racism and discrimination. New African diaspora women are active participants in existing organizations such as the Parent-Teacher Association (PTA) and also establish new organizations.[32] After all, many resettled in the United States to get better lives for themselves and their children, with education continuing to be key to social and economic advancement. They cannot afford to ignore the maltreatment of their children in schools. Such women then bring to the attention of school administrators and other parents issues of racism and discrimination against their children and seek solutions, often in alliance with historic African diaspora women, who can offer sage advice for pursuing educational battles at all levels of education, given that they have been on the frontlines for generations, especially in providing a multicultural curriculum including contributions of Africans and people of African descent in areas from science to history to music to math. Every victory won by the new and historic diaspora is a victory for all children of African descent and their communities.

A key problem faced by young new African diaspora women entering colleges and universities concerns identity in the face of continuing racial stereotyping by other students, faculty, staff, and administrators. Some students have adopted more defined and entrenched national and ethnic identities from Africa to distinguish themselves from being "black," while others identify as African American. Whether these students identify as Nigerian Americans, Somali Americans, or Ethiopian Americans, their experiences and treatment at predominantly white universities and colleges can enhance, broaden, or threaten deeper ties to the historic diaspora African student population.

Women's Self-Help Organizing

While the quality of their children's education is a major focus of new African diaspora women, it is not the sole focus. Many women have established or joined organizations pursuing reforms of health care, employment, immigration, and refugee laws. Women's health activism is necessary because many refugee and immigrant women arrive in the United States in ill health, especially if they have fled conflict, resided in refugee camps for years, undergone female genital cutting, or been raped. In addition, some women's health and lives are at risk even after they arrive in the United States because they find themselves in abusive marriages and relationships. New African diaspora women have formed organizations to help other immigrant women understand and exercise their legal rights in terms of leaving an abusive partner, divorce, alimony, and child support. African immigrant women and refugees, like others, often do not know their legal rights, especially if they believe that their immigration status and thus their right to remain in the country are dependent on their husband. They may not be employed or have a driver's license, may not speak English, and may wrongly believe that they will be deported if they contact the police and report an abusive husband or partner.[33]

As more women have migrated from Africa to the United States without a husband, partner, children, or other family members, the need for community organizations has expanded, and new African diaspora women have met this need. African women who migrate with a husband/partner or children also need assistance in finding employment and housing, navigating the school system to ensure that their children get access to educational opportunities, and gaining access to social, legal, and health services. Immigrant women of African descent from the Caribbean, especially those from countries where English is not the dominant language (Haiti, in particular), face the same types of educational and economic hurdles as African immigrant women due to the language barrier and are included in civic organizations formed by other African-descent women.

Pan-Africanism: Building Linkages between the New and Historic Diaspora

As seen above, immigrant issues in general and issues that pertain to women in particular have led new African diaspora women to establish community organizations and engage in civic activities. However, entrenched issues such as police brutality, economic inequality, the war on crime and drugs, anti-immigrant and anti-foreign sentiment, and the overall surveillance of communities of color following the terrorist attacks of September 11, 2001, have forged, broadened, and strengthened alliances between new and historic African diaspora members. Police officers killing unarmed African-descent men in particular has long been an issue. The murder by four New York police officers of Amadou Diallo, unarmed in the hall of his Bronx apartment building in

New York in 1999, brought this issue to the forefront of the new African diaspora. Diallo migrated to the United States from Guinea. The officers were charged with second-degree murder—and acquitted. Ordinary citizens along with well-seasoned civil rights activists such as Al Sharpton participated in ensuing demonstrations and acts of civil disobedience.[34]

Another earlier example from New York happened in 1997 when Abner Louima, of Haitian descent, was sexually brutalized by police, who were later charged with various offenses. Both of these cases brought out individuals and activists from the new and historic African diaspora because they illustrate that race trumps immigrant status in the eyes of the police, and that all communities of African descent are subject to unwarranted attacks for which police escape punishment.

More recent cases of police brutality—in 2015—include the killings of Freddie Gray, Baltimore, Maryland; Michael Brown, Ferguson, Missouri; Eric Garner, Staten Island, New York; Walter Scott, North Charleston, South Carolina; Tamir Rice, Cleveland, Ohio; and Sandra Bland, Prairie View, Texas; these cases were heard and watched by most African and African-descent people.[35] Although a racist vigilante killed Trayvon Martin in 2012, not the police, his death was viewed by many as being similar to those committed by the police. His killer was acquitted and went on to commit other crimes. These cases, along with other issues undergirding the Black Lives Matter movement, support promoting a new form of Pan-Africanism that includes members of the new and historic African diaspora. The use of social media to expose and report these violations of people's human rights has buoyed the Black Lives Matter movement and served to strengthen and broaden ties between the new and historic African diasporas in the United States that include women born in the Americas and Africa. The frequency of police killings that are viewed by their communities as unjustified and by law enforcement as justified helps promote closer ties between African and African-descent communities, forged in the experiences of racism and discrimination, especially when murderers are exculpated.

Conclusion

Women who make up the new African diaspora are faced with a number of hurdles as they navigate their way through educational institutions for their own education and their children's, the workplace, religious institutions, their communities, and their homes. They do this while facing racism and discrimination both at the individual and community levels. In order to thrive and survive under these conditions, such women have established community, state, and national organizations to address these issues while forging linkages and bonds with the historical African diaspora and women of African descent who are also a part of the new African diaspora. The diversity of the women who make up the new African diaspora is illustrated in their varied experiences and is dependent on issues of class, socioeconomic status, religious affiliation, and immigration status.

Any analysis of the "African American" community and "African American" women must take into consideration members of the new African diaspora as they become more prominent in metropolitan areas across the country. Small- and medium-sized cities and towns throughout the country are increasingly home to many new African diaspora women. Their impact and roles in future American politics, culture, economy, and schools will be felt more broadly as they join further in the multicultural American experiment now being undermined by those wishing to reverse it.

The first chapter in this book pointed out cultural similarities in diasporic experiences illustrated in African women's novels analyzed by Elizabeth Perego; this chapter goes into the real world of contemporary experiences and actions of African new diasporic women in the United States, showing that they bring along substantial organizational abilities that they are putting to use for their communities, as in Africa. The strengths of African-descent women and alliances across borders, races, ethnicities, religions, genders, ages, classes, and cultures may instead foster progress.

Notes

1. Jessica Lopes and Brandon Lundy, "Research Note: Secondary Diaspora: Cape Verdean Immigration to the Southeastern United States," *Southern Anthropologist* 36, no. 2 (2014): 70–102.

2. Mary J. Osirim, "African Women and the New Diaspora: Transnationalism and the (Re) Creation of Home," *African and Asian Studies* 7, no. 4 (2008): 367–94.

3. Cassandra R. Veney, *Democratization, Structural Adjustment, and Refugees: Forced Migration in Eastern Africa* (New York: Palgrave Macmillan, 2007).

4. Department of Homeland Security, "Green Card for Refugees," U.S. Citizenship and Immigration Services, June 26, 2017, https://www.uscis.gov/greencard/refugees.

5. Kwadwo Konadu-Agyemang, Baffour K. Takyi, and John Arthur, "An Overview of African Immigration to U.S. and Canada," in *The New African Diaspora in North America: Trends, Community Building and Adaptation*, ed. Kwadwo Konadu-Agyemang, Baffour K. Takyi, and John Arthur (Lanham, MD: Lexington Books, 2006), 1–12.

6. Cassandra R. Veney, "The Effects of Immigration and Refugee Policies on Africans in the United States: From the Civil Rights Movement to the War on Terrorism," in *The New African Diaspora*, ed. Isidore Okpewho and Nkiru Nzegwu (Bloomington: Indiana University Press, 2009), 196–214.

7. Veney, "Immigration and Refugee Policies," 201.

8. Cassandra R. Veney, "Redefining Citizenship: The Role of Refugees in Their Host Countries' Development," CODESRIA 11th General Assembly, Maputo, Mozambique, December 6–10, 2005, 1–19.

9. Veney, "Redefining Citizenship," 9–11.

10. Betsey Cooper and Kevin O'Neil, "Lessons from the Immigration Reform and Control Act of 1986," Migration Policy Institute, policy brief no. 3 (August 2005), https://www.migrationpolicy.org/research/lessons-immigration-reform-and-control-act-1986.

11. David M. Reimers, "Renewed African Immigration," in *Immigration and the Legislation of Harry S. Truman*, ed. Roger Daniels (Kirksville, MO: Truman State University Press, 2010), 151–71.

12. Joseph W. Scott and Solomon A. Getahun, *Little Ethiopia of the Pacific Northwest* (New Brunswick, NJ: Transaction, 2013), xix.

13. Reimers, "Renewed African Immigration," 151–71.

14. Konadu-Agyemang, Takyi, and Arthur, "Overview of African Immigration," 1–12.

15. Miriam Jordan, "U.S. Visa Lottery Attracts 11 Million Applicants," *Wall Street Journal*, November 6, 2014, www.wsj.com/articles/u-s-visa-program-attracts-11-million-applicants.

16. United States Department of State, "Cumulative Summary of Refugee Admissions," Bureau of Population, Refugees, and Migration, December 31, 2015, https://2009–2017.state.gov/j/prm/releases/statistics/251288.htm.

17. "United States Department of State, "Refugee Admissions."

18. Sanctuary for Families, "Female Genital Mutilation in the United States," 2013, https://sanctuaryforfamilies.org/gender-violence/related-forms-of-gender-violence/.

19. G. Oty Agbajoh-Laoye, "Lifting the Yoke of Tradition: New African Market Women-Diaspora: From Kaneshie, Accra to Harlem, New York," in Konadu-Agyemang, Takyi, and Arthur, *New African Diaspora*, 235–56.

20. Kevin J. A. Thomas and Ikubolajen Logan, "African Female Immigration to the United States and Its Policy Implications," *Canadian Journal of African Studies* 46, no. 1 (2012): 87–107.

21. Thomas and Logan, "African Female Immigrants, 88.

22. Sanctuary for Families, "Female Genital Mutilation in the United States."

23. Audrey Singer and Jill H. Wilson, "From 'There' to 'Here': Refugee Resettlement in Metropolitan America," Brookings Institution, September 1, 2006, https://www.brookings.edu/research/from-there-to-here-refugee-resettlement-in-metropolitan-america/; John W. Frazier, Joe T. Darden, and Norah F. Henry, *The African Diaspora in the United States and Canada at the Dawn of the 21st Century* (Albany: State University of New York Press, 2010), 329–37; Singer, "U.S. Immigration Demographics and Immigrant Integration," Brookings Institution, July 16, 2014, https://www.brookings.edu/wp-content/uploads/2016/06/Singer-WH-Integration-Convening-FIN5.pdf.

24. Asmaa Donahue, "African Immigrant Women and Girls in New York" (Female Migration Panel, Side event to the 54th Session on the Commission on the Status of Women, United Nations Headquarters, New York, March 2, 2010), http://www.unitar.org/ny/node.

25. Osirim, "African Women," 382; Agbajoh-Layoye, "Lifting the Yoke," 248.

26. Agbajoh-Laoye, "Lifting the Yoke," 242.

27. Sonja Brown Givens, "Mammies, Jezebels and Other Controlling Imagery: An Examination of the Influence of Televised Stereotypes on Perceptions of an African American Woman," *Media Psychology* 7, no. 1 (2005): 87–106.

28. Sulayman S. Nyang, "The African Immigrant Family in the United States of America: Challenges and Opportunities," Center for Islam and Public Policy, December 2013, http://www.cippusa.com/the-african-immigrant-family-in-the-us-of-america -challenges-and-opportunities.

29. Brenda L. Townsend, "The Disproportionate Discipline of African American Learners: Reducing School Suspensions and Expulsions," *Exceptional Children* 66, no. 3 (2000): 381–91; Russell J. Skiba, Robert S. Michael, Abra Carroll Narda, and Reece L. Peterson, "The Color of Discipline: Source of Racial and Gender Disproportionality in School Punishment," *Urban Review* 34, no. 4 (2002): 317–42; Russell J. Skiba, Choong-Geun Chung, Megan Trachok, Timberly L. Baker, Adam Sheya, and Robin L. Hughes, "Passing Disciplinary Disproportionality: Contributions of Infraction, Student, and School Characteristics to Out-of-and School Suspension and Expulsion," *American Education Research Journal* 51, no. 4 (2014): 640–70.

30. Alex Kumi-Yeboah, "Educational Resilience and Academic Achievement of Immigrant Students from Ghana in an Urban School Environment," *Urban Education* 5, no. 10 (2016): 1–22; Pamela R. Bennett and Amy Lutz, "How African American Is the Net Black Advantage? Differences in College Attitudes among Immigrant Blacks, Native Blacks, and Whites," *Sociology of Education* 82, no. 1 (2009): 70–99; A. C. Haynie, "Not 'Just Black' Policy Considerations: The Influence of Ethnicity on Pathways to Academic Success amongst Black Undergraduates at Harvard," *Journal of Public and International Affairs* 13 (2002):40–62.

31. William H. Frey, *Diversity Explosion: How New Racial Demographics Are Remaking America* (Washington, DC: Brookings Institution Press, 2014), 87–106.

32. Nyang, "African Immigrant Family."

33. Veney, "Forced Migration," 242.

34. Chelsea Rose Marcus Parascandola and Larry McShane, "NYPD Cop Involved in Amadou Diallo Shooting to Be Promoted," *New York Daily News*, December 16, 2016.

35. Peter Hermann and Johns Woodrow Cox, "A Freddie Gray Primer: Who Was He, How Did He Die, Why Is There So Much Anger?," *Washington Post*, April 28, 2015.

Suggested Readings

Arthur, John. *African Women Immigrants in the United States: Crossing Transnational Borders*. New York: Palgrave Macmillan, 2009.

Carter, Prudence L. *Keepin' It Real: School Success beyond Black and White*. Oxford: Oxford University Press, 2005.

Halter, Marilyn, and Violet Showers Johnson. *African and American: West Africans in Post–Civil Rights America*. New York: New York University Press, 2014.

Jones, Charisse, and Kumea Shorter-Gooden. *Shifting: The Double Lives of Black Women in America*. New York: HarperCollins, 2003.

Okomé, Mojubaolu Olufunke, and Olufemi Vaughan, eds. *Transnational Africa and Globalization*. New York: Palgrave Macmillan, 2012.

PART IV

LOVE, MARRIAGE, AND WOMEN'S
BODIES, PAST AND PRESENT

Figure 13.1. Togoland (?) portrait of a wedding party, ca. 1914–1924. Gelatin silver print. Image Af,A66.15, AN79112001. © Trustees of the British Museum.

13

LOVE, MARRIAGE, AND
FAMILIES IN AFRICA

Rachel Jean-Baptiste and Emily Burrill

W hy are the themes of marriage, household, and love so important to
understanding the histories of African women? In *"Wicked" Women
and the Reconfiguration of Gender in Africa*, Dorothy L. Hodgson and Sheryl
McCurdy write that marriage and household relations are "the primary locus of
production, reproduction, consumption, distribution and social control in societies."[1] An apt definition of marriage and household formation in Africa comes
from Henrietta L. Moore and Meghan Vaughan's study of Bemba society in
twentieth-century Malawi: "marriage was not an institution, but a set of processes" entailing "the shifting sands of negotiation, compromise, and interpretation on which it was based and through which it was constituted."[2] What is
missing in these analyses, however, is consideration of the affective realms,
affection and love, that cohere or disconnect women, men, and children to and
from each other. We argue that ideas and lived experiences of affect and sexuality are key to analyzing changes in marital forms over time, as well as factors
that have hastened shifts in family definitions and membership in Africa. In
analyzing changing relationships of marriage, households, and affect, we will
look first at precolonial Africa, then at the impact of European colonialism on
African family structures, and at postindependent and contemporary Africa.

Marriage and Motherhood in Precolonial Africa

In the *Epic of Sundiata*, the great praise poem that recounts the formation of the
Mali Empire in the thirteenth century, one of the central figures is the hero's
mother, Sogolon. Sogolon is described as a hunchbacked Buffalo woman, but
according to prophecy the king, Maghan the Handsome, must marry her in
order to reproduce the child who would become Sundiata. Maghan's marriage
to Sogolon unleashes the violent jealousy of his first wife, Sassouma. The sour

relationship between the two co-wives and their protection and promotion of their respective sons propel the story. Yet Sundiata prevails in the end, avenging the past suffering of both his mother and the Malinke people at the hands of corrupt kings. There are many morals within the *Epic of Sundiata*; one of them rests on the lesson that marriage serves a greater purpose than intimate love or attraction between married men and women. However, another moral of the great epic is that love and devotion—particularly filial love and devotion—and betrayal and jealousy are powerful emotional forces that drive women and men both to forge ties and to break with traditions.[3]

Though written sources exist for some precolonial African societies, knowledge of the deep precolonial past of many African societies is based mainly on oral traditions, such as the *Epic of Sundiata*, as well as folktales, origin myths, and songs. In many Central and East African societies, for example, remnants of the deep past are known through traditions describing chiefly and kingly lines and genealogies, the patrilineal, bilineal, and matrilineal paths of kinship.[4] However, as historian Rhiannon Stephens notes, most historians overlooked the fact that these traditions about succession and kinship are ultimately histories of marriage and motherhood, which determined succession to positions of power.[5] One element of marriage and household formation was the expectation that women would take on roles as mothers, raise children, and biologically and culturally reproduce kin. In the kingdoms of Buganda, Busoga, and the polities of Buswere in the North Nyanza region of present-day Uganda, motherhood—not the biological event of giving birth, but the social role of mothering and childrearing—was an essential element in the production and maintenance of political institutions, primarily through the role of the queen mother.

Queen mothers feature prominently in precolonial African histories, including Bugandan history, but also in many West African polities such as Asante, Oyo, and Dahomey (see chapters 3 and 4). While there are certain elements to the role of queen mother that seem archetypical across cultural and historical contexts, there is also variety over time and space in the meaning of the queen mother and the rise of her office. In Dahomey, for example, the queen mother, or *kpojito*, was a "reign mate" integral to the political authority of the king. The position originated in the eighteenth century, when the *kpojito* ruled in tandem with the king, a ruling partnership best exhibited in the reign of *kpojito* Hwanjile and King Tegbesu, in the mid-eighteenth century.[6] The *kpojito*, a woman who often came from a common background, sometimes even enslaved, was critical to the king's ability to consolidate authority in the expanding empire. The role of the *kpojito* as power sharer continued until the mid-nineteenth century, when the institution declined in power as other figures within the royal family became more critical to the consolidation and execution of political power. The example of the *kpojito* is instructive because it shows that family relations—between mothers and those whom they raised and husbands and slave and nonslave wives—were central to a patriarch's capacity to exercise authority in the first place. An interrogation of the institution of queen mother reveals in this case underlying gender complementarity within African patriarchy, or male dominance (see chapter 3), and complicates how we think about the social and political roles of mother and wife.

Historian Lorelle Semley tells us that the queen mother, as both an ideal and a real figure, provided a model for public motherhood in a precolonial context.[7] An excellent example of this is the Yoruba *iyalode*, a title meaning "mother owns the outside world." The *iyalode* derived her power from being a mother who has raised her children within a family and kin group, and as an elder she acquired knowledge and authority through that role, which could then be deployed in the larger community. *Iyalode*, as a public mother, nurtures and advises the community around her, both reproducing the conditions of a society and shaping new social networks.[8]

Both the role of the queen mother and the institution of public motherhood changed in dramatic ways as a result of an increase in the domestic and the export slave trade with the rise of the transatlantic slave trade (see chapter 9). In Oyo in the eighteenth century, kings became increasingly dependent on the counsel of queen mothers and royal wives, but by the mid-nineteenth century, Oyo had declined in size and power as a result of wars with neighbors and overdependence on the slave trade with European traders; queen mothers and royal wives declined in both number and status. Women who populated the Oyo court by the mid-nineteenth century were often wives who entered the court through enslavement, so that they could not count on lineages for support. Thus, the political authority of women and the influence of royal mothers and wives decreased as the numbers of women at court increased.

This dynamic unfolded in other parts of West Africa as well. Women in late eighteenth-century Kankan-Baté (present-day eastern Guinea) saw their power and influence that came with age and motherhood decline when male household heads derived power from new economic developments associated with long-distance trade. Elite men in Baté no longer had to rely on the work and expertise of the women in their families and households when slave women took on roles previously occupied by free women.[9] Just as the rise of internal African slavery and the export slave trade through the eighteenth century significantly affected African households and marriage, so too did the end of slavery and the process of slave emancipation (see chapter 9). Between the 1830s and the 1840s in the Western Cape of colonial South Africa, for example, a woman recently liberated from chattel slavery still had to navigate the world of marriage and a husband's authority over her formal labor.[10]

In parts of Africa, freewomen experienced the effects of slave emancipation as an increased demand for their labor within the household. The early years of formal slave emancipation in French Sudan (present-day Mali) witnessed an increase in divorce cases before colonial courts, the vast majority of which were initiated by women during harvest seasons and directly following massive slave exoduses.[11] This was in part because free women's agricultural labor was expected to replace that of those who left during the slave exoduses. Some women objected that this was beyond the scope of marital obligations and left their husbands. Still, some enslaved women used divorce claims before the colonial tribunal at the turn of the century to achieve manumission. What these cases show is that, at least in the early twentieth century, the bonds of slavery and the bonds of marriage were sometimes interconnected for women living in societies practicing slavery and in regions of massive political upheaval. Such interconnectedness resided in gendered labor expectations.[12]

Beyond entailing labor obligations for women and men, precolonial families in Africa were defined as all those descended from a common ancestor, which can be called a lineage family, usually patrilineal or matrilineal. Marriage was not the most important ritual since it was valued mainly for production of children to continue the lineage. Thus, the welcoming of babies to the lineage and funerals tended to be the most important rituals, not weddings. In contrast, weddings create conjugal families, which in the Western world are seen as defining family membership, centering on a couple or an individual with their children, parents, and further descendants. A lineage family will disappear if there are no descendants to carry it on, so childbearing is highly valued, while an ego-centered conjugal family can disappear with the death or divorce of those at its center, making divorce especially traumatic. In precolonial Africa in some societies divorce was common, especially where matrilinearity endowed women with full rights and maternity, not paternity, established lineage membership. In others marriage was supposed to be for life, with women often having lesser rights than men.

Marriage, Family Law, and Gender in Colonial Africa

The period of colonial rule, especially the 1930s through the 1960s, witnessed intense contestations and differing dynamics across Africa about the meanings and practices of marriage. Changing local and global economic processes,

European colonialism, opportunities for migration and mobility, transformations in laws and court systems, shifts in religious beliefs, and emotional attachments shaped women's everyday lives and actions. Flexibility in marital forms
and gender roles across Africa continued despite colonial impositions and
rigidities. What historian Stephan F. Miescher argues for Ghana in the 1930s
to 1970s can be said for the entire continent: "a multiplicity of requirements,
rules, and customs" circulated and engendered multiple forms of marriage.[13]
Among the Akan in Ghana domestic arrangements included monogamous
or polygynous (one husband with multiple wives) customary marriage, usually
arranged by elders, that involved bridewealth or other marriage payments,
cohabitation, and marriages legalized by European civil law or Christian
rites.[14] In Muslim communities (particularly in North Africa, parts of West
Africa, and coastal East Africa), various schools of Islamic *shari'a* law and figures of religious and political authority sought to regulate marriage, divorce,
and family formations and ensure that nearly all women entered into marriages arranged by elders.[15] In regions in Central Africa such as Gabon, some
women were betrothed as children, were raised by their mothers-in-law, and
consummated their marriages after puberty.[16] With increasing urbanization,
some women had sexual and domestic relationships with men through prostitution for which they earned money or other forms of payment. Such was
the well-known case of prostitutes in Nairobi, Kenya, from the 1930s to
the 1950s, documented by Luise White and summarized by Teresa Barnes in
chapter 11.[17]

Analyzing the Nigerian Aba Women's War of 1929 opens a window into
understanding the shifting sands through which African women waded in these
decades to create a variety of domestic arrangements. Kathleen Sheldon in
chapter 4 summarizes the dramatic process of the well-organized demonstrations and resulting reforms of the British colonial administration, emphasizing
that these women's protests occurred within the context of increasing moneti-
zation of the Nigerian economy. Some forms of protest included songs questioning the manhood of problematic chiefs. Women used the power of their
sexuality as a weapon—often by baring breasts and making threats to with-
hold sexual intimacy in response to political injustice.[18] However, at the heart
of these events were questions about the meaning of marriage and household
in changing historical circumstances. What was marriage? Could the state and
political figures regulate wives' mobility and work? Who would be able to
marry? What forms of economic exchange and control of material resources
did such a relationship entail? What were the expectations and rights of husbands, wives, and kin?

Many societies in West, East, Central, and southern Africa believed that heterosexual customary marriage conferred social adulthood. Bridewealth was often a cornerstone of the marriage agreement, legalized by the groom and his family giving cash, cattle, foodstuffs, and locally produced or imported goods to the bride's family (her family also sometimes gave goods of lesser value to the groom's family). However, economic booms and busts and the increased use of money in colonial daily life inflated bridewealth and made legal marriage less accessible.[19]

Beginning in the 1930s, African political leaders and British colonial personnel in areas such as rural Gusiiland in Kenya were concerned that young men could not afford to marry since fathers with daughters requested increased numbers of cattle as bridewealth. Many young men had earned money working in wage labor jobs, but wages stagnated in the 1930s and 1940s, along with the capacity of poorer young men to meet older men's requests for bridewealth. Meanwhile, young women decided with whom they would form intimate relationships and domestic arrangements, not their elders, resulting in increased numbers of elopements in which couples ran off or married women left their legal husbands' homes to live with a lover, who did not reimburse the husband's bridewealth. Legal cases over such situations appeared before Kenyan local courts presided over by chiefs, revealing debates about how women's individual ideas about love and quality of life determined marriage and generational shifts in which younger women and men challenged submission to the authority of elders.[20]

In Niger, the changing composition and meaning of marriage payments from the 1930s to the 1950s reflected collective and individual ideas about the social worth of the bride, as well as her and her female kin's wealth. Among Muslim Hausa in Maradi senior women played an active role in determining marriage payments, which were a series of gift exchanges between women and men, the bride and groom's kin, and juniors and seniors.[21] The groom's family gave gifts to the bride's family, and the bride's family was expected to meet or surpass the groom's offerings. After 1935, the content of brides' countergifts changed. Cash replaced cowries and imported cloth, enamel or Pyrex pots and bowls, and porcelain objects, and metal beds replaced locally supplied gifts from the giver such as calabashes, cloth, or grain. The capacity of a bride's relatives to give lavish gifts during marriage payment ceremonies signified her social ties and material wealth in the new political economy of increased global trade during French colonial rule. Women's ability to give cash and imported goods as wedding gifts for the marital home was an indication of female agency, women's purchasing power in the urban commercial economy, and insurance and savings for times of scarcity.[22]

The expansion of Christian beliefs and access to formal education in missionary schools also shaped how many African women and communities viewed and practiced marriage. Missionaries attempted to enforce Western ideals of Christian heterosexual conjugal marriage, sexuality, and parenthood (see also chapter 14). For example, in Southern Rhodesia, Christian ideas produced the idea of sexuality as regulated by "the realm of the moral" and potentially "sin."[23] Missionary schools taught women housewifery skills and that refraining from sex during pregnancy and lactation, common methods of spacing births used in precolonial Africa, was akin to disobeying their husbands.

However, African adaptations of Christian conjugal mores and household formation were selective. Christian Protestant women converts in Maragoli in Kenya adopted Christian marriage practices such as monogamous marriage and sent their children to be educated in mission schools, but they maintained other customary practices such as widow inheritance as an ethical means to ensure that widowed women and their children were not left materially bereft and socially isolated.[24] In Brazzaville and Pointe-Noire, Congo, from the 1930s to the 1960s thousands of women and men adopted the Catholic faith. Missionaries attempted to assert conformity to European norms of heterosexual monogamous marriages and decried "polygamy, concubinage, and free unions" and women's continued strong ties with their matrilineal kin as antithetical to Catholic morality.[25] Catholic Congolese women struggled to craft their own visions of domestic life, selectively adapting European Catholic norms and negotiating pressures from Congolese men in framing definitions of a good mother and wife.

A series of public scuffles that occurred in the 1930s illustrates the actions and intentionality of Congolese Catholic women. In May 1934, some five hundred women in monogamous marriages attended a religious retreat in Bacongo, leaving homes they shared with husbands at dawn and returning after dark. Husbands complained, stating that their wives were not attending to wifely duties of providing cooked meals and fetching water from public fountains for their children's and husbands' basic needs. Some men decided to prevent women from attending the retreat by blocking their passage, but women insisted on their rights and broke free of the blockade to continue on their way. A few months later, Catholic women in Brazzaville sought to celebrate the French National Holiday of Bastille Day with Congolese dances and songs. A local priest banned the women from performing at the celebration, stating that such local dances and songs were immoral for Christian wives and mothers. Women protested, taking their complaints against the priests' efforts to regulate their bodies and faith to the mayor's office.[26]

Adaptations of Christianity constrained some women but also provided tools for others to determine their own conjugal paths. In colonial Kenya, some young women viewed mission schools as a place of refuge from forced marriage to suitors chosen by their elders. Such was the case of a Kikuyu woman named Serah Mukabi. With the help of an uncle and her grandmother, she made her way to a mission school. Her father later withdrew from the marriage agreement and gave her a plot of land on which she grew food and earned money for her school fees and that of her brother. Unusually, Serah delayed marriage until twelve years after her puberty rite that established her as being of age to marry.[27]

Richard Roberts described the colonial state and the establishment of new native courts as contributing to "shifting landscapes of power" for women to shape their relationships and households and navigating these landscapes as involving "intentionality and action."[28] In francophone West and Equatorial Africa by the 1930s, various groups of European missionaries, medical personnel, colonial civil servants, and settlers declared African families "disorganized," resulting in low birth and high infant mortality rates that portended long-term demographic decline.[29] As a solution, local courts were to adjudicate marital conflicts to diminish divorce rates, punish women's adultery, and maintain stable households—that is, keep women in marriages, even if they were unhappy or abusive ones. Colonial representatives, along with senior African men in many regions, sought to enforce the control of senior men and husbands over women through codifying previously fluid customary marriage practices, in effect modifying customary laws in men's favor. In some regions in East and southern Africa, such as Malawi, chiefs and elder men invented new and rigid ideas of "customary" law to enforce control over women's marriage options, labor, reproductive capacities, children, and mobility, by newly created male authorities ensconced in native courts.[30]

In places such as Kenya and Gabon, customary law was never codified, and husbands, wives, lovers, and kin articulated competing visions of customary marriage and the rights it entailed into the 1940s and 1950s. In Ghana the 1935 restoration of the Asante Confederacy resulted in Asante chiefs presiding over customary law courts, which attempted to restrict women's extramarital sex, issuing new directives that women were to be faithful to their legal husbands and prosecuted for committing adultery, a criminal offence. However, Asante women were also active agents. Women in instances of divorce struggled to retain a portion of the cocoa farms they had helped their husbands establish, and some women opted out of marriage to secure their own income-earning capacity in the cash and cocoa economy.[31]

Into the 1950s in the French Sudan (now Mali), the colonial state continued to formulate interventionist projects and regulations to render African
marriage legible in European terms. African women continued to negotiate
interpersonal, economic, and political change, acting as bricoleurs to craft
their visions of health, wealth, and personal and collective well-being in their
marital relationships. In 1951 the French colonial state passed the Jacquinot
Decree for West and Equatorial Africa, which, among other stipulations,
attempted to regulate bridewealth payments by allowing each region to define
locally appropriate limits on their amounts. Some women appearing before
native tribunals seeking divorce for reasons of neglect or abuse were able to
win their cases on the grounds that their husbands had not completed promised bridewealth payments.[32]

However, increasing individual choice of spouse was not always a means
of strengthening families or spousal relationships and was cautioned against
in many folktales told to children. In precolonial Africa, romantic love and
sexual attraction were not supposed to be the basis for marriage but rather
the reason was promoting lineage interests and their children's prosperity.
Folktales and religious teachings said relationships based on romantic love
and sexual attraction only were dangerous and liable to bring trouble, not
in the interests of the family. Those who pursued them usually disobeyed
their parents' wishes, thereby sometimes deserving a dismal fate. A twentieth-
century parable can be found in the life history of Berida Ndambuki, a Kamba
woman from rural Ukambani. At the age of fourteen in 1950 she fell in love
with an assistant surveyor, entranced by his uniform. Meanwhile, her father
had arranged her marriage to a prosperous older man, but she rebelled, was
beaten for her disobedience, and threatened suicide. Her father relented; she
married for life a husband who turned out to be an alcoholic, an abuser, and
never a provider for their sixteen children. Imbued with Kamba belief in
lifelong monogamy for women, reinforced by Catholic missionary teachings,
Berida stayed married to him.[33] Romantic love and sexual attraction, which
youth were taught to avoid in folklore, in fact made a disastrous marriage
plagued with poverty and discord in this case.

Contrary to Western perceptions of Islamic law as male dominant, Muslim
African women usually had full property rights and the right to seek divorce,
and they approached courts to legitimize claims to certain rights, material
resources, and mobility. In Zanzibar after 1909, Muslim judges (*kadhis*) serving
in newly created British colonial courts adjudicated marriage and family cases
according to interpretations of Islamic law based on scripture. However, surviving court records of the 1930s reveal pragmatic decisions to allow spouses to

seek a divorce if they no longer wished to remain married and high rates of divorce.[34] Women of all socioeconomic classes, often represented by a male relative or lawyer if they followed seclusion (*purdah*), brought their grievances to seek divorce, reimbursement of their dowry, and their ex-husbands' financial support. Though *kadhis'* judgments often compelled wives to compensate their husbands for any financial resources provided at the time of marriage, the frequent decisions allowing for divorce then freed women to leave marriages they no longer desired and gave them the option to remarry a person of their choice.

Continuing a precolonial trajectory, marriage in the period of colonial rule remained a medium through which many societies articulated fluid gender roles, often decoupled from biological sex, and societies debated normative and transgressive ideas about what it meant to be male and female (see chapter 14). Essays in *Boy-Wives and Female Husbands* call into question the myth of Africa as heteronormative and demonstrate a range of same-sex relationships and flexible gender roles across the continent.[35] In many societies in East, West, and southern Africa, a woman could marry another woman by paying bridewealth and, as a female husband, become a "social male." Some scholars have suggested that such woman-to-woman marriages may have involved sex.[36] But historian Nwando Achebe (see chapter 3) argues that woman-to-woman marriage as practiced in West Africa did not involve sexual intimacy and was not a lesbian relationship, assertions supported partly by her study of Ahebi Ugbabe, Nigeria's sole British-appointed warrant chief in the 1920s and 1930s.[37] King Ahebi became the female husband of women who left abusive husbands, seeking refuge in her palace. Her wives and King Ahebi took male lovers according to their preferences. King Ahebi was the legal and social "father" of any children borne by her wives since she had paid the bridewealth. Such woman-to-woman marriages transformed her into "the female masculinities of female husband and father—elevated her standing in society."[38] Within a dominantly patrilineal society she founded a matrilineage.

In southern Africa from the 1930s to the 1950s, migrant men and boys from Mozambique, Malawi, Zimbabwe, and South Africa working in mines practiced *nkotshae* or *bukhontxana* (mine marriages), consensual or coercive male-male sexual affairs and domestic arrangements involving often young men as "wives" and older men as "husbands."[39] Some of these husbands and wives demonstrated feelings of emotional attachment, while other male wives may have viewed such relationships as a patron/client arrangement in which they received financial gifts and protection from violence by men other than their husbands.[40] Some men with boy wives also had sexual relationships with women prostitutes as well as biologically female wives left at their rural homes of origin. As argued by Marc Epprecht in his analysis of "dissident sexuality" in southern Africa, ideals of womanhood and masculinity allowed for a range of same-sex and heterosexual relationships, themes developed further by Signe Arnfred in chapter 14.[41]

Thus, while there are many different answers to the questions posed above (What is marriage? Who gets to marry? What are the expectations of marriage?), what is clear and constant throughout the history of marriage in colonial Africa is the linkage between changes in meanings and practices of marriage, the shifting power structures and new forms of wealth and authority that emerged in the colonial period, and the individual wants and needs of African women and men.

Love, Marital and Extramarital Relationships, and Divorce in the 1960s–1980s

The frenetic pace of urbanization in Africa (see chapter 11) has changed family life across the continent drastically. Some trends that began in urban colonial Africa intensified after the 1960s: self-selection of spouses by young women and men, the abandonment of bridewealth as a legal requirement for marriage; the tendency toward more interethnic marriages with a significant reduction in polygyny; and the reduction in the power of elder lineage members, left in the villages, whose experience as a foundation for knowledge was challenged by their juniors' access to Western-style formal education and media. In the magazine *Drum*, published in South Africa and widely circulated in anglophone Africa in the 1960s and 1970s, the column *Dear Dolly* dispensed advice to letter-writers and readers about youth and heterosexual and homoerotic courtship and desire.[42]

Many publications on marriage in contemporary Africa, often dominated by Western anthropologists and historians (see chapter 14), are nearly bereft of the concepts of sexual pleasure and desire; research perpetually portrayed African sexuality as "other."[43] More recent scholarship, popular literature, and fiction on postcolonial Africa has paid more attention to the emotional and interpersonal considerations of women's relationships. Where is the love? In a 2005 satirical essay assessing Western writings on Africa, Kenyan author Binyavanga Wainaina observed that taboo subjects included "ordinary domestic scenes, love between Africans (unless a death is involved)."[44] Scholars Jennifer Cole and Lynn M. Thomas suggest that writings about Africa for audiences outside of Africa have missed the popular discussions of love, emotion, and affect abundant in novels by African authors, popular music played and sung across the continent, movies, and soap operas and on billboards.[45]

Aidoo, Adichie, and Bâ on Love, Marriage, and Women's Challenges

Three African women novelists—Ghanaian Ama Ata Aidoo, Nigerian Chimamanda Ngozi Adichie, and Senegalese Mariama Bâ—narrate the postcolonial struggles of six African women to define their sexual fulfillment, emotional attachments, social and biological reproduction, and economic security in their heterosexual relationships. Female characters struggle to realize their individual aspirations in the face of pressure from their kin and society at large to conform to certain norms. In Bâ's *So Long a Letter*, Ramatoulaye and Aissatou, two Muslim Senegalese women of mature age who met while classmates in secondary school, write letters back and forth to each other from the 1960s to 1980. Aissitou lives overseas and is employed in a diplomatic post, having chosen to divorce her husband when he married a second wife and transformed their monogamous household into a polygynous one without her consent. From Dakar, Ramatoulaye informs her friend of her husband's death and the betrayal she felt when he decided a few years earlier to take a young woman the same age as their daughter as second wife. Though Muslim law permitted polygyny, Ramatoulaye had expected her husband to maintain a monogamous marriage based on the foundation of their mutual romantic love. Her husband financially abandoned her and her children and established a new home and life with the second wife. Ramatoulaye decided against divorce, reflecting that she wanted to adhere to her faith and the social respectability that marriage afforded (see also chapter 2). Upon his death, she rejected the offers of her deceased husband's brother and of a male friend to marry her, deciding that remaining a widow was the best way to take care of her children and her own self-realization.[46]

Aidoo's *Changes: A Love Story* describes the lives of three educated women living in Accra, Ghana, in the 1980s. Esi is a data analyst; her friend Opokuya works as a nurse; another woman, Fusena, cuts short her pursuit of education abroad to marry and have children. Esi is unhappy in her first marriage, which has resulted in one daughter, and she takes birth control pills to prevent the birth of more children. In the opening scene, Esi's husband forces her to have sex with him, which she considers marital rape, and she decides to divorce him. She meets a Muslim man from a neighboring francophone country for whom she feels sexual chemistry and companionship. She is content to remain lovers, but he desires marriage, and she agrees to become his second wife as he is already married to Fusena. For Esi, marital life is unhappy. She remains in her own home and her lover-turned-husband visits her less frequently than before; the sexual chemistry diminishes. Fusena feels a personal betrayal with her husband's decision to take on Esi as a second wife but chooses to remain in the marriage given that her husband continues to provide for her material needs and spends most of his time in their conjugal home.

Opukuya and her husband have a relationship of mutual companionship, but she resents that she had to reduce her work hours because she is responsible for all household and childcare duties. In the end, it is a combination of female friendship and renegotiation of marital expectations that allows the two friends to feel more fulfilled in the relationships with male partners. Esi gives Opukuya her reconditioned car, replaced by one given Esi by her husband. Opukuya then can go to work more often while still meeting household obligations. Though now married, Esi decides that being lovers and friends with her husband, rather than wife in sharing his bed every day and having children, is the most desirable daily norm.[47]

Shifting between cities in predominantly Muslim northern Nigeria and syncretic Christian and indigenous religion in southeastern Nigeria in the midst of the Biafran War in the 1960s, Adichie's *Half of a Yellow Sun* narrates the love and married lives of twin sisters Olanna and Kainene. The two sisters come from a wealthy household, were educated in Europe, and work as a university lecturer and businesswoman, respectively. The Biafran War, entailing ethnic, political, and religious violence, involved efforts of Igbo-speaking people to create a nation separated from Nigeria. When conflict breaks out Olanna moves in with her lover, a lower-class man from a rural village. Neither her family nor his approves of their relationship. Her lover's mother expected that the relationship would result in the birth of a child and accuses Olanna of being a witch and having cursed her son as the couple remain infertile. Her lover impregnates a young woman from his mother's village who gives birth to a daughter. The war intensifies, and Olanna and her lover are forced to flee and live as refugees in dire circumstances. Olanna adopts the baby, and she, her lover, and his child create a household amid the violence of the war.

Kainene also engages in a sexual and domestic partnership not in keeping with her parents' wishes for her to marry a high-ranking Igbo man. Kainene and her British lover maintain a constant domestic and sexual relationship throughout the war, during which they struggle over questions of fidelity, money, and racial and cultural prejudice.[48] The conjugal and sexual relationships of both women are metaphors for how the nation of Nigeria and its varied peoples seek to define gender roles, belonging, access to money and power, and individual emotional health and well-being.

It is noteworthy that divorce plays a prominent role in these novels. While statistics are rare, both novelists and scholars depicting African marriage since the 1960s have noted increases in divorces sought by women in particular, often due to men's lack of economic support of the family. Although divorce has been common across time in Africa, in some societies now both informal unions without marriage and divorce are common, even among those whose traditions condemned it. Men's provider roles have been greatly undermined by neocolonial economies that generate much unemployment and migrancy with globalization.

The Impact of the AIDS Epidemic, "Provider Love," and Same- Sex Relationships in the Late Twentieth and Twenty-First Centuries

Since the 1980s, the AIDS epidemic has tremendously transformed the political, medical, social, and emotional terrain through which societies and individuals maintain social and biological reproduction across the continent. In 2001 the United Nations Population Institute estimated that the African continent held 66 percent of the global AIDS cases, with women constituting 60 percent of HIV infections.[49] Southern Africa experienced one of the most rapid increases in HIV prevalence on the continent. In *Love in the Time of AIDS*, sociologist Mark Hunter traces how "a perfect storm of political economy, gender, and household trends resulted" when HIV came to the town of Mandeni, South Africa, in the 1980s. Due to high unemployment, the fragility of local economies in the wake of globalization, and the legacies of apartheid rule, marriage rates declined. Alternative sexual and domestic relationships of boyfriends and girlfriends, main and plural secondary lovers, in which people operated according to the "materiality of every day sex" emerged. In order to survive women became increasingly dependent on men and gifts that men provided. This dependency on "provider love" leaves women vulnerable to conditions for the increased spread of HIV through sexual violence and unsafe sex.[50] Ranging from Tamatave, Madagascar, to Dakar, Senegal, research in urban areas has similarly argued that young women in precarious economic contexts associate the expression of love with the gifting of money and material resources from men in conjugal and extraconjugal sexual relationships (see also chapter 14).[51]

The twenty-first century has also witnessed increased and intense debates across Africa about meanings and practices of same-sex desire, conversant with debates from past centuries. Ex-president Robert Mugabe of Zimbabwe demonstrated the idea of homosexuality as "unAfrican" espoused by some political leaders and public rhetoric across the continent. State-sponsored violence against same-sex desire is seen in legislation such as the presidential signing, and subsequent court invalidation, of the 2014 Uganda Anti-Homosexuality Act that made same-sex sexual acts or marriage punishable with prison.

Homosexuality is illegal in many African countries, and in some cities news-papers have "outed" individuals believed to be homosexual, who then have faced social marginality, violence, or murder.[52] Gay, lesbian, and other sexual minorities have mobilized to advocate for the rights of sexual minorities. For example, the organization Gays and Lesbians of Zimbabwe partners with inter-national organizations to protest imprisonment and violence against LGBT individuals and for the right for women who feel erotic desire for other women to love and live openly. Some governments have protected the rights of sexual minorities, such as the South African constitution of 1996, which prohibits discrimination based on sexual orientation. However, in day-to-day life these protections are sharply contested (see chapter 14).

Thus love, sexuality, and interpersonal intimacy were bound up with differ-ent sets of expectations between individuals, but also between individuals and institutions, which can change over time. One way that we can understand love as a historical topic of inquiry is by tracing changes in its expressions through choices that reveal both self-determination and obligation to others.

Conclusion

In order to construct a history of African women and men, studying marriage and households in the context of how affect and sexuality cohere and disjoin them is essential. Household and intimate relations are the site of so many essential forms of production and reproduction in society. These relation-ships differ according to gender and generation, and they are bound together through the expectations and obligations of marriage, even in relationships that are not recognized as marriage by customary or civil law or public opin-ion. Marriages are often deeply political, meaning driven by individual, famil-ial, and societal strategies tied to broad sets of goals and objectives. When marriages break down, webs of obligation and practices of accumulation and networking might be severely compromised, but where divorce is common societies normally evolve coping mechanisms to remedy precarity. Love bonds in family and conjugal relationships drive other types of strategic decision-making and are also bound up in power dynamics that we might otherwise understand as tied to the accumulative and political goals of marriage, and that should not be underrated.

Major global transformations, such as the rise of internal and external slave trades in the fifteenth through nineteenth centuries, had a direct impact on African marriages because slavery arose out of, and impacted, issues of pro-ductive and reproductive labor within and without households. Changing landscapes of colonialism—new economies, new forms of political control and dominance, changing access to resources, new forms of value and wealth—meant that changes in marriage practices, especially bridewealth, and expectations were also inevitable. Urbanization increased in most areas, fostering changes that became monumental after independence.

During the colonial period, young women and men made an increasing effort to wrest control over their marriages away from older generations. Generational struggles over marriage occurred, over who could control marriage arrangements including receiving bridewealth. Bridewealth was monetized and inflated, making legal customary marriages more difficult for increasingly impoverished populations, while missionaries touted monogamy, fidelity, and conjugal, ego-centered families. Urbanization increased in most areas, fostering changes that became monumental after independence.

Lastly, we see that love and desire are not immutable elements but creatively expressed and negotiated. While marriage rates according to customary, civil, and religious traditions in twenty-first-century urban Africa are declining, those who marry do so more and more based on romantic love and sexual attraction and emphasize egalitarian companionate relationships. These ideals of marriage are heavily influenced by mass media images. Into this mix in the last thirty years, as described by Ousseina Alidou in chapter 5, has come large fundamentalist Christian influence, in particular, that promotes male-dominant nuclear family structures, advertised as companionate, as well as more Muslim fundamentalist efforts to control women.

Where are marriage and families in Africa now? They are moving toward conjugal definitions of membership, sometimes with liberal helpings of male dominance, sometimes not, and definitely toward self-selection of partners. If many women now restrict their fertility with various forms of birth control, hoping to have only as many children as parents can support (average numbers of children borne by women in most countries have declined), many still, due to continuing high valuation of children, high infant mortality, and child labor needs, have as many children as they can. Homoerotic relationships generally take place outside of marriage, and some societies view them as compatible with heterosexual marriage, still valued for its procreative function (see chapter 14). Love and marriage are sought and reconciled, though not always successfully. Africans continue to innovate new relationships within the great challenges of globalization.

Notes

1. Dorothy L. Hodgson and Sheryl McCurdy, eds., *"Wicked" Women and the Reconfiguration of Gender in Africa* (Portsmouth: Heinemann, 2000), 7.

2. Henrietta L. Moore and Meghan Vaughan, *Cutting Down Trees: Gender, Nutrition and Agricultural Change in the Northern Province of Zambia, 1890–1900* (Portsmouth, NH: Heinemann, 1994), 156–57.

3. D. T. Niane, *Sundiata: An Epic of Old Mali* (London: Longman, 1971).

4. Jan Vansina, *De la tradition orale: Essai de méthode historique* (Turvuren: Musée royale de l'Afrique Centrale, 1961); David Henige, *The Chronology of Oral Tradition: The Quest for a Chimera* (Oxford: Clarendon Press, 1974).

5. Rhiannon Stephens, *A History of African Motherhood: The Case of Uganda, 700–1900* (Cambridge: Cambridge University Press, 2013), 10.

6. Edna Bay, "Belief, Legitimacy, and the *Kpojito*: An Institutional History of the 'Queen Mother' in Precolonial Dahomey," *Journal of African History* 36, no. 1 (1995): 1–27; Edna Bay, *Wives of the Leopard: Gender, Politics, and Culture in the Kingdom of Dahomey* (Charlottesville: University of Virginia Press, 1998).

7. Lorelle Semley, *Mother Is Gold, Father Is Glass: Gender and Colonialism in a Yoruba Town* (Bloomington: Indiana University Press, 2010).

8. Chikwenye Okonjo Ogunyemi, *Africa Wo/Man Palava: The Nigerian Novel by Women* (Chicago: University of Chicago Press, 1996).

9. Emily Lynn Osborn, *Our New Husbands Are Here: Households, Gender, and Politics in a West African State from the Slave Trade to Colonial Rule* (Athens: Ohio University Press, 2011), 71–73.

10. Pamela Scully, *Liberating the Family? Gender and British Slave Emancipation in the Rural Western Cape, South Africa, 1823–1853* (Portsmouth, NH: Heinemann, 1997).

11. Richard Roberts and Martin A. Klein, "The Banamba Slave Exodus of 1905 and the Decline of Slavery in the Western Sudan," *Journal of African History* 21 (1980): 375–94; Roberts, *Litigants and Households: African Disputes and Colonial Courts in the French Soudan, 1895–1912* (Portsmouth, NH: Heinemann, 2005).

12. Emily Burrill, *States of Marriage: Gender, Justice, and Rights in Colonial Mali* (Athens: Ohio University Press, 2015).

13. Stephan F. Miescher, *Making Men in Ghana* (Bloomington: Indiana University Press, 2005), 115.

14. Miescher, *Making Men in Ghana*, 115–16.

15. Elke E. Stockreiter, *Islamic Law, Gender, and Social Change in Post-Abolition Zanzibar* (Cambridge: Cambridge University Press, 2015), 4–19.

16. Rachel Jean-Baptiste, *Conjugal Rights: Marriage, Sexuality and Urban Life in Colonial Libreville, Gabon* (Athens: Ohio University Press, 2014).

17. Luise White, *The Comforts of Home: Prostitution in Colonial Nairobi* (Chicago: University of Chicago Press, 1990), 55–58.

18. Judith van Allen, "'Sitting on a Man': Colonialism and the Lost Political Institutions of Igbo Women," *Canadian Journal of African Studies* 6, no. 2 (1972): 165–81.

19. Jane I. Guyer, "Household and Community in African Studies," *African Studies Review* 24, no. 2 and 3 (1981): 87–137; Guyer, "The Value of Beti Bridewealth," in *Money Matters: Instability, Values, and Social Payments in the Modern History of West African Communities*, ed. Jane I. Guyer (Portsmouth, NH: Heinemann, 1995); Brett L. Shadle, "'Changing Traditions to Meet Current Altering Conditions': Customary Law, African Courts and The Rejection of Codification in Kenya, 1930–60," *Journal of African History* 40, no. 3 (1999): 411–31; Brett L. Shadle, "Bridewealth and Female

Consent: Marriage Disputes in African Courts in Gusiiland, Kenya," *Journal of African History* 44, no. 2 (2003): 241–62; Shadle, *"Girl Cases": Marriage and Colonialism in Gusiiland, Kenya, 1890–1970* (Portsmouth, NH: Heinemann, 2006).

20. Shadle, *"Girl Cases,"* 102–14.

21. Barbara M. Cooper, "Women's Worth and Wedding Gift Exchange in Maradi, Niger, 1907–89," *Journal of African History* 36, no. 1 (1995): 121–40; Barbara M. Cooper, *Marriage in Maradi: Gender and Culture in a Hausa Society in Niger, 1900–1989* (Portsmouth, NH: Heinemann, 1997), 90–109.

22. Cooper, "Women's Worth," 121–23.

23. Diana Jeater, *Marriage, Perversion, and Power: The Construction of Moral Discourse in Southern Rhodesia, 1894–1930* (Oxford: Clarendon Press, 1993), 31, 195–96.

24. Kenda Mutongi, *Worries of the Heart: Widows, Family, and Community in Kenya* (Chicago: University of Chicago Press, 2007), 64–68.

25. Phyllis M. Martin, *Catholic Women of Congo-Brazzaville* (Bloomington: Indiana University Press, 2009), 74–75.

26. Martin, *Catholic Women,* 88–90.

27. Tabitha Kanogo, *African Womanhood in Colonial Kenya, 1900–1950* (Athens: Ohio University Press, 2005), 202–22.

28. Roberts, *Litigants and Households,* 13–20.

29. Lorelle Semley, *Mother Is Gold,* 91–114.

30. Martin Chanock, "Making Customary Law: Men, Women, and Courts in Colonial Northern Rhodesia," in *African Women and the Law: Historical Perspectives,* ed. Margaret Jean Hay and Marcia Wright (Boston: Boston University, African Studies Center, 1982), 53–67; Martin Chanock, *Law, Custom, and Social Order: The Colonial Experience in Malawi and Zambia* (Cambridge: Cambridge University Press, 1998).

31. Jean Allman and Victoria Tashjian, "Marrying and Marriage on a Shifting Terrain: Reconfiguration of Power and Authority," in *Women in African Colonial Histories,* ed. Jean Allman, Susan Geiger, and Nakanyike Musisi (Bloomington: Indiana University Press, 2002); Allman and Tashjian, *"I Will Not Eat Stone": A Women's History of Colonial Asante* (Portsmouth, NH: Heinemann, 2000), xxxviii, 170–83, 145–61.

32. Emily Burrill, *States of Marriage: Gender, Justice and Rights in Colonial Mali* (Athens: Ohio University Press, 2015), 21–22, 154–56.

33. Berida Ndambuki and Claire Robertson, *We Only Come Here to Struggle* (Bloomington: Indiana University Press, 1999).

34. Stockreiter, *Islamic Law, Gender, and Social Change,* 167–99.

35. Stephen O. Murray and Will Roscoe, *Boy-Wives and Female Husbands: Studies in African Homosexualities* (New York: Palgrave, 1988).

36. Murray and Roscoe, *Boy-Wives and Female Husbands,* 266.

37. Nwando Achebe, *The Female King of Colonial Nigeria* (Bloomington: Indiana University Press, 2011), 13–14.

38. Achebe, *The Female King,* 148.

39. Patrick Harries, *Work, Culture, and Identity: Migrant Laborers in Mozambique and South Africa, c. 1860–1910* (Portsmouth, NH: Heinemann, 1994), 200–208; T. Dunbar Moodie with Vivienne Ndatshe, *Men, Mines, and Migration: Going for Gold* (Berkeley: University of California Press, 1994), 119–58.

40. Marc Epprecht, *Hungochani: The History of a Dissident Sexuality in Southern Africa* (Montreal: McGill-Queen's University Press, 2004), 67–80.

41. Epprecht, *Hungochani*, 81.

42. Kenda Mutongi, "'Dear Dolly's' Advice: Representations of Youth, Courtship, and Sexualities in Africa, 1960–1980," *International Journal of African Historical Studies* 33, no. 1 (2000): 1–23.

43. Signe Arnfred, ed., *Re-thinking Sexualities in Africa* (Uppsala: Nordic Africa Institute, 2004), 7; Stephanie Newell, *The Forger's Tale: The Search for Odeziaku* (Athens: Ohio University Press, 2006), 10.

44. Binyavanga Wainaina, "How to Write about Africa," *Granta* 92: "The View from Africa Essays and Memoirs." January 19, 2006.

45. Jennifer Cole and Lynn M. Thomas, *Love in Africa* (Chicago: University of Chicago Press, 2009), 1–30.

46. Mariama Bâ, *So Long a Letter*, trans. Modupé Bodé-Thomas (Portsmouth, NH: Heineman, 1989).

47. Ama Ata Aidoo, *Changes: A Love Story* (New York: Feminist Press, 1991).

48. Chimamanda Ngozi Adichie, *Half of a Yellow Sun* (New York: Anchor Books, 2009).

49. Ezekiel Kalipeni, Susan Craddock, Joseph R. Oppong, and Jayati Ghosh, eds., *HIV and AIDS in Africa: Beyond Epidemiology* (Malden, MA: Blackwell, 2004), 1–2; Mark Hunter, *Love in the Time of AIDS: Inequality, Gender, and Rights in South Africa* (Bloomington: Indiana University Press, 2010), 6; Ellen E. Foley and Fatou Maria Drame, "HIV/AIDS in Mid-Sized Cities in Senegal: From Individual to Place-Based Vulnerability," *Social Science and Medicine* 133C (2015): 296–303.

50. Hunter, *Love in the Time of AIDS*, 5–6, 16, 178–91.

51. Jennifer Cole, *Sex and Salvation: Imagining the Future in Madagascar* (Chicago: University of Chicago Press, 2010), 112–15; Ellen E. Foley and Fatou Maria Drame, "*Mbaraan* and the Shifting Political Economy of Sex in Urban Senegal," *Culture, Health, and Sexuality* 15, no. 2 (2013): 121–34.

52. World Organisation Against Torture, "Zimbabwe: Judicial Harassment against Ms. Ellen Chademana and Mr. Ignatius Muhambi," May 28, 2010, http://www.omct.org/human-rights-defenders/urgent-interventions/zimbabwe/2010/05/d20729/; Human Rights Watch, "South Africa: LGBT Rights in Name Only?," December 5, 2011, https://www.hrw.org/news/2011/12/05/south-africa-lgbt-rights-name-only.

Suggested Readings

Adichie, Chimamanda Ngozi. *Half of a Yellow Sun*. New York: Anchor Books, 2009.

Aidoo, Ama Ata. *Changes: A Love Story*. New York: Feminist Press, 1991.

Bâ, Mariama. *So Long a Letter*. Translated by Modupé Bodé-Thomas. Portsmouth, NH: Heinemann, 1989.

Mutongi, Kenda. *Worries of the Heart: Widows, Family, and Community in Kenya*. Chicago: University of Chicago Press, 2007.

Stephens, Rhiannon. *A History of African Motherhood: The Case of Uganda, 700–1900*. Cambridge: Cambridge University Press, 2013.

Figure 14.1. *Curtidoras* of tomorrow, Maputo, Mozambique. Photo by Jesper Milner Henriksen, copyright Christian Groes-Green.

14

GENDER AND SEXUALITY

Gradations, Contestations

Signe Arnfred

This chapter considers the variability of gender and sexuality in Africa while analyzing different lenses used in their study, differentiated by their contexts and goals. Most early scholarly writings on African social structure were produced by colonial anthropologists from the 1920s to the 1950s. This knowledge began to be contested in the early 1970s by Second Wave feminist scholars, who attacked the androcentricity of most anthropological texts and shifted focus to women.[1] From the 1980s onward an increasing wave of postcolonial scholarship has questioned colonial as well as feminist assumptions regarding gender and sexuality in Africa.

The first section of the chapter discusses these different approaches: colonial anthropology, interdisciplinary feminist scholarship, and postcolonial critique. The second section investigates implications of colonial constructions, considering particularly the provocative claim raised by postcolonial scholars that gender in Africa as perceived today is a colonial construction. The third section includes case studies selected particularly with relevance to rethinking gender and sexuality. Their authors investigate local historical and oral sources in order to provide new ways of seeing African societies.

Different Approaches to Studies of Gender and Sexuality in Africa

Colonial Anthropology

European colonialism framed most scholarship on Africa now recognized as foundational in disciplines such as anthropology, sociology, history, and political science. It was written by European missionaries and anthropologists, mostly men: European, white, Christian, middle-class men. Most scholarship relevant to gender (not a term they used) and sexuality was written by British social anthropologists at a point when Britain ruled the waves, roughly from the Berlin Conference of 1884–85, when European powers divided Africa among themselves, to the wave of decolonization from the late 1950s through the 1970s (excepting South Africa). British scholars were convinced of their superiority. Indeed, many studies were done by government anthropologists hired not just out of academic interest but also to provide help in explaining the workings of African societies to British civil servants interested in bettering their controls over those societies. Some of it was commissioned, for instance, immediately after the 1929 Aba Women's War (see chapter 4), intended to forestall any repetition of the disruptive "riots" (in the British view).

Early studies of gender and sexuality focused on kinship and marriage. An influential volume was *African Systems of Kinship and Marriage*, 1950, edited by A. R. Radcliffe-Brown and Daryll Forde, leading anthropologists of the structural-functionalist school.[2] In it Western notions of man/woman and sexuality were taken for granted and presumed to be valid in African contexts. What we see today as "gender," a constructed category that differs from one society to another, was generally seen as biological "sex": a man/woman binary, embedded in a hierarchical power relationship of male dominance/female subordination. "Sexuality" was heterosexuality; homosexuality (well known in Europe at the time) was taken to be a characteristic of overdeveloped decadent societies and thus not applicable to Africa.[3] Thus sex, gender, and sexuality were taken for granted and not discussed; what was discussed were forms of marriage: monogamy/polygyny, marriage with or without bridewealth, and so forth. Marriage was perceived to be a central institution and key to kinship studies. The assumption prevailed that patrilinearity was dominant and eventually would drive out matrilineal kinship systems, whose frequent occurrence in Africa anthropologists of the day found inconvenient and disturbing.[4] Behind all assumptions of colonial anthropology was the never-questioned master assumption of androcentricity: that the center of social structure and the proper subject of knowledge is a man.

Feminist Ways of Seeing Produce a Different Picture

Feminist anthropologists and others from the 1970s on started questioning these assumptions. Rethinking relations between women and men included prominently the introduction of the concept of "gender" as a socially constructed category to be distinguished from "sex," at that time seen as a biological category.[5] They also questioned the androcentric bias produced when male anthropologists selected only local men (not women) as informants, subsequently presenting male views as accurate representations of *the* unchanging culture of a particular place and people.

What happened to the study of African marital forms when feminists got involved? Marriage was seen as less foundational than assumed in classical anthropological studies (see chapter 13). For example, Karla Poewe in her 1981 study of male-female dynamics in Zambian matrilineal Luapula society found a structural contradiction between on the one hand siblings, womb-mates, and on the other hand relatives by marriage. The womb was seen as infused with spiritual power, guaranteeing the reproduction of Luapula social order. It symbolized "the Luapula universe, seen by Luapulans as unbounded, filled with an abundance of critical resources (especially land) to which everyone has access." *Balupwa*, often translated as "family," more correctly "connotes a plurality of individuals temporarily associated with one another for the purpose of enabling the reproduction of the social universe." If "family" in English connotes a basic social unit, in Luapula contexts there is nothing basic or stable about *balupwa*, rather the opposite. In contrast to relations to mother and siblings of the matrilineage, *balupwa* relationships are temporary: "Ties of intimate dependency between spouses are discouraged in many more or less subtle ways. While sexual enjoyment is valued, it is not limited to one specific partner. . . . A man's marital role is to sexually satisfy and impregnate the woman and to provide for her during her pregnancy. The man should not in any way be an object of exclusive emotional investment nor the focus of attention. Instead women are socialized to invest their emotions and material wealth in their respective matrilineages." From the point of view of the matrilineage, the aim of female sexuality is to "engulf male strangers and convert them into kin."[6] Women sought sexual pleasure and procreation, not emotional attachment to the husband. Women's primary emotional attachment was supposed to be to their matrikin. Similarly, men were supposed to care more about their sisters than their wives. Poewe demonstrated here also that structural-functionalist analysis could cast marriage in a different light, disputing the central position of marriage in classical anthropology.

Postcolonial Critique:
Gender, Race, and Sexuality as Colonial Constructs

In the 1970s much feminist literature followed Friedrich Engels's assertion that patriarchy, the rule of fathers—including male dominance/female subordination—was and is universal.[7] However, feminist scholars with knowledge of non-Western societies disputed this claim. Based on fieldwork in African societies, they uncovered phenomena such as dual sex organization (see chapters 3 and 7), successful business ownership by women and separation of property ownership by spouses allowing for women's economic autonomy, age being more important than gender in establishing authority, and other factors that militated against women's subordination.[8] Drawing on her Yoruba research and other Africanist studies, Oyèrónkẹ́ Oyěwùmí noted that Euro-American women's subordination is rooted in their role as *wives* in nuclear families, not in "womanhood" as such. The problem is that "wifehood" has become embedded in the very concept of "woman": "the woman in feminist theory is a wife—the subordinated half of a couple in a nuclear family," Oyěwùmí says, pointing to the fact that many Western feminists' analyses are vitiated by their assumption that nuclear families are universal.[9] In general Western epistemology the concept "woman" in itself denotes subordination; "woman" is defined in relation to "man," and woman is always already "the Other"—as pointed out by Simone de Beauvoir in her famous 1949 book *The Second Sex*.[10] Thus, even if feminist lines of thinking have critiqued these gendered structures of domination, they have also contributed to their continuation.

Maria Lugones, following Oyěwùmí, draws a parallel between gender and race as categories. Gender relations taken for granted in the Western world include the binary categories of women versus men, with men in a dominant position. This European construction, Lugones says, was introduced to the rest of the world by colonialism. Race is also a colonial construction.[11] Supporting this view is Kopano Ratele, who notes that "there were no black men before the introduction of whiteness in this country [South Africa], or anywhere else on the continent. In the early seventeenth century black men were other things: AmaZulu, AmaXosa; AmaNdebele, AmaSwazi, Basotho, Batswana, Khoi and San and so on. . . . They were [not yet] defined by blackness."[12] Similarly, Oyěwùmí argues that there were no "women" in Yorubaland prior to colonization. "I came to realize," she says, "that the fundamental category 'woman'—which is foundational in Western gender discourse—simply did not exist in Yorubaland prior to sustained contact with the West." She does not mean, of course, that human beings did not have male and female bodies in Yorubaland before colonialism. What she means is that the very concept of "woman" in Western thinking is so loaded with assumptions and implications, irrelevant and disturbing in African contexts, that any analysis using "woman" as a conceptual tool inevitably will lead investigations astray, ignoring key aspects of the subject matter.

Oyěwùmí supports this point by noting that prior to colonialism women could take up positions of power, as shown in chapters 3 and 7 in this volume.

Such a thing was, however, beyond colonial imagination; whenever the British saw a throne, they expected a man to be sitting on it. (This was in spite of the British monarch in the period of largest colonial expansion actually being a woman: Queen Victoria.) Thus, according to Oyěwùmí, "for females, colonization was a twofold process of racial inferiorization and gender subordination. The creation of 'women' as a category was one of the very first accomplishments of the colonial state."[13] The colonial state enforced and created a notion of "womanhood" along European lines; this notion was presented as given, based on bodies and biology, resulting in the naturalization and universalization of male/female gender hierarchies.

Like gender and race, sexuality is a colonial construction. According to Michel Foucault, sexuality should "not be thought of as a kind of natural given, which power tries to hold in check, or as an obscure domain, which knowledge tries gradually to uncover." Sexuality is historically constructed as "an especially dense transfer point for relations of power,"[14] a process that occurred from the sixteenth century onward with European colonial expansion. Ann Laura Stoler has pointed to the centrality of empire and race in the making of European bourgeois subjects as outlined by Foucault, emphasizing the mutual constitution of sexuality, race, and gender under colonialism as a two-way process: "Colonialism was . . . only partly an effort to import cultured sensibilities to the colonies, but as much about the *making* of them."[15] Furthermore, colonialist knowledge was privileged; the colonial gaze was given the character of scientific truth.

These insights regarding gender, race, and sexuality as concepts show that it is important to emphasize linguistic and conceptual accuracy in studying gender and sexuality in Africa (and elsewhere): To what extent is a colonial gaze embedded in apparently straightforward lines of thinking? How might alternative concepts and analytical approaches be developed? Questions such as these are taken up in the third section of this chapter. The second section investigates implications of colonial constructions for African social and political lives.

Implications of Colonial Constructions

Masculinities and Femininities

Aspects of masculinities and femininities in Africa were reworked with colonialism, influenced by Christian and European ideas of civilization. New constraints were introduced (such as passes or identity cards for men; only later for women). New possibilities opened: women as well as men migrated to new towns; some men became wage workers. Whereas previously a prime indication of manhood in southern Africa was to become a household head with a wife or wives, children, and cattle, colonialism created alternative routes to acquiring manhood, such as wage work on plantations or in mines, even if work conditions resembled slavery. Young men from Mozambique, for example, went to South Africa in the 1850s to work in the Natal sugar fields; later on, with the opening of gold mines in the Rand in the 1890s, the number of Mozambican wage workers multiplied. In some areas as many as half of the able-bodied men would be away at any one time.[16] Work in the mines became a symbol of manhood; young men were proud to go to work in the mines. Reflecting Africans' long history of female farming, they considered cultivation to be women's work; men should be wage workers.[17]

Meanwhile, wives and mothers were not allowed to accompany men to mines or cities in South Africa; unmarried women in cities without work permits were seen as prostitutes. Colonial exactions and racism made it impossible for African women to pursue the housewife ideal promoted by missionaries and administrators. Colonial ideas about gender roles were rooted in European middle-class ideals of a male breadwinner and a female housewife, ideals that flowered in the eighteenth century and were reinforced among elite classes by the Industrial Revolution.[18] Before that, women were active in urban crafts, were members of guilds, and performed essential labor in agriculture. According to Veronika Bennholdt-Thomsen, "Housework as performed by housewives does not represent a set of tasks which women have always carried out because of some natural predisposition. . . . [The housewife] was created—by the church, through legislation, medicine and the organization of the workforce (protective legislation, the 'family wage')."[19]

Although "housewifization" in Europe was the result of a specific historical process, this cultural artifact was constructed as natural and was imposed on Africa in a way that was particularly frustrating for many women. Girls who got access to the few girls' schools established by missionaries were instructed in Christianity, colonial languages, cooking, cleaning, and sewing. In white settler colonies this was in preparation for domestic service, where they would be separated from their families; their children were not allowed to visit them, much less live with them. In nonsettler colonies the idea was that these girls would be appropriate wives for a new class of mission-educated African men, trained as clergymen or clerks. In both cases, however, it was hard for African women to meet the housewife ideal. In African colonies there was no "family wage" where wife and children lived on the salary of the male breadwinner, which meant that even the wives of salaried male employees had to work outside the home to make ends meet. If some African women sought the respectability and status of being housewives, the prevailing low wages enforced by colonialists frustrated those aspirations. Seclusion was often the privilege of elite women, but even secluded Muslim women in West Africa earned money by employing junior girls and servants to sell goods for them, for instance.

Colonialists Change Rules for Marriage and Sexual Behavior

As shown in chapter 13, with colonialism and Christianity, missionaries pushed marriage to become the center of family relations, with nuclear conjugal families being the ideal and "social priority of the man over his wife, but equal dignity in front of God," as put by the Swiss Presbyterian mission in Mozambique.[20] Privileging monogamy and nuclear families was foreign to most African societies. Furthermore, Christianity introduced a moral policing of sex—female sexuality in particular—which was expected to take place only inside marriage, as per the sixth commandment, which describes "fornication," or adultery, as sin. Prior to Christianity, marriage involved control of fertility more than control of sexuality, with similar rules regarding sexual behavior for young unmarried women and men. Both could engage in sexual play, for example, in terms of *ukusoma* (thigh sex), as long as they made sure that no pregnancy would result.[21]

The new focus on monogamy set new standards of female subordination and dependence on men. Women were turned into wives; sex was turned into sin (unless it took place for the purpose of procreation); and sex as well as children were brought under male control. Moral judgments were profoundly altered in a gendered asymmetrical way. As put by Mark Hunter: "Women with more than one lover, particularly unmarried women, faced heightened public censure. . . . If pre-colonial society differentiated between sex and fertility, seeing the former as a legitimate source of pleasure, missionaries viewed any sexual act outside marriage as inherently 'sinful.'"[22] Missionary interventions also aimed at polygyny but in many cases merely drove it underground with male converts marrying a legal wife in a public ceremony while already married by customary law to another.

Sexual Diversity: A Silence in Colonial Constructions of African Lives

From the beginning of Western encounters with Africans, "African sexuality," male and female, was understood to be naturally heterosexual, since homosexuality and heterosexuality were defined as identities and seen as binary oppositions, definitive and distinct, much like binary oppositions of gender. In this view a person is, and remains, from beginning to end, either a man or a woman; fluctuating or ambiguous identities were condemned. Homosexuality was seen as a product of a decadent urban society and thus irrelevant to Africa. As stated by Marc Epprecht: "Since the prevailing prejudice was that Africans were uncivilized and close to nature, by definition they could not be decadent or exhibit social traits and behaviors that were assumed to come with a sophisticated level of culture. The emerging consensus on homosexuality thus required that Africans conform to the expectation of a supposedly natural heterosexuality."[23] Due to African peoples' presumed close relationship with nature, they were thought to be "ruled by instinct and culturally unsophisticated," for which reason they "had to be heterosexual, their sexual energies and outlets devoted exclusively to one purpose: biological reproduction."[24]

The colonial construction of Africans as heterosexual has deep repercussions even today. Now, when most Western countries are becoming increasingly open to nonbinary notions of sexuality and lesbian, gay, bisexual, transgender, and intersex (LGBTI) identities, when recognition of same-sex relationships is on the agenda of major Western donor agencies, and when sexual rights have been included in human rights and UN declarations, homophobia in Africa is increasing. While African presidents such as Robert Mugabe (Zimbabwe), Yoweri Museveni (Uganda), Goodluck Jonathan (Nigeria), and many others have made homophobic statements claiming that homosexuality is un-African, a vice imposed from the West, it is actually homophobia that has been imported. Colonial laws against homosexuality remain. Criminalization of homosexuality was usual in European legal systems, and the transference of laws condemning "carnal knowledge against the order of nature" (as the formulation goes in several previous British colonies) was part of colonialism's civilizing mission.[25] Exacerbating this situation is the homophobic interference of American fundamentalist missionaries, who have convinced Uganda's government to pass laws establishing the death penalty for homosexual acts (see chapter 5).

Since the publication in 1998 of Stephen O. Murray and Will Roscoe's pioneer volume, *Boy-Wives and Female Husbands*, there has been an upsurge of research on sexual diversity in Africa. Murray and Roscoe collected data from sources such as old anthropological writings and travelers' tales, as far back as 1732, which they supplemented with new research showing that the bulk of documented same-sex behavior takes place either at particular times during a lifetime or concurrently with heterosexual behavior, which illustrates a remarkably different sexual code of behavior compared to Christian morals: "This social code does not require that an individual suppresses same-sex desires or behavior, but that she or he never allows such desires to overshadow or supplant procreation."[26] For instance, there is ample evidence of "thigh sex" between men and boys, such as in the all-male compound life of workers in the gold mines of the Rand in South Africa, where this was the reported form of older men's sex with younger men. The younger "lovers" are also paid by the older men to perform domestic duties. Thus "men became 'wives' on the mines in order to become husbands and therefore full 'men' more rapidly at home."[27]

Evidence now abounds regarding female same-sex relations. Kendall reports from Lesotho how close and intimate relationships between married women, locally called *mpho*-relationships, were not categorized as "sexual" since no penis was involved ("no penis, no sex"). Husbands would often know about the *mpho*-relationship, since the wife's female lover sometimes had the status of a family friend. Woman-woman and woman-man relationships were conceived as differently constructed and thus not mutually threatening, especially since the former are nonprocreative (see chapter 13).[28]

Empirical Studies Rooted in Postcolonial Critique

Sex/Love/Money Entanglements: Provider Love and "Sugar Daddy" Relationships

Recent studies of intimate relations in Africa highlight the ways in which sex and love on one side and money and material goods on the other side are entangled rather than opposed. As pointed out by Jennifer Cole, missionary teachings "drove a conceptual wedge between the intertwined concepts of love and exchange," morally separating sex and love on one hand and money on the other.[29] According to the Bible, sex outside marriage—female sex in particular—is forbidden no matter how much love might be involved. Even worse is sex for money. In mainstream Western consciousness and morality even today, sex and money should be like oil and water: they should not mix. If they do, it is a moral transgression, condemned and stigmatized as prostitution. This moral approach has also tainted African studies, leading to derogatory terms such as "'transaction sex" employed by some nongovernmental organizations (NGOs), indicating women engaging in sex for money in situations of poverty as the only way out, or "sugar daddy relationships," referring to young (poor) women being manipulated into sexual relationships with older (rich) men in exchange for money for school fees or consumer goods.

Contemporary research goes behind this moral smokescreen, showing the ways in which sex and material exchange are interconnected, and how monetary considerations do not exclude affection and love—sometimes the opposite. Mark Hunter has coined the term "provider love" for capturing "a set of material and emotional links that encompassed a woman being *lobola*'ed (having bridewealth paid for her) and a marital couple 'building a home'" in KwaZulu Natal, South Africa. He contends further that serious emotional attachment and serious material intentions are interconnected, resembling the Western ideal of the breadwinner husband.[30] Other studies of marriage and divorce in Africa have emphasized the importance for wives of continued economic support from husbands, even minimal contributions.[31] The southern African custom of *lobola*—translated as bridewealth or "bride price"—has been systematically misunderstood and condemned as a material transaction, as noted already by Radcliffe-Brown in 1950. *Lobola*, he insisted, is a symbolic transfer, not unlike an engagement ring, which, though it may have considerable value, is not regarded as an economic transaction, but rather as engendering reciprocal relationships between lineages and affective ties over time.[32]

In addition to establishing the legitimacy of the children, *lobola* is a matter of emotions: sadness or pride. In Mozambique women explained how in the old days "a woman that had not been *lobolo*'ed had no value in society, she was not respected. . . . A woman in these conditions was to be pitied; when she was pounding grain or doing other domestic work, she would sing sad songs about her sorrowful fate of not being *lobolo*'ed."[33] Strong feelings relate to *lobola* payments, even today. According to Hunter, "a woman who is being *lobolo*'ed tends to be envied by her peers. Indeed, precisely because of *ilobolo*'s association with men's commitment and respectability, more young women than men often support the custom."[34] Properly understood, *lobola*—in addition to being a transaction between families—is also an emotional affair.

Hunter has investigated how the idea of "provider love" has traveled from the rural settings to modern urban lives. The Zulu term *isahluleki* (literally: a failure), previously a damning word used to describe a man who failed to support his marital home, is nowadays used "to scorn not only a married man who fails to support his family, but also an unmarried man who fails to support his girlfriend."[35] Sex and money go together inside and outside marriage, also connected importantly to child support. A man might have trouble establishing his paternity of children not only if he did not pay the bridewealth but also if he did not provide any child support, which has become a substitute for bridewealth in establishing the existence of a union.

Among matrilineal Makhuwa in northern Mozambique female initiation ceremonies include a session instructing young initiates regarding the proper ways to have sex in marriage, invariably ending with "the husband" (performed by the woman instructor) handing over money to "the wife" (the young initiate).[36] Similar transactions are described by Thera Rasing in Zambia: "A man should respect his wife. This is expressed in the wedding ceremony by teaching him that he should give her money in exchange for services. For instance on the wedding night the husband is required to pay when entering the room where his bride is waiting for the marriage to be consummated. He has to give money when the bride is placed on the bed and after intercourse. In addition he has to give money or a present, as a token of respect, when his wife washes him and shaves him."[37]

Insight into the entanglements of sex and money also cast the so-called sugar daddy relationships in a different light. Christian Groes-Green investigated such relationships in Maputo, Mozambique, between young, often fashionable, good-looking women, and older, often expatriate men. Maputo slang calls the young women *curtidoras* (women enjoying life), while the men are called *patrocinadores* (meaning "donors" or "sponsors"). Groes-Green approaches these relationships from the young women's points of view, linking the Maputo scenery of *curtidoras* and *patrocinadores* to the situation of general economic hardship for a majority of normal Mozambicans, in which younger men are unable to pay bridewealth and make a customary marriage, while young women are looking for new ways of getting money for themselves and their relatives. In this generally difficult economic situation, women "stand a better chance than male peers of achieving social mobility by utilizing their erotic resources in the thriving sexual economy." They are sexual agents with erotic skills, maintained and developed through their relationships with female elders, masters of these arts: "The erotic knowledge that female elders transmit to daughters and nieces is transformed into bodily capacities that women use to seduce *patrocinadores*. . . . Erotic powers are reproduced within a female space where secret knowledge is passed on from older to younger women."[38]

The type of knowledge transmitted depends on the religion and ethnicity of the instructor-relative. As Groes-Green further states, "Migrant families from the north . . . who belong to the matrilineal Makhuwa have much more detailed programs for initiation of girls and draw more on magic elements than families from other areas."[39] Young *curtidoras* learn from female kin how to seduce and retain *patrocinadores* so they will continue to contribute money and gifts. Even if young women sometimes call their lovers their "ATMs," for the ubiquitous cash machines in Maputo, such relationships are not without feelings. As part of erotic craftsmanship, however, they take care *not* to fall in love; the woman should make the man depend on her sexually and emotionally, while she herself keeps emotionally detached. This is not unlike the lessons of matrilineal ideology studied by Poewe, and not unlike my own findings from work among the Makhuwa of northern Mozambique: young women are instructed not to get too attached to their husbands; marital devotion is not encouraged.[40]

Like women in colonial Nairobi studied by Luise White, whose remittances were key to survival of their rural kin,[41] *curtidoras* distribute money and goods received from *patrocinadores* to mothers, aunts, and family members. They are part of what Groes-Green sees as "a broader moral economy of exchange, encompassing not only economic and social bonds, but also sexual favors, care, love and gender and kinship obligations."[42] In Nairobi as well as in Maputo such women are well respected by their kin because they redistribute their income.

Learning the Language of Love: Companionate Marriage

Even if "love" has not been the focus of older anthropological writings, love, emotion, and passion, in one form or another, have always been there (see chapter 13), now heavily influenced by mission teachings and mass media. Modern Christianity, from the eighteenth century on, framed love in terms of "romantic love" between a man and a woman, supposed to be the basis for life-long monogamous marriage: "to have and to hold, from this day forward; for better, for worse, for richer, for poorer, in sickness and in health, to love and to cherish, till death do us part."[43]

Christian missions in Africa introduced new modes of courtship, while at the same time, as Lynn M. Thomas puts it, "banishing initiation, promoting monogamy and condemning sexual practices that had previously been allowed, such as premarital sexual play (including 'thigh sex' . . .) and discreet extramarital affairs."[44] Christianity also brought "literacy, [which] . . . opened up rural lives to new ideas and practices of intimacy. By the mid-twentieth century images of romantic love circulated widely in magazines and newspapers that could be brought to rural areas from growing towns," as stated by Hunter.[45] The writing of love letters came to symbolize new modes of courtship. Authors of love letters had to learn a new language of love, to express their feelings verbally and in writing.

A key source of ideas regarding intimate life, unsurprisingly, was Christian missions. Early written media, such as the newspaper *Bantu World*, founded in Johannesburg in 1932, featured a women's page with articles on love and family life, where a useful vocabulary around this kind of issue could be developed. Thomas sees the conception of love advanced by *Bantu World* writers as coinciding with Victorian notions: "Modelled after the Christian conception of self-knowledge through love of God, Victorian conjugal love entailed an intense spiritual bond between a man and a woman. This bond, chosen and forged through courtship, provided the foundation for a monogamous union in which the husband and wife maintained a unique and future-oriented connection to one another."[46] In many ways this was a break from earlier forms of marriage, where exclusive emotional attachments between husband and wife were often discouraged.

The influence of mass media—initially newspapers and magazines, later videos and films—in creating a shared language regarding love and courtship, and a language for reflecting on the meaning of intimate relations in one's own life, can hardly be overstated. Rachel Spronk reported from Nairobi in the early twenty-first century how young professionals rely on lifestyle magazines for providing them with an appropriate language regarding emotional relations and problems in intimate life. At that point the style of weekly magazines had changed in the direction of an emphasis on self-reflexivity and greater communication between spouses. "A defining feature of young professionals' vision of love is that emotional investment and sexual intimacy in relationships is a means of individual development and self-fulfillment," she says. This new "therapeutic ethos" entered the Kenyan public sphere in the early 1990s, along with multiparty politics, media liberalization, and HIV/AIDS prevention campaigns. As elsewhere in Africa at that point, issues of sex and intimacy were high on the agenda. The therapeutic ethos insists that solutions to romantic problems lie in self-knowledge and reflexivity; spouses are expected to have a companionate marriage characterized by socializing together, equal decision-making, and emotional and sexual satisfaction.[47]

AIDS, Discretion, Silence, and Rhetorics of Ambiguity: Same-Sex Relationships under the Radar

According to much evidence it was the HIV/AIDS pandemic that "flung open the doors on sexuality," as put by Sylvia Tamale. "In particular it . . . forced into the open the myths and secrets in relationships and identities . . . often silenced or taken for granted."[48] The HIV/AIDS pandemic made possible—and necessary—a "putting into discourse of sex," which had not previously taken place in Africa, or certainly not to the same extent.[49] This putting into discourse of sex from the 1990s on has had a variety of results in different African contexts, such as a franker and more elaborate discussion of sex in the media and the creation of a language for talking and reflecting on intimate relationships, including their sexual aspects—that is, the therapeutic ethos that can be seen as an aspect of a new middle-class self-confidence of "being modern the African way."[50]

However, this creation of sexualized public discourse also allowed the condemnation of same-sex practices, practices previously often tacitly condoned. Same-sex discourse came into the open in contradictory ways, on the one hand as a steep rise in homophobic sentiments, voiced by presidents and normal citizens alike, ignited by Pentecostal-Charismatic churches—and on the other as a rising wave of donor-initiated and donor-funded nonprofit organizations involved in previously not-very-visible and tacitly tolerated same-sex communities. These communities have now been called on to organize and fight for their human rights against the intensification of public homophobia that rallied with the slogan "Homosexuality is un-African."

Nevertheless, in spite of intensified condemnations of so-called homosexuals and their organizations, same-sex practices, identities, and communities seem to survive "'under the radar," evident in a series of studies based on interviews with men and women who practice and enjoy same-sex relationships. Serena Dankwa studied *supi-supi* relationships in Ghana, a term that originally referred to affectionate relationships between girls at boarding schools. Usually there would be a senior and a junior *supi*, the senior protecting and supporting the junior, the junior fetching water and running errands for the senior. The borderlines between support, friendship, and erotic intimacies are blurred, but "regardless of whether or not erotic play occurred, neither the girls nor their environment considered these intimacies sexual."[51] This is the important point, recurring in Lesotho, South Africa, and other places. The basic rule of "no penis, no sex" applied; when no man/no penis was involved and pregnancy was not an issue, then whatever took place between the parties involved was categorized as "play," not "sex." This confirms the findings of Hunter and others discussed above regarding distinctions between sex and fertility: young men and women could engage quite freely in sexual play with one another so long as they made sure no pregnancies would result. The idea of sex in itself as inherently sinful when not linked to procreation was introduced by Christian missionaries.

The nonclassification as "sexual" means that such relationships stay free of policing by sexual discourse. Dankwa refers to the silence surrounding sexual relations as follows: "Sexual discourse in southern Ghana has been structured by norms of discretion and indirection that relegate non-marital sexual relations, including same-sex passions, to the realm of the unnamed and the unspoken. . . . Throughout West Africa same-sex practices have been concealed and celebrated through a 'language of allusion' and 'tactics of non-verbalization.'"[52] An important point about silence in sexual discourse is that "it maintains spaces for ambiguous expressions of homosociality and hence for building alternative community." Kathleen O'Mara focused on such communities in southern Ghana, where, she says, "a sense of LGBTI community forms around shared knowledge, individual and collective experiences, events and strategies of in/visibility in everyday life." In these contexts "a rhetoric of ambiguity" is a central tool, concealing sexual knowledge from outsiders, those who should not or do not want to know, while revealing it to insiders. She concludes that LGBTI communities in urban Ghana "tacitly challenge heteronormativity, instate intragender love as indigenous, and claim community and citizenship. Sexual identity is . . . intertwined with gender, community and nation, a strategy that disrupts the colonial and Christian argument that same-sex intimate relationships are a Western import [and] upends the Western narrative of 'coming out' with its emphasis on the individual."[53]

Another indication of difference between African and Euro-American conceptualizations of same-sex relationships is that African sexual identities and relationships are often not binary, one or the other, but simultaneous. Christophe Broqua found in Mali, "among men who engage in sexual relationships with other men, homosexual behavior, including identity, is not considered to be opposed to the dominant conception of parenthood and reproduction," which he links to the split between sex for pleasure and sex for procreation. "Malian men separate the reproductive and pleasurable aspects of sexuality, and consider it possible to construct a minority sexual identity, and at the same time respect the dominant order of parenthood and reproduction," he says.[54] Similarly, women interviewed by Dankwa were open to heterosexual marriage, "at least temporarily, 'because of the birth. Everybody wants to have a baby.'"[55] African variations in same-sex relationships thus challenge much common Western discourse such as the concept of "coming out," binary categories regarding sexual identity and practices, and what is defined as sexual or nonsexual practice.

Christianity, Islam, and Gender

In the above sections I have given priority to Christianity because European colonial powers dominating Africa from the late nineteenth century on were Christian. Colonialism—which came with powers of coercion and spiritual power in terms of Christian missions—did have tremendous impact. Islam, however, also had and continues to have an impact in Africa; Islam spread in Africa from the tenth century onward; Christianity (except in Ethiopia and Egypt) came centuries later, with the Europeans. According to recently collected data (and estimates) out of the total population on the continent, approximately 57 percent are Christian and 28 percent are Muslim, while the remaining 15 percent stick to African indigenous religions. African indigenous religions, however, often coexist with Christianity as well as with Islam.[56] Seen in relation to issues of gender and sexuality, there are more similarities than differences between Christianity and Islam, both Abrahamic religions, monotheistic, with holy scriptures, and with a Supreme Being—God, Allah— seen as male. In contrast, in most African indigenous religions, even when they are monotheistic, which is often the case, the Supreme Being is beyond gender, neither male nor female (see chapter 3). Another similarity is the growing influence of fundamentalist dogma in Christianity as well as in Islam; both limit freedom and equality of women (see chapter 5).

Of course, there are also differences between Christianity and Islam, one of the more obvious ones being rules regarding marriage, where the Christian prescription is strict monogamy, while Islam permits polygyny. Islam acknowledges the existence of female sexual pleasure, which should be exercised only in marriage and under male control—but under proper conditions women's sexual enjoyment is encouraged.[57] This is different from Victorian Christian mores, where respectable women were not supposed to experience sexual pleasure.[58] Among the Mahkuwa of northern Mozambique, perhaps because Islam has been established there for a longer time and did not come as an aspect of colonial power, African indigenous cultures and religion melded more smoothly with Islam than with Christianity. According to Sylvia Tamale, a major difference between the Abrahamic religions and African indigenous religions is that "while the former often view the female body as the seat of sin, moral corruption and a source of distraction from godly thoughts, African traditional religion celebrates and valorises the female body as a reproductive/sexual icon."[59]

Conclusion

This chapter has shown different ways of seeing and conceptualizing gender and sexuality in Africa, from the writings of colonial anthropologists and missionaries to feminist contestations from the 1970s onward, to examples of contemporary investigations inspired by (and contributing to) postcolonial critique. The first approach, rooted in colonial power structures, has had by far the most impact on Africans' social and political lives. Partly through its reinforcement by political power in colonial and later postcolonial states (the latter in many ways having followed in the footsteps of their colonial predecessors) and partly because upward social mobility depended on access to Western education taught in Christian mission schools, which still have widespread influence on the minds and lives of African populations. In sub-Saharan Africa there are now more foreign Christian missionaries (see chapter 5) than there were at the height of European colonial rule.

The second part of the chapter traced influences on African lives of colonial ways of seeing in terms of conceptions of masculinities and femininities, of ways in which marriage was transformed into a central institution, and finally how the colonial gaze also had its blind angles, for instance regarding same-sex intimacies, which were not supposed to exist.

Contemporary research on issues of sexuality and gender was the focus of the third section, including research on money and love, and how these are related in modern marriage, and on discretion, silence, and ambiguities in discourses surrounding sexuality. Findings stress sex/love/money entanglements inside and outside marriage; men are expected to hand over money or goods to women, and women are expected to be active and proficient in sex. Erotic skills passed from older to younger women demonstrate *female agency in matters of sex.* While sex/love/money entanglements have a long history, notions of "romantic love" are more recent, introduced by Christianity and connected to the Christian ideal of lifelong monogamous marriage. Romantic love implies the development of a language of love and emotions, which was constructed first in and by "women's pages" in newspapers and magazines and later in videos and films. Today, among young urban professionals romantic love has developed into "companionate marriage," with an emphasis on self-reflexivity and communication between couples, a so-called therapeutic ethos, with Christianity still lurking in the background.

Nevertheless, local patterns of same-sex intimacies, male as well as female, have managed to survive covertly in many places, in spite of the increasing homophobia fueled by fundamentalist religions. These findings regarding persistent same-sex cultures are—along with data demonstrating the resilience of female sexual agency—among the most remarkable results of recent studies of gender and sexuality in Africa. In different ways they challenge conventional notions, inspiring rethinking of gender and sexuality in Africa.

Notes

1. The First Wave was the women's suffrage movement in Europe and the United States.

2. A. R. Radcliffe-Brown and Daryll Forde, eds., *African Systems of Kinship and Marriage* (London: Oxford University Press, 1950).

3. A famous exception is a short paper by E. E. Evans-Pritchard on historical cases of homosexuality among the Azande (South Sudan). E. E. Evans-Pritchard, "Sexual Inversion among the Azande," *American Anthropologist* 72, no. 6 (1970): 1428–34.

4. Pauline Peters, "Revisiting the Puzzle of Matriliny in South-Central Africa," *Critique of Anthropology* 17, no. 2 (1997): 125–46.

5. Gayle Rubin, "The Traffic in Women," in *Toward an Anthropology of Women,* ed. Rayna Reiter (New York: Monthly Review Press, 1975).

6. Karla Poewe, *Matrilineal Ideology: Male-Female Dynamics in Luapula, Zambia* (London: Academic Press for the International African Institute, 1981), 56, 67, 68.

7. Friedrich Engels, *The Origin of the Family, Private Property and the State* (1884; repr., New York: International Publishers, 1972).

8. Kamene Okonjo, "The Dual-Sex Political System in Operation: Igbo Women and Community Politics in Midwestern Nigeria," in *Women in Africa: Studies in Social*

and Economic Change, ed. N. J. Hafkin and E. G. Bay (Stanford: Stanford University Press, 1976), 45–58; Claire Robertson, *Sharing the Same Bowl: A Socioeconomic History of Women and Class in Accra, Ghana* (Bloomington: Indiana University Press, 1984).

9. Oyèrónké Oyewùmí, "Family Bonds/Conceptual Binds: African Notes on Feminist Epistemologies," *Signs: Journal of Women in Culture and Society* 25, no. 4 (2000): 1094–95.

10. Simone de Beauvoir, *The Second Sex* (French, 1949; English trans., London: Vintage Classics, 1997).

11. Maria Lugones, "Heterosexualism and the Colonial/Modern Gender System," *Hypatia* 22, no. 1 (2007): 186–209.

12. Kopano Ratele, "Relating to Whiteness: Writing about the Back Man," *Psychology Bulletin* 8, no. 2 (1998): 38.

13. Oyèrónké Oyewùmí, *The Invention of Women: Making an African Sense of Western Gender Discourses* (Minneapolis: University of Minnesota Press, 1997), 124.

14. Michel Foucault, *The History of Sexuality* (French, 1976; English trans., London: Penguin Books, 1978), 105, 103.

15. Ann Laura Stoler, *Carnal Knowledge and Imperial Power* (Berkeley: University of California Press), 152.

16. Malin Newitt, *Portugal in Africa: The Last Hundred Years* (London: Hurst, 1981).

17. Signe Arnfred, *Sexuality and Gender Politics in Mozambique: Rethinking Gender in Africa* (Woodbridge, UK: James Currey, 2011), chap. 2, 39–61.

18. The Industrial Revolution began in the late eighteenth century in Britain.

19. Veronica Bennholdt-Thomsen, "Why Do Housewives Continue to Be Created in the Third World Too?," in *Women: The Last Colony*, ed. Maria Mies, Veronika Bennholdt-Thomsen, and Claudia von Werlhof (London: Zed Books 1988), 159.

20. Charles Biber, qtd. in Arnfred, *Sexuality and Gender Politics*, 59.

21. Jeff Guy, "Analysing Pre-Capitalist Societies in Southern Africa," *Journal of Southern African Studies* 14, no. 1 (1987): 18–37.

22. Mark Hunter, "Masculinities, Multiple-Sexual-Partners, and AIDS: The Making and Unmaking of Isoka in KwaXulu-Natal," *Transformation* 54 (2004): 126, 132.

23. Marc Epprecht, "The Making of 'African Sexuality': Early Sources, Current Debates," in *Sexual Diversity in Africa*, ed. S. N. Nyeck and Marc Epprecht (Montreal: McGill-Queens University Press 2013), 58–59.

24. Stephen O. Murray and Will Roscoe, *Boy-Wives and Female Husbands: Studies in African Homosexualities* (New York: St. Martin's Press 1998), xi.

25. Stoler, *Carnal Knowledge*.

26. Murray and Roscoe, *Boy-Wives*, 273.

27. Dunbar Moodie, "Black Migrant Mine Labourers and the Vicissitudes of Male Desire," in *Changing Men in Southern Africa*, ed. Robert Morrell (London: Zed Books, 2001), 305.

28. Kendall, "Women in Lesotho and the (Western) Construction of Homophobia," in *Female Desires, Same-Sex Relations and Transgender Practices across Cultures*, ed. Evelyn Blackwood and Saskia Wieringa (New York: Columbia University Press, 1999), 157–80.

29. Jennifer Cole, "Love, Money, and Economies of Intimacy in Tamatave, Madagascar," in *Love in Africa*, ed. Jennifer Cole and Lynn M. Thomas (Chicago: University of Chicago Press 2009), 118.

30. Mark Hunter, *Love in the Time of AIDS* (Bloomington: Indiana University Press, 2010), 42.

31. Robertson, *Sharing the Same Bowl*.

32. Radcliffe-Brown, introduction to Radcliffe-Brown and Forde, *African Systems*, 47.

33. Arnfred, *Sexuality and Gender Politics*, 75.

34. Mark Hunter, "Provider Love: Sex and Exchange in Twentieth-Century South Africa," in Cole and Thomas, *Love in Africa*, 150.

35. Hunter, "Provider Love," 148.

36. Arnfred, *Sexuality and Gender Politics*, chap. 7, 152–65.

37. Thera Rasing, *The Bush Burnt, the Stones Remain: Female Initiation Rituals in Urban Zambia* (Berlin: LIT Verlag 2001), 170.

38. Christian Groes-Green, "'To Put Men in a Bottle': Eroticism, Kinship, Female Power, and Transactional Sex in Maputo, Mozambique," *American Ethnologist*, 40, no. 1 (2013): 104, 106.

39. Groes-Green, "'To Put Men in a Bottle,'" 108.

40. Arnfred, *Sexuality and Gender Politics*, 261.

41. Luise White, *The Comforts of Home: Prostitution in Colonial Nairobi* (Chicago: University of Chicago Press, 1990).

42. Christian Groes-Green, "Journeys of Patronage: Moral Economies of Transactional Sex, Kinship and Female Migration from Mozambique to Europe," *Journal of the Royal Anthropological Institute* 20, no. 2 (2014): 242, 239.

43. Church of England wedding ritual.

44. Lynn M. Thomas, "Love, Sex and the Modern Girl in 1930s Southern Africa," in Cole and Thomas, *Love in Africa*, 38.

45. Hunter, *Love in the Time of AIDS*, 45.

46. Thomas, "Love," 47.

47. Rachel Spronk, "Media and the Therapeutic Ethos of Romantic Love in Middle-Class Nairobi," in Cole and Thomas, *Love in Africa*, 183, 187–88.

48. Sylvia Tamale, "Gendered Bodies, Sexuality and Negotiating Power in Uganda" (paper presented at conference organized by the Center for Global Gender Studies, University of Gothenburg, 2005), 1.

49. Michel Foucault, *The History of Sexuality*, 12.

50. Rachel Spronk, *Ambiguous Pleasures* (Oxford: Berghan Books, 2012), 13.

51. Serena Dankwa, "'It's a Silent Trade': Female Same-Sex Intimacies in Post-Colonial Ghana," *NORA, Nordic Journal of Feminist and Gender Research* 17, no. 3 (2009): 196.

52. Serena Dankwa, "'The One Who First Says I Love You': Love, Seniority and Relational Gender in Postcolonial Ghana," in Nyeck and Epprecht, *Sexual Diversity*, 172.

53. Kathleen O'Mara, "LGBTI Community and Citizenship Practices in Urban Ghana," in Nyeck and Epprecht, *Sexual Diversity*, 195, 196, 207.

54. Christophe Broqua, "Male Homosexuality in Bamako: A Cross-Cultural and Cross-Historical Comparative Perspective," in Nyeck and Epprecht, *Sexual Diversity*, 221.

55. Dankwa, "'The One,'" 178.

56. Sylvia Tamale, "Exploring the Contours of African Sexualities: Religion, Law and Power," in *Research on Gender and Sexualities in Africa*, ed. Sylvia Tamale and Jane Bennett (Dakar: CODESRIA 2017), 16.

57. Assitan Diallo, "Paradoxes of Female Sexuality in Mali," in *Re-thinking Sexualities in Africa*, ed. Signe Arnfred (Uppsala: Nordic Africa Institute, 2004), 173–89.

58. Nancy Cott, "Passionlessness: An Interpretation of Victorian Sexual Ideology, 1790–1850," *Signs: Journal of Women in Culture and Society* 4, no. 2 (1978): 219–36.

59. Tamale, "Exploring the Contours," 17.

Suggested Readings

Arnfred, Signe, ed. *Re-thinking Sexualities in Africa*. Uppsala: Nordic Africa Institute, 2004.

Cole, Jennifer, and Lynn M Thomas, eds. *Love in Africa*. Chicago: University of Chicago Press, 2009.

Nyeck, S. N., and Marc Epprecht, eds. *Sexual Diversity in Africa*. Montreal: McGill-Queen's University Press, 2013.

Oinas, Elina, and Signe Arnfred, eds. "Sex & Politics—Case Africa." Special issue, *NORA* 17, no. 3 (2009).

Tamale, Sylvia, ed. *African Sexualities. A Reader*. Nairobi: Pambazuka Press, 2011.

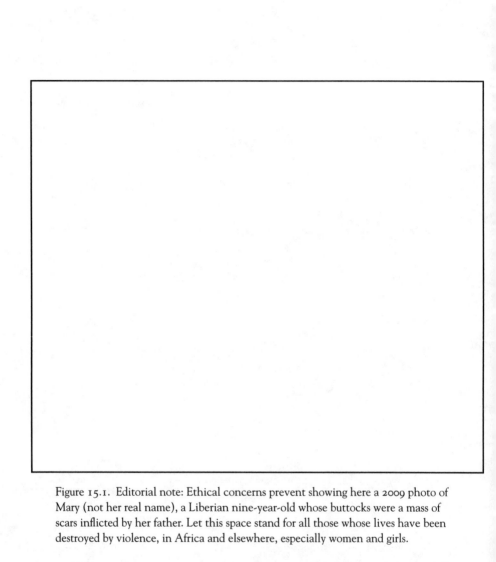

Figure 15.1. Editorial note: Ethical concerns prevent showing here a 2009 photo of Mary (not her real name), a Liberian nine-year-old whose buttocks were a mass of scars inflicted by her father. Let this space stand for all those whose lives have been destroyed by violence, in Africa and elsewhere, especially women and girls.

15

VIOLENCE AGAINST WOMEN

Households, Wars, Refugees, and Resistance

Henryatta Ballah and December Green

In 2000, when Mary was nine months old, her mother died, so she went to live with her father in Paynesville, Liberia. On Monday, September 7, 2009, when she was nine years old, she was severely beaten by him for failing first grade. Her father earned less than US$30 a month and considered her unsatisfactory performance a major economic loss. Enraged, he took her to his room, locked the door, and proceeded to beat her. Hearing her desperate cries for help, their landlord ran to the door and yelled for him to stop and open the door, but her father refused. Fearing the worst, the landlord broke down the door and found her unconscious on the floor, her father still beating her. He wrestled her father to the ground, saving her life. Her father was arrested but released within two hours of his arrest. Mary was returned to him. The healed scars on her buttocks indicate that she had frequently been brutalized by him; her survival was threatened.[1]

This case unfortunately typifies the issue of violence against girls and women in Africa in that it combines the various factors (economic, social, and male dominance) that perpetuate violence against them. This chapter examines two forms of gender-based violence in Africa: domestic and war-related. In various forms, violence against women and girls poses a major threat to their well-being both during peacetime and in war. Equally important, this chapter includes an analysis of women's agency, or their use of informal and formal mechanisms of power to resist violence, in both the private and public spheres.

According to the World Health Organization, approximately one in three of the world's women have experienced either physical or sexual intimate partner violence (IPV) or nonpartner violence. The most extensive study of its kind has found that the region with the highest combined prevalence rates for intimate partner and nonpartner sexual violence against women fifteen years or older is Africa, at 45.6 percent.[2] If these estimates are correct, then nearly half of all African females have experienced some form of abuse, a truly monumental human rights challenge.

Not unique to Africa, domestic violence and sexual assault share common functions worldwide. Although men and boys can be battered and raped, the vast majority of people victimized by these forms of violence are female, the perpetrators male. Even those who call for careful, context-specific differentiated analysis recognize that this is no coincidence.[3] The abuses discussed in this chapter can be considered routine and nonroutine; they occur in the public and private spheres and during times of war and peace. They share gendered aspects as forms of violence against women (VAW). The United Nations defines VAW as "any act of gender-based violence that results in, or is likely to result in, physical, sexual or mental harm or suffering to women, including threats of such acts, coercion or arbitrary deprivation of liberty, whether occurring in public or private life."[4]

However, violence is not gender-based simply because it targets women. Globally, VAW serves a specific social function: promoting and perpetuating hierarchical gender relations, or patriarchy. "Patriarchy" literally means "rule by the fathers," so some prefer the more general term "male dominance" since males of all statuses, related or unrelated to their victims, have engaged in violence against women. Male dominance/female subordination to varying degrees exists almost universally in families, communities, and nations, but not perhaps historically. It is all the more pernicious because it is cloaked in language making it seem natural, although its ubiquity is largely due to the impact of male-dominant European colonialism worldwide. For example, rape is often simply rationalized as due to "nature," and domestic violence is chalked up to "tradition"—and therefore condoned. Women and girls are often doubly victimized, blamed for provoking rape or deserving a beating. Nonpartner sexual assault is often treated as an attack not so much against an individual but against her family or (in war) her nation. Yet women are not only victims but agents or survivors resisting abuse: in their homes, as refugees, or as combatants in wars. Such violence comes in many forms; understanding it requires gender-specific analysis sensitive to context and complex realities. Fully confronting it requires moving this particular reality from the periphery to the center of national and international discourse.

Violence during Peacetime: Domestic Violence in Africa

Precolonially many African women had societal mechanisms that protected them from domestic violence, although not from war atrocities (precolonial warfare was not endemic in most areas), and socially recognized ways of protesting male misbehavior (see chapters 3, 4, and 6). However, colonial rule, with its failure to recognize female authority in the imposition of new laws or distortion of customary laws, enshrined and spread male dominance in new ways. Precolonial increases in the domestic slave trade subsequent to greater involvement in the transatlantic trade (see chapter 9) and colonial and postcolonial rapid urbanization (see chapter 11) caused much societal disruption. Urbanization removed young women from villages where their families could sometimes offer some protection, but in some situations women fled coercive violence from family members.

Now domestic violence is, for many, ingrained in the politics of everyday life, most commonly as spousal abuse, but it also includes child, sibling, and elder abuse. Whatever its form, violence within the home is often considered a private matter, minimized or explained away as a cultural practice or seen as an issue that can only be addressed later, after peace and development take hold. There is some evidence that the incidence of IPV has declined in Africa by nearly 10 percent since 2006.[5] Yet, according to the International Rescue Committee, it is not fighters with guns but rather husbands who are the biggest threat to women. For that reason intimate partner violence is increasingly recognized as a humanitarian issue—for its sociopolitical and economic ramifications. It is a leading cause of death for women worldwide and the most common type of violence against women.[6]

Although violence can exist among heterosexual and same-sex couples, and both males and females have victimized partners, females are the major victims of IPV. Regardless of debates over whether women are more or less likely to initiate aggression, multiple studies have shown female victimization to be more severe than male victimization partly because male-perpetrated IPV is associated with a much greater likelihood of serious injury.[7] In West Africa, it has been called the "most urgent, pervasive and significant protection problem women face."[8]

WHO defines intimate partner violence as "behaviour by an intimate partner or ex-partner that causes physical, sexual or psychological harm, including physical aggression, sexual coercion, psychological abuse and controlling behaviours."[9] Like torture, wife battery commonly involves escalating brutality and can have fatal results, ending in homicide or suicide. Another form of IPV, sexual abuse, is defined as coerced sexual intercourse or other sexual acts. Physical and sexual abuse almost always are accompanied by verbal abuse causing psychological harm, such as denigration of the victim, bullying, or humiliation. Economic abuse is also recognized as a form of IPV. Examples include controlling one's partner by refusing money to cover basic necessities, as well as limiting the woman's freedom to work, and constraining her mobility or access to friends, relatives, and services, including health care. Most of those abused describe domestic abuse as involving a combination of threats of violence, verbal abuse, economic controls, forced sex, and physical assault. The concept of violence is complex because often it is perceived not as violence at all but legitimate coercion reflecting men's rights and responsibilities. In all forms, IPV is often understood by men as taking what is theirs, establishing control over females, and punishing them for failure to obey.[10] An underlying societal belief that enables violence against women is that women belong to men as their property. In Europe and the United States and under colonial-imposed laws this was the case until legal reforms in the twentieth century. In societies where this assumption prevails, there are generally higher rates of violence against women.[11]

How big a problem is domestic violence in Africa? Although there has been some improvement in data collection, it is difficult to obtain reliable statistics on domestic violence allowing for comparisons of African nations—governments might not collect such information or the violence goes unreported. The available numbers are widely considered to be underestimates, given that women hesitate to report abuse because they are often stigmatized and blamed for it. Studies of IPV in Africa suggest that domestic violence is not manifested in the same way everywhere, nor is domestic violence equally widespread across the continent.[12] Evidence suggests that it varies within countries as well.

The available data indicate that levels of IPV in Africa appear to be quite high, described in every country as common to pervasive. Some recent estimates of the percentages of women experiencing IPV in their lifetimes range from a low of 25 percent of women in the Central African Republic and South Africa to 33 percent in Burkina Faso, Zimbabwe, and Liberia, 34 percent in Namibia, 39 percent in Kenya, 41 percent in Rwanda, and 47 percent in Tunisia and Egypt, to 64 percent in the Democratic Republic of the Congo (DRC). Several studies claim that the highest rates of IPV globally are found in Central Africa, where it is estimated that 66 percent of women have been abused by their partners.[13] These are truly astounding numbers but for the reasons cited above should be viewed with caution.

Risk Factors

Risk factors that tend to lead to IPV are witnessing parental abuse; the displacement associated with conflict settings (war and humanitarian disasters);

high levels of political violence; and "the crisis of masculinity," which occurs when men lack personal power but live in societies that expect them to be powerful.[14] Income, age, and education are also variously identified as correlated with abuse, but with inconsistent effects. However, the risk factor most often and consistently associated with IPV worldwide is social acceptance of wife beating as justified. According to a 2016 report, across Africa over the last decade, the acceptance of IPV has declined by nearly 10 percent, but the number of people who accept the practice is still extremely high, at 51 percent. However, Africa's varied complex political, economic, and cultural environments influence how violence is regarded in various societies. For example, acceptance of wife beating is much higher in Uganda and Mali (at 77 percent) than in Malawi (13 percent) or Mozambique (21 percent).[15]

At least part of the reason for the official silence on wife battery in much of Africa is acceptance of abuse as normal, natural, and inevitable. As in much of the rest of the world, such violence thrives where it is treated as "traditional," too culturally sensitive to tackle, because it belongs to the private realm. In many places an overwhelming coalition of social forces—family, community (including other women), and the state—combine to interpret acts likely to be considered assault if perpetrated against a nonfamily member as acceptable against a family member. In many societies, the injuries inflicted are excused, minimized, or dismissed as accidents.[16] A famous case from 1980s rural Kenya is instructive. Njoki, wife and mother of six daughters, had her eyes gouged out by her husband and a gang of neighbors he recruited to attack her. Why? She had not given him a son in patrilineal Kikuyu society. As a result, the court jailed him for five years and gave her a huge monetary settlement, which threatened his ownership of an extensive coffee plantation. They divorced. She then remade her life, and learned and taught Braille. When her husband was released, he wanted his plantation back so he begged her to remarry, getting support in this effort from both her and his family members, the local assistant chief, and four local churches (she agreed). This array demonstrates the strong societal forces condoning violence against women in Kenya.[17]

What is seen as domestic abuse varies from one culture to another. In many African societies, as in much of the world, when a husband beats his wife, he is doing his duty. Hilde Jakobsen illustrates this with her discussion of "good" (deserved and serving a justifiable social purpose) versus "bad" (undeserved or excessive) beatings in Tanzania. "Good beatings" are widely viewed as legitimate and treated as private matters beyond reproach, in that it is a husband's right and duty to preserve control and order and to correct his wife's unseemly behavior.[18] Often, wherever such beatings occur, they punish what are perceived as acts of resistance or transgression of gender norms. Supporters and detractors of such beatings agree that beatings (whether "good" or not) are used to reestablish order; they enforce the rules about expected gender roles.

Domestic Violence and the State

Just as family and community can protect against abuse or be complicit in it, so too can governments, particularly through the legal system, play a role in enforcing the rules about gender. Around the world, laws reflect norms about female sexuality—but they also can reflect changing gender norms and reshape gender relations (see chapter 14), as when colonial interventions in Africa made sex into sin and criminalized adultery. In the case of IPV, however, in much of Africa, European and African traditions came together to treat it not as a crime but as a private, family matter. As of 2018, twenty-seven African countries had adopted domestic violence laws. Even in these countries, though, IPV is commonly minimized or ignored by the legal system. In Nigeria and Burkina Faso, for example, the law allows husbands to use physical means to chastise their wives as long as they do not inflict grievous harm, which is defined as the loss of sight, hearing, speech, facial disfigurement, or life-threatening injuries. Even prosecution for severe battering is rare in Egypt because it requires multiple eyewitnesses, which is difficult with domestic violence.[19]

Moreover, where domestic violence is criminalized, many people are unaware of that because of lack of enforcement. Police, prosecutors, judges, and even health practitioners may doubt or minimize claims of abuse. Investigations are often impeded by lack of resources and inefficient judicial systems; it is not uncommon for the police to be poorly equipped or trained and greatly overstretched. Many countries do not issue restraining orders; even when they do, abusers rarely serve time or incur other penalties for violating them. South Africa has issued "protection" orders since 1992, but many men still literally "get away with murder." In South Africa 30 to 45 percent of all female homicides are perpetrated by women's male partners. In many countries, the rare cases of wife murder that go to trial are tried in family courts, which, as in Kenya, tend to acquit, accept minor pleas for serious offenses, or grant unusually lenient sentences; the case of Njoki cited above was an exception.[20]

Even in Sierra Leone, where domestic violence is now punishable by a fine of up to nearly $1,000 and up to two years in prison, three years after the passage of new laws only one person had been prosecuted for domestic violence. Why not more? As in many countries, including Chad, DRC, Mauritius, Nigeria, and Egypt, Sierra Leonean police do not take physical abuse seriously and handle it as a social, not a criminal, issue; often they just tell the couple to reconcile. Women's families may also push for reconciliation, leaving them with nowhere to go. In some countries no government-provided shelters or counseling are available. In Egypt, the few available safe houses are often empty because of the stigma of living outside one's home or the shelters' strict rules (such as health and police checks) that exclude many women.[21]

There are some efforts to remedy these problems. For example, the government of Namibia has been more proactive than most in partnering with civil society, which plays a leading role in advocacy and providing services there and elsewhere in Africa, although there is more to be done, particularly toward coordinating efforts. The country that has made perhaps the strongest effort is Rwanda, which experienced a social revolution of sorts after the 1994 genocide, when many women became heads of households. Since then the government has introduced laws to empower women, sensitize men, and treat IPV as a serious crime. There and in other countries, such as Ethiopia, police and military training includes a module on gender-based violence. Since 1993, South Africa has had courts that specialize in domestic violence, which have increased conviction rates while reducing the retraumatization of victims. In Rwanda, Namibia, and Tanzania, gender desks established at police stations have improved reporting and response to domestic violence crimes. Hotlines, as well as "one stop" centers in Rwanda, Tanzania, Namibia, and Morocco, provide police and legal assistance at no cost, along with medical and psychological aid. However, such services are usually not available outside of large cities, and change is slow. Inadequate resources and entrenched beliefs about gender relations and roles remain a problem in many places.[22]

Women's Agency in Relation to Violence: Domestic Violence and Informal Mechanisms of Power

As a result of the state's unwillingness, corruption, or inability to help them, most African women avoid turning to it for assistance.[23] Instead, they rely on their own resources. Contrary to stereotypes, women are often not passive victims, acquiescing in their abuse. In fact, as poet Nikki Giovanni puts it, "people are rarely powerless, no matter how stringent the restrictions on their lives."[24] A common way to mitigate abuse, especially in the past, was overt: women came together in single-sex organizations quite capable of organizing loud protests, reminding men of women's value to society (see chapters 3, 4, and 6). Women across Africa demanded respect for their role as mother and shamed men into stopping behavior harmful to women.

It is often assumed that African women suffer in silence, but confrontation is not the only means for achieving power over decision-making or resisting violence. Women often use both formal and informal power structures to cope with or resist IPV. Such responses may go unseen or be misinterpreted by outsiders as passive because they do not openly challenge male dominance. While hidden behind a mask of public compliance, women's strategies against domestic abuse can be both oppositional and subversive.[25] Women might use deference or placating as tools to manipulate men.[26] More strategies include adaptation, control of scarce resources, and the use of coercion to renegotiate gender relations. Such strategies work because they allow men to think that they are in control, to save face while changing their behavior. Women may turn inward to family or kin for support, withdraw into prayer groups or spirit cults to reaffirm their rights according to religious custom, or evade authority and mitigate suffering through "negative" activity (nonparticipation or the repudiation of wifely duties). Some strategies are direct; some work through modifications and recalibrations of existing social forms. Because most of these forms of resistance do not challenge established well-defined gender roles, they are by nature reformist rather than transformative. Still, analysts such as Christine Obbo point out that the cumulative effect may be gradual transformation of society. So, women use space available to them to take what control is possible, given their circumstances.[27]

Although the politics of everyday life play out differently for each individual, intimate partner violence is a very real problem in much of Africa. IPV has ramifications, not only for females but also for their children and communities because it seeks to enforce inequality, limiting the potential of half the population. Some governments have adopted reforms and proactive policies aimed to combat it, but in too many places, women and girls are clearly on their own. Their everyday forms of resistance draw on socially accepted protections that, much like judo, use "controlled surrender," turning patriarchy's own weight and strength against it in subverting the power of the men in their lives. As individuals or collectively, women have found their own ways of promoting their interests independent of state action. Sometimes even survival can be a form of resistance.

Gender Violence during Wartime:
Rape and Sexual Violence in Rwanda and Liberia

Since the 1960s many countries in Africa have been plagued by civil wars and unrest. During these conflicts, women and children invariably bear the brunt of hostilities and violence, especially rape and other forms of sexual violence. Moreover, they constitute the highest number of refugees and internally displaced people.[28] The dominant discourse about women's and girls' experiences during armed conflicts constructs them as hapless victims of male aggression. Although women bear much of the negative socioeconomic consequences of armed conflicts, they are not simply victims but also active agents who have developed strategies to ensure their families' survival. Here we analyze the multiplicity of women's experiences and roles in armed conflicts as survivors of sexual violence, as perpetrators of violence, and as peacemakers.

During wars, acts of rape and sexual violence against women and girls are not always random or solely for sexual gratification but can be "a deliberate form of torture, a tactic to humiliate and terrorize a perceived enemy."[29] The intended impact is to emasculate men by demonstrating their inability to protect their families from rape and other violence, as in Bosnia, and in Africa to damage the reproductive capacity of lineage families. During the Rwandan genocide of 1994, where an estimated 250,000 women and girls were raped, Hutu men raped and impregnated Tutsi women as a direct attack on Tutsi hegemony. Donatilla Mukamana and Petra Brysiewicz argue, "It is this ability to destroy community that makes rape such a powerful weapon of war."[30]

One reason women and girls are vulnerable to sexual violence during conflicts is because they bear responsibility for providing the subsistence needs of their families and must therefore venture into unsafe areas in search of food, firewood, and water. [31] Noting the critical importance of women's many economic activities in Africa (see chapter 8), Emmanuel Aning analyzed their involvement in trade during the Liberian and Sierra Leonean civil wars, noting that "women have engaged in this sort of activity in an effort to re-create forms of civil activity in war-destroyed areas as a means . . . of ensuring the supply of basic commodities." Women's trade in war zones involves major risks; during the Liberian and Sierra Leonean civil wars, their goods and money were routinely confiscated by rebels, and they experienced rape and other forms of violence, including murder.[32]

The consequences of rape and other forms of sexual violence against women also impact their lives postconflict. In Rwanda, an estimated five thousand infants, called *rape babies*, were born to women as a result of being raped during the genocide. Mothering them caused psychological trauma for many women since the child was a constant reminder of the attack, causing some to abandon their children.[33] Thousands of Rwandan women and girls, raped and impregnated during the conflict, contracted sexually transmitted diseases, including HIV/AIDS. In addition, many experienced humiliation and loss of respect and were stigmatized by community members once it was known that they had been raped. For some, finding a husband became difficult, as they were perceived to be "damaged goods."[34] These experiences of Rwandan women survivors of sexual violence are not unique but are shared by women in conflict zones across Africa, including Liberia and Sierra Leone.

During the Liberian civil war (1989–2003), an estimated 40 percent of women and girls experienced rape and other forms of sexual violence.[35] The most thorough study of the impact of sexual violence against women and girls during the Liberian civil war was published in 2008 by Isis-Women's International Cross Cultural Exchange (Isis-WICCE) in collaboration with the Liberian Ministry of Gender and Development and the Liberian chapters of West Africa Network for Peacebuilding (WANEP) and Women in Peacebuilding Network (WIPNET). It demonstrated that at the end of civil conflicts, women and girls suffer from an array of psychological problems such as post-traumatic stress disorder (PTSD), depression, anxiety, and insomnia. Among survey respondents, 93 percent reported having suffered at least one psychological symptom.[36] Of course, survivors of sexual violence also experience a host of diseases and other disabilities postconflict, often grave.

Refugee Women and Girls in Wartime

Between 1993 and 1998 approximately 1.3 million people from the Democratic Republic of the Congo, Burundi, and Rwanda fled to western Tanzania, only one example of the creation of refugees.[37] According to the United Nations High Commission for Refugees (UNHCR), in 2017, some 24.2 million people in Africa were in need of international assistance due predominantly to armed conflicts. From this number, 6.3 million are refugees, constituting 32 percent of the world's total refugee population, while 14.5 million are internally displaced, accounting for almost 40 percent of the world's 39.1 million internally displaced people.[38] The root causes of the majority of these conflicts lie in the colonial experiences of these countries, detailed earlier in this volume.[39] Although all ages and both genders are affected as refugees, women and children account for up to 80 percent, the majority residing in the Horn of Africa.[40] Women and children constitute a higher percentage of the refugees in Africa because most combatants are males; men are targeted and killed; and some men send their families away as a safety precaution while they remain behind. As refugees, women encounter a host of challenges and obstacles, which the cases of Uganda, Guinea, and Sierra Leone illuminate.

As a means of ensuring their family's survival, some refugee and displaced women and girls turn to prostitution, thereby exposing themselves to sexually transmitted diseases and physical and sexual violence. Thus, a gender-specific approach, which foregrounds the nutritional needs of women, children, and

the family as a whole, designed in consultation with refugee women, is absolutely required to ensure the success of international food ration programs.

Uganda, Guinea, and Sierra Leone

On their journeys to (presumed) safety, refugee women are vulnerable to sexual violence perpetrated by soldiers, warlords, border guards, armed gangs, and
even male refugees. In refugee camps, their vulnerabilities remain when they
search for wood and food, fetch water, and perform other subsistence tasks.
Meredeth Turshen explains, "Hundreds of thousands of Somali women crossed
into Kenya from 1991 to 1993 to escape political violence and rape, only to
face rape in the camps in which they sought shelter."[41] Similarly, during the
Ugandan civil war from 1987 to 1992, women and girls in refugee camps in
Teso were survivors of sexual violence committed by government soldiers.
Analyzing the experiences of these survivors, Joanna de Berry contends, "An
unknown but significant number of young girls experienced the humiliation,
terror and suffering of sexual violence at the hands of army personnel."[42] Currently, there exist over 180,000 internally displaced people in Uganda, many
of whom are women and children. The issue of sexual violence is a large concern for them and their advocates: at an international women's conference
held in Kampala at Makerere University in 2002 a Ugandan scholar, a male
activist for women's rights, broke down in tears while describing the many
atrocities committed against refugee women; then he apologized on behalf of
the men who committed them.

Malnutrition and starvation push some women and girls to exchange sex for
food, even with humanitarian aid workers. In the past few years, there has been
growing awareness of sexual exploitation by a different group of perpetrators:
humanitarian workers. In February 2002, UNHCR and Save the Children-
UK released a report titled "Sexual Violence and Exploitation: The Experience
of Refugee Children in Liberia, Guinea and Sierra Leone," which specifically
examined the issue of sexual exploitation of girls by aid workers and UN
peacekeepers operating in the aforementioned countries. Based on researchers' interviews with 1,500 individuals in the three countries, UNHCR and
Save the Children-UK acknowledged that the sexual exploitation of girls aged
thirteen to eighteen by aid workers and peacekeepers, perpetrated by making
access to food dependent on granting sexual favors, was endemic; 42 agencies
and 67 workers were implicated in this practice. In all three countries, workers
from international and local NGOs as well as UN agencies were reportedly
the most frequent sex exploiters of children, using the very humanitarian aid

and services intended to benefit the refugee population as a tool of exploitation. Items exchanged for sex included oil, rice, biscuits, plastic sheets, bars of soap, and cash often amounting to ten cents (U.S.), enough to buy a few pieces of fruit. It was reported that some peacekeepers pool their money to obtain a girl, with whom they all had sex. Teachers and community leaders in the camps were also implicated in exchanging passing grades and provisions for sex. Refugee women and girls are vulnerable to sexual violence and exploitation because "there are inadequate mechanisms for reporting abuses available to refugees and little prospect of doing so in a way that is safe and confidential."[43] As a result, the vast majority of rape cases and other forms of violence against refugee and displaced women go unreported.

In response to the findings of the 2002 report, the UN Inter-Agency Standing Committee (IASC), consisting of all UN agencies involved in humanitarian crisis and NGO networks, prepared a document in 2002 with specific mandates for combating the problem of sexual exploitation of refugee girls. Provided to all member agencies, it included a UNHCR Code of Conduct/ Child Protection Policy as a mechanism for preventing further abuses by employees.[44] The code of conduct applies to all employees, including volunteers; member agencies are required to provide training for staff regarding appropriate behaviors, standards of care, and staff responsibilities toward refugees. Despite these efforts, refugee and displaced women remain vulnerable to sexual and other forms of violence.

Scholars such as Nana Apeadu contend that the international community's response to the necessity for protection of refugee women and girls has been inadequate partly because of the way that the 1951 Convention on Refugees conceptualized the refugee problem when developing policy. They did not foresee that women and children would comprise a significant portion of the refugee population. No women were among the drafters, nor was the word "woman" ever mentioned.[45] The severity of rape and sexual violence against women and girls during conflicts only began to gain international attention in 1992 when Serbs raped white women in Bosnia.

Furthermore, the problem of impunity remains a driving factor perpetuating attacks not only on refugee women and girls but also in peacetime. For example, in 2008 in peacetime Liberia, thirteen-year-old Angel Togba was strangled to death by her aunt, with whom she resided, after the latter discovered that her husband had been having sex with the child. Instead of having compassion for abused Angel, her aunt murdered her and staged her death as suicide by hanging. Police acceptance of her aunt's claim and refusal to investigate the case outraged many, including Angel's teachers, who insisted that she was an A student and would never have killed herself, and demanded the case be investigated. The case gained national attention when women's activist groups, human rights organizations, and student activists at all levels held national protests demanding justice for Angel. Two independent autopsies conducted by Cuban and Ghanaian pathologists vindicated Angel by showing that she had not committed suicide and had been murdered. Due to the persistence of activists, the aunt and uncle were found guilty of murder on March 19, 2010, and sentenced to death by hanging. Five years later, they were set free.[46]

Women's Agency in Relation to Violence:
Women's Involvement in Africa's Wars

In chapters 3, 4, and 7, African women's involvement as combatants in precolonial wars and wars of liberation was described: as soldiers, leaders, and strategists. Since independence, the number of women and girl participants in armed conflicts has increased due to civil wars. Several factors motivate women and girls to participate in armed conflicts. Women may join rebel groups because they believe in a given cause; as a mechanism for protecting themselves and their families against violence; to get food after families and farms are destroyed; as an opportunity for upward socioeconomic mobility; and because many are forcefully conscripted through abduction and kidnapping to serve as fighters' "wives," cooks, and so forth.[47] Like men, female combatants also commit acts of violence, including murder, against civilians. For example, women from across the socioeconomic spectrum of Rwandan society participated in the genocide; close to two thousand are now imprisoned, convicted of genocide-related crimes.[48] While women can be perpetrators of violence during conflicts, men are still overwhelmingly its primary perpetrators.

Women Peacemakers and Survivors in Liberia, Rwanda, and Sudan

Holding perpetrators accountable is integral to protecting women and girls during peace and conflict. Because women are so negatively impacted by armed conflicts, many have become peace activists. The initiatives and activities in which African women engage during and after conflicts illustrate their agency and transcend the dominant trope of victimhood associated with women and armed conflicts. It can be argued that without such grassroots activism, peace and political stability in war-torn countries would be difficult to achieve. Some scholars, such as John Mutamba and Jeanne Izbiliza, argue, "Women are traditionally peacemakers because they give birth and raise children."[49] As mothers, they instill values in their children and work to maintain peace and harmony in their households, giving women the ability to be effective peace activists. Indeed, the politics of motherhood (see chapter 13) remain central to women's peace activism in Africa. In Liberia, for instance, women decided that relief work and advocacy alone were not enough and moved to direct political activism, taking to the streets in protest.[50] Women held rallies and called on the various factions to negotiate for peace. They also prayed and fasted for peace and called on all Liberians to do the same. Women activists also participated in peace conferences and demanded that their voices, concerns, and suggestions be taken seriously. In December 1994, after their request to the Economic Community of West African States (ECOWAS) to participate in the Accra Clarification Conference was denied, the Liberian Women Initiative (LWI) raised sufficient funds to send six delegates to Accra. Determined, the women sat outside the conference hall daily hoping for a chance to lobby delegates. Their efforts paid off when their exclusion from the conference gained national and international attention through Ghanaian and international news outlets. Feeling the pressure, ECOWAS officials, on the third day of the conference, made the women official delegates and gave them a place at the negotiation table.

The successes of women's peace initiatives in Liberia and across Africa require the active participation of rural women. In postgenocide Rwanda, rural women continue to play an integral role in the reconciliation and peacebuilding process. The fact that 20 percent of Rwanda's male population perished during the genocide meant that women constituted 70 percent of the country's population, leading to the significant ascent of women in parliament (see chapter 7) and increased women's participation in the reconciliation process.[51] Solidarity between women at the national and local levels has been significant to this success. Organizations such as Unity Club and Pro-Femmes Twese Hamwe in Rwanda are two examples of women's solidarity groups. Community-based organizations, including women's councils, have provided Rwandan women the opportunity to engage in communal developmental projects and other activities that involved the entire community as a method of promoting unity and solidarity. Women spiritual healers also performed rituals and cleansing ceremonies to help individuals and communities cope with the consequences of genocide.[52] Similar rituals and ceremonies were also performed after the Liberian, Sierra Leonean, and Mozambican civil wars to help individuals heal and to help reintegrate ex-combatant youths into the community.[53]

The creation of social networks and organizations has been a key survival strategy of refugee and displaced women in Africa. For example, in 1994 the

Sudanese Women's Association in Nairobi, Kenya (SWAN) was created by refugee women in Nairobi and Kisumu. Financial endowment for the formation of the organization was provided by foreign donors—the International Refugee Centre of Ireland (IRCI) and the Royal Netherland Embassy in Kenya. One of the primary goals of SWAN was to provide income-generating opportunities for refugee women by providing small loans for businesses and other self-help initiatives through the financial support of the UNCHR and other donor agencies.[54] International donor agencies, including governmental agencies and NGOs, are largely responsible for the funding of refugee projects. Without such funding, it is difficult for women to generate the necessary capital to engage in economic activities that could alleviate the burden of caring for their families. It is important to note that despite the institutional and structural constraints faced by refugee women across Africa, "they display a high degree of adaptability, resilience, creativity and resourcefulness."[55] As agents, refugee and displaced women labor to ensure the survival of their communities.

Conclusion

This chapter explores two forms of gender-based violence in Africa: domestic and war-related. We have shown that during both peace and war, violence in its various forms remains a significant impediment to the overall well-being of women in Africa. Moreover, we demonstrate that African women and girls are not simply objects of abuse but are also active agents who have deployed a series of survival and coping strategies, including becoming combatants themselves. Violence against women in Africa was facilitated by colonial disempowerment of women, including the remaking of African gender roles and ideas about sexuality, which have now become entrenched (see chapter 14) and perpetuated by the failure of many governments to establish and enforce domestic violence laws, so that most abuse cases go unreported. Across the world, women and girls are the primary survivors of rape and other forms of violence and constitute, along with children, the highest percentage of refugees and displaced persons.

Displaced and refugee women and girls remain vulnerable to sexual and other forms of violence due in part to the failure of the international community to protect them. The international community's inadequate response to female refugees' problems is attributable to male dominance resulting in the lack of women's participation in drafting international refugee policies. It is only recently, and in largely symbolic cases, that the international community has treated rape and other forms of violence against women as war crimes.

Integral to ending gender-based violence in all contexts is the making and enforcing of laws that will hold perpetrators accountable for their actions. Ending impunity must also include challenging complicity. Whether it occurs during times of peace or in war, violence against women will continue until and unless it is moved from the periphery to the center of national and international discourses because, ultimately, it is a changed public consciousness that will end what is too often denied or dismissed.

Notes

1. Henryatta Ballah, field interview conducted with Mary's father's landlord, Paynesville, Liberia, September 9, 2009.

2. World Health Organization, "Global and Regional Estimates of Violence against Women: Prevalence and Health Effects of Intimate Partner Violence and Nonpartner Sexual Violence" (London, 2013), https://www.who.int/reproductivehealth/publications/violence/9789241564625/en/.

3. Chandra Talpade Mohanty, "Under Western Eyes: Feminist Scholarship and Colonialist Discourses," in *Third World Women and the Politics of Feminism*, ed. Chandra Talpade Mohanty, Ann Russo, and Lourdes Torres (Bloomington: Indiana University Press, 1991), 67.

4. World Health Organization, "Violence against Women," November 29, 2017, http://www.who.int/mediacentre/factsheets/fs239/en/.

5. Kathleen Beegle, Luc Christiaensen, Andrew Dabalen, and Isis Gaddis, *Poverty in a Rising Africa* (Washington, DC: World Bank, 2016), 97–99.

6. Shamim Aleem, *Women, Peace, and Security* (Bloomington, IN: Xlibris, 2013), 19; Tamasin Ford, "Domestic Violence Is Biggest Threat to West Africa's Women, IRC Says," *The Guardian*, May 22, 2012.

7. Samson Olusina Bamiwuye and Clifford Odimegwu, "Spousal Violence in Sub-Saharan Africa: Does Household Poverty Matter?," *Reproductive Health* 11 (2014): 1–2; John Archer, "Differences in Aggression between Heterosexual Partners: A Meta-Analytic Review," *Psychological Bulletin* 126 (2000): 651.

8. Ford, "Domestic Violence."

9. WHO, "Violence against Women."

10. Liz Kelly, *Surviving Sexual Violence* (Minneapolis: University of Minnesota Press, 1988), 126.

11. WHO, "Violence against Women"; Kelly, *Surviving Sexual Violence*, 126; Martin Donohue, "Violence and Human Rights Abuses against Women in the Developing World," *Medscape* 8, no. 2 (2003).

12. Kelly, *Surviving Sexual Violence*, 126; U.S. Department of State, "2015 Country Reports on Human Rights Practices," 2016, https://www.state.gov/j/drl/rls/hrrpt/2015/; Ayanda Monyela, "Statistics on Domestic Violence in Africa," Women in Action, January 8, 2010, http://www.womeninaction.co.za/statistics-on-domestic-violence-in-south-africa/.

13. WomanStats Project, "Physical Security of Women," 2014, http://womanstats.org/laststatics/Physical%20Security%20°f%20Women%202014.jpg; U.S. Dept. of State,

"2015 Country Reports"; Amnesty International, "'Circles of Hell': Domestic, Public and State Violence against Women in Egypt," January 21, 2015, 25; WHO, "Global and Regional Estimates," 47; K. M. Devries, J. Y. T. Mak, C. Garcia-Moreno, M. Petzold, J. C. Child, G. Falder, S. Lim, L. J. Bacchus, R. E. Engell, L. Rosenfeld, C. Pallitto, T. Vos, N. Abrahams, and C. H. Watts, "The Global Prevalence of Intimate Partner Violence against Women," *Science* 340, no. 6140 (June 2013): 1528.

14. Catherine Campbell, "Learning to Kill? Masculinity, the Family and Violence in Natal," *Journal of Southern African Studies* 18, no. 3 (1992): 627.

15. Beegle et al., "Poverty in a Rising Africa," 97–99.

16. Bamiwuye and Odimegwu, "Spousal Violence," 2.

17. Claire C. Robertson, *Trouble Showed the Way* (Bloomington: Indiana University Press, 1997), 221.

18. Bamiwuye and Odimegwu, "Spousal Violence," 3; Hilde Jakobsen, "What's Gendered about Gender-Based Violence? An Empirically Grounded Theoretical Exploration from Tanzania," *Gender and Society* 28 (August 2014): 549–50.

19. Lee Hasselbacher, "State Obligations Regarding Domestic Violence: The European Court of Human Rights, Due Diligence, and International Legal Minimums of Protection," *Journal of International Human Rights* 8, no. 2 (Spring 2010): 1911; World Bank, "Protecting Women from Violence," Women, Business, and the Law, accessed October 30, 2018, http://wbl.worldbank.org/en/data/exploretopics/protecting-women -from-violence.

20. Merab Odero, Abigail M. Hatcher, Chenoia Bryant, Maricianah Onono, Patrizia Romito, Elizabeth A. Bukusi, and Janet M. Turan, "Responses to and Resources for Intimate Partner Violence: Qualitative Findings from Women, Men, and Service Providers in Rural Kenya," *Journal of Interpersonal Violence* 29, no. 5 (2014): 13; Shanaaz Mathews, Rachel Jewkes, and Naeemah Abrahams, "'So Now I'm the Man': Intimate Partner Femicide and Its Interconnections with Expressions of Masculinities in South Africa," *British Journal of Criminology* 55, no. 1 (2015): 108.

21. Ford, "Domestic Violence"; U.S. Dept. of State, "2015 Country Reports"; Amnesty International, "'Circles of Hell,'" 35.

22. UNAIDS, "Gender-Based Violence in Namibia: An Exploratory Assessment and Mapping of GBV Response Services in Windhoek" (Namibia, 2013), 5, 10, 19, 23, https://sisternamibiatest2014.files.wordpress.com/2014/07/gbvreport.pdf; Nishtha Chugh, "A Drive to Beat Rwanda's Gender-Based Violence," *The Guardian*, November 22, 2013; U.S. Dept. of State, "2015 Country Reports."

23. U.S. Dept. of State, "2015 Country Reports."

24. Giovanni, cited in Claudia Tate, *Black Women Writers at Work* (New York: Continuum, 1983), 68.

25. Christine Obbo, *African Women: Their Struggle for Economic Independence* (London: Zed, 1980), 147; James C. Scott, *Weapons of the Weak: Everyday Forms of Peasant Resistance* (New Haven, CT: Yale University Press, 1999).

26. Mary Allen and Muireann Ní Raghallaigh, "Domestic Violence in a Developing Context: The Perspectives of Women in Northern Ethiopia," *Affilia: Journal of Women and Social Work* 28, no. 3 (2013): 13; Obbo, *African Women*, 147.

27. Obbo, *African Women*, 5; Henrietta L. Moore, *Feminism and Anthropology* (Minneapolis: University of Minnesota Press, 1988), 3.

28. Nana Apeadu, "An Ignored Population: Female-Headed Households among Refugees in Africa," in *Where Did All the Men Go? Female-Headed/Female-Supported Households in Cross-Cultural Perspective*, ed. Joan P. Mencher and Anne Okongwu (Boulder, CO: Westview Press, 1993), 171–90; Piers Pigou, "Children and the South African Truth and Reconciliation Commission," in *Children and Transitional Justice: Truth-Telling, Accountability, and Reconciliation*, ed. Sharanjeet Parmar, Mindy Jane Roseman, Saudamini Siegrist, and Theo Sowa (Cambridge, MA: Human Rights Program, Harvard Law School, 2010), 116; Clotilde Twagiramariya and Meredeth Turshen, "'Favors' to Give and 'Consenting' Victims: The Sexual Politics of Survival in Rwanda," in *What Women Do in Wartime*, ed. Meredeth Turshen and Clotilde Twagiramariya (London: Zed Books, 1998), 101–17.

29. Joanna de Berry, "The Sexual Vulnerability of Adolescent Girls during Civil War in Teso, Uganda," in *Children and Youth on the Front Line: Ethnography, Armed Conflict and Displacement*, ed. Jo Boyden and Joanna de Berry (Oxford: Berghahn Books, 2005), 46.

30. Twagiramariya and Turshen, "Favors to Give," 102; Donatilla Mukamana and Petra Brysiewicz, "The Lived Experience of Genocide Rape Survivors in Rwanda," *Journal of Nursing Scholarship* 40, no. 4 (2008): 382, 379.

31. Judy El-Bushra and Ibrahim Sahl, *Cycles of Violence: Gender Relations and Armed Conflict* (Nairobi: Agency for Co-operation and Research in Development, 2005), 48.

32. Emmanuel Aning, "Gender and Civil War: The Cases of Liberia and Sierra Leone," *Civil Wars* 1, no. 4 (1998): 12–13.

33. Mukamana and Brysicwicz, "The Lived Experience," 382.

34. Twagiramariya and Turshen, "Favors to Give," 110, 104.

35. United Nations High Commission for Refugees, Reach Out: A Refugee Protection Training Project, November 1, 2005, accessed July 5, 2015, http://www.unhcr.org/reach-out.html.

36. Ruth Ojiambo Ochieng, *A Situation Analysis of the Women Survivors of the 1989–2003 Armed Conflict in Liberia* (Kampala: Isis-WICCE, 2008), 76.

37. Beth E. Whitaker, "Refugees in Western Tanzania: The Distribution of Burdens and Benefits among Local Hosts," *Journal of Refugee Studies* 15, no. 4 (2002): 329.

38. UNHCR, Global Report 2017, 58, 61–62, http://reporting.unhcr.org/sites/default/files/gr2017/pdf/GR2017_English_Full_lowres.pdf.

39. Ebenezer Q. Blavo, *The Problems of Refugees in Africa* (Aldershot, UK: Ashgate, 1999), vii, 6–12.

40. Apeadu, "An Ignored Population," 171.

41. Meredeth Turshen, "Women's War Stories," in *What Women Do in Wartime*, ed. Meredeth Turshen and Clotilde Twagiramariya (London: Zed Books, 1998), 14.

42. de Berry, "The Sexual Vulnerability of Adolescent Girls," 46.

43. United Nations High Commission for Refugees (UNHCR) and Save the Children-UK, "Sexual Violence and Exploitation: The Experience of Refugee Children in Liberia, Guinea and Sierra Leone" (London, 2002), 2–6.

44. Elizabeth G. Ferris, "Abuse of Power: Sexual Exploitation of Refugee Women and Girls," *Signs: Journal of Women in Culture and Society* 32, no. 3 (2007): 588.

45. Apeadu, "An Ignored Population," 175.

46. During Henryatta Ballah's fieldwork in Liberia (2009–10), she followed Angel's case closely, attended the trial of the accused, and was at the Temple of Justice on March 19, 2010, when the verdict was read.

47. Emmanuel K. Aning, "Gender and Civil War: The Cases of Liberia and Sierra Leone," *Civil Wars* 1, no. 4 (1998): 18; Susan McKay, "Reconstructing Fragile Lives: Girls' Social Reintegration in Northern Uganda and Sierra Leone," *Gender and Development* 12, no. 3 (2004): 24.

48. Nicole Hogg, "Women's Participation in the Rwandan Genocide: Mothers or Monsters?," *International Review of the Red Cross* 92, no. 877 (2010): 70.

49. John Mutamba and Jeanne Izabiliza, "The Role of Women in Reconciliation and Peace Building in Rwanda: Ten Years after Genocide" (Consortium on Gender, Security and Human Rights, Kigali, 2005), 12–13.

50. Irene Staunton, *Mothers of the Revolution: The War Experiences of Thirty Zimbabwean Women* (Bloomington: Indiana University Press, 1991); African Women and Peace Support Group, *Liberian Women Peacemakers: Fighting for the Right to be Seen, Heard and Counted* (Trenton, NJ: African World Press, 2004), 16.

51. Twagiramariya and Turshen, "Favors to Give," 102.

52. Twagiramariya and Turshen, "Favors to Give," 102.

53. Antoinette Errante and Junior Boia, "Failure Is an Orphan: Post-Conflict Peace Education and War-Affected Children in Mozambique," in *Post-Conflict Reconstruction in Africa*, ed. Ahmad Sikainga and Ousseina Alidou (Trenton, NJ: Africa World Press, 2006), 99.

54. Errante and Boja, "Failure," 120, 134.

55. Gaim Kibrea, "Eritrean Women Refugees in Khartoum, Sudan, 1970–1990," *Journal of Refugee Studies* 8, no. 1 (1995): 1.

Suggested Readings

Farah, Nuruddin. *From a Crooked Rib*. London: Penguin, 2006.

Journal of Refugee Studies. Volumes 1 through 8 specifically address the impact of wars on refugee women in Africa.

Reticker, Gini, dir. *Pray the Devil Back to Hell*. 2008. New York: Passion River Films, 2016. DVD.

United Nations High Commission for Refugees (UNHCR). www.unhcr.org/africa.

World Health Organization. "Global and Regional Estimates of Violence against Women: Prevalence and Health Effects of Intimate Partner Violence and Nonpartner Sexual Violence." London, 2013. https://www.who.int/reproductivehealth/publications/violence/9789241564625/en/.

Figure 16.1. Liberian Shoana Solomon started a social media campaign to help combat the stigma of Ebola. YouTube, October 13, 2014, https://www.youtube.com/watch?v=UEs8xHgBq7g. Reprinted with permission of subject.

16

AFRICAN WOMEN AND HEALTH

Evolving Challenges

Karen Flint

When the 2015 Ebola epidemic hit West Africa, underlying stereotypes informed the response of the Global North, causing them to ignore a crisis in an area prone to health challenges and then overreact when persons traveling from these regions came north. In the United States, the public made few distinctions between African communities afflicted by Ebola, stigmatizing and requiring travelers to take unnecessary precautions. When Shoana Solomon's daughters encountered bullying in American schools for identifying as Liberian, she began the "I am Liberian, not a virus" campaign. The image included here of Solomon, a proud and healthy Liberian woman, can be contrasted with many images dominating U.S. media of sick poor African women and children, often used to elicit sympathy and funds from northerners, that echo familiar stories of Africans' ill-health and vulnerability and represent Africa as in a continual state of crisis. Crises do exist, but what are often left unsaid and unexplored are their historical and contemporary causes, not to mention the various ways that Africans maintain well-being in the face of numerous health challenges and uneven scarce medical resources.

Since colonial times outsiders have blamed African ill-health and malnutrition on the environment and on African cultures, "superstitions," and agricultural practices. Such assumptions allowed colonial powers and corporations to ignore their contributions to creating such conditions and ways in which global and local structural inequalities maintain it. Because well-meaning outsiders expect that Africa has no indigenous viable or worthy medical practices, they often recommend culturally insensitive remedies and ignore medical and political allies with cultural capital that could help change hazardous behavior. So, news outlets covering the West African Ebola outbreak focused on African cultural practices (eating bush meat and funerary rites) and African skepticism of biomedicine. Journalists need to ask, how and why is the health-care infrastructure in many African countries broken and demoralized? Why did it take so long for the global health community to provide Ebola testing labs and create surveillance teams and treatment facilities? Structural inequities as well as assumptions about the types of diseases Africans suffer—STDs (sexually transmitted diseases), HIV/AIDS, and tropical diseases versus cancer and diabetes—affect the availability of current resources and influence the ability of researchers to promote viable strategies for future local and global afflictions.

To understand the roots of current health dilemmas, one must examine how environmental factors interact with people and culture. Among its highly diverse climates and ecology, Africa hosts a number of harsh disease environments. In West Africa, for example, early European explorers and traders, who survived on average less than six months due to malaria and yellow fever, dubbed it "the white man's grave." Historically the movements of people and goods both within and between Africa, Europe, and Asia meant the spread and proliferation of microbes, parasites, and pests. When contact intensified between the tropics and semi-tropics during the slave trade and colonialism, such long-standing exchanges meant that many contagious diseases were endemic rather than epidemic. Africans contended with tropical and zoonotic diseases including malaria, black water fever, yellow fever, sleeping sickness, bilharzia, typhoid, and river blindness, to name a few. Some people living in areas with high rates of malaria and yellow fever developed genetic defenses, including sickle cell anemia, but the latter also usually caused early death. Africans also encountered a number of parasites that not only created discomfort but also led to nutritional deficiencies, making them more susceptible to other ailments. More recently Africans have had to contend with Lassa fever, Ebola, and HIV/AIDS.

Socioeconomic and political encounters that both shaped and changed Africans' disease environment often have gendered implications. African women have always had to contend with health challenges related to childbirth and sometimes cultural practices such as female genital cutting (FGC), yet colonialism radically altered African women's health and well-being. Historically geographical features and indigenous environmental controls had kept many diseases and epizootics in check. Europeans introduced new diseases and enabled the spread of old ones by ignoring indigenous disease controls and by spreading disease vectors with new roads, railways, irrigation canals, migrant labor, and military and forced labor recruitment. Consequently African mortality increased through the 1930s as colonialism conquered, forcibly moved, taxed, and induced populations into migrant labor, underfed forced labor workers, and encouraged Africans to take up commercial agriculture. More subtle but equally important to health were the ways in which colonialism increased women's workload, reconfigured family and gender relations, and resulted in a decline in women's status and their marginalization from a cash economy (see chapter 8). These disruptions had long-term demographic implications, which later prompted colonialists to target African women's sexuality and reproductive practices for intervention.

Often it is assumed that colonialism had a silver lining, that it helped diminish harmful cultural practices like child marriage and FGC and introduced biomedicine. Sometimes this was true, though efforts rarely impacted significant numbers of Africans, and some Africans resisted interventions, finding them intrusive and possibly dangerous. Instead, "traditional" medicines proved more accessible and effective at coping with local diseases, while biomedicine remained focused on preserving the health of the colonizers. Biomedical treatment and vaccines were sometimes administered to Africans to prevent contagious diseases or when colonialists feared disruption in the flow of necessary labor. Only after the 1930s, however, did colonialists consider how to maintain the health of the colonized and create a health-care infrastructure that could provide effective vaccines for common childhood diseases. These results, however, were highly uneven.

Meanwhile, colonialism helped distort local economies and societies such that inequalities were exacerbated, with disproportionate impacts of poverty on women's and children's health. Lack of cash affects access to not only medical resources such as facilities and medicines but also clean water and air, good nutrition, and long-term health. Daily survival now might include gathering water from parasite-infested sources, exposure to pollution from cooking over open fires, or living in crowded conditions increasing susceptibility to diseases such as tuberculosis. While extreme poverty (living on less than $1.25 a day) has decreased globally, including modest percentage declines in Africa, steep increases in population growth mean growing numbers of poor. In 2013 Africa's population included a third of the world's extreme poor compared to only 11 percent in 1981.[1] Compounding individual poverty is the lack of public health infrastructure to ensure safe food and drinking water and accessible health-care providers and facilities. Finally, endemic hunger is a major contributing factor to disease. While the causes of hunger are multiple and complex, undernutrition (getting insufficient calories and food) and malnutrition (insufficient nutrients) jeopardize overall health by weakening the body's immune system.

Here I assess why African women have borne the brunt of Africa's health challenges, beginning by examining changes in African agriculture disproportionately affected by women's nutrition and workloads, then investigating missionary and government interventions in sex socialization, female genital cutting, and childbirth (see also chapter 14) that impacted the sex lives and reproduction of African women. I conclude by discussing how patients and healers have negotiated the sometimes uneasy relationship between biomedicine and indigenous health care. While African women have made some gains in the postcolonial period, many processes that have radically altered women's health and access to health resources remain or intensified in the face of a predatory world capitalist economy that treats women's bodies as disposable commodities. Although highly relevant, women's vulnerability to political violence, war, and domestic abuse and rape is fully discussed in chapter 15.

Transforming African Farming: Impacts on African Nutrition and Women's Health

When Europeans first came to Africa they remarked on the fecundity of the land and the large varieties of foods cultivated and gathered, yet by the 1920s and 1930s colonial reports complained that African health had greatly deteriorated and that much of this could be attributed to diet.[2] Changes to African agricultural practices begun during the colonial era and continued through the postcolonial period radically disrupted African forms of farming and have had long-term implications for Africa's food security, gender relations, and women's health. While Europeans noted African women's key role in agricultural labor, they thought it culturally strange—if not cruel—and made legal and agricultural interventions that favored European gender roles such as male-headed households and male farmers. In fact, most of Africa is considered to be, historically and now, a female farming area, where women did much of the farming. The destructive impacts of colonialism and then globalization, fully described by Gracia Clark in chapter 8, withdrew land and male labor from local food production, forcing women farmers to adapt and create new strategies to meet these challenges. Gender inequalities meant women often bore the burdens of overwork and declines in nutrition and food production, forcing reliance on imported foods.

Historians note that one can measure the relationship of African communities to colonialism by looking at their nutrition levels. Cynthia Brantley revealed that Kikuyu women eating a "traditional" vegetarian diet suffered the fewest nutritional diseases, while Kikuyu men, who had been largely absorbed into plantation labor and subsisted on colonial rations, showed the greatest nutritional abnormalities. Employers throughout southern Africa preferred to feed laborers a diet of maize meal and cassava, crops that were cheap to produce, transport, and store. The Maasai, however, less incorporated into migrant and forced labor, relied heavily on meat and milk and had better nutrition than Kikuyu men but worse than Kikuyu women. Nonetheless, Maasai cattle were decimated by colonial introduction of diseases such as rinderpest and bovine pleuropneumonia in the 1890s. Nutritional changes thus reflected the introduction of new crops, foods, epizootics, urbanization, and changed African food preferences. In Central Kenya the British forced local farmers to grow white maize (to feed plantation laborers) and abandon beans as a major staple, changing the diet permanently and harming nutrition.[3] Many Africans came to associate customary foods with poverty and new "European" foods, despite their less nutritious nature, with "modernity." Most long-term nutritional changes, however, resulted from modifications in indigenous farming and food strategies.

As described in chapter 8, the seizure of African land and introduction of cash crops resulted in the depletion of the soil, reduced biodiversity, and decreased food production. In settler states such as Algeria, Kenya, and South Africa, white farmers dispossessed Africans of the most productive farm land, forcing Africans to work as laborers on their own land, move to less productive land, or become laborers in urban or industrial areas. In nonsettler colonies Africans were coerced and encouraged through taxation, the distribution of seeds, and price incentives to grow cash crops on land formerly used for domestic food consumption or allowed to lie fallow. Monocropping meant giving up intercropping and biodiverse crops, made plants more vulnerable to diseases and pests, and increased farmers' reliance on expensive inputs such as pesticides and fertilizers. Since cash was needed to pay taxes, food production decreased when farmers abandoned edible crops and organic farming methods in favor of new cash crops—cotton, peanuts, tobacco, coffee, tea, cocoa.[4]

Historians Steven Feierman and John M. Janzen argue that the "hungry-season," when farmers finished the remains of last year's crop while awaiting the new one, can be traced to colonial changes in cultivation. In Genieri, Gambian women rice farmers relied on men working collectively to harvest millet to feed them during the period when maturing rice crops required extra labor for weeding. After World War II, men took up peanut farming, enabling men to own land individually for peanut growing. While some men continued to grow millet, others used peanut profits to buy food during the hungry season. Privatization of land and crop ownership meant that collective cultivation became unreliable; large compounds that had successfully managed food risks before broke up into smaller separate households, leaving poor women-headed households particularly vulnerable since they lost hungry-season food. Working for others to earn money or food meant time away from their crops and children and a decline in their own harvests.[5]

Women's increased labor obligations related to cash cropping, forced labor, and loss of male migrant labor strained gender and family relations. Demands on women's labor already included growing and producing family food as well as most of the extensive domestic labor required to maintain households: laundry, cooking from scratch, gathering water and firewood, child care, cleaning, and so on. Having many children was and is useful for both men and women to share the labor, but raising children to an age of being economically useful fell to women. Colonialism determined that cash crops were male crops; while many Africans expected women to produce food crops, they assumed that "women's responsibilities"—like weeding—extended to cash crops. Taxing male-headed households further increased men's desire to gain control over the best land and African women's labor for the benefit of men's fields.[6] In precolonial Bemba communities, women could depend on men to cut trees to create new agricultural fields, yet migrant labor withdrew male labor from farming communities already short on people.[7] Some women farmers adapted to the loss of male labor by drawing on kinship networks and growing cassava. Others worked for millet, eating some while brewing the rest to host "beer" parties that mobilized collective labor for clearing new fields.[8]

Colonial and postindependent governments often did not recognize women's land claims; European-type farming schemes provided African men with land, training, seed, and fertilizer, jeopardizing women's informal access to land.[9] Because advances of seed and fertilizer had to be repaid at harvest regardless of a poor harvest or low market price, many male farmers fell into debt, risking loss of land. Women fought to maintain access to arable land or were forced to use marginal land or land that should have been left fallow. Women's insecure land tenure meant they had little incentive to invest in long-term maintenance and regeneration of the land. In any case, since women farmers received little of the cash crop profits paid to men, they rarely had capital to invest in agricultural improvements. The loss of good land and male labor meant African women often worked harder and longer days with lower yields.[10]

At independence African governments continued to encourage commercial growing in hopes of gaining tax revenue and export earnings to bolster other parts of the economy, often retaining colonial marketing boards that required farmers to sell export crops to them at reduced prices. In Tanzania, the government adopted campaigns to encourage maize and wheat cultivation while discouraging that of indigenous grains such as sorghum and millet, referring to them as a "famine" crops.[11] Initially, marketing boards helped farmers by guaranteeing crop prices, subsidizing fertilizer and seeds, and building up food crop reserves for emergencies. Yet poor infrastructure and competition with northern markets made it difficult for African producers to compete globally. International players gained greater leverage over African markets and government agricultural policies during the 1970s and 1980s, when indebted nations turned to international financial institutions for loans. Lenders required the termination or decrease of government farm subsidies, dismantling marketing boards, and selling food reserves. It is now cheaper to import a ton of grain from Chicago, Illinois, into Mombasa, Kenya, than from neighboring Uganda. Local food insecurity increased with reliance on food imports.

Overall, colonialism and the commercialization of agriculture led to a decline in women's status, decreased their access to a cash economy, and consequently changed family dynamics and increased women's dependence for basic provisions and medical aid. Today, women still predominantly produce domestic food crops while men farm cash crops. In 2013 a six-country study showed a productivity gap between men's and women's fields. Researchers attributed this gap to the by-now-familiar factors afflicting women farmers: lack of reliable labor, tenuous land rights, and limited access to cash. Women cannot afford to hire labor or purchase the same quality inputs—seeds and fertilizers—as male farmers. Technical training continues to be oriented toward men and their needs, meaning women get such information secondhand or not at all, so, for instance, if they do acquire fertilizer they might apply it incorrectly.[12] Food security and sovereignty are clearly more than just a women's issue. Undernourishment and malnutrition have obvious ramifications for all Africans' health.

Changes, Challenges around Sex, Reproduction, and Childbearing

Sex and reproduction have historically been fraught with societal anxieties (see chapter 14). After all, childbirth was dangerous; access to land and status often depended on bloodlines; and a healthy and growing population assured prosperity. Many patrilineal African societies, in particular, valued women's virginity at marriage, given that lineage membership often determined title and land tenure. Since the status of individuals, lineages, and communities could rise and fall with marital connections and the birth of children, lineages often intervened in matters concerning sexuality and reproduction. African rituals marking the transition from childhood to adulthood were important for instilling gender expectations and educating initiates about issues of sexuality and reproduction. In some areas these included initiation rites, such as the seclusion and fattening of girls as they entered marriage age or male and female genital cutting (see chapters 6, 14). Various African societies approached sexuality differently; some encouraged or tolerated premarital sexual play while others forbade interactions between sexually maturing boys and girls. European mission schools, colonial laws, public health campaigns, urbanization, and the availability of biomedical aid and hospitals changed the way Africans practiced and talked about sex and how they gave birth. In the age of HIV/AIDS a new type of anxiety has emerged around sexuality and reproduction, encouraging African communities to reexamine their sexual practices and ways in which they have historically approached sex.

AIDS and Sexual Socialization

"AIDS came into my house on the afternoon of the sixth of June 1986." Ugandan physiotherapist and educator Noerine Kaleeba recounted how she learned that her husband, Chris, then studying in London, fell ill with AIDS. In the six months before his death in Uganda, they experienced the stigma of AIDS, which began at the airport when he was gawked at, and continued at the hospital, where nursing staff refused to care for him. Thus, Kaleeba founded TASO (The AIDS Service Organization) to educate and support those impacted by the disease, including creating peer counseling groups. Reflecting on "traditional" sex education for girls given by paternal aunts, Kaleeba argued that TASO also had to teach girls and women new ways of talking to male partners about sex, contraception, and HIV/AIDS.[13]

Prior to the twentieth century, many southern Africans assumed that youngsters would be sexually curious and active. Strict societal rules sought to prevent penetrative intercourse and pregnancy, while still permitting sexual play. Older relatives, peers, and siblings as well as elders who conducted rites of passage instructed youngsters on the importance of these rules and corrected and shamed transgressions. This included the notion that girls and women were to be protected and that birth should be within marriage. When premarital pregnancy occurred, the man generally paid a penalty, the couple could be socially ostracized, and every effort was made to wed the parents. This sexual and reproductive socialization began to break down in the 1920s and 1930s, particularly among Christian converts and urban residents,[14] as noted by Patience Tyalimpe, born in the 1920s and interviewed in 1992, who explained thigh sex (see chapter 14): "Yes, I knew about something which is like contraception. I had a boyfriend . . . but there were strict rules in the rural community. . . . These girls who came straight from town, well, they fell pregnant. They did, and we knew it was because they were not doing the right thing. We, from the rural areas, we also had boyfriends, but it was not sexual intercourse."[15] This form of indigenous birth control existed alongside others. Female relatives, friends, and healers passed along knowledge of herbs that induced abortions.[16]

By the 1930s and 1940s these practices, which had minimized premarital births and protected the health of women and children, came to be seen by many as "backward," unnecessary, and largely unenforceable. Because Christian churches saw sexuality and premarital sex as sinful, they told young people to practice abstinence until marriage, after which birth control was also discouraged. Puberty rituals continued, but sex became a taboo subject no longer discussed. Familial and peer mentoring faltered when boys and men went to work in mines or cities or on plantations. With independent access to the cash economy, young men freed themselves of parental control and social obligations. In essence, there was a breakdown of social conventions that had reduced premarital sex and pregnancies. Marriage declined or was delayed when bridewealth became more expensive. Illegitimate children often got no support from their fathers, especially since urbanization removed many young people from their elders' supervision, and preventing pregnancy became increasingly a woman's responsibility.[17] Though couples might cohabit or have children, they did so without the checks on abuse provided by family intervention that a legal marriage confirmed by bridewealth sometimes conferred. Peter Delius and Clive Glaser argue that in southern Africa the breakdown of older forms of sexual socialization, combined with new family formations and perceived emasculation that accompanied white rule, led men to seek greater dominance over women's bodies in often violent ways (see chapter 15).[18] Missionary and colonial governments complained about increases in premarital sex and a rise in sexually transmitted diseases, tending to view Africans as sexually promiscuous without taking stock of how their own actions contributed to the situation.

In the late twentieth century when HIV/AIDS rates soared, these changes in sexual socialization, dismissal of condoms, distrust of national governments, silences induced by taboos and fear, and governments' early denial of the virus made it difficult for many Africans to talk about prevention. Asking a partner to wear a condom often became synonymous with accusing him of cheating or having AIDS. Fertility was widely prized, and many urban women had moved quietly to intra-uterine devices and chemically induced birth control beginning in the 1940s. While such contraceptives offered women some control over their own fertility without the knowledge of men, later they offered no protection from STDs and HIV. Africa's high rates of the virus also resulted from its largely heterosexual transmission, multiple and more virulent strains, and because many African bodies were vulnerable due to undernourishment or malnutrition and compromised immune systems. Eastern and southern Africa also contended with a destructive migrant labor system that separated families and enabled the virus's extensive reach, resulting in an area with over half of the world's HIV-positive persons. This is in contrast to Western and Central Africa with 17 percent of the globe's infected population, of which half live in Nigeria.[19] Women are particularly vulnerable to HIV/AIDS because their bodies are more susceptible to the disease than men, while their socio-economic status makes them particularly dependent on men and less willing or able to demand condom use. Consequently, women make up 61 percent of all HIV-positive Africans and tend to acquire the disease much earlier in life.[20] In South Africa, 2008 HIV rates differed between men and women ages 20–24, from 5.15 percent for men to 21.1 percent for women.[21] In an effort to curb the pandemic, some South African communities turned to older forms of sexual socialization, namely "virginity testing." While some celebrated this as an African solution to a modern problem, others deemed it discriminatory and harmful to girls, particularly as it emphasized girls' responsibility for preserving sexual morality. South Africa's 2005 Children's Bill later banned this practice for all girls under the age of 16.[22]

In light of African nations' public health campaigns, sexual socialization has changed, and condom use has steadily increased. The greatest impact on HIV transmission, however, resulted from better and, more importantly, affordable medical treatments that emerged in the early twenty-first century. As of 2016, 83 percent of Western and Central Africans and 79 percent of Eastern and Southern Africans living with HIV were receiving treatment, exceeding the global average of 50 percent. Successful treatment not only keeps people alive; it lessens a patient's viral load, making transmission less likely, and it provides an incentive to get tested.[23] Women are more likely than men to be tested and seek treatment, largely to prevent transmission of HIV to their children but also because prenatal care and their role as caretakers means greater exposure and knowledge of treatment options. Prenatal testing combined with antiretroviral therapy has greatly lowered mother-to-child transmission through birth and during breastfeeding, and when treatment is offered free, women are more inclined to seek and comply with treatment. Willingness to disclose one's status to her partner, however, varied widely, with 43 percent of women in Côte d'Ivoire sharing prenatal tests versus 86 percent of Cameroonian women.[24]

Female Genital Cutting

In *The Hidden Face of Eve*, Nawal El Saadawi argued that she lost her child-hood when at age six, female relatives stole her from her bed to perform the time-honored ritual of clitoridectomy experienced by most Egyptian girls. This experience, combined with her work as a doctor that included treating rural young girls for complications following infibulation and women refugees from Sudan, who had more extensive genital damage, led to her activism combat-ing FGC. Saadawi drew attention to the harmful physical and psychological impacts of infibulation in the hopes of changing Egyptian attitudes, but simul-taneously she became an ardent critic of Western feminists who sought to "save" Africans from their traditions.[25]

Material concerns coupled with notions of colonial progress and moral responsibility led colonial powers to intervene in African sexuality and repro-duction. Demographic shifts affecting World War I porter recruitment and the influenza pandemic that followed, which killed as many as a third of the popu-lation in some places, alarmed colonialists who depended on African labor. This was particularly true for Central and East Africa, where colonial admin-istrators and doctors began to consider the demographic impact of FGC and other factors.[26] Some forms of FGC (see chapters 6 and 14) were dangerous, leading to infections, infertility, labor complications, and death. Colonial intervention in such cultural practices was then justified by missionary and colonialist arguments that they were morally repugnant. Therefore, missionar-ies pushed colonial administrators to end FGC, including in their own congre-gations with the help of medical missionaries and mission schools. Colonial states, however, not wanting to alienate those who practiced any of its forms, sometimes supported reforms rather than abolition. In the 1920s among the Meru in Kenya, marriage and excision ceremonies were delayed because of lack of community resources to support bridewealth and expenses associ-ated with excision. Consequently, pre-excision births and abortions increased. Local colonial officials worked with Meru chiefs to decrease the age of exci-sion and mandate a milder form. With little notice, male chiefs and police officers selected and rounded up girls for mass operations, who were then cut by a government-certified exciser.[27]

At the same time in Sudan, the British supported introducing a modified form of FGC by training midwives who (like local qualified midwives, or *dayas*) assisted in labor and FGC. Midwifery schools sought local respectable women, that is, older married women, with a preference for local midwives, and taught them anatomy, hygiene, and a modified form of FGC. In both cases, colonialists allied with local communities and sought to accommodate local ideas of respectability while reforming FGC but failed. In Kenya this was largely because FGC reinforced hierarchies and conferred title and status on a variety of women—mothers included. The new practice was seen as male colonial meddling in the affairs of women, punishing unruly girls, and literally leaving a mark on girls' and women's bodies. Older women and midwives undermined the credibility of the "government" excision by issuing a "second cut" that corrected the first. In the Sudan, new government-trained midwives could not compete with local ones because midwifery licensing was not enforced. Furthermore, Sudanese clients continued to request unaltered infibulation, and government-trained midwives incurred greater expenses maintaining sterile supplies and equipment.[28]

In the 1940s and 1950s, the British attempted to ban FGC altogether, another tactic that failed with unintended consequences. Criminalizing FGC inspired resentment and made women's bodies into a site of resistance against colonialism. In 1956 when colonialists banned FGC among the Meru, 2,400 girls responded by cutting themselves while older women again quietly issued a second cut, acts praised as anticolonial expressions of cultural nationalism.[29] Likewise, in Sudan when the British banned infibulation in 1946, supporting the ban was condemned as condoning the imposition of Western imperialism. One religious leader even led crowds to free a jailed midwife.[30] Bans thus had the unintended effect of provoking resistance, resulting in more cases of FGC.

In the postcolonial period, FGC remained a sensitive issue, in part because of a history of moralizing missionaries and intervening colonialists, yet a rising tide of African women emerged to engage in eradication efforts (chapter 6). Since the mid-1970s a number of African states such as Egypt have passed laws that ban infibulation or FGC entirely. This demonstrated their concern in a global arena that increasingly called for intervention even if governments had little intention of enforcing such bans. In Ghana, legislation against FGC proved politically popular because those who practiced excision belonged mainly to a northern minority group. Expressing anti-FGC sentiment thus became a means of demonstrating one's modernity, while viewing those who practiced it as "backward" and undeveloped.[31] Yet many Africans historically and contemporarily interpret the international anti-FGC movement as the imposition of pro-Western, secularist, and imperialist agendas that perpetuate international assumptions about an exotic and ignorant Africa. In Egypt, a number of *fatwas* were issued during the 1980s encouraging FGC as a means to support local traditions while demonstrating against the West. When a national Kenyan women's organization worked with a U.S. NGO to perform a girls' initiation without cutting in the mid-1990s, some suspected foreigners for wanting to encourage immorality and the use of birth control among unmarried girls. For many communities, however, FGC remained a private family affair to be tackled quietly. In newly independent Kenya, politicians favoring reform argued for change through education, not banning.[32] In the 1990s in Sudan, a number of religious debates conducted primarily by men discussed the "value" of various types of FGC (infibulation versus *sunna*—a modified form) or if it was even mandated by Islam.[33]

African women have been clear that FGC is their fight to lead (see chapter 6). Nawal El Saadawi warned in 1980 that outside intervention was patronizing and could not succeed.[34] While many local activists argued that FGC is a violation of human rights, others detailed its painful and deleterious health effects. Health arguments have proved more compelling; many families turned to biomedicine to provide a more sterile setting with surgical instruments and anesthetic. By 2005 over 70 percent of Egyptian FGCs were performed by biomedical staff.[35] In Kenya, medicalized FGC comprised 46 percent of all procedures.[36] In Sudan, 35 percent of operations were performed by biomedically trained personnel, with a move toward *sunna* cuts rather than infibulation.[37] Likewise, medicalization trends can be seen in Eritrea, Mali, and Mauritania. When local midwives and excisers were trained in other vocations, their work was generally taken over by biomedically trained personnel. The medicalization of FGC does reduce harm and over time has been linked with more "modest" forms of FGC, yet anti-FGC advocates fear it will normalize and institutionalize the practice.[38] Saida Hodzic argues that the health hazard argument proved more politically palatable since it asked governments to save women from their own customs rather than view women as citizens entitled to full rights and protection.[39] It certainly ignored any male preferences or responsibility for the continuance of FGC.

FGC continues to affect over two million girls aged 4 to 12 in Africa every year, but a 2013 UNICEF analysis showed a strong decline in FGC rates over the past twenty years.[40] By 2014, Egypt, which historically had one of the highest rates of FGC at over 95 percent, decreased the practice among 20- to 24-year-old married women to 87 percent.[41] Among the Meru, the rate has declined from 52.4 percent of females aged 15 to 49 in 1998 to 39.7 percent in 2008, while in Nairobi puberty rites are disappearing altogether.[42] In Sudan, where infibulation has been modified, the rate nevertheless remains steady at about 88 percent.[43]

There is a clear consensus among anti-FGC advocates that legislation needs to be complemented by broad-based efforts to increase girls' and women's overall status. In Egypt, researchers found that increasing education and economic opportunities for women also changed societal attitudes toward FGC. Education and employment both exposed women to people and ideas outside their direct local communities and enabled them to gain status through other means than marriage.[44] In Kenya, decline in FGC seemed tied to the spread of Christianity, as well as access to education and economic prosperity. In some ways schooling created a new type of initiation, but when economic downturns meant fewer girls in school, activists implemented the ritual without cutting. In Sudan, midwives devised less damaging ways of doing surgery, while men have gotten involved by pledging to marry uncircumcised women and not cutting their daughters.[45] In the long run, it seems the most effective means of limiting FGC are a combination of the demonstrated success of uncircumcised girls and women—particularly those of higher status—education, urbanization, and the political and economic empowerment of women more generally.

Childbirth

In the late 1920s, Balau, a "traditional" midwife of the Yakusu district of Congo, attended a childbirth in which the baby was born not breathing. Unable to do anything, Balau gave the baby to an observing missionary nurse, who then resuscitated the baby. Balau's willingness both to teach biomedical nurses local midwifery skills and in turn to allow a patient to be treated by biomedicine opened the possibilities of a new type of medicalized birth. Balau later converted to Christianity and came to work as a hospital midwife in Yakusu's hospital. She acted as a cultural intermediary between patients and biomedical staff and later eased the acceptance of young women trained in maternal health.[46]

Missionaries and colonial powers were highly successful in changing African birthing practices, though this intervention was initially viewed with suspicion. Missionaries introduced medicalized childbirth through biomedically trained midwives and later maternity hospitals. Childbirth was a dangerous time, especially where child marriage was common, since young teens might give birth before they were fully grown. A successful birth was celebrated not only for a new life and lineage member but also for the survival of the mother and the increase in status that parenthood brought. Given the importance of birthing rituals performed by midwives and family members, visiting a biomedical doctor was usually a last resort. Biomedical doctors were seen as culturally foreign, and hospitals as places of death, especially since people only went there when in extremis. For instance, biomedicine prescribed semi-reclining births (now seen as being for the convenience of doctors and not conducive to encouraging labor) rather than squatting, new ways of breathing and push-ing during labor, different obstetric tools, and often a hospital setting. After World War II, sulfonamide, blood transfusions, and antibiotics became more widely available, as did Cesarean sections.[47] Also culturally awkward was that male doctors employed young, single, childless, and potentially menstruating midwives and nurses' aides—considered to be low status and potentially "pol-luted." Biomedicine thus had to tread carefully. In 1936 a failed C-section that killed the mother and saved the child in the Yakusu district of Congo resulted in community anger, suspicion, and rejection of the baby. For fear of further alienating this community, this mission hospital avoided C-sections until the 1950s, preferring embryotomies that killed the fetus in order to save the mother.[48] Yet between the 1920s and 1950s increasing numbers of African women began having medicalized births.

Such births became a more viable option as Africans themselves became involved in biomedicine during the 1920s to 1940s, and communities wit-nessed the success of difficult cases. Colonial governments followed the lead of missionaries and began their own training of midwives. The early acceptance of biomedical births often depended on the success of early African nurses and midwives, who served as cultural mediators, understood African ideas of the body and health, and could negotiate or intervene on behalf of patients and doctors. African biomedical workers tolerated a certain amount of what they considered benign cultural practices within the homes of Africans, yet once births moved to clinics and hospitals in the 1930s to 1950s, local prac-tices were largely replaced with prayer or denied altogether.[49] This usage not only showed the acceptance of medicalized childbirth but became a way that Africans, particularly Christian, urban, educated, or salaried employees, signi-fied their "modernity" and status in society.[50]

Despite the successful introduction of biomedicine into birthing, childbirth still remains a dangerous time in women's lives. In 2010 Africa accounted for half of the world's maternal deaths, with maternal mortality at 480 per 100,000 live births compared to Europe's 20.[51] More than half of maternal deaths in Africa occur within twenty-four to forty-eight hours after delivery from pre-ventable conditions that could be handled by emergency obstetric care.[52] However, even nominal user fees, combined with transportation costs, often discourage prenatal visits.[53] Even where maternal death is prevented, pro-longed and obstructed labor often results in obstetric fistulas, an embarrassing condition that leaves women leaking urine and feces. In Africa, between

30,000 and 130,000 new cases emerge each year. The long-term effects of this condition are often social isolation, discrimination, and loss of income and independence.[54]

Access to medicalized births varies between African countries and urban and rural areas in 2009; in Ethiopia over 80 percent of births occurred without trained health workers, whereas in South Africa under 25 percent did. Yet rural South Africa, home to 46 percent of the total population, is served by only 12 percent of the doctors and 19 percent of the nurses. Likewise, rural Nigerian women are twice as likely as their urban counterparts to give birth without a trained health worker present.[55] In Tanzania, where only half of births occur in clinics, there were only 822 doctors in the country, or .02 doctors per 100 persons in 2009, and pregnant women were expected to bring their own delivery kits. Shortage of personnel and drugs meant C-sections were often performed with ether by assistant medical officers rather than surgeons.[56] These circumstances reflect the larger problem of both individual and structural poverty.

In an era of declining resources, many governments rely on foreign medical personnel (missionaries and those recruited through NGOs) as well as international financing to provide basic health care. Without central administration and coordination, however, services and data collection can be quite uneven, meaning it is difficult to determine success rates of treatments, future needs, and funds. In recent years there have been efforts to eliminate user fees for prenatal and childbirth services or to mandate prenatal visits to access free childbirth. Improvements are uneven, with great progress in places like Rwanda, which reduced the maternal mortality rate from 952 to 383 per 100,000 births between 2000 and 2008. Overall, African maternal deaths declined an average of 2.7 percent from 1990 to 2010, a positive step but well below the 5.5 percent reduction target of the 2015 Millennium Development Goals.[57]

Conclusion

Historically and currently, African health care has come from a variety of sources: grandmothers with folk remedies, healers and midwives, and, more recently, the formal biomedical sector—government, missionary, NGO clinics and hospitals, and the informal biomedical sector—nurses and patent medicine sellers, who provide advice and care within their own communities. Nowadays, Africans weave their way through a variety of therapeutic options and have no problem utilizing biomedicine, homeopathy, and folk healers and remedies, sometimes simultaneously. Choice is often based on people's understanding of their ailment or predicament, their access to and affordability of a treatment, and the reputation of a healer or medicine. Ironically women, who are often the caregivers, repositories of folk medical knowledge, healers, and midwives, have faced gender-based inequalities in land, education, status, and income that in turn impact their own health and access to health care.

At independence African countries established medical schools and put money into primary health care, yet demographic pressures threatened goals such as free or affordable health care. Poor transportation infrastructure made it difficult to access clinics, while poor pay caused high rates of turnover among medical personnel. In the 1980s and 1990s, international financial institutions pushed structural adjustment programs that mandated countries' reduction of government expenses, decreasing people's access to health services and forcing government clinics to institute or increase user fees. Many challenges remain for African women's health; there is a growing recognition that the best way to improve women's health is to tackle larger inequalities.[58] Africa suffers more than 24 percent of the global disease burden but has only 3 percent of the world's health workers and less than 1 percent of the world's financial resources.[59]

Solutions include a robust health infrastructure serving everyone and improved access to girls' education and to women's economic empowerment and rights to land. Providing or improving basic infrastructure such as safe and accessible drinking water helps protect women from water-borne diseases and parasites and cuts down on labor. Guinea worm, which affected 3.5 million people in 1986 with painful lesions, has since been eradicated in twenty-one African countries through filtering drinking water and changing the behavior of the infected. In 2017 there were only 30 cases worldwide.[60] Devices such as food processing mills and solar stoves require less labor and prevent burns and pollution from cooking fires.[61] Income generation for women can be improved by such means as training women farmers with consideration of their childcare obligations, land requirements, and economic constraints. Finally, more research on African health conditions is needed, preferably by locally trained and highly skilled scientists and researchers, to help fill the knowledge gap and enrich the lives, talents, and potential of Africans endangered by healthcare deficits.

Notes

1. World Bank, "Remarkable Declines in Global Poverty, But Major Challenges Remain," April 17, 2013, http://www.worldbank.org/en/news/press-release/2013/04/17/remarkable-declines-in-global-poverty-but-major-challenges-remain.

2. Michael Worboys, "The Discovery of Colonial Malnutrition between the Wars," in *Imperial Medicine and Indigenous Societies*, ed. David Arnold (Manchester: Manchester University Press, 1988), 208–25.

3. Claire Robertson, *Trouble Showed the Way* (Bloomington: Indiana University Press, 1997), chap. 2.

4. Parker Shipton, "African Famines and Food Security," *Annual Review of Anthropology* 19 (1990): 359–60.

5. Steven Feierman and John M. Janzen, eds., *The Social Basis of Health and Healing in Africa* (Berkeley: University of California Press, 1992), 6–7.

6. Emily Burrill, Richard Roberts, and Elizabeth Thornberry, *Domestic Violence and the Law in Colonial and Postcolonial Africa* (Athens: Ohio University Press, 2010); Sarah Berry, *No Condition Is Permanent: The Social Dynamics of Agrarian Change in Sub-Saharan Africa* (Madison: University of Wisconsin Press, 1993), 33.

7. Berry, *No Condition Is Permanent*, 87.

8. Henrietta Moore and Megan Vaughan, *Cutting Down Trees: Gender, Nutrition, and Agricultural Change in the Northern Province of Zambia, 1890–1990* (London: James Currey, 1994), 46–78.

9. Moore and Vaughan, *Cutting Down Trees*, 110–39.

10. Berry, *No Condition Is Permanent*, 94–95.

11. Cymone Fourshey, "The Remedy for Hunger Is Bending the Back: Maize and British Agricultural Policy in Southwestern Tanzania, 1920–1960," *International Journal of African Historical Studies* 41, no. 2 (2008): 69.

12. Michael O'Sullivan, Arathi Rao, Raka Banerjee, Kajal Gulati, and Margaux Vinez, *Levelling the Field: Improving Opportunities for Women Farmers in Africa* (Washington, DC: World Bank Group, 2014), http://documents.worldbank.org/curated/en/2014/01/19243625/levelling-field-improving-opportunities-women-farmers-africa.

13. "Interview with Noerine Kaleeba," *Frontline*, May 5, 2005, PBS, http://www.pbs.org/wgbh/pages/frontline/aids/interviews/kaleeba.html#1.

14. Peter Delius and Clive Glaser, "Sexual Socialization in South Africa: A Historical Perspective," *African Studies* 61, no. 1 (2002): 27–54; Catherine Burns, "Controlling Birth: Johannesburg, 1920–1960," *South African Historical Journal* 50, no. 1 (2004): 170–98; Catherine Burns, "Sex Lessons from the Past?," *Agenda: Empowering Women for Gender Equity*, no. 29 (1996): 79–91.

15. Patience Tyalimpe, quoted in Burns, "Sex Lessons," 88.

16. Helen Bradford, "Herbs, Knives and Plastic: 150 Years of Abortion in South Africa," in *Science, Medicine and Cultural Imperialism*, ed. Teresa Meade and Mark Walker (London: Macmillan, 1991), 120–47.

17. Burns, "Sex Lessons," 174.

18. Delius and Glaser, "Sexual Socialization," 27–53.

19. Joint United Nations Programme on HIV/AIDS, "Ending AIDS: Progress Towards the 90-90-90 Targets" (Geneva, 2017), http://www.unaids.org/sites/default/files/media_asset/Global_AIDS_update_2017_en.pdf.

20. Institut de Recherche pour le Développement (IRD), "African Women Reacting against AIDS," *Scientific Newssheet* 332 (November 2009), https://en.ird.fr/the-media-centre/scientific-newssheets/332-african-women-reacting-against-aids.

21. Republic of South Africa, "Global AIDS Response Progress Report, 2012," 33, http://www.unaids.org/sites/default/files/country/documents//ce_ZA_Narrative_Report.pdf.

22. Fiona Scorgie, "A Battle Won? The Prohibition of Virginity Testing in the Children's Bill," *Agenda: Empowering Women for Gender Equity*, no. 68 (2006): 9–28.

23. Joint United Nations Programme, "Ending AIDS."

24. IRD, "African Women Reacting."

25. Nawal El Saadawi, *The Hidden Face of Eve: Women in the Arab World* (1980; repr., London: Zed Books, 2007), 13–19.

26. Heather Bell, "Midwifery Training and Female Circumcision in the Inter-War Anglo-Egyptian Sudan," *Journal of African History* 39, no. 2 (1998): 293–312; Lynn Thomas, *Politics of the Womb: Women, Reproduction and the State in Kenya* (Berkeley: University of California Press, 2003), 53–55.

27. Thomas, *Politics of the Womb*, 45.

28. Thomas, *Politics of the Womb*, 47.

29. Thomas, *Politics of the Womb*, 25.

30. Ellen Gruenbaum, *The Female Circumcision Controversy: An Anthropological Perspective* (Philadelphia: University of Pennsylvania Press, 2001), 208–9.

31. Saida Hodzic, "Gender Violence as a Site of Friction in Ghanaian Advocacy," in *Domestic Violence and the Law in Colonial and Postcolonial Africa*, ed. Emily S. Burrill, Richard L. Roberts, and Elizabeth Thornberry (Athens: Ohio University Press, 2010), 220–38.

32. Thomas, *Politics of the Womb*, 177–84.

33. Gruenbaum, *The Female Circumcision Controversy*, 185–88.

34. Saadawi, *The Hidden Face of Eve*, preface.

35. Carla Obermeyer, "The Consequences of Female Circumcision for Health and Sexuality: An Update of the Evidence," *Culture Health and Sexuality* 7, no. 5 (2005): 457; Ronan Van Rossem et al., "Women's Position and Attitudes towards Female Genital Mutilation in Egypt, 1995–2014," *BMC Public Health* 15, no. 1 (2015): 874–87.

36. 28 Too Many, "Country Profile: FGM in Kenya, May 2013," http://28toomany .org/media/uploads/final_kenya_country_profile_may_2013.pdf.

37. Obermeyer, "The Consequences of Female Circumcision," 457; Gruenbaum, *The Female Circumcision Controversy*, 102.

38. Obermeyer, "The Consequences of Female Circumcision," 457.

39. Hodzic, "Gender Violence," 224.

40. UNICEF, "Female Genital Mutilation/Cutting: A Statistical Overview and Exploration of the Dynamics of Change" (New York, 2013), 1–184, http://data.unicef. org/resources/female-genital-mutilationcutting-statistical-overview-exploration-dynam ics-change/.

41. Van Rossem et al., "Women's Position and Attitudes."

42. 28 Too Many, "Country Profile."

43. UNICEF, "Female Genital Mutilation/Cutting."

44. Van Rossem et al., "Women's Position and Attitudes."

45. Gruenbaum, *The Female Circumcision Controversy*, 184.

46. Nancy Hunt, *A Colonial Lexicon: Of Birth Ritual, Medicalization, and Mobility in the Congo* (Durham, NC: Duke University Press, 1999), 201–19.

47. Hunt, *A Colonial Lexicon*, 224.

48. Hunt, *A Colonial Lexicon*, 204, 224; Thomas, *Politics of the Womb*, 53; Bell, "Midwifery Training," 296.

49. Bell, "Midwifery Training," 311; Thomas, *Politics of the Womb*, 59–62; Hunt, *A Colonial Lexicon*, 227.

50. Thomas, *Politics of the Womb*, 62.

51. Chimaraoke O. Izugbara and Eleanor Krassen Covan, "Research on Women's Health in Africa: Issues, Challenges, Opportunities," *Healthcare for Women International* 35, nos. 7–9 (2014): 697–702.

52. World Health Organization (WHO), "Addressing the Challenge of Women's Health in Africa: Report of the Commission on Women's Health in the African Region" (Brazzaville, 2012), 26–27, http://apps.who.int/iris/handle/10665/79667.

53. WHO, "Addressing the Challenge," 30–31.

54. Lilian T. Mselle and Thecla W. Kohi, "Living with Constant Leaking of Urine and Odour: Thematic Analysis of Socio-cultural Experiences of Women Affected by Obstetric Fistula in Rural Tanzania," *BMC Women's Health* 15, no. (2015): 107.

55. World Health Organization (WHO), "Maternal Health: Investing in the Lifeline of Healthy Societies and Economies" (Geneva, September 2010), 8, https://reliefweb .int/report/world/maternal-health-investing-lifeline-healthy-societies-and-economies.

56. D. Grady, "Where Life's Start Is a Deadly Risk," *New York Times*, May 23, 2009. In 2010 only 50 percent of Tanzania women gave birth in health facilities. Mselle and Kohi, "Living with Constant Leaking," 107.

57. WHO, "Maternal Health," 10–19.

58. WHO, "Maternal Health," 10–19.

59. World Health Organization (WHO), "World Health Statistics 2006," http:// www.who.int/whosis/whostat2006/en/index.html.

60. Carter Center, "Guinea Worm Eradication Program," accessed March 7, 2017, http://www.cartercenter.org/health/guinea_worm/index.html.

61. World Health Organization (WHO), "Women and Health: Today's Evidence, Tomorrow's Agenda," (Geneva, November 2009), Executive Summary, 3, https://www .who.int/gender-equity-rights/knowledge/9789241563857/en/.

Suggested Readings

Burns, Catherine. "Sex Lessons from the Past?" *Agenda: Empowering Women for Gender Equity*, no. 29 (1996): 79–91.

Moore, Henrietta, and Megan Vaughan. *Cutting Down Trees: Gender, Nutrition, and Agricultural Change in the Northern Province of Zambia, 1890–1990*. London: James Currey, 1994.

Saadawi, Nawal El. *The Hidden Face of Eve: Women in the Arab World*. London: Zed Books, 2007.

Thomas, Lynn. *Politics of the Womb: Women, Reproduction and the State in Kenya*. Berkeley: University of California Press, 2003.

CODA

Transforming Visions

Abena P. A. Busia

This is what we know—and here we show it:
Cracked mirrors refract light: clear ones reflect it:
These our new points of view—
What was dim is made bright, so wrongs can be set right:
Changed perspectives, visions transformed,
While holding the world together.

CONTRIBUTORS

Nwando Achebe, the Jack and Margaret Sweet Endowed Professor of History, is an award-winning historian at Michigan State University and the founding editor in chief of the *Journal of West African History*. Achebe's books include *Farmers, Traders, Warriors, and Kings: Female Power and Authority in Northern Igboland, 1900–1960* (2005), *The Female King of Colonial Nigeria: Ahebi Ugbabe* (2011), *History of West Africa E-Course Book* (coauthor, 2018), *A Companion to African History* (coeditor, 2019), and *Female Monarchs and Merchant Queens in Africa* (2019). Achebe has received prestigious grants from the Rockefeller Foundation, Wenner-Gren Foundation, Woodrow Wilson Foundation, Fulbright-Hays Program, Ford Foundation, World Health Organization, and National Endowment for the Humanities.

Ousseina Alidou is a professor of linguistics, gender, and African studies at Rutgers University New Jersey–New Brunswick. She teaches in the Department of African, Middle Eastern and South Asian Languages and Literatures and Comparative Literature. She is the author of *Engaging Modernity: Muslim Women and the Politics of Agency in Postcolonial Niger* (2005, a runner-up for the Aidoo-Snyder Book Prize of the Women's Caucus of the African Studies Association) and *Muslim Women in Postcolonial Kenya: Leadership, Representation, and Social Change* (2013) and the coeditor of *Writing through the Visual and Virtual: Inscribing Language, Literature, and Culture in Francophone Africa and the Caribbean* (2015).

Signe Arnfred is an associate professor in the Department of Social Sciences and Business at Roskilde University, Denmark. She is a sociologist and gender scholar working with issues of gender and sexuality in Africa and postcolonial feminist thinking. In 2000–2007 she was the coordinator of the research program "Sexuality, Gender and Society in Africa" at the Nordic Africa Institute, Uppsala, Sweden. Her books include *Re-thinking Sexualities in Africa* (2004), *African Feminist Politics of Knowledge* (with Akosua Adomako Ampofo, 2010), and *Sexuality and Gender Politics in Mozambique* (2011).

ANDREA L. ARRINGTON-SIROIS is an assistant professor in the Department of History and the African and African American Studies Program at Indiana State University. She is the author of *Victoria Falls and Colonial Imagination in British Southern Africa: Turning Water into Gold* (2017) and the coauthor of *Africanizing Democracies: 1980–Present* (2015).

HENRYATTA BALLAH is an assistant professor of history at Connecticut College. Her research interests include nineteenth- and twentieth-century Africa, the Atlantic world, civil wars, labor and social movements, women's history, and youth history. She is the author of "Politics Is Not for Children: Student Activism and State Repression in Liberia, 1944–1990" (2017).

TERESA BARNES is an associate professor of history and gender and women's studies at the University of Illinois at Urbana-Champaign, where she also serves as director of the Center for African Studies. A graduate of Brown University and the University of Zimbabwe, she was a resident of Zimbabwe and South Africa for twenty-five years. Her major publications include *To Live a Better Life: African Women in Colonial Harare, Zimbabwe* (1989), *"We Women Worked So Hard": Gender, Urbanization, and Social Reproduction in Colonial Harare, Zimbabwe, 1930–56* (1999), *The Restructuring of South African Higher Education: Rocky Roads from Policy Formulation to Institutional Mergers, 2001–2005* (2009), and *Uprooting University Apartheid in South Africa: From Liberalism to Decolonization* (2019).

JOSEPHINE BEOKU-BETTS is a professor of women, gender, and sexuality studies and sociology at Florida Atlantic University. Her research focuses on African women academic scientists and women's political activism in Sierra Leone since the 1990s. She is currently working on a coedited book about the politics of women's empowerment in postwar Sierra Leone. She is a former co-president of the Research Committee on Women and Society of the International Sociological Association.

EMILY BURRILL is an associate professor of history and women's and gender studies at the University of North Carolina at Chapel Hill, where she also directs the African Studies Center. She is the author of *States of Marriage: Gender, Justice, and Rights in Colonial Mali* (2015) and the coeditor of *Domestic Violence and the Law in Colonial and Postcolonial Africa* (2010).

ABENA P. A. BUSIA has been the ambassador of Ghana to Brazil since January 2018, with concurrent accreditation to the other twelve Republics of South America. Prior to that she served as chair of women's and gender studies at Rutgers University, where she is also a professor of English and a former director of the Center for African Studies. She is past president of both the Association for the Study of the Worldwide African Diaspora and the African Literature Association. The author of over fifty articles and chapters in books, her major academic achievements include being project co-director and editor of the four-volume Women Writing Africa series (2002–8), coeditor of *Theorizing Black Feminisms* (1993) and *Beyond Survival: African Literature and the Search for New Life* (1994), and the author of two collections of poems, *Testimonies of Exile* (1990) and *Traces of a Life* (2008).

GRACIA CLARK is a professor emerita in anthropology at Indiana University in Bloomington. Her Ghanaian fieldwork in and around Kumasi Central Market began in 1978. Major publications include two books, *Onions Are My Husband* (1994) and *Asante Market Women: Seven Life Histories from Kumasi Central Market* (2010), and a web gallery, "Everyday Islam in Kumasi" (http://aodl.org/islamictolerance/kumasi).

ALICIA C. DECKER is an associate professor of women's, gender, and sexuality studies and African studies at the Pennsylvania State University, where she also co-directs the African Feminist Initiative with Gabeba Baderoon. Decker is the author of *In Idi Amin's Shadow: Women, Gender, and Militarism in Uganda* (2014) and the coauthor with Andrea Arrington-Sirois of *Africanizing Democracies: 1980–Present* (2015). She is the coeditor of the *Oxford Encyclopedia of African Women's History* (2019) and the series coeditor of War and Militarism in African History.

KAREN FLINT is an associate professor of history at the University of North Carolina at Charlotte and the author of *Healing Traditions: African Medicine, Cultural Exchange, and Competition in South Africa, 1820–1948* (2008). She has written a number of articles and chapters on African medicine and healing and is currently examining how biomedicine and doctors both empowered and disrupted the system of South African indenture.

DECEMBER GREEN is the chair of the School of Public and International Affairs and a professor of political science at Wright State University. Her publications include *Gender Violence in Africa: African Women's Responses* (1998), *Contentious Politics in Brazil and China: Beyond Regime* (2016), and *Comparative Politics of the Global South: Linking Concepts and Cases* (4th ed., 2017).

CAJETAN IHEKA is an assistant professor of English at the University of Alabama. His research focuses on African literature and film, postcolonial studies, ecocriticism, and world literature. He is the author of *Naturalizing Africa: Ecological Violence, Agency, and Postcolonial Resistance in African Literature* (2018) and coeditor of *African Migration Narratives* (2018).

RACHEL JEAN-BAPTISTE is an associate professor of history at the University of California, Davis. Her articles have been published in the *Journal of Africa History*, the *Journal of the History of Sexuality*, the *Journal of Women's History*, *Cahiers d'Etudes Africaines*, and edited volumes. She is the author of *Conjugal Rights: Marriage, Sexuality, and Urban Life in Twentieth-Century Colonial Libreville, Gabon* (2014).

ELIZABETH M. PEREGO is an assistant professor of history at Shepherd University, where she teaches courses in African, Middle Eastern, and gender history. She has authored articles for the *Journal of North African Studies* and *Hawwa: Journal of Women of the Middle East and the Muslim World*. Her current book-length project maps Algeria's comedic landscape and the influence of satire on national politics and individual subjectivities in the country's post-independence era.

CLAIRE ROBERTSON is a professor emerita of history and women's, gender, and sexuality studies at the Ohio State University. She has published more than sixty articles; this book will be her eighth one, adding to *Sharing the Same Bowl*, which won the African Studies Association's Herskovits Award, and *Transnational Sisterhood and Genital Cutting: Disputing U.S. Polemics*, coedited with Stanlie James, winner of the PCA/ACA Peggy Koppelman Book Prize.

KATHLEEN SHELDON is an affiliated research scholar at the Center for the Study of Women at the University of California, Los Angeles. She has published widely on Mozambican history and on African women's history, including coediting with Judith Van Allen a special forum on gender in *African Studies Review* (2015 and 2016) and serving on the editorial board of the online *Oxford Research Encyclopedia in African History* and the print edition, *Oxford Encyclopedia of African Women's History* (2019). Her books include *Pounders of Grain: A History of Women, Work, and Politics in Mozambique* (2002), a reference work, *Historical Dictionary of Women in Sub-Saharan Africa* (2nd ed., 2016), and *African Women: Early History to the 21st Century* (2017).

AILI MARI TRIPP is the Wangari Maathai Professor of Political Science and Gender and Women's Studies and the chair of the Department of Gender and Women's Studies at the University of Wisconsin–Madison. She is the author of several award-winning books, including *Women and Power in Postconflict Africa* (2015), *Museveni's Uganda: Paradoxes of Power in a Hybrid Regime* (2010), *African Women's Movements: Transforming Political Landscapes* (coauthored with Isabel Casimiro, Joy Kwesiga, and Alice Mungwa, 2009), and *Women and Politics in Uganda* (2000).

CASSANDRA VENEY is chair of the Department of International Relations and a professor of International Relations at the United States International University-Africa. Her publications include *Leisure in Urban Africa* (coedited, 2003), *Forced Migration in Eastern Africa: Democratization, Structural Adjustment, and Refugees* (2007), *African Democracy and Development: Challenges for Post-Conflict African Nations* (coedited, 2013), and *US-Africa Relations: From Clinton to Obama* (2014).

INDEX

The letter *f* following a page number indicates an illustration; the letter *t* indicates a table.

Women in Africa and the Diaspora